THE TEMPLE OF MUKTĒŚVARA AT CAUḌADĀNAPURA

A little-known 12th-13th century temple in Dharwar District, Karṇāṭaka

To the revered memory

of

Shivadeva Wodeyar

who was "Ajja" grand father to all of us and the real source of inspiration for this monograph.

Pl. I 2: Temple of Muktēśvara seen from south-east angle. Old photograph published in *Śivadēvavijayam*.

THE TEMPLE OF MUKTĒŚVARA AT CAUḌADĀNAPURA

A little-known 12th-13th century temple in Dharwar District, Karṇāṭaka

by

Vasundhara FILLIOZAT

architecture by

Pierre-Sylvain FILLIOZAT

INDIRA GANDHI NATIONAL CENTRE FOR THE ARTS

ABHINAV PUBLICATIONS

First Published in India 1995

Publishers
Indira Gandhi National Centre for the Arts
Janpath, New Delhi-110 001
Abhinav Publications, E-37, Hauz Khas, New Delhi-110 016
Tel.: 666387

ISBN 81-7017-327-2

Printed at
D.K. Fine Art Press (P) Ltd., Delhi-110052.

CONTENTS

FOREWORD

"The Temple of Muktēśvara at Caudadānapura", a monograph incorporating the studies undertaken by Vasundhara Filliozat at her own initiative, has been included in scheme of publications of the Indira Gandhi National Centre for the Arts (IGNCA) under the *Kalāsamālocanā series* for its significant contents concentrating on regional structural and cultural idioms in the context of Karṇāṭaka. The IGNCA views the regional architectural tradition of India as the basic source of any artistic expression; and such an approach becomes highly relevant in regard to a particular shrine or group of shrines which have not been analyzed in the light of available evidence of *Vāstu* and *Āgama* texts. Thus, in this respect the Muktēśvara temple at Caudadānapura (District Dharwar), which is associated with Vīraśaivism as a living shrine, makes an ideal choice.

IGNCA is aware of the importance of the cultural heritage of Karṇāṭaka and has already brought out Pierre-Sylvain Filliozat's *'Svāyambhuvasūtrasaṃgraha'*, a Śaiva *āgamic* text, and will be publishing soon a monograph by Adam Hardy on the Karṇāṭaka temples. Vasundhara Filliozat's monograph on Muktēśvara temple, devoted to and inspired by Vīraśaivism, may offer a different regional perspective on the subject combining cultural ethos, artistic creativity and spiritual idealism.

Perhaps on account of its moderate proportions and, relatively, an unpretentious character, in comparison with structurally conspicuous shrines of Karṇāṭaka cast in northern, southern and blended styles, the Muktēśvara temple at Caudadānapura could not receive much attention of well-known art-historians. Some references, no doubt, are available to the temple in the older publications, yet these do not cover all the necessary details. The inscriptions at the site, however, have been deciphered and studied but only limited attempts seem to have been made to analyze them in the context of the shrine under reference, without much relevance to the textual traditions. Built in the twelfth century A.D., the Muktēśvara shrine at Cauḍadānapura is a living temple with Vīraśaiva affiliations and preserves a long standing tradition of rites and rituals.

We are thankful to Vasundhara Filliozat and Pierre-Sylvain Filliozat, reputed Indologists and Sanskritists, who have authored the present monograph, for undertaking integrated and detailed investigations on this little-known shrine covering the history, epigraphs, architecture, iconography and local religious (Vīraśaiva) traditions and *āgamic* concepts. The monograph is intended to present, relatively, an integrated picture of various aspects of the Muktēśvara temple in the light of the sources available including those connected with Vīraśaivism. The epigraphical material available throws interesting light on the Pāśupata and Vīraśaiva traditions as also its interface with more crystallized and textually articulated *āgamic* tradition.

It appears from an inscription (Inscription I, p. 27) that the Muktēśvara temple was built under the influence of Pāśupatas with possibly *sabhaṣma dvijas* (brāhmaṇas smearing ashes on various parts of their body) serving as priests under the Śaiva *yogins*. While the brāhmaṇas recited sacred hymns using seven notes like the *Sāmaveda* and chanted the *Gāyatrī* hymn and the sacred Ṣaḍakṣarī (*Śiva*) *mantra* (*Oṁ namaḥ Śivāya*) to propitiate the Lord and offered *tarpaṇa* as a part of daily *pūjā* to the God, *ṛṣis* (sages=*gurus*) and the directions; the *yogins* (*pāśupatācāryas*) were engaged in the practice of (Haṭha) Yoga using diverse sitting poses like *padmāsana, vajrāsana* and *svastikāsana* and followed different precepts like *nādabheda, bindubheda, śaktibheda* and *ātmabheda* as a part of some specific system, in their *sādhanā.*

Initially, the temple under reference, although of Pāśupata (Śaiva) origin, recognized and accepted some elements of Brāhmaṇical tradition in regard to certain rituals as evidenced by inscriptions and iconographic representations. Possibly the system underwent some modification, under a puritanical Vīraśaiva saint (*siddha*) Śivadeva who arrived at this site, i.e., Muktikṣetra, around the middle of the year A.D. 1225 and introduced some amended or purified system of worship in the temple. According to the epigraphical references, he (Śivadeva) chased and dispersed the trembling *bhūtas* (evil spirits) and pounded Bhairava (Inscription III, p. 49). He has also been mentioned as the one who destroyed the prestige of those who worshipped other (than Śiva) gods, and that he carried nothing else but his overflowing weight of devotion to Śiva (Inscription V, p. 74). Such expressions suggest that on account of his great devotion to Śiva, with the knowledge of *Śiva-tattva,* he might have prevented the priests to make offerings to various deities like *bhūtas* and Bhairava, as a part of the *vighnotsāraṇa kriyā* and giving *bali* (offering) which is a normal item of Hindu *pūjā* tradition to make the ritual free from obstructions. Śivadeva appears to have rightly discarded the system with a spirit of total surrender to the Supreme Lord, i.e., Śiva. It is not unlikely that the Saint might have even simplified the rituals as a staunch follower of the doctrines of Vīraśaivism.

The Muktēśvara temple according to the local tradition symbolizes Kailāsa, the eternal abode of Śiva and his divine assembly. An inscription (III, p. 48), although Vīraśaiva in character, explains the concept beautifully: 'the excellent Tuṅgabhadrā is a divine river, the congregation of the brāhmaṇas is the assembly of gods, the temple of Śiva is Meru making thus the Muktikṣetra like Kailāsa on the earth.'

The *liṅga* installed inside this shrine is regarded to be a *svayaṁbhū-liṅga* representing Śiva with his own consciousness (creative power). The concept could be better understood in the light of a reference in *Kriyāsāra* of Śaivācārya Nīlakaṇṭha (*circa* 1400 A.D.), quoted by Pierre-Sylvain Filliozat, which reads as under:

Pṛthivyantargataḥ śambhurbījaṁ vaināda rūpataḥ /

Sthāvarāṅkuravadbhūmim-udbhidya vyakta eva saḥ //

[*Translation:* Śambhu inside the earth is like a seed in the form of *nāda,* simulating an immobile germ, which bursts from the ground and becomes manifest.]

The Vīraśaivas of Karṇāṭaka do not seem to have totally discarded pre-Basava concepts and elements of the main stream of Hindu thought including the sacredness of the Vedas and Śāstras and recognized even thirty gods of Vedic origin. It appears that there was a constant flow of ideas from one part of India to the other, and it is on this account that poet Bāṇabhaṭṭa's invocatory verse from *Harṣacaritam* (I.1), a non-religious text, reached Cauḍadānapura where it has been used as *maṅgalācaraṇa* in four out of eight epigraphs perhaps for the reason that it preserved the concept of Śiva as a cosmic column:

Namastuṅgaśiraścumbi-candracāmaracārave /

Trailokyanagarārambhamūlastambhāya śambhave //

[*Translation:* Salutation to Śiva, serving as the foundation-column (*mūla-stambha*) in the construction of a city comprising the three worlds (*Trilokas*), whose lofty head is decked with a charming fly-whisk in the form of the moon kissing it.]

Most probably the Pāśupatas were responsible for the origin of the concept of Śiva-*linga* as cosmic column which itself is derived from the Vedic notion of *skambha* as the source of life. The reference to *linga* being the basis of creation also appears to have been accepted by the Vīraśaivas. Theoretically, Śiva as a cosmic *linga* represents his *niṣkala* as well as *sakala* state.

The great saint Basava, the founder of Vīraśaivism, who strongly commended the worship of *iṣṭa-linga,* that is, a tiny *linga* to be worn around the neck by every one of his followers, believed in a totally casteless society. This idea has its source in the earlier Pāśupata doctrines as reflected in the undernoted verse preserved in the *Pañcatantra* (*Mitralābha,* verse 178):

Śūdrovā yadi vānyopi cāṇḍālo' pijaṭādharaḥ /

Dīkṣitaḥ Śiva-mantreṇa sa bhaṣmāṅgī Śivobhavet //

[*Translation:* If anyone whether a Śūdra or otherwise or even a *Cāṇḍāla* (lowest of the lowly) wears matted locks, smears ashes on his body and is initiated in *Śiva-mantra,* he turns into Śiva himself.]

A significant point about Siddha Śivadeva was that he was not just a Śaiva teacher but a builder also. He constructed a shrine in honour of Rudra at Mukti Tīrtha and also carried out conservation of the old temple of Muktēśvara. Besides, he established a monastery at Cauḍadānapura which survives even today.

An important reference recorded in some of the Cauḍadānapura epigraphs is about the migration of some members of the famous Gupta dynasty of north India to Karṇāṭaka, perhaps some time during or after the fall of the imperial line. The term Gupta was Kannaḍized as Gutta in Karṇāṭaka inscriptions. The Gutta chieftains, who were the main patrons of temples in Mukti Kṣetra, vividly record the tradition about Vikramāditya of Ujjayinī and name Candragupta as their ancestor. The Guttas used several titles to denote their connexions with the Guptas like *Guptānvayarājabhavana-kalaśa, Guptānvaya-Tilaka, Vikramāditya-Vaṁśodbhava, Candragupta Mahārājādhirāja-Kula Sampūrṇa, Gupta-Kula mārtaṇḍa,* etc. supporting their Gupta origin. It is not unlikely that elements of Gupta artistic idiom in Cālukyan sculpture might have been transported to Karṇāṭaka with the migration of the Guptas from northern India.

The Cauḍadānapura epigraphs, which refer to various cultural and political aspects of local history, contain interesting data about development of Kannaḍa language during the twelfth and thirteenth centuries in the area.

Another point, which deserves special attention in the context of architecture of the Muktēśvara temple, is Pierre-Sylvain Filliozat's discussion on theological concepts unfolding the mystery of unmanifested and manifested *Śiva-tattva.* Similarly, Vasundhara Filliozat, in connexion with her iconographic studies, records a custom of keeping a stick by the side of Śiva-*liṅga* or Vīrabhadra figure in the Liṅgāyata temples of Karṇāṭaka, which in her view may be a lingering influence of earlier Lakulīśa (Pāśupata) tradition.

The work, thus, is a fine specimen of integrated studies on a living shrine and enlightens us about the real purpose of a temple intended to serve as a multifaceted cultural entity in accordance with the needs and aesthetic awareness of a society. The credit for initiating such studies in India goes entirely to Dr. Kapila Vatsyayan, Academic Director of the Indira Gandhi National Centre for the Arts, who, over a decade ago, stressed upon the need to assess the age-old Indian shrines as a whole as symbols of a living culture in all their aspects. The present monograph, with this new approach to the study of an ancient temple, we hope, would be welcomed by scholars and students alike.

December 6, 1994 M.C. Joshi

PREFACE

A temple dedicated to a great Hindu God is the product, not only of a technical knowledge of building, but also of metaphysical and theological concepts, of artistic and literary culture and of characteristic religious practices and attitudes. We possess a revealing literary documentation on all these aspects. That which may be useful for the study of the temple of Muktēśvara at Cauḍadānapura is naturally circumscribed in works of Śaivite inspiration, as it is a monument dedicated to Śiva, erected by individuals inspired by the ideals of this religion and belonging to communities who characterise themselves by the pursuit of these ideals. It belongs to a period of transition in the history of Śaivism in Karnāṭaka, i. e. the 12th and 13th century when the predominant Pāśupata and Kālamukha movements were gradually integrated in what was to become the Vīraśaiva faith inspired by Basava. The prevalent Śaiva literature of that time, in that region, is the Śaivasiddhānta school of *Tantras* and of course the first period of Vīraśaiva literature, which appears itself as deeply rooted in the Tantric and Puranic lore.

The Śaivasiddhānta *Tantras* are claimed as scriptural authorithy by the Śaiva communities of that time in Karnāṭaka The *Vātulaśuddhāgama*, a version of the last text in the consecrated list of twenty-eight *Āgamas* has always been held in high reverence in this group. There are also Sanskrit Vīraśaiva *compendia* of Śaiva concepts, tenets and practices, such as the *Śaivaratnākara* of Jyotirnātha (c. 1100), the *Vīramāhēśvarācārasaṃgraha* of Nīlakaṇṭha Nāganātha (c. 1300), the *Kriyāsāra* of Nīlakaṇṭha Śivācārya (c. 1400). They contain a host of quotations from the same Śaivasiddhānta *Āgamas* and from *Purāṇas*. References to Vedic scriptures come only in the latest of these works.

These diverse communities, their organized religious institutions, their pontiffs and heads, are known to us through allusions in inscriptions found in the precincts of the temples. These inscriptions contain also references to āgamic sources, sometimes direct quotations. They express many facts of the religion, ideas about the deities, about the abodes offered to them on earth in the form of temples. The inscriptions and their tantric background are, indeed, the best source for the correct understanding of a Hindu temple.

The present study is based on the direct observation of the monument and remains on the site, on inquiry with all those who are to-day concerned with the life of the temple, descendants of the founder, villagers etc., on the examination of the inscriptions and on research in the literary sources. It aims at collecting and correlating informations of different sources. The section on history places the monument in its historical setting. The full text of the inscriptions is given and a translation is proposed. That appeared as an attempt to be done. These inscriptions provide the most authentic material about the temple. They are also refined literary pieces. And it appears necessary to correlate this poetic art with the plastic art of architecture and sculpture. Both, the inscribed chart and the monument, are objects of beauty, products of a same culture. The unity of this culture is based on philosophical and religious concepts, the origin of which we have searched in Sanskrit Tantric, Puranic and Vīraśaiva literature. The section on architecture includes an attempt to correlate the philosophical concepts of God and the world with the proper architectural forms and spaces. A brief description of particular features has been given, only to indicate the general structure of the monument. Features of style have not been studied as such. Any study of a temple style implies comparison of as many samples and items as possible. At the present stage it cannot be conducted satisfactorily, because the high number of later Cālukyan temples has not yet been systematically surveyed and very little material is easily accessible. In spite of the pioneering work done by Cousens and others the survey is still at its initial stage. The section of iconography is also shortened for the same reason.

The sections on history, epigrapghy and iconography are authored by Vasundhara Filliozat; the architecture has been dealt with by Pierre-Sylvain Filliozat.

The period of construction of the temple of Muktēśvara has been the thirteenth century, when a saintly figure, Śivadēva, inspired the religious life by his faith and his actions. His memory has been preserved in the inscriptions. The temple is still a testimony to the grandeur of the religion and art he inspired. His memory is also kept alive by a family in which are traditionally selected the heads of the local Vīraśaiva Maṭha and which claims Śivadēva himself as its most famous member. We had the good fortune to get our first acquaintance of this temple and of Śivadēva, through Sri Sadashiva Wodeyar, former Vice-Chancellor of Karnatak University, Dharwar, who not only gave us hospitality, informations, but also demonstrated to us the profound feeling that this holy place and monument raise in the heart of the Vīraśaivas. He invited us to work on the site in his family home, where his father, Shivadeva Wodeyar lived in retirement, like the saint of yore. They both helped us in many ways, with friendly services as well as with informations. We regret very much that Shri Shivadeva is no more in this world to see this book, which he wished so much to help. Like his predecessor Saint Śivadēva, our Ajja also left this world to enter that of Śiva as a nonagenaire. We evoke his memory with reverence and nostalgy. We extend our most hearty thanks to Sri Sadashiva Wodeyar and to all those in his entourage who helped us and sympathised with our work. We have a special debt of gratitude to Professor K. Krisnamurthy who has explained us difficult poetical passages of inscriptions and thanks to whom our translation was greatly improved. Our special thanks are due to my guru, Dr. G. S. Dikshit, for his timely advices and suggestions.We have a thought for all those whom we consulted like Drs. M. M. Kalburgi, Raghunath Bhatt, Katti from Karnāṭak University, Dharwar, and who gave us willingly precious informations. Also we will not fail to remember the participation of Mr. Basavaraj and Mr. Hiremath, two students of architecture and our daughters Miss Manonmani and Bhamati at the initial stage of this work. We will no forget to evoke the precious advice given by Prof. K. R. Hayagreevachar and his better half Vanamala Achar; both, being professors of English, went through the first draft of this text and gave us some valuble hints to improve our style of English. We also express heart felt gratitude to The Indira Gandhi National Centre for the Arts, New-Delhi, for accepting to make our work available to the world of scholars and indologists.

We lack in words to express our heartfelt gratitude to Dr. (Mrs.) Kapila Vatsyayan, Academic Director of IGNCA, New Delhi, for accepting to publish this work. We thank also Mr. M.C. Joshi, Ex-Director General of ASI, now Member Secretary of IGNCA, for his valuable suggestions and finally Dr. Lalit Gujral of IGNCA for making our work available to the world of scholars and indologists in a short time.

Paris, 20 August 1993 Vasundhara & Pierre-Sylvain FILLIOZAT

I

HISTORY

To-day, though reduced to a small village, Cauḍadānapura, with its temple of Muktēśvara, is a celebrated pilgrim centre for Śaivaïtes, and undoubtedly it has played an important role in the 12th and 13th centuries. Cauḍayyadānapura or Cauḍadānpura are different orthographs of one and the same modern village (Long. 75° 42' and Lat. 14° 48') situated on the Southern bank of Tuṅgabhadrā river, in the Ranebennur Taluk, Dharwar District, Karnataka State in South India, at a distance of about 23 kms to the north-east of Rāṇebennūr. It can be reached by route from Rāṇebennūr, Hāvēri, Hāvanūr via Guttala. It is seven kms from Guttala and lies between Honnatti and Guttala.

To the north of the village flows Tuṅgabhadrā, one of the most beautiful rivers of India. The spot where the temple of God Śiva is built is endowed with exquisite scenic beauty with the meandering stream of the river flowing westwards. Sitting on the parapet wall of the temple, the visitor meditates over the landscape of Narasipura on one side, Kuruvatti on the other and the gently flowing Tuṅgabhadrā in the front.

Sources.

The reconstitution of the history of Cauḍadānapura is not an easy task because of scanty documentation. Although the surrounding region abounds in inscriptions and monuments, the establishment of historical facts gets hindered due to the rehabilitation of the village and recent repairs or re-arrangements made in the temple complex. There are eight inscriptions in the temple. *Śivadēvavijaya*, a *kāvya* probably written in the 19th century or even later by a certain Śarīf Kavi, and a few documents in the archives of a Maṭha are the only sources which come in handy to the historians.

The above mentioned *Śivadēvavijaya* by Śarīf Kavi is a very good example of *kāvya* in Kannaḍa. It deals with the life and activities of the saint Śivadēva who was responsible for the glory of the present village of Cauḍa-dānapura. It is evident that the poet had a high command over Sanskrit and classical Kannaḍa, but was unaware of the life history of the saint. For example, while extolling the greatness of Śivadēva, by pure devotion the poet makes him travel from place to place and credits him with many miraculous powers, whereas in the inscriptions it is said that Śivadēva took the vow not to cross the four limits of Muktikṣētra. There are many such disparities between the contents of the *kāvya* and the epigraphs. Therefore, we decided it is better not to rely much upon this literary work. Besides, it has been published on the basis of only two incomplete manuscripts and each one with only two cantos.

About an inscription dated Śaka 821 Siddhārthi saṃvatsara, the *Dharwar Gazetteer* published in 1884 and *Śivadēvavijaya* (appendix p.41) refer to an article in the *Journal of the Bombay Branch of Royal Asiatic Society* vol IX. But there is no question of this inscription in the said article[1]. Dates of the available inscriptions engraved on stone slabs *in situ* range from 1100 to 1292. On the ghats, i. e. the steps leading to the river, there are a few fragmentary records. Among them one is dated Śaka 1486 Raktākṣi saṃvatsara corresponding to 1565, and it records the visit of some pilgrims to Muktikṣētra. Another inscription from Narasipura, dated 1556 A.D., mentions the name of Muktikṣētra while enumerating the boundaries of fields donated to God Narasiṃha. These are the last known records which mention Muktikṣētra. The other inscriptions in the temple of Muktēśvara furnish very valuable historical information and some are literary pieces par excellence. If one mentions the name of Basavēśvara the founder of the Vīraśaiva sect, another mentions Rēvaṇasiddha, probably the author of *Siddhāntaśikhāmaṇi.* Both the persons are of great importance to the Vīraśaivas. Moreover, the information recorded in the inscriptions on social and religious conditions of this period is inexhaustible.

Other documents such as *kaḍita*s and papers in the archives of the Maṭha deal with the history and other accounts of the institution. As they are not of much use for us to re-write the early history of the temple, we have not used them here.

---

1 "Report on Photographic Copies of Inscriptions in Dharwar and Mysore" by Dr. BHAU DAJI in *Journal of the Bombay Branch of Royal Asiatic Society* IX, 1867, p. 326-327.

The name of the place.

In the inscriptions, the place is called, chronologically, Gōpe, Mukti-kṣētra and Śivapura. Cauḍadānapura appears to be a later appellation, though a legend attributes it to the twelfth century.

The history of Cauḍadānapura centres around the temple of Muktēśvara and the saint Śivadēva Voḍeyar who lived there in the 13th century. According to the *kāvya*, the place was donated to Cauḍayya, a great devotee of Śiva, by Śivadēva pleased with his devotion; hence the name Cauḍayyadānapura (*dvitīya āśvāsa* verse 109 ff., p. 54). This Cauḍayya belonged to the community of boatmen (*ambiga*).

Although the *vacanas* of Ambigara Cauḍayya are available to us, there is no historical evidence to give credit to the above mentioned story. However, even to-day the local boatmen play an important role during the festivities of the Maṭha. This proves that there must be some truth somewhere in the legend. Perhaps, in the subsequent centuries there might have been a Cauḍayya belonging to the caste of boatmen who must have played an important role on some occasion. But the absence of documents hampers the research progress. So let us leave the legend and look at the past history of Cauḍadānapura through the inscriptions.

In its primitive days Gope was the name of Cauḍadānapura. Whether it was "Gope" or "Gōpe" is not known. "Cave, grotto" is the meaning of the former word, whereas the meaning of the latter is doubtful. The reading of the inscription No. II gives an idea that Gope was located somewhere in between the present villages of Cauḍadānapura and Honnatti. So it is not wrong to say that Cauḍadānapura is not the exact location of the ancient Gope.

In *Vīrāgamottara*[1] there is a reference to a place called Muktinilaya:

तुङ्गभद्रानदी गौरि अस्ति पापहरा नृणाम् । तत्तीरे मुक्तिनिलयं ब्रह्मविष्णुप्रपूजितम् ।।

tuṅgabhadrānadī gauri asti pāpaharā nr̥ṇām ।
tattīre MUKTINILAYAṂ brahmaviṣṇuprapūjitam ॥

"O Gauri (listen), the river Tuṅgabhadrā steals away the sins of mankind; on its bank is Muktinilaya "abode of Mukti" revered by Brahman and Viṣṇu."

Taking into account the epigraphical evidences, it may not be wrong to think that the *āgama* makes here an allusion to the temple of Muktēśvara on the bank of Tuṅgabhadrā.

---

1 *Vīrāgamottara* paṭala 4, stanza 374, p. 264.

There are many versions with regard to the name Muktikṣētra. According to one given by a Svāmi who lives in Mailāra, because the river Tuṃgabhadrā takes a curve and the meandering stream runs westwards, then turns to the North, the place where one course ends and the other begins.is called "Muktikṣētra"

Turning to the epigraphical evidences the term Muktitīrtha (line 45) is met with right from the first inscription. The second inscription states that in the year 1191 an ascetic named Muktajīyar was at this place and was performing the *pūjā* of Muktinātha. During this time the god came to be known as Muktēśa (l. 67):

ಮುಕ್ತೇಶ್ವರನಾಮಾರಂಭನೆಸೆವುತಿರ್ಪ್ಪನೀಶನುಮೇಶಂ

Muktēśvara nāmāraṃbhanesevutirppanīśanumēśam.

So, appropriate was the name of god Muktēśvara as he was bestowing *mukti* on his disciples. The remaining inscriptions provide abundant information with regard to Muktikṣētra and Muktēśvara.

In India river banks, seashores and the summit of mountains are considered to be very sacred for the construction of temples. Especially the sites where the river runs northwards are regarded as holier. As Tuṅgabhadrā starts her northward course from this place no wonder the site was considered as holy and chosen for building temples. It is worthy of note that in other inscriptions also the term Muktikṣētra occurs. That means not only Cauḍadānapura village but also the surrounding localities such as modern Guttala, and its suburb Haraḷahaḷḷi were parts of Muktikṣētra (S.I.I. XVIII No.295, l. 77-78). Nevertheless, Cauḍadānapura holds a higher rank in the matter of sanctity

Śivapura. When Muktajīyar left this mundane world to enjoy the pleasures of the world of Śiva, a Śaiva saint named Śivadēva residing at Śrīparvata (Śrīśailam in Āndhra), under the orders of Lord Śiva, entered Muktikṣētra in 1226 A.D. and occupied the pontifical seat. Leading a very pious life he must have lived there beyond 1292. As his influence grew, the place came to be known as Śivapura. From this date onwards, in the inscriptions, the names of Muktikṣētra and Śivapura begin to occur simultaneously

The river Tuṅgabhadrā is compared to the sacred river Gaṅgā in the North and Cauḍadānapura is called Southern Vārāṇasi. Like Vārāṇasi this place also carried the name Śivapura. From time immemorial, Vārāṇasi is exalted for its merits. Cauḍadānapura stood equal to this holy place in all respects.

Śivadēva was very much impressed and influenced by the philosophy of Basava, the founder of the Vīraśaiva movement which was gradually gaining the terrain then. Śivadēva established a Vīraśaiva Maṭha at Śivapura. His descendants, the Wodeyar family in Dharwar, who belong to Vīraśaiva community, still have control over the Maṭha. They are in posession of some historical doccuments and our well-wisher patron was also called Śivadēva Voḍeyar like the saint of the thirteenth century.

The Historical background.

Out of the many dynasties that have contributed to the glory of Karnāṭaka, the Kadaṃbas from Banavāsi, the Cāḷukyas from Bādāmi and Kalyāṇa, the Rāṣtrakūṭas from Maḷakhēḍ, the Kaḷacūris from Kalyāṇa, the Yādavas from Dēvagiri, the Hoysaḷas from Bēlūr and Haḷebīḍu, and, of course, the Karnāṭaka kings from Vijayanagara are very important. After the fatal battle of Tāḷikōṭa in 1565, though the Hindu kings were routed from the present Karnāṭaka, the name of the kingdom of Karnāṭaka was heard in the extreme South. If in *Kavirājamārga* the boundaries of Karnāṭaka were from Kāvēri to Gōdāvari, after 1565, it was limited only to the banks of the river Kāvēri streching up to Tañjāvūr in Tamiḻnāḍu.

As stated earlier, there were two dynasties amongst the Cāḷukyas. The early Cāḷukyas ruled from their capitals Bādāmi, Paṭṭadakallu and Aihoḷe (6th to 8th century). The Rāṣṭrakūṭas succeeded them and ruled over the kingdom for more than two centuries, from their capital at Maḷakhēḍ and Verūḷa (8th to 10th century). In the latter half of the 10th century, around the year 973 A.D. Taila II of the waning Cāḷukya stock succeeded in overthrowing the last weak Rāṣṭrakūṭa king and restored the power.to his own dynasty. For some time, he even ruled from Maḷakhēḍ and then transferred his capital to Kalyāṇa from where the dynasty exercised power for more than two centuries. The reigns of Cāḷukya Sōmēśvara I (1043-1068) and Vikramāditya VI (1075-1126) are considered to be an Augustan age in the history of literature and art in Karnāṭaka. Between 1150 and 1186, for a short period, the Cāḷukya power was eclipsed. Bijjaḷa of Kaḷacūri stock triumphed in overthrowing the sovereign ruler Taila III in 1157, but occupied the royal throne only in 1162. His reign is remarkable in the history of Karnāṭaka because of the new movement led by Basavēśvara the founder of Vīraśaiva community. This topic will be dealt with later, in the section about Śivadēva at Cauḍadānapura.

In 1186, some agitation followed by the assassination of Bijjaḷa, favoured the accession of Cāḷukya Sōmēśvara VI to the throne (S.I.I. XVIII, No. 163). But the victory did not last long because the king was too weak to face the Hoysaḷas rising into power on one side and the Sēvuṇas of Dēvagiri on the other. Together Hoysaḷas and Sēvuṇas caused the final downfall of the Cāḷukyas. With the end of this dynasty the beautiful Banavāsidēśa, the pupil of Karnāṭaka, became the bone of contention between the Hoysaḷas and the Yādavas of Dēvagiri.

The Hoysaḷas began their career as feudatories of Cāḷukyas, and in no time gained importance. Viṣṇuvardhana, the first great monarch of Hoysaḷa family began to expand his power already in the glorious days of Vikramāditya VI. Though the latter tried to check him, Viṣṇuvardhana successfully established his secondary residence at Baṅkāpura in the heart of the Cāḷukya dominion. They never stopped strengthening their position and finally became overlords of the whole empire with the extinction of Cāḷukyas. But peace was not at their doors. The incessant feuds with the Yādavas of Dēvagiri for the control over the extinguished Cāḷukyan kingdom turned the attention of Hoysaḷas from temple construction to military garrisons and that resulted in impoverishment of temple art in the region of Banavāsidēśa.

Minor dynasties.

Guttas of Guttavaḷal.

To day Guttala is a small village in Hāvēri tālūk but it played an important role in the early years of 11th century. Guttas were the rulers of Guttala. The first inscription to mention Gutta and Dāsa is the one which hails from the Gaḷagēśvara temple at Gaḷaganāth and is dated 1080 A.D. (S.I.I. XVIII, No. 88). Dāsa was in the service of Cenna, a subordinate of Vikramāditya VI. In the same inscription.a stray reference to Gutta occurs in l. 52

A record speaking of Guttas and the family of Dāsa in more details is an undated inscription from Muktēśvara temple at Cauḍadānapura (No. I; S.I.I. XVIII, No. 112).While crediting the Guttas with the patronage of the temple at this place, it says that Gōvindarasa was governing the region of Banavāsideśa. Fleet has assigned the date of this inscription of Cauḍadānapura to 1115 on the basis of other epigraphical statements that Gōvindarasa was administering Banavāsidēśa between 1110 and 1120 when king Vikramāditya VI adorned the Cāḷukya throne. Some modern historians fully agree with him. However there are other inscriptions dated right from 1101 A.D. which mention the name of the same Gōvindarasa as governor of the same Banavāsidēśa, while king Vikramāditya VI was on the throne. It is probable that the king might have created the principality of Guttavaḷal and put the Guttas in charge of its protection, perhaps after the events recorded in an inscription dated 1104 A.D (S.I.I. IX, pt. i No. 169).

There is some confusion with regard to the origin of the Gutta family. The name appears to be a Kannaḍisation of "Gupta", because the descendants of this family say that they belong to Gupta dynasty. At the same time, in the same inscription of Cauḍadānapura No. 1 there is an allusion to the legendary king Vikramāditya who ruled from Ujjayinī, who was blessed by the Goddess Kālī and was familiar with ghosts and goblins. This confusion is due to the lapse of time and distance. Guptas were in the north and ruled from Pāṭaliputra from fifth to seventh centuries. The most powerful king of this dynasty was Candragupta Vikramāditya. For their namesake, a confusion was created between the legendary king Vikramāditya devotee of God Mahākāla and king Candragupta Vikramāditya of Gupta dynasty.

From an inscription dated 1124 we gather that the Gutta chieftains had control over the Beṇṇevūru 12, Beḷahuge 70 and Honnavarti 12 seignories. It also confirms the fact that the Guttas were descendants of Guptas of Central India (S.I.I. XVIII, No. 124). The Cauḍadānapura inscription, being the first to be issued by the Guttas, there is some confusion about their descent, whereas there is no room for such doubts in the inscriptions of Haraḷahaḷḷi and other places dated 1105 and after. This fact makes it clear that Cauḍadānapura inscription was issued prior to 1105 A.D.

Māgutta according to Cauḍadānapura inscription, was the founder of the family. To him was born Gutta, a "tilaka" on the forehead of the family of Guttas. Like a jewel amongst the kings, his son Mallidēva was shining like a moon on the eastern ocean. Jōma I was the younger brother of Mallidēva. Vikramāditya I was the son of Mallidēva. Jōyidēva or Jomma II and Gutta II were the two sons born to Vikramāditya I. With his queen Padmaladēvi Gutta II begot one son Vīra Vikramāditya II and a daughter Vijayamahādēvi. Paṭṭamahādēvi and Sōvaladēvi were two queens of Vikramāditya II. His sister Vijayamahādevi was married to Siṅgidēva of Sāntali-maṇḍala or Sattaḷige which is identical with modern Sātēnahaḷḷi. Vikramāditya II had three children namely Gutta III, Jōyi or Jomma III, Vikramāditya III and a daughter called Tuḷuvaladēvi. She was married to Ballāḷa son of Siṅgidēva of Saṃtaḷimaṃḍala. Vikramāditya IV, Gutta IV, Hiriyadēva and Joyidēva IV were the four progenies of Vikramāditya III. After Vikramāditya V son of Jōyidēva IV the name of Guttas is heard no longer. Nothing is known as to what happened to the family.

Close matrimonial alliances of Guttas with the chieftains of Raṭṭihaḷḷi and Sātēnahaḷḷi are revealed from epigraphs. Sōvaladēvi, wife of Vikramāditya II, was the daughter of Vijayapāṇḍya of the Raṭṭihaḷḷi royal family. Laḷiyādēvi, one of the princesses of Guttas was married to a Raṭṭihaḷḷi chieftain. The influence of these happy alliances is reflected in the art and architecture of these regions The temples at Raṭṭihalli, Cauḍadānapura, Sātēnahaḷḷi and Haraḷahaḷḷi make one unit. Probably one common architectural treatise or *āgama* must have been followed for the construction of these monuments.

Religious conditions.

Prior to the date of Śivadēva at Śivapura or Cauḍadānapura the Śaiva movement of Pāśupatas and Kāḷāmukhas was very powerful in Karnāṭaka. Many Kāḷāmukha and Pāśupata saints were "rājagurus" or royal preceptors of ruling monarchs and their vassals. They were followers of Lākuḷasiddhāṃta or Lakuḷīśamata and were generally known as Lākuḷaśaivas.

The name Lakulīśa is variously spelt as Lakulēśa, Nakulīśa, Lakuḷin, etc. and it is derived from *lakula, lakuṭa* or *laguḍa* the club which represents the four vēdas, carried by Śiva in his hands. In the iconography, by and large Lakulīśa is characterised by two hands, one of them holding this *laguḍa* or *daṇḍa.*

About Lakulīśvara the founder of the Lākuḷapantha there are no definite records to fix his date and his origin. He is supposed to be none but Śiva.and the author of many *āgama*s or basic texts known under the title *Lākuḷāgama.* It is really our misfortune that we have lost them all. This loss handicaps much the progress of research work.

Lakuḷīśa may have hailed from Kāśmīr. According to various sources he is an incarnation of Śiva himself who came to the earth in human form to "bestow favour on the universe"[1]. Dr. Lorenzen, in conclusion says thus: "It

---

[1] See David Lorenzen, *The Kāpālikas and Kāḷāmukhas,* Thomson Press ltd, New-Delhi, 1972, p.176. About the tradition locating Lakulīśa in Kāyārōhaṇa (modern Kārvāṇ in Gujrat) and the relevant epigraphical documents, see *Corpus Inscriptionum Indicarum,* vol. III, *Inscriptions of the early Gupta Kings,* 1981, revised by D. R. Bhandarkar, B. Ch. Chhabra and G.S. Gai,

is evident that not much solid historical information can be derived from these accounts. They are however unanimous on two points, that Lakulīśa was regarded as an incarnation of Śiva and that he settled at a place called Kāyāvarōhaṇa in the Lāṭa or Bhṛgukaccha region. It also seems that Lakulīśa belonged to a brāhmaṇa family and that he travelled at least as far as Ujjayinī to preach his doctrine" (*ibidem* p. 177). As this is not the main point of our book we shall leave this problem here and proceed to study Kāḷāmukhas and Pāśupatas.

A few general remarks have been made by previous historians with regard to Kāḷāmukhas and Pāśupatas in general but nothing much has been done in particular about this movement in Karnāṭaka. A special study on this subject is worthwhile, because features of these movements in Karnāṭaka appear to be different from that of other regions. In this connection, ample material is available in inscriptions from Shimoga, Dharwar and Bijapur districts.

Some scholars are of the opinion that Kāḷāmukhas of Lakuḷīśapantha came to Karnāṭaka from Kāśmīra, and the earliest reference in this connection is found in an inscription dated in the 9th century. Usually their names end with the term "Jīya, Śiva, Śakti" etc. and on the basis of this Dr. G. S. Dikshit dates the presence of Kāḷāmukhas back to 755 A.D. In support of his views he quotes an inscription from Paṭṭadakallu which mentions that "Jñānaśiva came there from Mrigathanikāhāraviṣaya on the north bank of the Ganges"[1].

Other epigraphical records relate that the Kāḷāmukhas and Pāśupatas came to Karnāṭaka from the four corners of India. For example the Kāḷāmukha gurus at Noḷambavāḍi claim a relationship with Malayāḷapaṇḍita from Rāmēśvaram. The Gurus of Śaktipariśe of Kōḍimaṭha at Baḷḷigāṃve show their origin at Śrīśailam, though the Gurus hailed from Kēdār in the North. At Kuḍatini near Bellary, there was a school whose teachers came from Bengal. So, taking into account the information furnished by these examples it appears that by the 10th century, almost the whole of Karnāṭaka was dominated by Kāḷāmukhas and Pāśupatas of Lākula doctrine from the four corners of the country, settled in different parts of the kingdom after choosing for their base the headquarters of royal and feudatory families. The majority of the Śaiva

---

Introduction p. 133 sq. These sources suggest that Lakulin flourished in the first quarter of the 2nd c. A.D.

[1] Dr. G. S. Dikshit, "Social and Religious Conditions before Basava" in *Sri Basavēśvara Commemoration Volume*, p. 121.

temples were built under the orders of Kāḷāmukha and Pāśupata religious leaders in Karnāṭaka. And monuments were also provided with inscriptions giving facts about the purport of the construction, the name of the donee(s) and the donor(s), of spiritual leaders and so on These inscriptions never fail to mention that the establishment and the religious heads were followers of the Lākuḷa doctrine propounded by Lakuḷīśa.

In the absence of documents it is difficult to point out the difference between Kāḷāmukhas and Pāśupatas. Some inscriptions record the fact that the former were *naiṣṭhikas*, attached much importance to celibacy and observed *guruśiṣya-paramparā* in the matter of succession to a pontifical throne (E.C. VII, Shikarpur ins. 99 and onwards), whereas the Pāśupatas in many cases were married and practiced *pitāputra-paramparā* for a pontifical seat (S.I.I. XVIII No. 133). But there are also inscriptions, which mention that Kāḷāmukhas were married and Pāśupatas were *naiṣṭhika.* So in such contradicting cases of factual records, it is difficult to draw any definite conclusion about their religious life. This topic can be an object of special study[1]. Epigraphical source makes it clear that in Karnāṭaka Kāḷāmukhas and Pāśupatas were following *Lākuḷāgamas* and held in high reverence Lakuḷiśvara.

Though it is an indication but to be used with much care and caution, generally it is believed that the persons who bear names ending with "jīyar, śakti, paṇḍita" etc. are Lākuḷaśaivas. With regard to their physical appearance, from sculptures and epigraphic data it appears, that, irrespective of the changes of climate, they were clad with just a pagne. Their whole body was smeared with cinder. Their head was never shaved and dressed with knotted hair. They were growing beards and moustaches.

As they were followers of Lakuḷīśa, naturally they followed the *Lākuḷāgamas* for building temples. All the scholars unanimously agree that the *Lākuḷāgamas* are different from the *Śaivāgamas* of *Śaivasiddhānta.* If this is the case, then how far can the latter be used in the study of the architecture of these temples ? However the architectural elements mentioned in the *Śaivāgamas* of Śaivasiddhānta are amply prevalent in these temples. Therefore, it may not be wrong to presume that there was a close affinity between the texts of *Śaivasiddhānta* and *Lākuḷāgamas*. To corroborate this an inscription from Sālōṭṭagi mentions the name of Sōmaśaṃbhu (S.I.I. XVIII, No.

[1] Some treatises make difference between Kāḷāmukha, Pāśupata and Lākuḷaśaivas. Others differentiate between Pāśupatas and Kāḷāmukhas.

179). Another inscription from Gadag cites *Siddhāgama.* In Cauḍadānapura inscriptions verses from *Candrajñānāgama* occur (see ins. No III).

Vīraśaivism.

It is difficult to say whether Vīraśaivism is an offshoot of the Lākuḷa-śaivism or a totally independent movement by itself. Under the influence of Lākuḷaśaivas temple building became very active in Karnāṭaka during 12th-13th centuries. However, temples are treasures of arts and culture; their maintenance means a heavy taxing to the public. A few changes that Basava, the finance minister of Bijjaḷa, tried to introduce in the society, were to control the proliferation of construction of temples, of huge grants in cash and kind, of exaggeration in the modes of conduct. Religious heads of Lakuḷīśapanthins were walking almost naked execept a piece of cloth to cover the secret parts of the body, had knotted hair, their body smeared with ashes. They used to produce a kind of *ḍuṃ ḍum* sound[1], at the time of rituals, and at times behave like madmen etc. Probably Basava and his followers wanted, if not to abolish, at least to bring under control such abnormal activities.Though it was not his intention, the revolution begun by Basava on the principle "Work is worship" ended up with the birth of the new religion called "Vīraśaiva" or "Liṅgāyata".

He preached his followers to respect work and duty, to worship *iṣṭaliṅga* the symbol of Śiva and carry it on their body. This practice of wearing a *Liṅga* existed already amongst the Kāḷāmukhas. Nevertheless he did not oppose the building of temples. He allowed those who are fortunate enough to build temples, but told that those who could not, should be contented with the worship of *iṣṭaliṅga* and rendering services to *Jaṅgamas.* The latter are known as *caraliṅgas.*Worship of *Iṣṭaliṅga* and *Jaṅgama* were emphasised thus. Gradually, this new faith began to gain terrain and its propounders started replacing the Kāḷāmukha and Pāśupata pontiffs. In the subsequent centuries, those who carried a *liṅga* on their body came to be known as *liṅgin* or *liṅgāyata* and finally Liṅgāyata or Vīraśaiva. It may not be wrong to say that the Vīraśaivism is a refined version of Lākuḷaśaivism.

Basava and his followers preached the value of "work is worship" through *vacanas* or "paroles", which can be either set to music and sung or recited. This *vacanasāhitya* occupies a unique place in Kannaḍa literature.

---

1 At the times of main *pūjā*s in the temple of Jagannāth in Puri I was surprised to hear the sound produced by the devotees by tapping on their mouth with three or four fingers.

By the end of the 13th century mentions of Kāḷāmukha or Pāśupata became rarer and rarer. In the year 1292 Ballāḷa III mounted on the throne of Hoysaḷas. Soon after his accession the whole of South India witnessed a drastic event, i. e. Malik Kāfūr's invasion. During the following three-four decades the muslim invasion persisted, leaving the whole of South India in chaotic conditions till 1346, when the Saṅgama brothers under the leadership of Harihara and Bukka took the reins of protection of the Hindu kingdom. Their principal religious protectors were the pontiffs of Śāradāpīṭha and the two renowned Vedic scholars Mādhava and Sāyaṇa at Śṛṅgēri in Karnāṭaka. As a result of their joint efforts the whole of south India was united and came under the banner of the "Karnāṭaka Empire" with its capital at Vijayanagar which is modern Haṃpi. These political changes led to the decline of Lākuḷa-śaivas and even to the extent of their total disappearance.

Saṅgamas the new kings of Karnāṭaka empire requested Sāyaṇa and Mādhava to revive vedic studies. During this period only, the new Śaivism also came to prominence.The ideals of Basava received due recognition. The *Vacanas* of Basava and other saints were collected, arranged under the headings of *ṣaṭsthalamārga, Śūnyasampādane,* etc.

Śivadēva happens to be the last Śaiva saint to propagate the principles of Basava before the invasion of Malik Kāfūr in the south. Owing to the services rendered by Śivadēva and his disciples the principles of Basava were still lingering in the memory of people. And that helped the revival of new Śaivism in the 14th century. To designate the followers of this new Śaivism terms such as Vīraśaiva or Liṅgāyat came into usage and never vanished. In reality, the present day Vīraśaivas owe much more to Śivadēva than to Basava, because the latter is the founder, whereas the former is the protector.

History of Cauḍadānapura.

The beginning of the 12th century was an auspicious dawn in the history of Guttala. In the early 1120s a certain Attirāja of Jaṭācōḷa family, a relative of Guttas, built a temple on the spot known as Muktitīrtha on the southern bank of Tuṅgabhadrā near Guttala, the residential town of Guttas. The inscription recording this event is, unfortunately, incomplete. However it informs that the place was inhabited by brahmins reciting *Sāmavēda, Gāyatrījapa* etc. and there were many *liṅgāśrayas*. The meaning of this word is not clear. Probably they were the numerous small shrines or shelters dedicated to Śivaliṅgas.

In the following years, the place came to prominence. In 1191-92 Muktajīyar became the temple head. From his name it appears that he was a Lākuḷaśaiva. Inscription No. II mentions that Śiva began to be called by the name Muktēśvara (l. 67). It is not clear whether Muktajīyar had another temple built or he worshipped the Liṅga which was installed by Jaṭācōḷa and was rechristened by this new name.

The same inscription ends with the phrase :
ಕಲುಹಂದರಾದಿಯಾಗಿ ಹೊರಥರ ಸಹಿತ ರೇವೋಜನ ಕೆಲಸ
kaluhaṃdarādiyāgi hoṟathara sahita rēvōjana kelasa.

First the meaning of the two terms *kaluhaṃdara* and *hoṟathara* requires to be made clear. In Kannaḍa a *manṭapa* or pavillion is called *handara.* In that case, a *manṭapa* which was built of stone might be the meaning of *kaluhandara. Thara*[1] is a coating and *hoṟa* means "external". Including the external coating, the building of a pavillion in stone was carried out by the architect Rēvōja.

With the arrival of Śivadēva at Muktikṣētra begins the second phase of the history of this holy place. The inscription No. III, in the style of the epics, relates the events that lead Śivadēva, the worshipper of Dhavaḷaliṅga at Śrīśailaṃ, to go to Muktikṣetra. His guru Śivamuddudēva believed that in the four worlds of Brahman, one has to undergo the six *vikṛtis*. Whereas in the case of Śivadēva it looked as if Śiva himself was born in the best of the family as Śivadēva who appeared like a *gaṇeśvara* (l. 21 to 23, verse 11). The Guru advised his disciple thus : "The river Tuṃgabhadrā is a holy river. There are assemblies of brahmins and Gods. The real Kailāsa is there where is the abode of Śiva and that is Muktikṣētra, you should go there and disclose the greatness of Śivabhakti". Accordingly, Śivadēva entered Muktikṣētra at noon, on Monday, 15th day of the bright fortnight of the month of Bhādrapada in the cyclic year Pārthiva, Śaka 1148, corresponding to 1225 August 19th. No sooner he entered the place he engaged himself in writing the story of Kaiḷāsa. Unfortunately, this poetical work is not available to-day. Remembering God's holy feet Śivadēva built a shrine to Rudra. He took vows (*vīravrata*) i. e. not to cross the four limits of his residential town, not to lie down on the floor, not to embrace women with the arms with which he em-

---

[1]The term *thara* (ಥರ) occurs in other inscriptions also (E.C. V, Arsikere 8).

braced the *liṅga* and not to accept anything unless given by Mahādēva. Śivadēva was like Basava, the founder of the Vīraśaiva community. His main aim was to propagate Śivabhakti or devotion towards Śiva. He built a *Śiva-kaṭṭe* in order to convince the world that this is the only way to acquire Śivapada. Like the three Vedas as body of the three worlds created by Brahman, Śivadēva built a temple in propitiation of Rudra, as if it were the Kaiḷāsa on the earth, where Śiva himself had descended down with his *gaṇas*. His way of worshipping the *liṅga* was different from those of the ancestors (*purātanaru*). In what way his method of *pūjā* differed from that of the ancestors is not explained. Besides what is the meaning of *Purātana* ? Is it an allusion to the *triṣaṣṭi Purātanas* "63 Śaiva saints" or the Kāḷāmukhas and Pāśupatas ? In the context the latter reference seems more appropriate.

The place was named Śivapura after Śiva which was also the saint's name. Thus it became equal to Vārāṇāsi even in name. Another very important work that Śivadēva accomplished was the restoration of the old temples at Muktikṣētra. The temple which was known in the three worlds as Śivabhavana was dilapidated upto the pinnacle. Once again he had it done upto the finial in stone (l. 36 to 37, verse 21).

Here again readers are left in doubt. The record is not explicit in mentioning the temple which underwent the repairs. As late as in 1191-92 Rēvōja had worked on a temple and made it in stone. In the lapse of 35 years had this temple fallen to that state of ruins ? Or was there another temple, equally important, which needed repairs ? These questions remain answerless.

In style, the inscription No. IV excels all the others. In the manner of a *Sthaḷamāhātmya* it begins with the description of Śiva in his assembly where *gaṇas* praise him. On coming to know the reason of their visit, hearing their eulogy and the cause of their anxiety Śiva assured them that on the earth, in the name of Muktīśa He will reside with Umā, at Muktikṣētra. He also ordered his *gaṇas* to come down to the earth (*bhūraṅgakke baralikke*.l. 18) with Him. So, Śivadēva appeared in the best or highest family.

Little explanation will not be out place here. The previous inscription clearly mentions that Śivadēva came from Śrīśailam. The word *udaya* in the inscription No. IV should not be taken in the sense of "born" but "hailed". The word *agraja* may be interpreted as the best of the families, probably priestly class

In the inscriptions Śivadēva's observance of severe vows and particularly of celibacy. are emphasised. Those were the days when great importance was attached to celibacy by Kāḷāmukhas and Pāśupatas. Śivadēva opted for this practice. Like Saṅgana Basava he also accepted to serve not only Liṅga but also Jaṅgamas. Through *vīravrata* he achieved the same *siddhi* which Saṃgana Basava had obtained (l. 48b to 49, verse 22).

It shows that Śivadēva adopted an intermediary way of devotional life between the declining Lākuḷaśaiva system and the rising Vīraśaiva movement. Like Lākuḷaśaivas he also built one more shrine to Śiva at Muktikṣētra itself and attended to the repairs of a dilapidated temple to save it from further decay, though building temples is not Vīraśaiva. However he too worshipped Liṅga and Jaṅgama like Basava. Probably, Vīraśaivism must have suffered from backdrops.following the chaotic conditions in Kalyāṇa after the death of Basava. So, it may not be wrong to say that saints like Śivadēva gave a boost to the movement started by Basava and yet did not go against the existing practices of Kāḷāmukhas and Pāśupatas. On discovering his ascetic values, a Gutta king was convinced that his blessings were necessary for his welfare. Owing to the vow of the saint not to cross the four limits of the agglomeration, in 1263-64, the king decided to visit Śivadēva every year. Apart from many more grants to the temple provisions were made for the feeding of one Jaṅgama in the temple (ins. No. III, l. 70).

The inscription No. V discloses the name of Siddha Rēvaṇadēva, one of the Pañcācāryas of Liṅgāyat community. On the advice of Siddha Rēvaṇadēva Kannādēvi, wife of Kallarasa of Toṟagale, went to Muktikṣētra, where she had a temple built and called it Kallēśvara in memory of her defunct husband. This Toṟagale can be identified with Torgal in the modern Belgaum district. It shows that the fame of the virtues of the saint had already spread far and wide.

In the south-east corner of the temple complex there is an empty shrine and the local people call it Kalleśvara guḍi. There is a piece of interesting information in the old *Dharwar District Gazetteer* (*ibidem*), according to which this inscription (No. V) was found in the shrine of "Gōpālamuni gadduge" which is identical with what is now known as "Gomunigaḷa gadduge" (a tomb-monument of Gōmuni). Also, *Bombay Revised List of Antiquarian Remains* mentions that the inscription is "behind the image of Vīrabhadra in the temple of Gōpadēvamuni, Śaka 1184" (p. 142). Effectively, an image of Vīrabhadra has been carved on the back of this inscription. This image of Vīrabhadra can be seen on one of the old photos published in *The Chālukyan Architecture of Kanarese Districts* by Henry Cousens and in *Śivadēva*

Vijaya. In Walter Elliot's collection, *Inscriptions of Canerese country,* it is clearly mentioned that the inscription is in the Gopadēvara guḍi. If the inscription was installed there, because its contents were coherent with the activities of the shrine, we may conclude that this was in medieval times the Kallēśvara shrine built by the pious lady Kannādēvi who spent the remaining days of her life in the *kāruṇya kaṭākṣa* (compassionate grace) of Śivadēva.

In 1288 A.D. July 5th, in the days of Yādava kings of Dēvagiri, a monolithic granite stone pillar was installed in front of the temple as *kīrtistaṃbha* "pillar of fame" by a general of the Sevuṇas probably to commemorate a victory over the Hoysaḷas. Recently struck by thunderbolt, it suffered from damages and the broken parts have been reinforced by iron bars. Though locally it is known as *dīpastaṃbha,* in the inscription it is called *kīrtistaṃbha.*

The last inscription is dated 1292 A.D. It begins with *śrī śivadēvaprabhuvē śaraṇu* "salutation to Śivadēvaprabhu". The previous inscription says :
ಮುಕ್ತಿಕ್ಷೇತ್ರೆ ಶ್ರೀ ಶಿ(ಸಿ)ದ್ಧಸಿ(ಶಿ)ವದೇವನಾಮ್ನಿ ಮುಕ್ತೇಸ್ವರದೇವಸಂನ್ನಿಧೌ
muktikṣētre śrī siddhaśivadēvanāmni muktēśvaradēvasaṃnidhau
"in Muktikṣētra in the presence of Muktēśvara called Siddha Śivadēva"

This shows that Śivadēva became one with Muktēśvara. In the following inscription there is the expression *siddhaśivadēvara prāṇaliṅga* "prāṇaliṅga of Siddhaśivadēva". It implies also that Śivadēva was no more in this world. He must have become one with Śiva at the ripe age of a nonagenaire.

After 1292 there are no more important inscriptions in Cauḍadānapura, only a few grafitti on the stairs of the ghat leading to the river. Though they just record the names of the pilgrims who rendered homages to Muktīśvara, they hold their own place in the history. Amongst them one is dated śaka 1485, cyclic year Raktākṣi corresponding to 1565 A.D., the year of the fatal battle of Tāḷikōṭe in which the Karnāṭaka king of Vijayanagara suffered a severe defeat, and the empire disintegrated. With this disruption and the ensuing chaos neither the name of Muktikṣētra nor of the chieftains of Guttala are heard of any longer. A few miles from Cauḍadānapura there is a village called Narasiṃhapura. Muktikṣētra is mentioned in its inscription dated in the times of Sadāśivarāya of Karnāṭaka empire with his capital Vijayanagara. Practically this is the last mention of the name of Muktikṣētra.

II

Epigraphy

In all, there are eight inscriptions in the compound of Muktēśvara temple. Except one which is on the *kīrtistambha*, all are written on well polished steles specially prepared for engraving. An image of Vīrabhadra has been carved on the back of the ins. No. V. The sixth inscription is written on the back of the inscription No. III. Except the one on the *kīrtistambha* all are kept in the shade of a shed which was recently built to shelter them. Judging from old photographs, it was not their original place. Originally they were installed near the temples, to the activities of which their contents refer.

The top portion of each stele, except the sixth and the seventh, is decorated with a small replica of a temple with a *liṅga* and a couchant Nandin. The representation of the temple is in conformity with the text of the chart. More details will be given in the introduction to each inscription. In most of the cases the *Liṅga*, in the replica of the temple, is covered with garlands of *rudrākṣa*. On the top of either side of the shrine are carved the sun and the crescent moon suggesting the eternity of the chart. Also a cow with a sucking calf represents Kāmadhēnu which realises all desires. In the shrine there is a devotee engaged in worshipping the *liṅga*. In the first two inscriptions of pre-Śivadēva period, the devotee is carved in standing position, whereas in the other four, contemporaneous with Śivadēva, he is in a sitting position.

There is also a difference in the physiognomy of the worshippers. In the first two inscriptions they are in standing position and almost naked except a pagne on their loins. Their matted hair is tied up on their head forming a turban. They have beards like that of a he-goat (*hōtina gaḍḍa*) or Brahman in sculptures. Whereas fully clad are the devotees in the effigies of the seated images in the remaining steles. Beards and moustaches are no more visible. This change in the representation is significant because Kāḷāmukha saints were covered with a negligible piece of cloth and stood up to worship Liṅga, whereas the Vīraśaiva saints, by and large, are clean shaven and sit on the ground for their *iṣṭaliṅgapūje.*

It is interesting to note that in almost all the inscriptions the land donated is of black soil (*yerebhūmi*). Because in Karnāṭaka the black soil land is considered as more fertile and more crop yielding than the red one.

All the eight inscriptions are written in Kannaḍa characters of 12th and 13th centuries. The letters are well incised and beautifully engraved. Texts are a good combination of prose and poetry. Seven inscriptions are in Kannaḍa interlaced with Sanskrit verses, whereas the one on the stone pillar is entirely in Sanskrit. As in most of the inscriptions, the *praśasti* part of the text is in poetry and the details of the grants are in Kannaḍa prose.

Inscription No. I. (S.I.I. XVIII No. 112)

The stele containing the text of inscription No. I, now installed in the shed specially built to shelter the inscriptions, is the second from the right and faces the East. Formerly, according to the *Dharwar District Gazetteer*, this stele was in the shrine of Muktēśvara. This inscription is also published in *Śivadēva Vijayaṃ* as No. VII, p. 33 in Appendix; then in *Cauḍadānapura Monograph* as No. 1 and in S.I.I. XVIII, No. 112. There are a few variants in these different publications. S. C. Nandimath had already given a full description of these steles in his monograph (p. 66-67). We have mainly followed his reading and verified the printed text directly on the stone. S. C. Nandimath gives the description of the stone slab as follows: "It (the stele) measures 7'-6" in height and 3'-8" in breadth. The written space covers 5'-6" by 3'-6" leaving a margin of 1" space on both sides. At the top of the slab there is an arc of a circle. In the centre of the arc there is a Liṅga. To the left of the Liṅga is a man, a devotee with beard and matted hair tied to form the shape of a turban. He is in the act of worshipping the Liṅga i. e. offering a garland of *rudrākṣa* on the top of the Liṅga. Above the Liṅga there is a cow and sucking calf. Above them there is the Sun. Just below this whole scene there is a band, 2 1/2" in breadth, consisting of one and a half line. Round the arc of a circle at the top there is a band of 4 1/2" breadth".

There are 63 lines, but the inscription is incomplete. The portion containing the date and the purport of the grant is missing. The inscription is written in Kannaḍa characters of 12th century with round and legible letters. "The text is in prose and poetry and the language is Kannaḍa interlaced with

Sanskrit verses. There are totally 32 verses in various metres such as *anuṣṭubh, utpala, campaka, mahāsragdharā, mattēbha* and *kanda*." (*ibidem* p. 67)

The composition of the text is as follows. As in most of the epigraphs of this epoch, it begins with the famous *ślōka* "Namas tuṅgaśiraścumbi..." followed by another in praise of God Śiva. Then follow the titles of the Cāḷukya king Tribhuvanamalla Vikramāditya VI. The description of his realm and the name of Gōvindarasa the governor of Banavāsi come next. This is followed by the history of the feudatory chiefs of the Gutta family starting from their origin, namely from the days of the legendary king Vikramāditya of Ujjayinī. From l. 10b to 14 there is a *praśasti* of the legendary king Vikramāditya in Sanskritised Kannaḍa enumerating his epithets and achievements. Māgutta was a descendant of this family. His son was Gutta whose son was Mallidēva or Mallugi or Mallabhūpa. From l. 30b to 48a, in a very beautiful poetical style, a long description of the river Tuṅgabhadrā, of a temple of Śiva built by one of the descendants of Jaṭā Cōḷa family, relatives of Guttas, are given. In the family of Jaṭā Cōḷa was born Joṃma whose son was Dāsa. From his wife Candabbarasi, Dāsa begot two sons, Attinṛpāla and Canda. It appears from the inscription that the feudatory chieftain Mallabhūpa of Gutta family was the father-in-law (*māva*) of Attirāja, the author of a Śiva temple at Cauḍadānapura. The portion between lines 37b-45a is full of double meanings: e. g. *dānōcita sthāna* means a place fit for donation and another meaning of *dāna* is the rut of the elephant; *bhitti* is a wall and also the temple of elephants; *nāga* means snake and elephant and according to the Hindu mythological conception snakes are in the Pātāḷa or subterranean world; *rambhā* stands for the banana tree and also is the name of a celestial nymph who was in the court of Indra; the waves of the sea are called *tāḷa* which is also the rhythm in music; *sumana* means the gods whose mind is good and also flowers which beautify the body and make it well-appreciated.

In l. 54b-55a the poet extols the king's generous qualities and compares him with the *cintāmaṇi* (celestial wish granting stone) and the *kalpavṛkṣa* (heavenly wish granting tree) and says that these are inferior to the king, because the monarch invites meritorious people and honours them with rich grants, whereas the other two satisfy the desires of the wishers. So these two remain barely a tree and a stone when compared to the king.

Though there is no date, Fleet has assigned this inscription to 1115 on the basis of other documents which evoke the governorship of Gōvindarasa in Banavāsi between 1110 and 1120 under Vikramāditya VI. But there are other inscriptions, namely from Ablūru and Baḻḻigāve, which record the governorship of Gōvindarasa in Banavāsi as early as 1101 A.D. Consequently, the date of construction of this Śiva temple by Jaṭā Coḷa at Cauḍadānapura can be taken back to a date slightly earlier than 1115 and it may not be wrong to say that the temple might have been built after 1101 but before 1120 A.D.

With regard to orthographical peculiarities Dr. Nandimath's remarks are valuable. For example:

1. Syllable *ri*, in 'mriṇmaya' (l. 1), 'prithivi' (l. 3) etc., for vowel *ṛ*.
2. *śa* for *sa* in 'śahasra' (l. 2), 'śamadhigata' (l. 7).
3. *śa* for *ṣa* in 'śaḍakṣari' (l..43) for 'ṣaḍakṣari'.
4. *sa* for *śa* in 'silā' (l. 2), 'sikhamaṇi', 'saraṇāgata' (l. 8), sauca (l. 14).
5. *ba* for *va* in 'brāta' (l. 26).
6. Consonant before r is doubled in 'tūrttada' (l. 30).

Text	Translation
೧. ನಮಸ್ತುಂಗಶಿರಶ್ಚುಂಬಿಚಂದ್ರಚಾಮ- ರಚಾರವೇ । ತ್ರೈಳೋಕ್ಯನಗರಾರಂಭ ಮೂಲಸ್ತಂಭಾಯ ಸ(ಶ)ಂಭವೇ ॥ (೧) ॥ ತ್ರಿಣಾನಿ ಕೋಟಿವರ್ಷಾಣಿ ಮ್ರಿಣಾ(ಣ್)ಮಯಂ	1a. Homage to Śaṃbhu, lovely with a *cauri*, the moon kissing his lofty head, foundation column of the construction of a city, the three worlds.(1)
೨. ದಶಕೋಟಿಭಿ: ದಾರೇಷ್ಟುಶತಂಕೋಟಿ ಶಹಶ್ರ(ಸಹಸ್ರ) ಕೋಟಿ ಶಿಳಾ(ಲಾ)- ಮಯಂ[1] ॥ ೨ ॥	1b-2. Grass [for building a temple, procures] one crore of years [in heaven], mud ten crores, wood hundred crores, stone thousand crores. (2)
೩. ಸ್ವಸ್ತಿ ಸಮಶ್ತ(ಸ್ತ) ॥ ಭುವನಾಶ್ರ- ಯಂ ಶ್ರೀ ಪ್ರಿಥ್ವೀವಲ್ಲಭಂ ಮಹಾರಾ- ಜಾಧಿರಾಜಪರಮೇಶ್ವರ ಪರಮಭಟ್ಟಾ- ರಕ ಶ(ಸ)ತ್ಯಾಶ್ರಯ ಕುಳತಿಳಕಂ ೪. ಚಾಳುಕ್ಯಾಭರಣಂ ಶ್ರೀಮತ್ತ್ರಿಭುವನ- ಮಲ್ಲದೇವರ ವಿಜಯರಾಜ್ಯಮುತ್ತ- ರೋತ್ತರಾಭಿವೃದ್ಧಿಪ್ರವರ್ದ್ಧಮಾ- ನಮಾಚಂದ್ರಾರ್ಕ್ಕತಾ- ೫. ರಂಬರಂ ಸಲುತ್ತಮಿರೆ ॥	3-5a. The refuge of all the world, master of the earth and fortune, king of great kings, great seigneur, great lord, glory of the family of Satyāśraya, ornament to the family of Cāḷukyas, Tribhuvanamalla's victorious kingdom extending on all sides, to continue as long as the sun, moon and stars,

[1] Cf. *Śaivaratnākara* of Jyotirnātha : mṛṇmayāt koṭiguṇitaṃ puṇyaṃ syāt dārubhiḥ kṛte । koṭikoṭiguṇam puṇyaṃ dārukād iṣṭakālaye ॥ iṣṭakād dviguṇam puṇyaṃ śailake syāc chivālaye ॥ "A temple made of wood gives a crore times more of merit than a temple made of mud; a temple of bricks a crore of crores times more than the wooden one; a temple of Śiva made of stone two times more than the brick temple." (V. 5- 6a).

ಕನ್ದ ॥ ಪಡುವಲು ಪಡುವಣ ವಾರಿಧಿ
ಗಡಿ ಮೂಡಲು ಮೂಡಣಬ್ಧಿ ಗಡಿ
ಬಡಗಲು ಹಿಮಂ । ಗಡಿ ತೆಂಕ ಸೇ
೬. ತುವೆರೆಗಂ । ಗಡಿಯಾಗಿರೆ ವಿಕ್ರ-
ಮಾಂಕನಾಳ್ವಂ ಧರೆಯಂ ॥ ೩ ॥

5b-6a. (*kanda*) King Vikramāditya, ruled over the earth, with the western ocean to the West, the eastern ocean to the East, to the North the snow[1], and to the South the bridge (sētu) as boundaries; 3

ಜಳನಿಧಿ ಪರಿವ್ರಿ(ವೃ)ತ ಧಾತ್ರೀತ-
ಳಮೆಲ್ಲಮಂ ತನ್ನ ಹಸ್ತತಳಮೆನೆ
ಪೆಂಪಂ । ತಳೆದೀ ಚಾಳುಕ್ಯಾನ್ವಯ
೭. ಕಳತಿಳಕಂ ವಿಕ್ರಮಾಂಕನಾಳ್ವಂ
ಧರೆಯ ॥ ೪ ॥

6b-7a. This king Vikramāṅka, *tilaka* of the family of Cāḷukyas after having made the entire stretch of the ocean-bound earth contained in the palm of his own hand[2], ruled it in glory. (4)

ವ ॥ ಆ ಪರಮೇಶ್ವರನ ಶ್ರೀ ಪಾದ-
ಪದ್ಮೋಪಜೀವಿ ಶ(ಸ)ಮಧಿಗತಪಂಚ-
ಮಹಾಶಬ್ದ ಮಹಾಸಾಮನ್ತಾಧಿಪತಿ
ಮಹಾ-
೮. ಮಹಾಪ್ರಚಂಡ ದಂಡನಾಯಕ ವೈ-
ರಿಗಿರಿವಜ್ರಸಾಯಕ ಸುಭಟಸೇನಾನಾಥ
ನಿ(ಶಿ)ಖಾಮಣಿ ಸ(ಶ)ರಣಾಗತರ-
ಕ್ಷಾಮಣಿ ಶ್ರೀಮನ್ಮಹಾಪ್ರಧಾನಂ
ಗೋವಿಂದರಸರಾ
೯. ಜಂ ಬನವಾಸಿ ಪನ್ನಿಛ್ಛಾರ್ಸಿರಮು-
ಮಂ ಸುಖದಿಮಾಳುತ್ತಮಿರೆ ॥

7b-9a. While the fortunate Gōvindarasa, dweller at his (King's) lotus feet, having all five great titles, great chieftain of vassals, great general, an arrow like Indra's thunderbolt to the mountains which are the enemies, commander of great warriors, protecting jewel to those who seek refuge, great minister, was administering in pleasure the Banavāsi 12000,

[ಎಱ]ಗದವರಂ ಕೊಂದು ಸಲೆ ತನ ।
ಗೆರಗಿದರಂ ಕಾದು ದಕ್ಷಿಣಾಪಥಮೆ-
ಲ್ಲನೆ ಬೆಸಕೆಯ್ವಂತಾಗಿರೆ ಮೆಱೆದಂ
ಶ್ರೀ
೧೦. ಕೀರ್ತಿಲಕ್ಷ್ಮಿಯಂ ಗೋವಿಂದಃ ॥
(೫)

9b-10a. killing those who were not submissive, protecting those who prostrated (to him), Gōvindarasa displayed his fame in all grandeur in company of Kīrti-Lakṣmī, while the whole South obeyed his orders. (5)

10b-15a. Hail. To tell the grandeur of Guttas, descendants of Vikramāditya :

---

[1] I. e. Himālaya.

[2] I. e. having brought the earth under his sway.

[3] ಗೋವಿಂದಂ.

ವ ॥ ಸ್ವಸ್ತಿ ಸಮಸ್ತಭುವನಜನವಿನ್ಯ-
ಸ್ತಮಸ್ತಕಸಂಸ್ತೂಯಮಾನಚಾ-
ರುಚರಣಾರವಿಂದವ್ವೈರಿಬಳವಿಳಯಗೋ
ವಿಂದನುಜ್ಜನೀಮಹಾಕಾಳ
೧೧. ದೇವತಾಲಬ್ಧವರಪ್ರಶಾ(ಸಾ)ದ
ಸಮಸ್ತವಿದ್ಯಾವಿನೋದ । ಪಾಟಳೀಪು-
ರವರಾಧೀಶ್ವರ । ಕೀರ್ತ್ಯಂಗನಾಧೀ-
ಶ್ವರ ವಟವ್ರಿ(ವೃ)ಕ್ಷಧ್ವಜ । ಧೈರ್ಯ-
ಗರುಡಧ್ವಜ । ಸೋಮ-

೧೨. ವಂಶಲಲಾಟಲೋಚನ । ಮೃಗ-
ರಾಜಲಾಂಛನ । ಗುತ್ತರ ಭೀಮನಂ ।
ಛಲದಂಕ ರಾಮ । ಅರಿಕುಮರಮ-
ಕುಟಘಟ್ಟಿತಚರಣ । ಗುತ್ತರಾಭರ-
೧೩. ಣ । ರಿಪುಬಳತಿಮಿರಮಾರ್ತ್ತಂಡ।
ವೈರಿಕುಳಕಾಳದಂಡ। ಹಯವತ್ಸರಾಜ।
ರೂಪಮನೋಜ । ಭ್ರಿತ್ಯಚಿಂತಾಮಣಿ ।
ಸುಭಟಚೂಡಾಮಣಿ ವಂದಿಜನ ಕಳ್ಪ-
(ಲ್ಪ)ವ್ರಿ(ವೃ)ಕ್ಷ
೧೪. ಶರಣಾಗತ ರಕ್ಷ । ಚಂದ್ರಗುಪ್ತ
ಮಹಾರಾಜಾಧಿರಾಜ ಕುಳ(ಲ)ಸಂಪೂ-
ರ್ಣ್ಣ । ನನ್ನಿಯಲುಕರ್ಣ್ಣ । ಮನು-
ಮಾರ್ಗ್ಗಮಾನಿ । ಸನುಮಾನದಾನಿ ।
ಸೌ(ಶೌ)ಚಾಂಜನೇಯ ಸಂಪಂನ್ನ ।
ನುಡಿದು ಮ

೧೫. ತ್ತೆನ್ನ । ಅಯ್ಯನ ಚಕ್ರ । ಭೂ-
ಚಕ್ರಶಕ್ರ ವಿಕ್ರಮಾದಿತ್ಯವಂಶೋದ್ಭವ-
ರಪ್ಪ ಶ್ರೀಮತ್ ಗುತ್ತಾನ್ವಯರ
ಮಹಿಮೆಯಂ ಪೇಳ್ವಡೆ ॥

ಕನ್ದಂ ॥
೧೬. ಅಲ್ಲಿಗೆ ಮನ್ನೆಯ ಲಕ್ಷ್ಮೀ । ವ-
ಲ್ಲಭರೆನಿಸಿದ್ದರ್ ಗುತ್ತಭೂಪಾನ್ವಯ-
ರೊಳ್ ॥ ಬಲ್ಲಿದನ ಜಯನಪ್ರತಿಮ-
ಲ್ಲಂ ಮಾಗುತ್ತ ಭೂಪನೆಂಬ ನೆಗಳ್ದ
॥ ೬ ॥

the foreheads of the people of the earth prostrated extolling highly his lotus-feet; he was destroyer of groups of enemies, blessed by God Mahākāḷa of Ujjaini, taking pleasure in all branches of learning, master of Pāṭaḷīpura, Lord of the Lady of Celebrity, having banyan tree as a banner, in courage like Him (Viṣṇu) who has an eagle as his banner,

an eye on the forehead of Sōma's family, having lion as emblem, Bhīma of Guttas, firm like Rāma in battles, with feet touched by the crowns of royal princes, ornament of Guttas, Sun to the darkness which is the army of enemies, club of the god of death to the enemy clan, King Vatsa to horses, in beauty Cupid, wish yielding jewel in protection, jewel among disciplined army, wish granting tree to those who compliment him, protector of the submissive, full (moon) to the family of king of kings Candragupta, Karṇa in truth, follower of Manu, donor of honours to the deserving, in chastity like Hanumān, never withdrawing a promise once made, Disk of Ayya (Viṣṇu), Indra of the entire circle of the earth.

16. (*kanda*) There, in Gutta family who were like Lords of Lakṣmī, was born king Māgutta known as unrivalled and invincible (6)

(ಕಂ) ಅಂತಾ
೧೭. ನ್ರಿಪ(ನೃಪ)ತಿಗೆ ಸುತ ವಿಕ್ರಾಂ-
ತಧನಂ ರಾಜವಂಸ(ಶ) ಚೂಡಾಮಣಿ
ಮಾ । ಊಂತರಿಗಂತಕ ವಂದಿಗೆ
ಚಿಂತಾಮಣಿ ಗುತ್ತಭೂಪನಂಗಜರೂ-
ಪಂ ।। (೭)

16b-17a. To such a king (was born) a son, treasure of valour, crest jewel of the royal family, god of death to adversaries, wish granting stone to the subdued, like Cupid in beauty. (7)

ವ್ರಿತ್ತ ।। ತಂದೆಯ ತಂ
೧೮. ದೆಯಿಂದಮೆವಗಾಳುವ ಮಹೀತ-
ಳವಜ್ಜವಜ್ಜರಿಂ ಬಂದುದೆ ಸಾಲುಗು-
ವೆಂದಿರದೆ ವಿಕ್ರಮದಿಂದಿರಾಂತ
ಭೂಪರಂ ಕೊಂದು ।। ಧರಿತ್ರಿಯಂ
ಪಡೆದನರ್ತ್ಥಿಗೆ ಬೇರ್ಮ್ಮದನಿತ್ತು
೧೯. ಕೀರ್ತ್ತಿಯಂ ಮಂದಿರವಿರ್ಪ್ಪಿನಂ
ಪಡೆದ ಗುತ್ತನ್ರಿ(ನೃ)ಪಾಳಿಸಿದೇಂ ಕ್ರಿ-
(ಕೃ)ತಾರ್ತ್ಥನೋ ।। ೮ ।।

17b-19a. (*vṛtta*) Glory of the Gutta family, not satisfied with the kingdom inherited from his forefathers, he acquired more territories by slaying heroically the enemies who came to face him; and by granting wishes to one and all who desired, King Gutta attained everlasting celebrity as his own palace. What a fulfilment king Gutta achieved in life! (8)

।। ಕಂದ ।। ಗುತ್ತಾನ್ವಯ ವಂಶಾಗ್ರ-
ಣಿ । ಗುತ್ತಾನ್ವಯ ರಾಜಭವನಮಂ-
ಗಳ ಕಳಶಂ ।। ಗುತ್ತಾನ್ವಯ
೨೦. ಚೂಡಾಮಣಿ । ಗುತ್ತಾನ್ವಯತಿ-
ಳಕನೆನಿಸಿದಂ ಗುತ್ತನ್ರಿ(ನೃ)ಪಾಳಕ ।।
೯ ।।

19b-20a. (*kanda*) Best in the dynasty of Guttas, sacred finial of the royal palace of Gutta family, crest jewel amongst Gutta descendants; (thus) Gutta appeared like *tilaka* on the forehead in the line of Guttas. (9)

ಆತನ ತನಯಂ ಜಗದೊಳು ನೀತಿಪ-
ರಂ ರಿಪುಕರೀಂದ್ರ ಕಂಠೀರವ ।।
ಭೂತಳ ಕ್ಷತ್ರಿಯರೊಳಜಾ
೨೧. ತಭಯಂ ಮಲ್ಲಿದೇವನದಟಂ
ದೇ ವ।। ೧೦ ।।

20b-21a. His son, Mallidēva, Lord of mighty lords, respecter of rules of polity in the world, lion to mighty elephants the enemies, fearless amongst kṣatriyas on the earth. (10)

ವ್ರಿತ್ತ ।। ಎಣಿಸಲು ಭೂಪಾಳರೀಗಳು
ಪಲಬರುಮೊಳರಾ ಭೂಪವರ್ಗ್ಗಂಗ-
ಳಿಳ್ದೇಗಣಿದೇಂ ಪೂರ್ವ್ವಾದ್ರಿಯೊಳು
ಚಂದ್ರಮನೆನೆ
೨೨. ವ ಸರೋಮಧ್ಯದೊಳು ಪಂಕ-
ಜಂ

21b-23a. (*vṛtta*) What is the use of other kings? Now Mallidēva shines like a moon on the Eastern mountain, a lotus in the midst of an ocean,

ಕೇವಣದೊಳು । ಮಾಣಿಕ್ಯವಿರ್ಪಂತಿರೆ
ಭುವನಜನಕ್ಕಾಶ್ರಯಂ ರಾಜಚೂಡಾ ।
ಮಣಿಯಿಪ್ಪಂಮಲ್ಲಿದೇವಂತ್ರಿಭುವನತಿಳ
೨೩. ಕಂ ರಾಜಮಾನ್ಧಾತಬೂಪಂ ॥
೧೧ ॥

ruby in a ring, refuge to the inhabitants of the earth, crest jewel amongst kings, (like) Mandhāta (son of Yuvanāśva) to three worlds[1]. (11)

ಭಂಡಣದೊಳು ರಿಪುಭೂಪರ । ತಂ-
ಡಮನವಯವದೆ ಗೆಲ್ದು ಜಯಲಕ್ಷ್ಮ-
ಯ ದೋ । ರ್ದ್ದಂಡದೊಳಿರಿಸಿದ
ಧೀರದ । ಗಂಡಂ। ಕೇವಳ
೨೪. ಮೆ ಮೇರುಗಿರಿ ನಮ್ಮ ಮಲ್ಲ-
ನ್ರಿ(ನೃ)ಪಾಳ ॥ ೧೨ ॥ ಕಂದ ॥

23b-24a. (*kanda*) Our brave hero who conquered the entire host of enemy kings by the might of his limbs, bore the goddess of Victory on his arms, who is like Mēru, our king Malla, is he an ordinary king ? (12)

ನುಡಿಯದಡೆ ನುಡಿಯದಿಕ್ಕಮೆ ಕುಡು-
ವೆಂ ನಿಮಗೆಂದು ನುಡಿದನಪ್ಪಡೆ ಮ್ರಿ
(ಮೃ) ಡನೊಳು । ಪಡೆದ ಬರ
೨೫. ಮೇರುಗಿರಿಯೊಳು । ಕಡೆದಕ್ಕರ
ಮಲ್ಲಭೂಪ ನುಡಿದಿಂ ಬಳಿಕಂ (೧೩)

24b-25a. The words of Malla are such that if not uttered, there is no issue; if he says "I will", they are like boons of Śiva; letters engraved on the celebrated mountain Mēru if once uttered (by him) . (13)

॥ ವ್ರಿ ॥ ಪದಪಿಂ ನ್ರಿ(ನೃ)ಪಾಳ(ಲ)
ನಿನ್ನ ರಣಕೇಳೀಲೀಳೆ(ಲೆ)ಯಂ ಪಕ್ಷ-
ಪಾತದಿ ನಾಂ ಪೇ । ಳದೊಡೇನೊ
ಮೋದಪ-
೨೬. ಲವುಂ ಸುಗ್ರಾಮದೊಳು ಪುತ್ತನೆ।
ತ್ತಿದ ಪುಲ್ಗರ್ಚಿದ ಕಯ್ದುವಂ ಬಿಸುಟ
ನೀರಂ ಪೊಕ್ಕ ನಿಗ್ರನ್ಧಮೋ । ಡಿದ
ನಿಂದಾಡಿದ ಕೆಯ್ಗಳಂ ಮುಗಿದರಾತಿ-
ಬ್ರಾತ
೨೭. ವೇಂ ಪೇಳವೇ ॥ ೧೪ ॥

25b-27a. O king Malla, should I be alone to eulogise your sports in the battlefield, I could be accused of partiality. However, will not the host of enemies in many a battle speak eloquently about you : in dispair the enemies mounted on an ant-hill, bit the grass, you slew those who threw their sword, hid under water, made others flee, others to join hands for protection.[2] (14)

---

[1] The letter read *ndha* by other epigraphists looks to me like *nya*. In that case the text should read as *rājamānyātabhūpa* and the meaning will be "honoured by all kings".

[2] Mounting on an ant-hill, throwing one's sword, biting grass etc. are signs of surrender. The poet compares the king with Bhīma by saying that he killed those who hid under the water. This is an allusion to the fight between Bhīma and Duryōdhana as narrated in the *Mahābhārata*. Also it reminds us of the stories of Viṣṇu in Matsya and Varāha-avatāra.

ಕಂದ ॥ ಆಜಿಯಂ ಧರಣಿಯನೇಱೆ-
ದ । ವಾಜಿಯಖುರದಿಂದ ಮುತ್ತುರ್ರಿ-
ಮುಸಿರಮೆಂಬೀ ಬೀಜಮನೆ ಬಿತ್ತಿ ಬೆ-
ಳೆವಂ ರಾಜಿ
೨೮. ಕ ವಿಖ್ಯಾತ ಕೀರ್ತ್ತಿಯಂ ಮ-
ಲ್ಲನ್ರಿ(ನೃ)ಪ ॥೧೫॥

27b-28a. (*kanda*) Brilliant Mallanṛpa mounted on his horse, tilled the soil of the battlefield with its hooves, to reap a crop of shining, celebrated glory by sowing heads of enemies as seeds. (15)

ವ್ರಿತ್ತ॥ದೆಸೆಪೊಸ(ವುಣ್ಣ)ದಿಂದೆಸೆವ ನೆ-
ತ್ತರ ಸುಟ್ಟುರೆಯಿಂ ನಭಸ್ಥಳಂ ಪ-
ಸರಿಸಿ ಬಿಳ್ದ ವೀರ ಭಟ್ಟರಟ್ಟೆಗಳಿಂ
ಹಯ
೨೯.ಖಂಡಖಂಡಿಯಿಂ ಕುಸುರಿವೊಲಾ-
ಗೆ ವೈರಿಬಲಮಂ ತಱಿದೊಡ್ಡಿದಗುರ್ವ್ವು
ತಾನುಗು । ರ್ವಿಸಿದುದು ಮಲ್ಲಿದೇವ-
ನಿಱಿದಾಹವರಂಗದ ವೈರಿಸೇನೆ
೩೦. ಯ ॥ ೧೬ ॥

28b-30a. (*vṛtta*) The terrific nature of the battlefield was increased very much indeed by the blood of the killed enemy force newly painting the quarters, and by the severed heads of slain soldiers and mutilated body bits of slaughtered horses enveloping the entire sky. (16)

ವಚನ॥ಆ ಗುತ್ತಾನ್ವಯರ ಹ್ರಿ(ಹೃ)-
ದಯಾಳ[ವ]ಳಂಬಿಗಳಪ್ಪ ಜಟಾಚೋ-
ಳಾನ್ವಯರು ಮಾಡಿಸಿದ ಶಿವಾಲಯದ
ಮುಕ್ತಿತೀರ್ತ್ಥದ ವ್ಯಾವರ್ಣನ ॥ಕ॥

30b. Description of the temple of Śiva at Muktitīrtha built by the descendants of Jaṭā Cōḷa dear dependent of the descendants of Guttas :

೩೧. ಹರನ ಜಟಾಗ್ರದಿ ನೆಲಸಿದ ಸು-
ರನದಿಗಂ ವೇದಶ್ಶೈಳ(ಲ)ಸಿ(ಶಿ)ಖರಾ-
ಗ್ರದಿ ನೀ। ಧರೆಗಿಳಿದ ತುಂಗಭದ್ರಾ ।
ವರನದಿಗಂ ದೊರೆಯೆ ಜಗದ ನ-
ದಮುಂ ನದಿಯುಂ ॥ ೧೭ ॥

31. (*kanda*) Is there any river or *fleuve*[1] in the world equal to Tuṃgabhadrā descending from Vēdaśaila and the celestial river (Gaṅgā) residing in Śiva's matted hair ? (17)

೩೨ ॥ ವ್ರಿ ॥ ಸುದತೀಕುಂಕುಮಪಂ-
ಕಿತಾರುಣಜಳಂದಾಭಿದಾ.[2]ನಾಜಳಂ ವಿ
। ದಳತು ಪಂಕಜಪ್ಪುಱರಂಜಿತ
ಜಳಂವೇದಾಚಳೇಂದ್ರೋಪಕ। ಣ್ಯದಿ-
ನೆತ್ತಂ ಸುರಿ
೩೩. ದಿಂದುಕಾನ್ತದ ಜಳಂ ಪೇರರ್ವ್ವ
ಸಂದೋಹದಿಂ ಪು । ದಿದೆತ್ತಂ ಲಹ-
ರೀದಿಶಾಬಧಿರಿತಂ ಶ್ರೀತುಂಗಭದ್ರಾ
ಜಳಂ ॥ ೧೮

32a-33a. The water of holy Tuṅgabhadrā dripping from the mountain appears as if oozing from moonstones on the slopes of Vēdaśaila, embellished with full blown lotuses turned into red by the saffron powder used by damsels during their water sports, deafened all directions with a multitude of high waves. (18)

---

[1] In the text there are two words *nadī* (f.) and *nada* (m.). But in English there is no word for *nada* as the French word *fleuve* which is masculine.

[2] Space for one letter is left blank.

||ಕ|| ಗಂಗೆಸಮಾನ ದಕ್ಷಿಣಗಂಗಾನ
೩೪. ದಿ ಮಿಂದ ಮರ್ತ್ಯರಘಸಂಕುಳ-
ಮಂ ಪಿಂಗಿಸುವ ಗಂಗೆಯುಂ ತಿರಿ-
ಪಿಂಗಿಪಳಘಕುಳಮ ನಮ್ಮ ದಕ್ಷಿಣ
ಗಂಗೆ || ೧೯.||

33b-34a. Equal to river Gaṅgā, (Tuṅgabhadrā is) southern Gaṅgā; like Gaṅgā this southern Gaṅgā too washes off loads of sins of mortals who bathe there. (19)

ಪಾವನವೆನಿಸಿದ ಗಂಗಾದೇವಿಗೆ
೩೫ ಸರಿದೊರೆ ಸಮಾನ ದಕ್ಷಿಣಗಂ-
ಗಾದೇವಿಯನೆ ತುಂಗಭದ್ರಾದೇವಿಯ-
ನಿನೆಱಿಯ ಪೊಗಳಲಾವಂ ನೆಱಿವಂ
||೨೦||

34b-35a. In sacredness this southern Gaṅgā (Tuṅgabhadrā) is equal to Gaṅgā. Who is able to eulogise the sanctity of Tuṅgabhadrā ? (20)

ವ್ರಿತ್ತ || ಸುರಸ್ರ
೩೬.ಳೇಂ(ಲೇಂ)ದ್ರದ ಹಿಮ್ಯಾ[ಮಾ]ಚಳ-
(ಲ)ದ ಮಹಿಮೆಗಂ ತಾರಶ್ಶೈಳ(ಲ)-
ಕ್ಕಂ ನೋಡಲು ದೊರೆವೆತ್ತಿವೇದಶ್ಶೈ-
ಳೇಂ (ಲೇಂ)ದ್ರದಲಮರನದಿಸಂನಿಭಂ
ಮೇಘಬ್ರಿಂದೋತ್ಕರದಿಂದಂ
೩೭. ಭತ್ತಥಿದಣ್ಣದ ಬಹಳತೆಯೆಂಬಂ-
ದದಿಂ ಬಂದು ತಾ ನಿಕರದ ಪಾಪ-
ಕ್ಷಯ ಮಾಡುವ ವಿಮಳ ಜಳಂ
ತುಂಗಭದ್ರಾ ಪ್ರವಾಹ|| ೨೧ ||

35b-37a. The flow of Tuṅgabhadrā, is the purifier of all sins, with its clean water (poured by) clouds having come in large quantity near the source of the river on the summit of the Vēdaśaiḷ(l)a which is comparable to Mēru and Himācala, lord of mountains.(21)[1]

ಗದ್ಯ|| ಅದೆಂತೆಂ
೩೮. ದೊಡ್ಡೈರಾವತಗಂಡಮಂಡಳಭಿ-
ತ್ತಿಯಂತೆ ದಾನೋಚಿತಸ್ಥಾನಮುಂ
ಹರಜಟಾಗ್ರದಂತೆ ನದೀವಿರಾಜಿತಮುಂ
| ಪಾತಾಳಲೋಕದಂತೆ ನಾಗ

೩೯ ಸಹಿತಮುಂ | ಸುರೇಂದ್ರನ(ಶ)-
ಯನದಂತೆ ರಂಭಾಯತಮುಂ |
ದೇವಲೋಕದಂತೆ ಸುಮನಾಭಿರಾ-
ಮಮುಂ ಸಂಗೀ ತಕದಂತೆ ತಾಳ

37b-45a. Like the fluid flowing from Airāvata's temples, Muktikṣētra, encircled by walls, is fit for the flow of water libation; like the top of Śiva's matted hair, it shines with a river; like the netherworld with snakes (*nāga*), it is an abode of a mighty race of elephants (*nāga*); like the bed of Surēndra with Rambhā, it is embellished with (*rambha*) banana groves; like the world of celestial beings with (*sumana*) gods, it is delightful with (*sumana*) flowers; like music with rythm (*tāḷa*), it is delightful with waves (*tāḷa*);

---

[1] In *Cauḍ. Monograph* '22' is a mistake for '21'.

೪೦. ಸಹಿತಮುಂ ಬ್ರಹ್ಮಸಭೆಯಂತೆ
ದ್ವಿಜವಿರಾಜಿತಮುಂ। ಅಂತಲ್ಲಿ ಮೂ-
ಱುಂ ಕಾಲಮುಂ। ಆರುಂ ರಿ(ಋ)-
ತುಗಳುಂ। ಸರ್ವ್ವರ್ತ್ತುಕಮಪ್ಪ ಮು
೪೧. ಕ್ತಿತೀರ್ತ್ಥ(ರ್ಥ)ದ ಸ್ಥಾನದೊಳು
ಸು(ಶು)ಕಸಾರಿಕಾರಮಣಮುಂ।
ಮತ್ತಮಧುಕರಗೀತಾರಮಣಮುಂ ।
ಪುಗಲ ಪುಗಲೆಂಬ ಕೋಕಿಳ(ಲ)ಸ್ವ-
ನಾರಮಣಮುಂ
೪೨. ನಮೇರು ಮಂದಾರ ಪಾ[ರಿ]ಜಾ-
ತಾದಿ ಸಕಳ ಪುಷ್ಪ(ಷ್ಪ)ರಾಜಿತಮುಂ
ಸಾಮವೇದ ಸಪ್ತಸ್ವರ ಮಂತ್ರಾಕ್ಷ-
ರಂಗಳಿಂ ಹೋಮಂ ಗೆಯ್ವ ದ್ವಿ-
ಜೋತ್ತಮರ

like the *dvija* in Brahmasabhā it shines with brahmins (*dvija*); (and) in such Muktikṣētra blessed in all three times (*kālas*) and six (*ṛtus*) seasons[1], he and she parrots play, intoxicated bees sing sweet songs, echoed with the sweet musical sound "pugal, pugal"[2] of cuckoo; it is delightful with flowers like *namēru, mandāra, pā(ri)jāta,* with thick smoke of *homa* performed by the best of brahmins (who recite) *maṃtrākṣara* in the *saptasvaras* of Sāmavēda,

೪೩. ಹೋಮಧೂಮಸ್ತೋಮಮುಂ ।
ದೇವತಾತರ್ಪ್ಪಣ ರಿ(ಋ)ಷಿ ತರ್ಪ್ಪಣ
ದಿಕ್ತತರ್ಪ್ಪಣ ಗಾಯತ್ರೀ
ಶ(ಷ)ಡಕ್ಷರ ಜಪಂಗಳಂ ಮಾರ್ಪ್ಪ
ಸಬ್ರಾಹ್ಮಣರಿಂ ವ
೪೪. ಜ್ರಾಸನ ಪದ್ಮಾಸನ ಸ್ವಸ್ತಿಕಾಸ-
ನಂಗಳಿಂ । ನಾದಭೇದ । ಬಿಂದು-
ಭೇದ। ಸ(ಶ)ಕ್ತಿಭೇದ । ಆತ್ಮಭೇದ-
ಮೆಂಬ ನಾಲ್ಕು ತೆಱ(ರ)ದ। ಯೋಗ-
ಲಕ್ಷಣ ಲಕ್ಷಿತರಪ್ಪ ಯೋಗಿಗ
೪೫. ಳಿಂ । ಮುಕ್ತಿಮಾರ್ಗ್ಗಮೆ ಮೂ-
ರ್ತ್ತಿಗೊಂಡಿರ್ದ್ದ ಮುಕ್ತಿತೀರ್ತ್ಥದ
ಬಹುವಿಧ ಲಿಂಗಾಶ್ರಯಂಗಳೊಪ್ಪು-
ಗುಮಲ್ಲಿ॥೨೨॥

with the good brahmins engaged in offering *tarpaṇa* to gods, to ṛṣis, and to the directions repeating *japa*s of Gāyatri, Ṣaḍakṣari, with *yogin*s engaged in performing difficult yogic exercises (such as) *vajrāsana, padmāsana, svastikāsana,* and four ways (of *mantroccāra*) *nādabhēda, bindubhēda, śaktibhēda, ātmabhēda*; Muktitīrtha which is like an embodiment of the way to liberation, shines with many shelters for numerous Liṅgas. (22)

ಕಂದ ॥ ಅಜನಸಭೆಯಂತೆ
೪೬. ಸದಾ ದ್ವಿಜಪರಿವ್ರಿತ (ವೃತ)
ಮಿಂದ್ರನಂತೆ ಸುಮನಾಶ್ರಯಮಾ

45b-46. (*kanda*) Like Brahmā's assembly it shelters *dvijas*[3], like Indra's court *sumana* (gods, flowers);

---

[1] The flowers and fruits of all seasons (are) found simultaneously.

[2] *Pugal*: "don't come in, don't enter" (see Kittel). The meaning is : as if to say "don't enter, don't enter, O! you trespasser, because the place is too holy for you".

[3] *Dvija* means twice born. Brahmins are called *dvija* because they undergo the thread ceremony which is equal to a rebirth. Birds are called *dvija* because they are born once in the egg and then come out of its shell.

ತ್ರಿ(ದ)ಸಗಜದಂತೆ ದಾನಬ್ರಜಮಯ-
ಮುಮುಕ್ತಿತೀರ್ತ್ಥಮದು ಕೇವಳಮೇ ||
೨೩ ||

like the heavenly elephant's (ichor), here flow water libations (of donations). Is Muktitīrtha ordinary ?(23)

೪೭. ||ವ್ರಿತ್ತ|| ಕುಸುಮಿತ ಮಲ್ಲಿಕಾ
ಭಿನವ ಪಾಟಳಸಂಕುಳದಿಂ ಕೊನ-
ರ್ತ್ತು ತಳ್ತಸದಳಮಾಗಿ ಬಂದ ಮೊ-
ಸಮಾವುಗಳಿಂ ಮೊರೆವುನ್ಮದಾಳಿಯಿಂ
ಮನ
೪೮. ಗಿತ [ಮ]ಷ್ಟ ಬಗ್ಗಿಪ ಪಿಕಾಳಿಗ-
ಳಿಂ ನಯದಿಂದ ತೆಂಕಣಂದೆಸಪಲ-
ರಿಂದಮೀ ಮುಕ್ತಿತೀರ್ತ್ತ(ರ್ತ್ಥ)ವದೊ-
ಪ್ಪು ಗುಮೆಂತು ನೋರ್ಪಡ ||೨೪||

47-48a. (*vṛtta*) With full-bloomed jasmins, *pāṭalis*, newly come unaccountable ripe new mangoes, the buzzing of bees, the passionate cooing of cuckoo couples, the gentle breeze of south passing through render Muktikṣētra lovely to look at. (24)

ವಂಸಾ(ಶಾ)ವತಾರ
೪೯. ಕಂದ || ಶ್ರಿಗೆನೆಲೆ ದಾನಧರ್ಮ್ಮ-
ಕಾಗರವೆನೆ ನೆಗಳ್ದ ನೀ ಜಟಾನ್ವಯ
ಕುಲದೊಳು ಭೋಗಪುರಂದರ ನೆಯ-
ಪಿದ ಸಾಗರ ಪರಿವ್ರಿ(ವೃ)ತ
೫೦. ಧರಿತ್ರಿಯೊಳ್(ಳ್)[1] ಜೊಮ್ಮನ್ರಿಪಂ
||೨೫||

48b. The family descent of (Jomma) :
49-50a. (*kanda*) On this earth encircled by oceans, in Jaṭā(Cōḷa's) family was born Jomma, abode to the goddess of fortune, refuge to the making of grants and good laws, Indra in enjoyment and statecraft. (25)

ಕಂದ|| ಆತಂಗೆ ಪುಟ್ಟಿದ ವಿಖ್ಯಾತಿ
ಪರಂ ರಾಜಸುತರೊಳಮಳಚರಿತ್ರ
ಭೂತಳದಲರ್ತ್ಥಿಗಮ

೫೧. ರಕುಜಾತಂ ಕೇವಳಮೆ ದಾನ
ವೀರವಿಳಾಸಂ || ೨೬||

50b-51a. Amongst the celebrated princes (was) born Dāsa pure in character, an ornament to heroes, like the wish-fulfilling celestial tree to the seekers on the earth; is he an ordinary person ? (26)

ಸರಸೀರುಹವದನ ಚಂದಬ್ಬರಸಿರು-
ಗುಣನಿಳಯನೆನಿಪ ದಾಸನ್ರಿ(ನೃ)ಪಂ-
ಗಂ ಪರಹಿತ ಚರಿತಂ
೫೨. ಪುಟ್ಟಿದ ಹರಚರಣಪಯೋಜ ಭ್ರಿ-
(ಭೃ)ಂಗನತ್ತಿನ್ರಿ(ನೃ)ಪಾಳಂ । ೨೭ ||

51b-52a. To the lotus-faced Candabbarasi and Dāsa, abode of good qualities, was born Attinṛpa, bee on Hara's lotus feet, renowned for taking interest in other's welfare. (27)

1 ಳ್ (ḷ) is written above the line.

ಆತನ ತಮ್ಮ|| ಚಂದಗವಜ್ಜ(ಬ್ಜ)
ನಾಭನ ಕಂದಂಗೆ ಸೇತುಗಟ್ಟಿ ಲಂ-
ಕೇಶ್ವರನ ಕೊಂದಂಗೆ ಸುರನದಿ
೫೩. ಯಂ ತಂದಂಗೆ ದೊರೆಯೆ
ಮನುಜರವನೀತಳದೊಳು || ೨೮ ||

52b-53a. Can there be an equal to his younger brother Canda on earth ? He is like Lakṣmaṇa, brother of he who has Brahmā in his navel (Viṣṇu), who built the bridge and killed Rāvaṇa, like (Bhagīratha) who brought the heavenly river to the earth. (28)

(ವಚನ) ಮಾವಂ ಮಹಾಮಂಡಳೇ-
ಸ್ವ(ಶ್ವ)ರಂ । ವೀರಾರಾತಿಮದನಮ
ಹೇಸ್ವ(ಶ್ವ)ರ । ಮೂಱುರಾಯ
೫೪. ಮಂಡಳಿಕಮದಗಜೇಂದ್ರಕಣ್ಠೀ-
ರವಂ ರಾಯನ ಮಹಿಮೆಯ ಪೇಳ್ವಡೆ

53b-55a. His father-in-law is Mahāmaṇḍaḷēśvara; as Lord Śiva to Cupid he is to the army of valourous heroes, *māṇḍaḷika* of three kings, lion to the elephants, the enemies.To tell his glory :

|| ಕಂದ || ಮರವಟ್ಟಿವುದು ಸುರ-
ತರು ಪರಳಾಗಿಯೆ ಕುಡುತಮಿ
೫೫. ಕರ್ಕ ಚಿಂತಾಮಣಿಯಾ ಮರ-
ನುಂ ಕಲ್ಲುಂ ಪ್ರಿಯದಿಂ ಕರದೆನಿ-
ಪ್ಪುವೆ ರಾಯನಂತಿರೆ ಜಗದೊಳು ||
೨೯.

(*kanda*) In inviting and endowing donation with affection to those who deserved it the king cannot be compared to the tree of plenty or the wish-fulfilling stone (*cintāmaṇi*), (because) do they call and give ? (29)

ವ್ರಿತ್ತ || ಪರಮಾರ್ತ್ಥಕ್ಕಿಷ್ಟದೆಯ್ವಂತೆ
೫೬. ನಗಖಿಳಜಗತ್ಸ್ವಾಮಿಸಂದಾದಿ
ದೇವಗಿರಿಜಾಳ್ವಂಗಾನುಸಂಗಂ ಶಿವನೆ
ಗಡ ಕುಲಸ್ವಾಮಿ ಕಾರುಣ್ಯದಿಂದು
ಮೊರೆದಾಳ್ವಂ ವಿಕ್ರಮಾಂಕಾನ್ವಯ
೫೭.ಕುಳ(ಲ)ತಿಳ(ಲ)ಕಂ ಮಲ್ಲಭೂ-
ಪಂ ಗಡಿಂತೀ ಧರೆಯೊಳು ಧನ್ಯಂ
ಜಟಾಚೋಳರೊಳು ಮಳಯಸೋ-
(ಶೋ)ರಾಜನೀಯತ್ತ(ತ್ತಿ)ರಾಜಂ||೩೦||

55b-57a. Mallabhūpa, an *iṣṭadaiva* to *paramārtha*, master of the whole world, *tilaka* in the family of king Vikrama, under the protection of Śiva and his consort Girijā, rules the (kingdom) with compassion. Blessed on the earth, this Attirāja, a mountain in the family of Jaṭā Cōḷa. (30)

ಕಂದ|| ಧರೆಯೊಳಗೆ ವಾರಣಾ
೫೮. ಸಿಯ ದೊರೆಯೆನಿಸುವ ಪುಣ್ಯನ-
ದಿಯ ತೀರದ ಸಮುದಂ ಹರನಿಳ(ಲ)
ಯಮನಘಕುಳ(ಲ)ಸಂಹಾರನಿಳ(ಲ)
ಯಮನರ್ತಿಂದಮತ್ತಿನ್ರಿ(ನೃ)ಪಾಳಂ
||೩೧||

57b-58a. (*kanda*) (In Muktikṣētra) equal to Vāraṇāsi on the bank of the celestial river, with pleasure, Attirāja made to be built a temple for Hara, destroyer of loads of sins. (31)

ಉತ್ತಮರ
೫೯. ಕೆಲದೊಳಂ ಭೂಪೋತ್ತಮರಾ-
ಸ್ಥಾನರಂಗದೊಳು ಸುಜನಕವಿತ್ತೋ-
ತ್ತಮರಸಭೆಯೊಳಮತ್ಯುತ್ತಮನೀ
ಯತ್ತಿರಾಜನಂ ಪೊಗಳದರಾರೋ ||
೩೨||

58b-59a. Who will not praise this excessively good king Attirāja, the best in the assembly of the best of kings, best amongst people of good conduct, highest in the congregation of the learned poets ? (32)

ಧರೆಯೊ
೬೦. ಳನೇಕರಿಲ್ಲ ಸುಜನರ್ಕ್ಕಲಿಕಾಲ-
ದೊಳಂತೆ ಭದ್ರಸಿಂಧುರಘಟೆಯಿಲ್ಲ-
ದಂತೆ ಸುಜನೋತ್ತಮನಕ್ಷರ ಪಕ್ಷ-
ಪಾತಿ ನಂಟರ ಬೆಳೆಗೆಯಿ ಧರಾ-
ಮರರ ಕಯ್ಗನ್ನಡಿ
೬೧. ಸಿಷ್ಟನಿಧಾನನಿರ್ದ್ದಪಂ ವರಗು-
ಣೆಯತ್ತಿರಾಜನೆಳೆಗೋರ್ವ್ವನೆಕಳ್ಪ(ಲ್ಪ)-
ಕುಜಾತನಿರ್ಪ್ಪ ಪೊಲ್ || ೩೩ ||

59b-61a. (*campaka*) There are not many good people on the earth in this iron age, just as there are no white elephants. Indeed he is the foremost among good men, a patron of letters, harvest in the hands of his kinsmen, hand mirror to the gods, a treasure house of virtues; a man of sterling character, he is singular on the earth like the wish-fulfilling tree. (33)

ಸ್ವಸ್ತಿ ಶ್ರೀಮನ್ಮಹಾಸಾಮಂತ ವೀರಲ-
ಕ್ಷ್ಮೀಕಾನ್ತಂ ಜಟಾನ್ವಯ ಚೋ
೬೨. ಳ ವಂಶಾಗ್ರಣಿ ಶಿಷ್ಟಚಿಂತಾ-
ಮಣಿ ಗೋತ್ರಪವಿತ್ರ ನಬಳ ತ್ರಿಣೇತ್ರ
ವೀರವಿಳಾ(ಲಾ)ಸಂ ಗುತ್ತರ ಚಂದ್ರ-
ಹಾಸಂ ಹರಚರಣ ಸರಸೀರುಹ
೬೩.ಮಧುಕರ ವಿನಯರತ್ನಾಕರಂ...[1]

61b-62. Mahāsāmanta, lord of the goddess Vīralakṣmī; wish-granting stone to the *śiṣṭas*, best amongst the descendants of Jaṭā Cōḷas, of pure *gōtra*, Candrahāsa of Guttas, bee on the lotus feet of Śiva, jewel in politeness...

1 The inscription is left incomplete here.

Inscription No. II. (S.I.I. XVIII No. 299. In Elliot's collection vol. II . No. 17, folio 345 verso - 347 recto)

This inscription is now set up in the special pendal built to shelter all the engraved steles, which means that it is not in its original place. In the shed it stands second from right and faces East. According to *Dharwar District Gazetteer*, it was found standing in "Īśvara temple on the bank of Tungabhadrā" (p. 390). This Īśvara temple probably is the main temple, i. e. Muktēśa. Also in the collection of inscriptions by Sir Walter Elliot it is mentioned "in the village of Caḍāmpura in the temple of Ishvara near the river". From a photograph of the inscription taken somewhere in the middle of the last century by Dixon it can be noticed that this stele was planted next to the main temple. Judging from a photograph published in Col. Meadows Taylor's book, *Architecture of Dharwar and Mysore*, we may say that it was installed to the South of the main shrine not far from the others (p. 57, photo 39). The text on the stele was facing west. From these above mentioned facts it is clear that the Liṅga which was worshipped by Muktajīyar began to be called Muktēśvara and even to-day the temple goes by the same name. Otherwise, only in the European documents it was known as Īśvara temple.

"On the slab of 7'-5" x 3'-4" the inscribed area covers 7'-5" x 3'-2" leaving a margin of one inch on either side. The arc at the top measures 2'-4" in the centre and 3'-2" at the base" (*Cauḍadānapura Monograph* p. 74). The figure of the temple in the centre of the arc resembles in structure that of the main temple of Muktēśvara. In the centre of the temple a replica of the Liṅga is represented in cylindrical form but on a high *pāṇipīṭha* . Whereas in the main temple, the Muktēśvara Liṅga being an *udbhavamūrti* is very small and not much elevated from the floor level. The devotee who is engaged in the worship of Liṅga looks like the one in the inscription No. I. Behind the personage is a couchant Nandin and the sun above. To the left of the temple is a cow and a sucking calf. The crescent moon is carved above the cow and calf.

Totally there are eighty two lines, of which the first five are engraved on a band of 7" below the arc. Each line contains 30-35 round and legible Kannaḍa letters of 12th century. The text of the inscription is strewn with some beautiful decorative motifs viz *śaṅkha, cakra,* etc. The language of the inscription is Kannaḍa prose and poetry except the beginning and a few imprecatory verses which are in Sanskrit. The inscription is complete and preserved in a very good condition. There are 34 verses containing *kanda* and *vṛtta* as follows: *anuṣṭubh* 1, *mahāśragdhara* 4, *campaka* 6, *utpala* 2, *mattēbha* 6, *śārdūla* 1, *kanda* 14. Orthographical peculiarities are there but not worth mentioning (*Cauḍadānapura Monograph* p. 75).

The inscription begins with an invocation to Śiva in Sanskrit and continues in the style of a *kāvya* describing oceans, mountains, Jaṃbudvīpa, Bhārata, and finally Māḷava with its capital Ujjayinī. Further it speaks of the supernatural powers of Vikramāditya the ruler of Ujjayinī. With the descendants of Vikramāditya, the history of Guttas of Guttavaḷal begins. Then it describes the Gutta chieftain, his officer Kāmeya Nāyaka and his relationship with Jaṭā Cōḷa family. A grant was made by Kāmeya Nāyaka after laving the feet of Muktajīyar, the ascetic who was in charge of the religious activities of the temple. The last line of the inscription gives the name of Rēvōja who was the architect and sculptor of the temple.

Also, there is a piece of information which is very important from the point of view of history. To-day, Guttala is a small and insignificant village without any trace of its past glory. But the inscription records that there was a fort and it was a *jaladurga* or "water-fort"; that means it was encircled by water. Effectively, the river Tuṅgabhadrā flows not far from there. As Guttaḷa was the principal residence of Gutta chieftains, it is but normal that it had a fort. As the river flows in its vicinity no wonder the fort was encircled by water. According to other inscriptions (S.I.I. XVIII, nos 296, 297) Guttala was lying in the limits of Muktikṣētra.

With regard to the text of the inscription a few words may not be out of place here. The poetry that we read here is of a high rank and the poet uses many *alaṅkāras* such as *śliṣṭopame, utprēkṣā* and so on. For example in l. 5b to 11a the poet points out the superiority of the earth over all the worlds by using *utprēkṣālaṅkāra.* In l. 17b-19a the poet shows his talents in *parisaṅkhyālaṃkāra* by using the same word in two different meanings: e. g. nobody speaks ill of others; if words are spoken they are only in the sense of lotus. With regard to *jāti* the pun is excellent. *Jāti* stands for caste as well as jasmin flowers. So *jātisaṅkara* was only in the garlands of jasmin with an admixture of various other flowers and not in the sense of mixture of castes in marriages. Similarly, the word *karagrahaṇa* also has double meaning. *Kara* is tax as well as hand. *Karagrahaṇa* may mean holding the hand in marriage ceremonies as well as levying taxes. Here the poet says that *karagrahaṇa* used to take place only in marriages and no new taxes were levied. Also *kaṟe* means milking animals as cows etc., or black stigma. Black stain is the sign of spreading anti-propagandas, calumnies. In Mālava *kaṟe* was used for milking animals and there was no place for evil.

In lines 29b-31a king Jomma is compared with Indra, Sūrya and Viṣṇu because he shared with them common epithets. *Vinatānandanasaṅgataṃ* : the king was "endowed with the quality of pleasing those who bow down to him", Viṣṇu is *Vinatā naṃdana* "he who causes pleasure to Vinatā", i. e. her son, Garuḍa, Viṣṇu's vehicle. *Sajanitōdyat kāmavarṣapravardhanaharṣaṃ*: King's joy was increasing by fulfilling, literally raining down, the wishes of devotees. Of the three Gods Indra, Divasendra and Upendra, Indra is associated with the rainbow, the Sun with light, Viṣṇu with Kāma. In this way the poet extols the qualities of his patron King Jomma through *śliṣṭōpame*, a means to exhibit his poetic talents.

The date, Śaka 1113, Virōdhikrit, Mārgaśira amavāsya, Budhavāra, Sūryagrahaṇa, corresponds to A.D. 1191, December 18, Wednesday. And the other date mentioned in line 80, namely Virōdhikritu saṃ, Puṣya amavāsye, brihaspativāra corresponds to A.D. 1192, January 16, Thursday.

ಶ್ರೀ ಮುಕ್ತೇಷಂ[ಶಂ] । ನಮೋ ಯ-
ನ್ಯ ಜಟಾಜೂಟೇ ವಿಧೋ: ಕಳಾ ।
ತುಂಗಗಂಗಾನದೀತೀರಬಾ
೨. ರೇ ಹಂಸೀವ ರಾಜತೇ ॥ ೧ ॥
ಪದಪಿಂ ಮುಕ್ತೇಶ್ವರಂ ಮಾಳ್ಕಭಿಮ-
ತ ಸುಖಮಂ ಭಕ್ತ
೩. ಲೋಕಕ್ಕೆ ಭಕ್ತ್ಯಾಸ್ಪದಚಂದ್ರೋ-
ಪೇಂದ್ರವೃಂದಾರಕನಿಕರನುತ ಶ್ರೀ
ಪದದ್ವಂದ್ವನುದ್ದಾಮದಷಾ(ಶಾ)ಸಂ
೪. ಭೂತಭೂತಿಪ್ರದನಖಿಳಜಗತ್ಸ್ವಾಮಿ
ಸಂಬದ್ಧಗೌರೀಹೃದಯಾನಂದೈಕಕಂ
೫. ದಂ ವಿಷದತರಯಶ:ಪ್ರಾಪ್ತಸ-
ಚ್ಛಾಂಸನಾಕಂ (ಬ) ॥ ೨ ॥

1-2a. Obeisance to Muktēśa on whose knotted hair is the moon crescent which shines like a swan swimming in the divine river Gaṃgā. (1)

2b-5a May Muktēśvara bless us with zeal and pleasure, place of worship of the world of devotees, whose sacred feet are praised by the Moon and Viṣṇu, master of the whole world, bestower of sovereignty born of unfettered prosperity, sole root of pleasure to the heart of Gaurī ever associated with Him; his very bright fame has reached the heaven in the form of the praise of the good. (2)

ವಿಷದತರೇಶ್ವರಾಜ್ಞೆಯೊದವಿಂ
೬. ದಮೆ ಸಂಭವಿಸಿರ್ದ್ದವೀ ಚತುರ್ದ್ದ
ಷ(ಶ)ಭುವನಂಗಳಷ್ಟತನುಧರ್ಮ್ಮದ-
ನೇರ್ಮ್ಮದಲ್ಲಿಯುಂ ಮನ:ಕುಷ(ಶ)
೭.ಲಮನಿತ್ತು
ಭೂಭುವನಮಾಭುವನಂಗಳನೇಳಿಕುಂ
ರಮಾವಷರಭಿವಾಂಛೆಯಂಸಲಿಪ ಸ
೮. ತುಕ್ರಿ(ಕೃ)ತಿಯಂ ಸಲೆ ತೋರ್ಪ್ಪ-
ನೆಪ್ಪಿನಿಂ|| ೩ ||

5b-8a. On the orders of Viṣadatarēśvara (?, Śiva) indeed all the fourteen worlds have come into being. Earth is the most pleasing to the mind, created following the rules of Śiva-dharma[1]; and to raise the beauty of the world to a higher level the seven splendid oceans were made to encircle them. (3)

ಕಂ|| ಸಪ್ತಸಮುದ್ರದ ಬಳಸಿಂ ಸಪ್ತ-
ದ್ವೀಪಪ್ರದೇಶದಿಂ ಭುವನಂ
೯.ಗಳ್ವ್ಯಾಪ್ತಿಯನುಳಿದೀರೇಳುಮವಾಪ್ತ-
ಸುಖಾವಳಿಗಳಿರ್ದ್ದವೆನಲ್ಕಿಳೆಯೆಸಗುಂ
||೪||

8b-9a. Encircled by seven oceans, with seven continents, the earth shines as if it had acquired for itself all the joys of the rest of the fourteen worlds. (4)

ದ್ವೀಪಾವಳಿಯೊ
೧೦. ಳ್ಜಂಬೂದ್ವೀಪವೆ ಸೂಗಯಿಕ್ಕ-
ವಲ್ಲದೆಂದುಳಿದಾಱುಂ ದ್ವೀಪಗಳುಮಂ
ಮೋಱಗಣ ಕಾ
೧೧. ೦ಪಿಂಗಿರಿಸಿದ ವಿಧಾತ್ರನೇನಱಿ-
ಯದನೇಮ ||೫||

9b-11a. Amongst the seven dvīpas Jaṃbudvīpa is the most beautiful one, and it appeared as if the other six have been assigned to protect it around. Who knows the rules of the Creator[2] ? (5)

ಇವಿ ಜಂಬೂದ್ವೀಪಲಕ್ಷ್ಮೀವಿಳಸಿತಲಾವ
೧೨. ಣ್ಯಮೆಂಬನ್ತೆ । ದೇವದ್ರುಮಾವಿಂ
ಚನ್ದನೋರ್ವ್ವೀರುಹದ ಸೊವಡಿನಿಂ ।
ರತ್ನಭೂಪಾಳಿಯಿಂಫೇನವಿನಿವಿಬದ್ಧಮಾ
೧೩. ದಾ ತೆರೆಗಳ ನಿಱೆಯುಂ ನನ್ಮ-
ಹಾಮಚ್ಛ್ಯಮಂಚ್ಛಾತ್ರವಿಚಿತ್ರೋರುಪ-
ತ್ರದಿಂ ರಾಜಿಸಿ ಬಳಸಿದ ಲಾವಣ್ಯ
೧೪. ವಾರಾಸಿ ತೋರ್ಕ್ಕುಂ ||೬||

11b-14a. The beautiful ocean with rows of waves full of foam, of giant fishes and other aquatic reptiles, appeared as if it were the beautiful girdle of Goddess Lakṣmī of the Jaṃbudvīpa resplendent with the fragrance of Dēvadāru, sandal wood trees and a number of gems. (6)

ಕಂದ || ವಾರಿಧಿ ತಿಳಿಗೊಳನದಱ ।
ಳ್ನೀರಜದವೊಲೆಸಗುಮಲ್ತೆ ಜಂಬೂ-
ದ್ವೀಪಂ । ಮೇರುವೆ ಕ
೧೫. ರ್ಣಿಕೈದೆಸೆಯೆಸಳಾರಯೆ ಬಲ-
ವರ್ಪ್ಪ ರಾಶಿಚಕ್ರಂ ಭ್ರಮರಂ ||೭||

14b-15a. In the midst of the ocean(s) Jaṃbudvīpa (is like) a lotus in a pond of clear water, Mēru being the stalk, the directions the petals, whirlpools armies of bees. (7)

---

[1] Śiva is called here Aṣṭatanu "having eight bodies": *pṛthvī,* (the earth) *appu* (water), *vāyu* (wind), *tējas* (fire), *ākāśa* (sky), Sūrya (Sun), Candra (Moon) and *jīvātma* (soul).

[2] What is there which the creator does not know ?

(ಕಂ) ಸುರಗಿರಿಯಿಳಾವೃತ್ತ(ತ)ಂ
ಕಿಂಪುರು
೧೬. ಶ(ಷ)ಂ ಹರಿವರ್ಷಮೆನೆವ ಹಿಮ-
ವದ್ಗಿರಿಯಂ ಭರತೋರ್ವಿವರ್ಷಖಂ-
ಡಂ ತರತರದಿಂ ತೆಂಕಲಲ್ಲಿ ಮಾಳ-
ವಮೆಸ
೧೭. ಗುಂ ॥೮॥

15b-17a. Mount Mēru with six islands is encircled : Suragiri, Iḷāvṛtta, Kiṃpuruṣa, Harivarṣa, Himavadgiri, (and) Bharatavarṣa with Himālaya, and to their south shines Māḷava. (8)

ತಾವರೆಯಂದೆನಿಪ್ಪ ಕಮಳಂಗೆಳಸಾ-
ಲ್ಕೆಮ ಜಾತಿಸಂಕರಂ ಪೂವಿನೊಳಕ್ಕೆ
ನೂತನ ಕರಗ್ರಹಣಂ
೧೮. ವಿವಾಹದಲ್ಲಿತೋರ್ಕ್ಕುವರವೆಂಗ-
ದಲ್ಸುರಭಿಯಂಕಱಯೆಂಬದೆನಿಪ್ಪಲ
ಕ್ಷ್ಮೀಕಾಮಾವಳಿ ರಾಜನೀತಿಹ್ರ(ಹೃ)ದ-
ಯ ಸ್ಥಿತಿ
೧೯. ಮಾಳವದೊಳು ವಿರಾಜಿಕುಂ॥೯॥

17b-19a. Spoken words are used only in the sense of "lotus"; *jātisaṅkara* is in jasmin garlands only; and *karagrahaṇa* in marriages; *kaṟe* used only in milking the cow. In such Māḷava *rājanīti* shines with multitudinous desires of Lakṣmī (prosperity). (9)

॥ಕ॥ ಮಾಳವದೊಳಗುಜ್ಜಯನಿಯೆ ।
ಪಾಳಿಸುಗುಂ ಕರ್ಣ್ಣಮಣ್ಯಮಂ ಕ-
ಣ್ಬೆಳಗಿಂಬಾಳೆವೋ
೨೦.ಸರಿಸೆ ಚಂದ್ರಶಿಳಾ(ಲಾ)ಲಯಮಂ
ಮಳೆಯನುಳಿದು ಬಳೆಯೆ ಬನಂಗಳ-
ಿಂ ॥೧೦॥

19b-20a. The merit of ears is to hear about Ujjayinī, (capital) city of Māḷava (where) the mansions made of moon-stone exceed in lustre that of the blackness of the eyes of fishes[1]; without rains grow woodlands. (10)

ಅಮರ್ದಂ ತತ್ಪುರದೊಳ್ನೃಪೋತ್ತಮ-
ನೆನಿಪ್ಪಾ ವಿಕ್ರಮಾ
೨೧. ದಿತ್ಯನ । ಪ್ಪ ಮಹಾಸಿದ್ಧಿಯ
ನೆಯ್ದೆ ಸಾಧಿಸಿ ಜಗಕ್ಕಾನನ್ದಮಾಗಿತ್ತ
ಭೀಷ್ಟಮ ನಿಂಶಂಕನಾಗಿ ಮೂಜಗಮು
ಮಂ ಸತ್ಕೀರ್ತಿಯಿಂ ಮುಚ್ಚಿ
೨೨. ಭೂರಮೆಗಿಂ ತಂನೆಯ ತೋಳ-
ಬಾಳೆ ಮಱವಾಳಿಲ್ಲೆಂಬಿನಂ ತಾಳ್ದು-
(ಳ್ವು)ತುಂ ॥ ೧೧ ॥

20b-22a. Vikramāditya the best of the kings of that city, having achieved great *siddhis*, without hesitation bestowing pleasure to his subjects by fulfilling their desires, covering the three worlds with his glory, ruled the beloved Earth with his mighty arm, as if She had a glorious life only in his arms and nowhere else. (11)

ಉಗುಗುಂ ರತ್ನಾಳಿಗಳ್ಕಂಥೆಯಿನೆಸ-
ಗಿಕ್ಕುಮಿಷ್ಟಾನ್ನ
೨೩. ಮಂ ಖರ್ಪರಂ ಪಾಹಗೆವೊ-
ಯ್ದುಂ ಪೇಳ್ದ ತಾಣಕ್ಕೆ ಸಪುದಸುವ-
ನಂಟಂಟು ಚಿತ್ರಕ್ಕೆ ಬೆತ್ತಂ ।

22b-24a. Owing to his magical merits Vikramāditya's bundle gives gems, his bowl supplies best food, his sandals take him where he wants, his brush paints what he desires,

---

1 *Bāḷe*, a kind of fish: *Trichiurus lepturus.*

ಬಗೆದಾಗಳ್ತೀಚ್ಚುಗುಂ ಶತ್ರುವನಸಿರಸ
೨೪. ದಿಂ ಪೊಂಗಳಕ್ಕು ಪಟಂ ದಿಟ್ಟ-
ಗದ್ರಿಶ್ಯವಕ್ಕೆಯಕ್ಕುಂ ಘುಟಿಕೆಯ ಸ-
ದಳಂ ವಿಕ್ರಮಾದಿತ್ಯಪುಣ್ಯಂ ॥ ೧೨ ॥

his sword slays enemies heads at will, his clothes turn into gold, he becomes invisible by force of magic pills; his merit is unaccountable.(12)

ಕಂ. ಎನಲೆಸೆದ ವಿಕ್ರಮಾದಿ
೨೫. ತ್ಯನೆನಿತ್ತಲ್ಚಂದ್ರಗುಪ್ತವಂಷ(ಶ)-
ದೊ[ಳ]ಂನ್ಯರ್ಜ್ಜನಿಯನತಿನಿಪಿದ
ನೋಡಿಸಿ ಜನಿಯಿಸಿದಂ ವೀರವಿಕ್ರ-
ಮಾದಿತ್ಯ ನ್ರಿ(ನೃ)ಪಂ ॥೧೩॥

24b-25. While it was said thus about Vikramāditya, here, in the family of Candragupta, after defying the belief that no one will be born (equal to him), was born Vīra Vikramāditya. (13)

೨೬.ಚರಿತಂಗಂ ನೀತಿಗಳ್ಗಂ ಘನಮೆ-
ನಿಸುಪುವಾಪ್ತರ್ತ್ಥಿಗಿಷ್ಟಾರ್ತ್ಥದಿಂದಂ
ಪಿರಿದುಂದಚೌಬ್ಯರ್ಯ್ಯಮುಬ್ರ್ಬೀ(ರ್ವ್ವೀ)
ವಳಯದ ಬಳಸಿಂದ
೨೭. ಗ್ಗಳಂ ಲಕ್ಷ್ಮೀಸಾಮ್ರಾಜ್ಯರಮಾ-
ವಿಸ್ತಾರದಿಂದತ್ಯಧಿಕ ಮನುವಿನೋದಂ
ಮನೋಜಂಗಮಾಯ್ತುಬ್ಬರಮಾ ನ
೨೮.ತುಕೀರ್ತ್ತಿ(ರ್ತಿ) ಲೋಕಕ್ಕತುಳಮೆ
ನಿಸಿದಂ ವಿಕ್ರಮಾದಿತ್ಯದೇವಂ ॥೧೪॥

26-28a. His good character, good conduct, great desires, entertainments, matchless heroism, the expansion of his rich empire made god Cupid to suffocate. The good fame of Vikramādityadēva made the world to think that he is unique. (14)

ಕಂ ॥ ಆ ವೀರ ವಿಕ್ರಮಾದಿ । ತ್ಯಾವ
ನಿಪಂಗುದಯಗಿರಿ
೨೯. ಯೊಳುದಯಿಸುವಂದಿನ ಶ್ರೀವರ-
ನೆನೆ ಜೊಮ್ಮನ್ರಿ(ನೃ)ಪಂ । ಭೂವಧುಕ
ಣ್ದೆಱೆಯೆ ಪುಟ್ಟಿದಂ ಕಮಳೇ(ಲೇ)ಶಂ
॥೧೫॥

28b-29a. To this valourous king Vikramāditya was born Joṃmanṛpa, as the lord of lotuses the Sun (rose) in Udayagiri (eastern direction), when the bride Earth opened her eyes. (15)

ವಿನತಾನಂದನ ನಂ
೩೦.ಗತಂ ನಜನಿತೋದ್ಯತ್ಕಾಮುವರ್ಷ-
ಪ್ರವರ್ದ್ಧಮಾನಹರ್ಷಂ ವಿಬುಧಾಶ್ರ-
ಯಸ್ತುತ ಪದಂ ಶ್ರೀಮಣ್ಣಳಾ(ಲಾ)ವ-
ಳೋ(ಲೋ)ಕನರಾಗೋದಯ
೩೧. ನಾ ಸುದರ್ಷ(ರ್ಶ)ನಕರಂಗಾಶ್ಚ-
ರ್ಯ್ಯರೂಪಂ ಸುಜೊಮ್ಮಂ ನೃಪಂ-
ರಾಜಿಸುತಿರ್ಪ್ಪನಿಂದ್ರದಿವಸೇಂದ್ರೋಪೆಂ
ದ್ರವೊಂದಂದದಿಂ॥೧೬॥

29b-31a. He treats humbly and courageously in company, accrues the joy through a shower of genuine good wishes, deserves the praise of protector of literates; affection rises through casting a glance on his realm; he excells in beauty He who holds Sudarśana cakra (Viṣṇu); such Jomma shines like Indra, Divasēndra (Sun) and Upēndra. (16)

ಅರ
೩೨. ಸಗ್ಗಿರ್ಗ್ಗಲ್ಲರಸಪ್ರಶಕ್ತಿ ರಸಿಕತ್ವಂ
ಕೂಡೆ ಕೂರ್ಪಿರ್ಗ್ಗಿಲ್ಲ ಕೂರ್ಪ್ಪಿರ್ಗ್ಗರೆ ವಿದ್ಯಾ-
ವಳಿಯಿಲ್ಲ ವಿದ್ಯೆಯಿರೆ ನೇರ್ಪ್ಪಿರ್ಗ್ಗಲ್ಲಾಗೆ
ನೇರ್ಪ್ಪಿರ್ಗ್ಗಲ್ಲ ಸಚ್ಚರಿತಂ । ಮೊದಲ್ಗಿ
೩೩. ರೆ ವಿಳಾ(ಲಾ)ಸ ಪ್ರೀತಿಯಿಲ್ಲ
ಗುಣೋತ್ಕರವೆಲ್ಲಂ ನೆರೆದಿರ್ದ್ದವೆಂ
ದೆನಿಸಿದಂ ಶ್ರೀ ಜೋಯಿದೇವೊರ್ಬ್ಬಿ
(ರ್ವಿ) ಪಂ ॥೧೭॥

31b-33a. Many kings have no perseverance for literary taste; if endowed with refined taste, they have no sharpness; if endowed with sharpness they have no spirituality; without spirituality they have no good conduct, without good conduct they have no grace, whereas all these good qualities are united in King Jomma lord of the earth. (17)

॥ಕಂದ॥ ಆ ಜೊಮ್ಮನನುಜ
೩೪. ಗುತ್ತಂ ರಾಜಾಚಾರಪ್ರಶಸ್ತಿಯಂ
ಕುವಳೆಯಲಕ್ಷ್ಮೀಜಾಪ್ಯಮಂತ್ರವಿಳಸ-
ದ್ಬೀಜಾಕ್ಷರಮಂ ಬುಧಾಳಿಯಿಂದೋದಿ
ಸುವಂ ॥೧೮।

33b-34a. Gutta, younger brother of Jomma, with the eulogy of *rājācāra* was delighted by the reading of *jāpyamantra* of shining *bījākṣaraman tra* of Bhūlakṣmī by the priests. (18)

ಮನಸಿ
೩೫. ಜನೊಲಗಿಪ್ಪೆಸಕದಿಂ ಪಡೆದಂ।
ನೆಱಕೆಟ್ಟಮೆಯ್ಯನೀತನನಿವುದ್ಧ್ಯಕೀರ್ತ್ತಿ
ಯನೆ ಪೊರ್ದ್ದಿ ಹಿಮದ್ಯುತಿ ತತ್ಕ
ಳ(ಲ)ಂಕ ವರ್ತ್ತನಮನಿದಿರ್ಪ್ಪದಂ
೩೬. ಯಮನುಮೀತನ ಖಳ್ಗದೊಳಿಪ್ಪ-
ನಲ್ತೆ ಭೋಜನಸುಖದಿಂದಮೆಂದೆನಿಪು-
ದುತ್ತಮಗುತ್ತನೃಪಾಳವೃತ್ತಕಂ ॥೧೯॥

34b-36a King Gutta with his charming body appeared as Cupid having himself entered into his body after having been bodyless; by uniting with his fame the Moon could face the attacking clouds; Yama lives in his sword for the pleasure of a sumptuous food. (19)

ಎನಿಸಿದ ಗುತ್ತ
೩೭. ಭೂಮಿಪನ ವಲ್ಲಭೆ ಪದ್ಮಲದೇವಿ
ಜಾತಿ ಪದ್ಮಿನಿಯೆನೆ ಲಕ್ಷ್ಮಿಯಂತಳದಿ-
ನಂಗನುರಾಗಿಸಿ ರಾಜಹಂಸವರ್ತ್ತನದೆ
ಡೆಯಾಗಿ ಸೇಬ್ಯ (ಸೇವ್ಯ)
೩೮.ಕವಿಚಕ್ರದೆ ಸಂಸ್ತುತೆಯಾಗಿ ಕಾ-
ಮರಾಜನ ಜಲದುರ್ಗ್ಗಮಂ ರಸವಿ-
ಶೇಷ ವಿನೋದದಿ ಮಾಡಿ ರೂಢಿಪಳು
॥೨೦॥

36b-38a. The beloved spouse of King Gutta, Padmaladēvi, lady of Padmini class, of charming grace and wit, dazzling like Lakṣmī, having graceful walk like a royal swan in love with the sun, celebrated with honours by a circle of poets, made (Guttala) into a waterfort of Cupid and pleased her husband with charm and wit. (20)

॥ಕಂ॥ ಪದ್ಮೆಯ ನಿ
೩೯. ರ್ಮ್ಮಳನೋದರ ಪದ್ಮದಿನೀ ವೀ-
ರವಿಕ್ರಮಮಂ ಪುಟ್ಟಿದನಾ ಪದ್ಮಭವ-
ನನ್ತೆ ಕ್ರಿಷ್ಯ(ಕೃಷ್ಣ)ನ ಪದ್ಮೋದರದಲ್ಲಿ
ಪುಟ್ಟೆ ನಯವಿನುತುಂಟೇ ॥೨೧ ॥

38b-39a. In Vīra Vikramāditya born in the pure lotus like stomach of Padmā, like Padmabhava in the lotus stomach of Kṛṣṇa, (now) will there be any limit for diplomacy. (21)

ವಿನ
೪೦ ಯಂ ವಿಕ್ರಮಶಕ್ತಿ ಪುಣ್ಯವೆನಿಪೀ
ಮೂಱುಂ ಗುಣಂ ರಾಜ್ಯಮಂಡನ
ದೇಹಾಂಶುಗಳೆನ್ತನಲ್ಸಿರಿಗೆ ಪುಣ್ಯಚೇತ
೪೧. ನಂ ಬಲ್ಪು ಮೇಯ್ಪಿನಯಂ
ಭೂಷಣಮೆಂದು ಷಾ(ಶಾ)ಸ್ತ್ರಂ ರುಚಿ
ಶಸ್ತ್ರಾಭ್ಯಾಸಧರ್ಮಪ್ರವರ್ತ್ತನಮೆಂದಿಂ
ತಿವು ವೀರ ವಿಕ್ರಮನೊಳಿರ್ಕ್ಕುಂ
೪೨. ಪ್ರಾಜ್ಯಸಾಮ್ರಾಜ್ಯನೊಳು ||೨೨||
ಮೊನೆಯೊಳ್ಖಳ್ಗಸಹಾಯವ್ರಿತ್ತಿತನಗಾ-
ಬ್ರಿಂ(ವ್ರಿಂ)ದಂನರೇಂದ್ರಾಯತೇ
ಯೆನೆಸಲ್ಸೇನೆಮನಂ ಸತತ್ವಮೆ
೪೩. ಯಥಾರೂಪಂ ತಥಾ ಶೀಲಂ-
ಮೆಂದೆನಿಸಲ್ಕಾವ ಸುಖಂ ಯಾವಿಳನೆ
ತಾಂ ತೇಜ:ಫಳಂ ರಾಜ್ಯಮೆಂದೆನೆ
ನಿಸಲ್ವಿಕ್ರಮಶಕ್ತಿ ರಾಜಿಸು
೪೪. ಗುಮಿಂತೀ ವಿಕ್ರಮಾದಿತ್ಯನೊಳು।
||೨೩||
ಜಯವಧುವುಂ ವೊರ್ಮೆಯುಂ ಬ-
ಯಸುತಿರ್ಪ್ಪದಟಂಗನೆಯುರ್ವ್ವಿಳಾ -
ನದಿಂ। ಬಯಸು
೪೫. ವಚೆಲ್ಪು ನೀತಿತತಿಗಳ್ನಡೆಯಲ್ಸು-
ಪಥ ಪ್ರಪಂಚಮುಂ ಬಯಸುವ ಮಾ-
ರ್ಗ್ಗವರ್ತ್ತಿಗಳಪೇಕ್ಷ್ಯಗಳಂ ಬಯ-
ಸುತ್ತವಿರ್ಪ್ಪತಿಪ್ರಿಯ
೪೬. ವೆನಿಪಾರ್ಪ್ಪ ರಾಜಿಸುದಿನಂ ಮಿ-
ಸುಪಂ ವಿಭು ವೀರ ವಿಕ್ರಮಂ ||೨೪||

ಸ್ವಸ್ತಿ ಸಮಧಿಗತಪಂಚಮಹಾಶಬ್ದಮ
೪೭. ಹಾಮಂಡಳೇಶ್ವರಂ ಉಜ್ಜಯನೀ
ಪುರವರಾಧೀಶ್ವರಂ ವಟಕಲ್ಪವ್ರಿ(ವೃ)
ಕ್ಷಲಾಂಛಿತವಿಜಯಧ್ವಜಂ ಭುವನ
[ರ]ಕ್ಷ
೪೮. ಣೈಕದಕ್ಷದಕ್ಷಿಣಭುಜಂ ಚಂದ್ರ-
ಗುಪ್ತಾನ್ವಯ ಸುಧಾರ್ಣ್ನವಪೂರ್ಣ್ನ
ಚಂದ್ರಂ ವಿಭವಾಮರೇಂದ್ರಂ

39-42a. Vīra Vikrama is possessed of three qualities, humility, heroism and merit, the ornaments of administration to the goddess of the kingdom, strength, humbleness, liking for all *śāstras*, promotion of *dharma* were all present abundantly in Vikramāditya the great king. (22)

42b-44a. The sharp edge of the sword as his friend, he enters the battlefield, the enemy feels that the king has become an entire army; as the saying goes "as the form, so the conduct"; his will is so firmly set on victory, what is the use of any other joy; the only goal worth seeking by a king is a kingdom which comes as a fruit of valour in war. These qualities adorn king Vikramāditya. (23)

44b-46a. Occcasionally, even the goddess of victory would long for his beauty which is such that women would crave for; so is his munificence in statecraft and good conduct which people on the road look as perfection; he shines with his greatness manifest in everything (24)

46b-53a. Be it well. Vīra Vikramāditya, *mahāmaṇḍaḷeśvara* of five great titles, lord of Ujjaini, having *vaṭakalpavṛkṣa* as emblem on his victorious banner, unique right arm in protecting the earth, full moon to the nectar ocean of Candragupta's family, eternal Indra in magnanimity,

೪೯.ಹರಣಚರಣನಖಕಿರಣಸಾಂದ್ರಚಂ
ದ್ರಿಕಾಚಕೋರಂ ಗುರುಪದಪಯೋಧ
ರಧ್ವಾನಾನಂದಿತ ಮ
೫೦. ಯೂರಂ ಮಾನಿನೀ ಮಾನ-
ಸಬ್ಬ(ರ್ವ್ವ)ಸ್ವ ಸೂಱೆಕಾರಂ ರಣ-
ದೊಳ್ವೀಱಂ ಮಂಡಳಿಕಭೈ ರವಂ
ಆನಂದಿತ ಯುವತೀನ
೫೧. ಯನಕೈರವಂ ಪನ್ನಿಬ್ಬರ ಗ-
ಣ್ಡಂ ಸಮರಷೌ(ಶೌ)ಂಡಂ ಆಹವಾದಿ
ತ್ಯಂ ವೀರ ವಿಕ್ರಮಾದಿತ್ಯಂ। ಬನವಾ-
ಸೆನಾಡಂ
೫೨. ದುಷ್ಟ ನಿಗ್ರಹ ಶಿಷ್ಟಪ್ರತಿಪಾಳನದಿ
ಪಾಳಿಸುತ್ತಂ ಗುತ್ತವೊಳಲ ನೆಲೆವೀಡಿ-
ನೊಳ್ಸುಖಸಂಕಥಾವಿನೋ
೫೩. ದದಿಂ ರಾಜ್ಯಂಗೆಯುತ್ತಮಿರೆ॥
ಆ ಭೂಪಾಳಪದಾಬ್ಜಭೃಂಗನೆನಿಪಂ
ಸದ್ಭಕ್ತಿಯಿಂ ಯುಕ್ತಿಯಿಂದಾ ಭೂಪಾ
೫೪. ಳನ ಮಂತ್ರಯೋಗ್ಯನೆನಿಸಿಪಂ
ತಂನ್ನುದ್ಧವೀರತ್ವದಿಂದಾ ಭೂಪಾಳನ
ದಕ್ಷದಕ್ಷಿಣಭುಜಾದಂಡ ನಿಜಂ
೫೫.ತಾನೆನಲ್ಕಾ ಭೂಪಾಳನ ನಾಯ-
ಕಾಗ್ರಣಿ ಜಗದ್ವಿಖ್ಯಾತನೀ ಕಾಮೆಯ
॥೨೫॥

cakōra to the moonlight shooting off from toe-nails of Hara, peacock enjo ying the sound of clouds, Guru's words, plunderer of the proud property (husband) of women, brave in battles, Bhairava to vassals, white lotus to the eyes of joyous young damsels, overlord of twelve, fond lover of fighting, Sun in wars, Vīra Vikramāditya governed Banavāse-nāḍu from his residence Guttavoḷal, in pleasure and pleasant conversation, in good pursuits, chastising the wicked and protecting the chaste.

53b- 55a Like a bee on the lotus feet of his overlord, with his deep dedication and talents fit to be called appropriate minister to the king, through his own valour he became the true dexterous right arm of the king, the world famous Kāmeya, chief amongst the generals of the king. (25)

ವಚನ ॥ತದನ್ವಯಮೆಂತೆನೆ । ಅತ್ಯ

55b. To tell about his geneaology :

೫೬. ರಸಂ ಚಂಡರಸಂ ಸತ್ಯದ ಕ-
ಣೆಯೆನಿಸಿ ಮಿಸುಪ ಧರ್ಮ್ಮದ ಧುರ-
ಮಾ ನಿತ್ಯೋತ್ಸವದಿಂ ಧರಿಯಿಪ ।
ಕ್ರಿ(ಕೃ)ತ್ಯೌಚಿತ್ಯ
೫೭.ಮೆ ಸಮಸ್ತ ಗುಣವೆನಲೆಸೆದರು
॥೨೬॥

55c-57. Atyarasa, fiery king, mine of truth, shining as the shaft of Dharma, with daily festivities and appropriate actions made to feel as an abode to all (good) qualities; (26)

ತತ್ಸುತೆ ಮಾಚಲದೇವಿಯ ಹ್ರಿ(ಹೃ)ತ್ಸ
ರಸೀರುಹದೊಳೆಸೆವ ರಸಮಧುಲಹರೀ
೫೮. ಪ್ರೋತ್ಸುಕನೆನಿಸಿ ಕರಗ್ರಹಸತ್ಸು
ಖಮಂ ಪಡೆದನಂದು ನಾಯಕ
ಮಾರಂ ॥೨೭॥

57b-58a. of his daughter, Mācaladēvi, causing waves of fluid of sweet sap in a lotus pond, her heart, Nāyaka Māra obtained the good pleasure of holding the hand. (27)

ಮಾರೆಯನಾಯಕಂಗೆ ನುತ ಮಾ
೫೯. ಚಲೆಗಂ ಜನಿಸಿರ್ದ್ದಾ ಶಂಕ-
ರೋದಾರಪದಾಬ್ಜ ಭೃಂಗನತಿ ಮಂ-
ಗಳ ಚೇಷ್ಟಿತನಂಗನಾಜನಕ್ಕೀ ರತಿವ-
ಲ್ಲಭಂ ಜನಿತನೆಂಬಿನವಿಂಬಿನ
೬೦.ಸದ್ಗುಣಂಗಳಿಂದಾರುಸಮಾನವಿಂದ
ಮಮ ನೋೞ್ಪಡೆ ಕಾಮೆಯನಾಯ-
ಕಾಗ್ರ್ಯೇಯನೊಳು|: ||೨೮||
೬೧.ಭೀಮನ ಬಲ್ಪಿಂ ನೆಗಳ್ದಾ| ರಾಮ
ನ ಸಾಹಸದಿನಣುವನಿ | ನ ಸದ್ಭಕ್ತಿ
ಪ್ರೇಮದಿನಾದ್ಯನೆನಿಪ್ಪಂ| ಕಾಮೆಯ
೬೨. ನುದಾತ್ತಚಿತ್ರಚರಿತ್ರ ||೨೯||
ಜವದಿಂ ಶ್ರೀ ವಿಕ್ರಮಾಂಕಸ್ಥಿ(ಕ್ಷಿ)
ತಿಪತಿತಿಳಕಂ ಶತ್ರುಸೇನಾಂಗಮಂ
೬೩. [ತಾಂ] ತವಿಪುಲ್ಕುದ್ಯೋಗಮಂ
ಮಾಳ್ಪನೆಗೆವತಿಮದೋಚ್ಚಂಡವೇ
ದಂಡಷಂಡಂ ನವವೇಗಬ್ರಾಜಿ
೬೪ಳವಾಜಿಬ್ರಜವತಿಬಳಪಾದತವನ್ನೆ||
ಕ್ರಿ(ಕೃ)ಪಾಣಾಹವದೊಳ್ಕುಂತಿರ್ದವಿನ್ನೇ
ಕೆ ನಿನಗೆ ಭರವೆಂದೆಂಬನಾಳ್ದಂಗೆ
೬೫. ಕಾಮಂ ||೩೦||
ಕಂದ || ಆ ನರನಾಥನ ವಿಶ(ಷ)ಯ
ದ ದಾನಜಳಂ ಕೂಡಿ ಪರಿದುವೆಂಬ
ವೊಲುಬ್ಬಿರ್ವಮಾನಿನಿಯ ಹಾರದಂತಿರೆ
೬೬. ತಾನೆಂದುಂ ತುಂಗಭದ್ರೆ ತದ್ದೇ
ಶದೊಳಂ ||೩೧||
ಭೂರಮಣೀತರಳದವೊಲೀರೇಳುಂ
ಭುವನಂಗಳೂಳಗೆ ಸವಿತತಮಹಿ
೬೭.ಮಾಧಾರಂ ಮುಕ್ತೇಶ್ವರನಾಮಾ
ರಂಭನೆಸೆವುತಿರ್ಪ್ಪನೀಶನುಮೇಶಂ
|| ೩೨ ||
ಸ್ವಸ್ತಿ ಸಮಸ್ತ ಪ್ರಶಸ್ತಿಸಹಿತಂ
೬೮. ಶ್ರೀಮನು ಮಹಾಮಂಡಳೇಶ್ವರಂ
ವೀರ ವಿಕ್ರಮಾದಿತ್ಯಾದೇವರಸರು ಗು
ತ್ತವೊಳಲ ನೆಲೆವೀಡಿನೊಳು

58b-60. Kāmeya Nāyaka was born to Māraya Nāyaka and Mācale; he was like a bee on a lotus the noble feet of Śaṅkara, play of good omens, made women to feel that the lord of Rati (Kāma) was born. Kāmeya Nāyaka, the best of heroes, is there anybody equal to him in good qualities ? (28)

61-62a. With Bhīma's puissance, Rāma's courage, Hanumān's devotion and affection, the illustrious Kāmeya Nāyaka was of brilliant nature. (29)

62b-65a. As king Vikramāṅka, *tilaka* of earthly kings, when set to reduce quickly the armies of enemies, he used strongly his shining sword, quickly raised the ranges of elephants in rut, speedily running cavalry, (placed) the strong infantry in the front; to rule "why should you worry", said Kāma. (30)

65b-66a. Swollen by the flow of water pouring for grants by the lord of men, the Tuṅgabhadrā flows in that land as if saying "I am the necklace of the respectable lady Earth".(31)

66b-67a. The children of the beautiful woman Earth's twice seven (fourteen) worlds; as a support to them Śiva with Umā present there was called by the name Muktēśa; (32)

67b-69a. With all praśastis, while Ārīmanu mahāma~ḍaḷēśvara Vīra Vikramādityadēva, was ruling from his residence Guttavoḷal in pleasure, discourse and divertissement,

೬೯.ಸುಖಸಂಕಥಾವಿನೋದಿಂ ರಾಜ್ಯಂ
ಗೆಯ್ಯುತ್ತಮಿರೆ|| ತತ್ಪಾದಪದ್ಮೋಪಜೀ
ವಿಯೆನಿಪ ಖಂಡೆ ಯ
೭೦. ಕಾಱ ಕಾಮೆಯನಾಯಕಂ ತಂ-
ನ ಸ್ವಾಮಿಯ ಚಿತ್ತವನುಪಾರ್ಜ್ಜಿಸಿ
ಪಾರಿತೋಷಿಕಮಾಗಿ ಪಡೆದ ಹೊನ್ನವ
೭೧. ತ್ತಿಯ ಹೊಲದೊಳು ಚಾಮೇ-
ಶ್ವರದೇವರ ಕೆಯ್ಯಿಂ ಮೂಡಲು
ಗೋ(ಗೊ)ಪೆಯ ಓಣಿಯಿಂ ತೆಂಕಲು
ಚತುರಾಘಾಟ
೭೨. ಶುದ್ಧಮಾಗಿರಲಾಱು ಮತ್ತರು-
ಮಂ ಸ(ಶ)ಕವರ್ಷಂ ೧೧೧೩ನೆಯ
ವಿರೋಧಿಕ್ರಿ(ಕೃ)ತು ಸಂವತ್ಸರದ ಮಾ
೭೩.ರ್ಗ್ಗಶಿರದಮಾವಾಸೆ ಸೂರ್ಯ್ಯಗ್ರ-
ಹಣದಂದು ಶ್ರೀಮನು ಮುಕ್ತೇಶ್ವರ
ದೇವರ ಅಂಗರಂ
೭೪.ಗಭೋಗಕ್ಕೆ ಜೀರ್ನ್ನೋದ್ಧಾರಕ್ಕೆ-
ನ್ದು° ಮುಕ್ತಜೀಯರ ಕಾಲಂ ಕರ್ಚ್ಚಿ
ಧಾ
೭೫. ರಾಪೂರ್ವ್ವಕಂ ಮಾಡಿಕೊಟ್ಟ||[೨]
|| ಶ್ರೀ ವಿಶ್ವನಾಥಾಯ ನಮ: || ಶ್ರೀ
ಮುಕ್ತೇಶ್ವರಾಯ ನಮ:||

69b-75. Khaṃḍeyakāṟa Kāmeya Nāyaka dwelling at the lotus feet of the king, after conquering the good will of the master, as trophy obtained a field of six *mattaru* at Honnavatti, the four limits[1] of which are : to the east the field of God Cāmēśvara, to the south the road to Gope, thus four limits of six *mattaru* of land being defined, on the date of the solar eclipse of new moon day in the month of Mārgaśira, in the cyclic year Virōdhikṛtu, Śaka 1113, for the pleasure of the decoration of the Lord's body and stage, and for the repairs of what is worn out, …, after bowing down at the feet of Muktajīyar, … making the field tax free, offered it with water libation (to the God). Salutation to the Lord of the Universe. Homage to Śrī Muktēśvara.

೭೬. || [೩] || ಈಂತೀ ಧರ್ಮ್ಮವಪ್ರತಿ-
ಪಾಳಿಸ(ಸಿ)[೪]ದವರು ಪ್ರಯಾಗೆಯಲ-
ರ್ಘ್ಯತೀರ್ತ್ಥ ವಾರಣಾಶಿ(ಸಿ)ಯಲು

೭೭. ಕವಿಲೆಯಂ ಕೊಂಡು ಕೊಳ-
ಗುಮಂ ಪೊನ್ನಲು ಕಟ್ಟಸಿ ನಾಸಿ-
ರ್ಬ್ಬ(ರ್ವ್ವ)ರು ವೇದಪಾರಗರಿಗೆ
ಕೊಟ್ಟ ಫಲ ||

76-77. By protecting this dharma one obtains the fruit of buying a Kapilā cow(s) at the *arghyatīrtha* of Prayāga, setting up its (their) hooves with gold, giving it to 1002 brahmins versed in Vedas.

---

1 Some letters here are completely erased.
2 Some decorative motifs.
3 Decorative motif.
4 In the *Cauḍadānapura Monograph* sa (ಸ) is a mistake for *si* (ಸಿ).

ಇ (ಈ) ಧರ್ಮ್ಮವ
೭೮. ನಾವನಾನುಂ ಕಿ(ಕೆ)ಡಿಸಿದನಾ-
ಬ್ರಾಹ್ಮಣರುಮಂ ಕವಿಲೆಯುಂ
[ಕೊನ್ದ] ಮಹಾಪಾತಕನಕ್ಕು|| ಸ್ವದ
ತ್ತ(ತ್ತಾ)ಂ ಪರದ
೭೯. ತ್ತಂ (ತ್ತಾಂ) ವಾ ಯೋ ಹರೇತಿ
(ಹರೇತ) ವಶು(ಸು)ಂಧರಾ(ಂ)||
ಷಷ್ಟಿರ್ವ್ವರ್ಷಸಹಸ್ರಾಣಿ ವಿಷ್ಟಾಯಾಂ
ಜಾಯತೆ ಕ್ರಿಮಿ: ||೩೩||

...[1]ಕಬ್ಬ
೮೦. ವಿರೋಧಿಕೃತು ಸಂವತ್ಸರದ ಪು-
ಶ್ಯ(ಷ್ಯ)ದಮವಾಸೆ ಬ್ರಿ(ಬೃ)ಹಸ್ಪತಿ ...
ಸಂಕ್ರಮಣ ...ಕೂಡಿದಲ್ಲಿ ಶ್ರೀ
ಮುಕ್ತೇಶ್ವರದೇವರ ತ್ರಿಕಾಲ
೮೧.ದುಪಹಾರಕೆ[2] ಶ್ರೀಮನ್ಮಹಾಮಂಡ-
ಳೇಶ್ವರಂ ವೀರ ...[3] ವಿಕ್ರಮಾದಿತ್ಯ-
ದೇವರ ...[4]ಮಹಾಜನಂಗಳ
ಸಂನಿಧಾನ
೮೨. ದಲು ಕೊಟ್ಟ ಗದ್ದೆ ಶ್ರೀಮದ-
ಗ್ರಹಾರಂ ಹೊಂನವತಿಯ ಹಾಳ ಶ್ರೀ
ಕಲಿದೇವರ ಗದ್ದೆಯ ತೆಂಕ ಆ ದೇ-
ವರಿಂ ಮೂಡ ಬಿಟ್ಟ ಗದ್ದೆಕಂಬ
||೨೦||
ಇನ್ತೀ ಧರ್ಮವಂ
೮೩. ತಪ್ಪದೆ ಪ್ರತಿಪಾಳಿಸುವದು||

[ಕ]ಲುಹಂದರಾದಿಯಾಗಿ ಹೊಱಧರ
ಸಹಿತ ರೇಓಜನ ಕೆಲಸ ||
ಮುಕ್ತೇಶ್ವರಾಯ ನಮ: ||

77-79a. He who destroys this dharma, will incur the great sin of killing a brahmin, a Kapilā cow in Vārāṇasī. He who steals the earth given by him or another, is reborn as a worm in dirt for sixty thousand years. (33)

79b-83. On the eclipse and vyatīpāta of the new moon day of the dark fortnight of the month of Puś(ṣ)ya in the cyclic year Virōdhikṛtu ... for the three main food offerings of Lord Muktēśa Śrī Vīra Vikramāditya ... in the presence of the assembly of Mahājanas was granted a field measuring 20 kaṃba; the limits are : to the south the temple in ruins of Śrī Kalidēva in Śrīmadagrahāra Honnavatti, to east of the same God. In this manner (the clauses of) this chart should be executed without any derogation.

83b. Including the stone pendal the execution of external work (was) by Rēvōja.

Salutations to Muktēśa.

[1] A few letters are worn out.
[2]. *Cauḍadānapura Monograph*'s reading *dagrahārakke* ದಗ್ರಹಾರಕೆ is incorrect.
[3].Some letters are worn out.
[4].Some letters are missing.

Inscription No.III. (*Cauḍadānapura Monograph* No. IV; S.I.I. vol. XVIII, No. 244. In Sir Walter Elliot's collection : no. 52, folios 240 *vo* to 242. In *The Inscriptions of Dharwar and Mysore* photographed by Pigou and Biggs, edited by T.C. Hope No. XXXVII)

Chronologically this inscription comes third.

"The stele is kept along with the others in the same pendal in the South Western part of the temple complex. It is 7' 10" high and 3' broad. The carved space occupies 5' 4" from top to bottom, 2' 10" from left to right leaving a one inch margin on both sides and an unwritten space of 8" at the bottom. The letters are pretty good and belong to the 13th century Kannaḍa script. The whole is in fairly good condition except the damaged last few lines" (*Cauḍadānapura Monograph* p. 94). *Viḷāsa* is the term employed by Walter Elliot's copyists to designate the top of the stele in semi-circular shape. Like in other inscriptions, here too a shrine has been represented with a Liṅga in the centre. To the right of the Liṅga is the figure of a devotee in seated posture unlike in the two previous incriptions, other details being same except for a kind of crooked sword carved above the cow and calf. Two lines are written in the space left as margin round the semi-circle and the name of the engraver on the pedestal of Naṃdin : Dēvaṇa of Guttavoḷal who recited and wrote the text of the inscription. The language is mainly Kannaḍa, interlaced with Sanskrit and Prākrit ślōkas. The text begins with *śrī muktēśvarāya namaḥ* and *namas tuṅga*... "There are 26 verses : Nos. 1, 2 and 22 are in Sanskrit and *anuṣṭubh* metre, 23 is in Prākrit and the rest in Kannaḍa. Of these three are in *mahāsragdharā*, four in *mattēbhavikrīḍita*, five in *śārdūlavikrīḍita* and eleven in *campaka* metre." (*Cauḍadānapura Monograph* p. 95)

After invocatory verses on Śiva and Muktēśvara, the inscription proceeds with the description of Kailāsa and the glorification of *bhakti*. Pārvatī the consort of Śiva requests Her Lord to impart *bhakti* to the world. Śiva looks at Nandin and the latter answers that, as Basava the son of Saṃgamēśa did, similarly he would accomplish the mission in the name of Śivadēva. First he goes to worship Dhavaḷaliṅga at Śrīśailam where he meets Śivamuddudēva and then he proceeds to Muktikṣētra This part of the text is not very clear. In the following inscription the same matter is recounted in a different fashion. At Muktikṣētra he becomes a great saint, imposing on himself many restrictions such as not to lie down on a bed, not to embrace women, not to beg anything from anybody etc. In l. 29 one of his vows is mentioned in very concise style : *svāmi mahādēvanittoḍallada nēmaṃ*, i. e. he will not accept anything except given by Lord Śiva. A *śivakaṭṭe* was built by him at Muktikṣētra to stop the river Tuṅgabhadrā from advancing up to the Liṅga.What it is and where it is, is not specifically indicated. Dr. M. M. Kalburgi and Dr. Katti suggest that it may be identified as an embankment of the river.The architecural plan of the temple strengthens this opinion. On the northern side of the shrine there is no door whereas there is one to the east and another to the south. This blindness is due to the embankment built checking the rising up of the river water. He also built a shrine to Rudra, most probably Vīrabhadra. Moreover, the main temple to Śiva was repaired by him and was entirely lined with stone panels. The inscription mentions that he wrote *Kaiḷāsa caritre*, which unfortunately is not available to us to-day.

There is a piece of interesting information in l. 15 and 16. Here we come across with two important names. Not only Basava the son of Saṃgamēśa is mentioned but also his companion and fidel follower Baṅkaya. The exact name of the latter occurs in the literature as Baṅkanātha. He was from Iñcal in Torgal which is the same as Toragale in the inscriptions. Baṅkanātha while fighting with the army of Bijjaḷa during the troubled days of Kalyāṇa finally reached Iñcal where he built a temple which goes by the name of Baṅkanāthana Guḍi even to-day. He was a staunch defender of the principles of Basavēśvara. Here in this inscription there is an allusion to Baṅkanātha and Śivadēva says that he will defend the principles of Śaivism of Basava like Baṅkanātha.

A series of dates are mentioned here. The first one marks the arrival of Śivadēva at Muktikṣētra and the rest are the dates of grants to the temple. The first is Śaka 1148, Pārthiva saṃ, Bhādrapada Śu 15, lunar eclipse, corresponding to Monday, 19th August 1225. The inscription says precisely that Śivadēva made his entrance at Muktikṣētra in the afternoon. Then in Kāḷayukta saṃ. on Kārtika Śu. 8, Sō, which corresponds to A.D. 1258, November 4th, Monday, Śivadēva bought some lands from *mahājanas* of Gope and Kuṟuvatti. Another grant was made in the reign of Yādava Siṅghaṇadēva in the year Siddhārthi saṃ., Caitra Ba. 15, solar eclipse, corresponding to Tuesday, 25th March 1259 (according to S. K. Pillai's *Ephemeris* there was no solar eclipse). In the sixth year of Vīramahādēva, Dundubhi saṃ, on Vaiśākha Śu. 15 pūrṇimā, corresponding to Friday, 5th May 1262 (date declared irregular by S.I.I. vol. XVIII 244), one more grant was made. It is the latest date, but occurs first in the list of grants to the temple at Muktikṣētra.

೧. ಓಂ ನಮ: ಶಿವಾಯ । ನಮ-
ಸ್ತುಂಗಶಿರಶ್ಚುಂಬಿಚಂದ್ರಚಾಮರಚಾ-
ರವೇ । ತ್ರೈಲೋಕ್ಯನಗರಾರಂಭಮೂ
೨. ಲಸ್ತಂಭಾಯ ಶಂಭವೇ ॥ ೧ ॥

1-2a. Salutation to Śiva. Homage to Śambhu, lovely with a *cauri*, the moon kissing his lofty head, foundation column of the construction of a city, the three worlds. (1)

ಶಬ್ದಾದಯೋಽಪಿ ಗೃಹ್ಯಂತೇಕ್ರಿಯಂತೇ
ವಚನಾದಯ:॥ಅವಿಲಂಘ್ಯಾ ಹಿ ಸರ್ವೇ
೩.ಷಾಮಾಜ್ಞಾ ಶಂಭೋರ್ಗ್ಗರೀಯಸೀ
॥೨॥

2b-3a. Indeed his command is inviolable and the mightiest of all. His very words are received and his rules too are obeyed. (2)

ಸ್ವಸ್ತಿ ಶ್ರೀಜಯಮಂಗಳಪ್ರದಮಹಾದೇ-
ವಶ್ಯ(ಶ್ರು)ತಿಬ್ರಾತದಿಂ ಪ್ರಸ್ತುತ್ಯ ಪ್ರಭು
ಸಂ
೪.ಸ್ಥಿರಾಯವನಖಂಡಾನನ್ದಸಂಪ್ರೀತಿ-
ಯಂ ವಸ್ತುಸೋಮನುಡುಪಕೀರ್ತಿಯ-
ನುದಾರೈಶ್ವರ್ಯ್ಯಮಂ ಶೌರ್ಯ್ಯಮಂ
೫. ವಿಸ್ತೀರ್ಣಾವನಿಮಂಡಳಕ್ಕನುದಿನಂ
ಕೂತ್ತೀರ್ಗೆ ಮುಕ್ತೀಶ್ವರನುಂ ॥೩॥

3-5a. Be it well. May Muktīśa who is praised in a multitude of *śrutis* with immeasurable love and pleasure bestow on this large globe incalculable wealth, undiminishing celebrity, exalted power and valour. (3)

ಸ್ವಸ್ತಿ ಸಮಸ್ತಸುರಾಸುರಕಿರೀಟಕೋ-
ಟಿಖಚಿತಮಣಿಮರೀಚಿರೋಚಿಧಾಮ
೬. ವಿರಾಜಿತಚರಣಂ। ಅಚಿಂತ್ಯಗುಣಾ
ಭರಣಂ। ಅನಂತಬ್ರಹ್ಮಾಂಡಷಂಡನಿ-
ವಾಸನಿಜಭವನಂ । ಇಚ್ಛಾಮಾತ್ರಕೃತ
ಚತುರ್ದ್ದಶಭುವನಂ।
೭. ರು(ಋ)ಗ್ಯಜು:ಸಾಮಾಥರ್ವವೇದಾ-
ರ್ತ್ಥಸ್ಮ್ರು(ಸ್ಮೃ)ತಿಪುರಾಣಧರ್ಮ್ಮಶಾ
ಸ್ತ್ರೋಪಗೀಯಮಾನಶುಭಚರಿತಂ। ನಿಜ
ಶಕ್ತಿಕಳಾಮಾತ್ರವಿಮೋಹಿತ
೮.ಲೀಲಾಚರಿತಂ। ಪ್ರಮಥಗಣಮನ:-
ಸರೋಜರಾಜಹಂಸಂ । ಸಮುತ್ತುಂ-
ಗಜಟಾಜೂಟವಿಭೂಷಿತಚಂದ್ರಕಳಾವ-
ತಂಸಂ ಶ್ರೀ ಪಾರ್ವತೀ

5b-12a. Be it well. Along with Pārvatī seated on a celestial throne on Kailāsa, his handsome feet illuminated with reddish light emerging from the rays of rows of rubies and gems embedded in the high crowns of the entire class of gods etc. who came to render service unto Him, adorned with countless good qualities, dwelling place to the entire galaxy of innumerable worlds, he who just by his will created fourteen worlds, whose auspicious actions are sung by *dharmaśāstra, purāṇa, smṛti*, who is the kernel of *Vedas, Ṛk, Yajus, Sāma, Atharva*,

---

[1] *Candrajñānāgama,* I.21; also see S.C. Nandimath, "A broken stone inscription from Chauḍadānapura" in *P. B. Desai Feli Vol. Studies in Indian History and Culture,* Karnatak University Dharwar, 1971, p. 76-84. See p. 75, n. 1.

೯.ವದನಪಂಕಜರಾಜಮಿತ್ರಂ। ಶರಣಾ
ಗತತಾಪತ್ರಿತಯರೌದ್ರವಿದ್ರಾವಣಕಾ-
ರುಣ್ಯಛತ್ರನಪ್ಪ ಶ್ರೀಮನ್ಮಹಾದೇವಂ
ದಿವ್ಯಸಿಂಹಾಸನಾರೂ
೧೦. ಢನಾಗಿ ಪಾರ್ವತೀಸಹಿತಮಿರೆ
ನಂದಿ ನಂದಿನಾಥ ವೀರಭದ್ರ ಭದ್ರ-
ಕಾಳ ಮಹಾಕಾಳ ಭೃಂಗೀಶ ಪ್ರಮು-
ಖಾಸಂಖ್ಯಾತ ಗಣಂಗಳಿಂ ಸಂಸೇ-
ವ್ಯಮಾ
೧೧. ನನಾಗಿ ಶ್ರೀಕಯಿಳಾಸದಲ್ಲಿ ವ-
ಡ್ಡೋಲಗಂಗೊಟ್ಟು ಸುಖಸಂಕಥಾವಿ-
ನೋದದಿಂದಿರ್ದ್ದ ಸಂಪ್ರಸ್ತಾವ ಸಮ-
ಯದೊಳು।ಆ ಉಮಾಮಹೇಶ್ವರಂ ಗ
೧೨. ಣಂಗಳಿಗೆ ಪ್ರಸನ್ನನಾಗಿ ಯಿಂ-
ತೆಂ ದಂ
ಕಂದ॥ ಇದೆ ನಾಲ್ಕುಂ ವೇದಪಾರಂ
ಬಗೆವಡೆ ದಿಟದಿಂ ಸರ್ವ್ವಶಾಸ್ತ್ರಾರ್ತ್ಥ
ಪಾರಂ ಪದಪಿಂ ಸ್ಮೃ(ಸ್ಮೃ)ತ್ಯರ್ಥ
ಪಾರಂ ತ್ರಿಭುವನಭುವ
೧೩. ನಜ್ಞಾನವಿಜ್ಞಾನಪಾರಂ । ಸ-
ದ್ವಾಕ್ಯಾರ್ತ್ಥೈಕಪಾರಂ । ಪ್ರಣವಸಮು-
ದಿತಂ ಧ್ಯಾನಭಾವೈಕಪಾರಂವಿದಿತಂ
ಶ್ರೀ ಜ್ಯೋತಿರ್ಲ್ಲಿಂಗಾಮರಗಣಕರು-
ಣೋತ್ಪಂನ್ನಭಕ್ತಿಪ್ರ
೧೪. ಸಾದವು
ಎನೆ ಕೇಳ್ದದ್ರಿಜೆ ಬಿನ್ನಪಂ ಶಿವ ಜಗ-
ಕ್ಕೀಮಾರ್ಗ್ಗಮನ್ತೋಱಬೇಳ್ಕೆನಲನ್ತಾ
ಪ್ರಭು ನಂದಿನಾಥನ ಮೊಗನ್ನೋಡಲ್ಕೆ
ಶ್ರೀ ಸಂಗಮೇಶನಪುತ್ರಂ
೧೫. ಬಸವಯ್ಯ ಬಂಕನದಱಿಂ(ದೆ
ಱಿಂ) ಶಿವಮುದ್ದುದೇವಂ ಜನಕ್ಕನಿ-
ಮಿತ್ತಂ ಶಿವದೇವನಾಗಿಯು ಗಣ
ಶ್ರೀಪಾದಮನ್ತೋಱುವೆಂ ॥ ೫ ॥
ಅದೆಂತೆಂದಡೆ

whose sportive acts are illusions of just a particle of his power, who is a royal swan in the midst of the lotus lake, the mind of his *pramathagaṇas*, the top of whose matted hair is adorned with the moon, friend of the king of lotus which is the face of Pārvati, true shelter of compassion to those who surrender, victims of threefold troubles[1], surrounded by Nandi, Nandinātha, Vīrabhadra, Bhadrakāḷa, Mahākāḷa, Bhṛṅgīśa,

(while) amusing himself in his court, in joy, Mahēśvara said to his *gaṇas* :

12b-14a. "It is evident that *bhaktiprasāda* born of compassionate *amaragaṇas* and Jyōtirliṅga is the only solution to go to the other end of four *vēdas*, of the meaning of all *śāstras*, the meaning of *smṛtis*, the spiritual and material knowledge of the three worlds, the sole meaning of the sacred utterances, the deep sense of meditation arising out of *praṇava*." (4)

14b-15a. Having heard this, the daughter of the mountain, requested : "Oh! Śiva, may this path be made known to the world"; Śiva looked at the face of Nandinātha who said : "as Baṃkanātha (did) to Basavayya son of Saṅgamēśa, similarly, I shall show to people the holy feet of *gaṇas* in the name of Śivadēva". (5) If asked how :

---

1 *Tāpatritaya: ādhidaivika, ādhibhautika* and *ādhyātmika* in *Sāṅkhyayōga*.

||ಕಂ|| ಅವನ
೧೬.ತಕಂಧರರಾಗಿಯೆದಿವಿಜರ್ಶಿವರಾತ್ರಿ
ಮಾಡಿದಾ ತತ್ಪದದೊಳ್ ಧವಳೇ-
ಶ್ವರಾಖ್ಯ ಲಿಂಗದೊಳವಿರಳ ಶಿವಮು-
ದ್ದುದೇವಮುನಿಪತಿಯಿಪ್ಪನಂ||೬||

15b-16a. At (Śrīśailam), where, on the day of Śivarātri, the gods, with their head bowed down installed the Liṅga called Dhavaḷēśvara, stays as an ascetic Śivamuddudēva. (6)

ಅ
೧೭.ಭ್ಯ(ವ್ಯ)ಕ್ತಶಂಕರನನತಿಸುಭ್ಯ(ವ್ಯ)-
ಕ್ತಂಮಾಡಿತೋರ್ಪೆನೆನುತೀಜಗದೊಳ್।
ದಿಬ್ಯಧವಳೇಶಲಿಂಗನಬ್ಯಯ ಶಿವಮು-
ದ್ದುಮುನಿ ವರಂ ಭಾವಿಸುವನು ||೭||

16b-17a. Śivamuddudēva who says : "I shall show to this world that the invisible Śiva is manifested here in Dhavaḷēśaliṅga" believes in it firmly. (7)

ಶಿವಮುದ್ದು
೧೮. ಬ್ರತಿಪತಿಗೀದಿವಿಜೇಂದ್ರಪದಗಳೆಂ-
ಬಿವೇಂ ಪಾಸಟಿಯೋ ಭವನೆ ಕಲಿಕಾ-
ಲಕಲುಷವ ತವಿಸುವೆ ನೆವದಿಂದ
ಮೂರ್ತಿಯನ್ತಾಳ್ದಿರ್ದ್ದನು|| ೮||

17b-18a. These supernatural positions are no wonder to Śivamuddudēva; it looks as if Śiva had manifested himself (in him) in order to wash off the sins of Kaliyuga; (8)

ಕೇಶವ ಜಿನ
೧೯. ಬೌದ್ಧಾದಿಗಳೀಶನ ಕಿಂಕರರು
ಬೇಱೆ ದೇವತೆಯಲ್ಲೆಂದಾ ಶಿವಮುದ್ದು
ಬ್ರತಿಪ ಮಹೇಶನೊಲಿದಾಲಿಸಿದಂ ಜಗ-
ತ್ರಯವಱಿಯಲು||೯|| ಅಮ

18b-19a. he proclaimed to all the three worlds : Kēśava, Buddha, Jina are the servants of Lord Śiva and they are not gods; thinking thus Śivamuddudēva pleased Lord Śiva. (9)

೨೦. ರಗಣಚರಣಕೋಮಳವಿಮಳದ-
ಳೋತ್ಫುಲ್ಲಕಮಳಯುಗಳಪರಾಗಪ್ರ-
ಮೋದಿತಮನದ್ವಿರೇಫೋಪಮೆಯಿಂ ಶಿ-
ವಮುದ್ದುದೇವಮುನಿಪತಿಯಿಪ್ಪಂ||೧೦||

19b-20. Śivamuddudēva is like a bee intoxicated by the union with the pollens of tender, spotless, fully blossommed lotuses, the holy feet of Amaragaṇa. (10)

೨೧.|| ವ || ಅನಂತರವು ಶ್ರೀಗಿರಿನಿ
ವಾಸನಾಜ್ಞೆಯಿಂ ಬಂದ ವೀರಬ್ರತಿ
ಯಂನೋಡಿ ||ವೃ||ಹವಣಿನಬಾರದಗ್ರಜ
ಕುಲೋದ್ಭವನಾಗಿ ವಿಧಾತ್ರಿ(ತ್ರ)ನಿಂ

21a. Then, on seeing this eminent saint (who) had come there by the orders of Śrīgirinivāsa (Dhavaḷaliṅga of Śrīśaila),

೨೨. ದ ನಂಭವಿಸಿದ ನಾಲ್ಕು ಸೃಷ್ಟಿ-
ಯೊಳು ಪುಟ್ಟದನೆಂಬಡೆ ಜಾಯತೇಸ್ತಿ-
ಯೆಂಬವು ಮೊದಲಾದ ಷಡ್ವಿಕೃತಿ
ಯೊಳ್ಸಲೆ ಕೂಡಿದನಲ್ಲ ಭಾವಿ

21b-23a "in the creation of four worlds by Brahmā, one who is born (must undergo) six *vikāras* such as taking birth, being etc.[1] —,

---

[1] Stages of being according to Vārṣyāyaṇi quoted in Yāska's *Nirukta* : "to take birth, to exist, to evolute, to grow, to decrease, to die" (I.2).

೨೩. ಸದ್ಭವನೊಲವಿನ್ದ ವೀರ ಶಿವದೇ-
ವ ಗಣೇಶ್ವರನಾಗಿ ತೋರಿದನ್
॥೧೧॥

it seemed that not being united with them, with pleasure Śiva himself appeared as Vīra Śivadēva Gaṇēśvara", (11)

||ವ|| ಎನ್ದು ತನ್ನೊಳ್ಪರಿಭಾವಿಸಿ
ಮಿಂತೆನ್ದಂ || ಸುರನದಿಯ ತುಂಗ
೨೪. ಭದ್ರಾವರನದಿ ಸುರಸಮಿತಿ ವಿಪ್ರ-
ಗಣನಿಕರವು ಆ ಸುರಗಿರಿ ಮಹೇಶ-
ಭವನವು ಧರೆಯೊಳ್ಕವಿಳಾಸ (ಕೈಲಾ
ಸ)ವೆನಿಪ ಮುಕ್ತಿಕ್ಷೇತ್ರವು ||೧೨||

23b-24. thinking thus in himself then the (Guru) said : "the excellent Tuṃgabhadrā is the divine river; the congregation of brahmins is the assembly of gods; the temple of Śiva is Mēru ; thus Muktikṣētra is like Kailāsa on the earth." (12)

೨೫. ಆ ಮುಕ್ತಿಕ್ಷೇತ್ರದುಳಿದ್ದಿರ್ದೀ ಮ್ಮ-
ಮೆಯಮೆಱಯಬೇಕೆನುತ ಗುರು ನು-
ಡಿಯಲ್ । ಸ್ವಾಮಿ ಮುಕುತೇಶನೆ ಪ-
ರಂಧಾಮ ಶ್ರೀಜ್ಯೋತಿನೆಂದೊಲ
೨೬. ವಿನ್ದಂ ||೧೩||

25-26a. When Guru said : "You should go there and exhibit the greatness of this (*bhakti*)", "Lord Mukutēśa is the Resting Place and highest Light" quoth he with affection (13)

ಶಕವರ್ಷ ೧೧೪೮ನೆಯ ಪಾರ್ತ್ಥಿವ
ಸಂವತ್ಸರದ ಭಾದ್ರಪದ ಶುದ್ಧ ೧೫
ಸೋಮವಾರ ಚಂದ್ರೋಪರಾಗ ಪುಣ್ಯ-
ತಿ
೨೭. ಥಿಯ ಮಧ್ಯಾಹ್ನ ಸಮಯದೊಳು
ಬಂದು ಪೊಕ್ಕು ||ಕಂ|| ವಿರಚಿಸಿದಂ
ಕೈಳಾ(ಲಾ)ಸದ ಚರಿತ್ರಮಂ ವೀರಭ-
ದ್ರನ ಶ್ರೀ
೨೮. ಪದಮಂ । ಸ್ಮರಿಸುತ ವೀರಬ್ರ-
ತಮಂ ಧರಿಸಿದನತುಳವಿಕ್ರಮಂ ಶಿ-
ವದೇವಂ ||೧೪||

26b-28a. On Monday the 15th day of the bright fortnight of Bhādrapada in the year Pārthiva Śaka 1148, auspicious date of a lunar eclipse[1], in the afternoon, having entered Muktikṣētra the heroic Śivadēva composed the story of Kaiḷāsa and, worshipping mentally the fortunate feet of Vīrabhadra, took heroic vows of matchless valour : (14)

ಸೀಮೆಯನುಲ್ಲಂಗಿ(ಘಿ)ಸದುದ ನೇಮ
ಧರೆಗೊಱಗದಿಪ್ಪು
೨೯.ದೆ ಸಲೆ ನಿಯಮವು । ಕಾಮಿಸದಿ-
ಪ್ಪುದೆ ನೇಮಂ ಸ್ವಾಮಿ ಮಹಾ
ದೇವನಿತ್ತೊಡಲ್ಲದ ನೇಮಂ ||(೧೫)||

28b-29a. not to tresspass the limits (of his residential town) is the vow; nor to lie-down on earth; nor to desire for anything; nor to accept anything except given by the Great Lord. (15)

---

[1] Monday, 19th August 1225.

ಅದಱುಟದ ಭೂತಂಗಳ ಬೆದಱಿಸಿ ಬೆನ್ನ
೩೦. ಟ್ಟಿಕುಟ್ಟಿದಂ ಭೈರವಂ। ಕೆದಱುವ ಭಂತರದೈವವನೊದೆದಂ ವೀರೇಶನಾ ತ್ಮಜಂ ಶಿವದೇವನು ॥೧೬॥

29b-30a. Śivadēva son of Vīrēśa chased and dispersed the trembling *bhūtas*, followed and pounded Bhairava, kicked the provocative evil spirits of transmigration. (16)

ಮಾರಿದೊಱೆಯಾಗಿ ಲಿಂಗದ ನಲೆವ- ರಂ ಬ
೩೧. ರಲು ತುಂಗಭದ್ರೆಯ ಪಡೆ ಹೊ ಸಾನ್ತು ಜಱಿದು ನೂಕಿದ ವೀರ ಗ- ಣಂಗಳ ಕುಮಾರನೀ ಶಿವದೇವನು ॥೧೭॥

30b-31a. Śivadēva, (God) Kumāra of Vīragaṇa, insulted and pushed away the army of waves of Tuṅgabhadrā who like Māri (goddess of death) came up to Liṅga. (17)

ಶಿವಪದಮನೆಯ್ದು
೩೨. ಪಡೆ ಮಾರ್ಗವಿದೆಯೆನುತ್ತಖಿಳಜ- ಗಕೆ ತೋರುವ ನೆವದಿನ್ದವಿರಳವಾಗಿರೆ ನಲವಿಂ ಶಿವಕಟ್ಟೆಯಕಟ್ಟಿ ತೋರಿದಂ ಶಿವದೇವನು ॥೧೮॥

31b-32. In order to show to the whole world that to obtain a place near Śiva this is the only way, he proved it, with pleasure, by building up a huge śivakaṭṭe[1]. (18)

೩೩. ಹವಣಿಸಲಱಿಯದೆನಿಸುವ ಶಿವಕ- ವಿಳಾಸವನಖಿಳ ದೇವತಾಪದಸಹಿತೀ ಭುವನಕ್ಕೆ ತಂದು ಶಿವಸುಖಭವನದ ನೆವದಿನ್ದ ರಚಿಸಿದಂ ಶಿವದೇವನು ॥೧೯॥

33. Śivadēva having brought the Kailāsa, said to be beyond imagination, with the army of all gods, to the earth, had a pleasant abode built to Śiva, to produce Śiva's pleasure.(19)

೩೪. ತ್ರಯಿಯಂ ನೆಲೆಗೊಳ್ಸಿದವೊಲ್ತ್ರ ಯಂಗದಿಂ ಮೂಱು ಭುವನಮಂ ನಿಲಿಸಿದವೊಲ್ತ್ರಯಿಭುವನಿಕೆಯಿಂ ರುದ್ರಪ್ರಿಯಭವನವನೊಲಿದು
೩೫. ಮಾಡಿಸಿದ ಶಿವದೇವನು ॥೨೦॥

34-35a. With pleasure Śivadēva built this abode pleasant to Rudra, with three *bhuvanas*, like the implantation of the three worlds, and with three *aṅgas* like the instauration of the triad (of Vedas). (20).

ಆ ಕಳಶಾಂತಂಬರೆ ಮೂಲೋಕವ- ಱಿಯೆ ಜೀರ್ಣ್ಣವಾದ ಶಿವಭವನವ ಮತ್ತಾ ಕಳಸಂಬರೆ ಶಿಲೆಯಿಂ ಲೋ- ಕೋತ್ತಮವಾಗಿ ಮಾ
೩೬. ಡಿಸಿದ ಶಿವದೇವನು ॥೨೧॥

35b-36a. That abode of Śiva dilapidated up to its finial, known to the three worlds, Śivadēva had it built in stone up to the finial, as the best in the world. (20)

---

[1] A dam across the river, probably the embankment on the left bank.

ಶಿವದೇವಬ್ರತೀಂದ್ರಸ್ಯ ಲಿಂಗಾರ್ಚ್ಚನ
ಕಳಾಲವಂ । ಅಚಿಂತ್ಯ ಸರ್ವ್ವಶಾಸ್ತ್ರಾ-
ದ್ಯೈರನೌಪಮ್ಯಮಗೋಚರಂ । ಅಳ-
ಖ್ಖಿಳಖ್ಖಿಯರೂ
೩೭. ಣ್ಣೈಕಳದ್ದ ದಿಡಭಕ್ತಿಭಾವಸಂ
ಪಣ್ಣಾಕಳಿಬಳಕುಳಣಿಮ್ಮಹಣೋ ಭಳ-
ನಗ್ಗುಣಸಾಯರೋಭವೆವೂಖ್ಖು ಶಿವ-
ದೇವ ॥೨೩॥

36b-37a. Even a minute part of Śivadēva's Liṅga worship is inconceivable, incomparable, out of the scope of scriptures. (22)

O! Śivadēva, bursting with constant sentiment of devotion, capable of churning away all the hosts of evils in this age, like an ocean of spotless virtues. (23)

ಆಱುಂ ದರ್ಶನಮಂ
೩೮. ನಲೆ ಮೀಱೆ ಶಿವಗಣಾಜ್ಞಾಚಿಂ-
ತಾಮಣಿ ಕಯಿಸಾರೆ ಶಿವದೇವಮು
ನಿಪತಿ ತೋಱೆ ಮೆಱದ ಲಿಂಗಜಂಗ-
ಮವೈಕ್ಯಕ್ರಮವಂ ॥೨೪॥

37b-38a. To the hands of Śivadēva has come a magic gem, the scripture of Śivagaṇas, beyond the reach of the six systems, as he showed the identity of Liṅga and Jaṅgama. (24)

ಮತ್ತಂ ಪುರಾತ
೩೯. ನರ ಚರಿತ್ರಕ್ಕತಿವಿಚಿತ್ರಮಾಗಿ
ಲಿಂಗಾರ್ಚನಂಗೆಯ್ಯುತಮಿರೆಯಿರೆ ॥

38b-39a. And thus while he was immersed in Śiva's cult in a way, most of which was different from the way of the ancients (24bis)

ಸ್ವಸ್ತಿ ಶ್ರೀಮತು ಯಾದವನಾರಾಯ-
ಣಂ ಭು
೪೦. ಜಬಳಪ್ರತಾಪಚಕ್ರವರ್ತಿ ಶ್ರೀವೀರ-
ಮಹದೇವರಾಯ ವಿಜಯರಾಜ್ಯೋದ
ಯದ (ಮೂ)ಱನೆಯ ದುಂದುಭಿ
ಸಂವತ್ಸರದ ವಯಿಶಾ
೪೧. ಖ ಸು(ಶು)ದ್ಧ ೧೫ ಸೋಮವಾರ
ಸೋಮಗ್ರಹಣದಲ್ಲಿ

39b-41a. –be it well– at the time of a lunar eclipse on Monday, 15th day of bright fort-night of Vaiśākha in the year Dundubhi, in the third regnal year of Śrī Vīra Mahādēvarāya, bhujabaḷapratāpa cakravarti, Yādava Nārāyaṇa,

ಸ್ವಸ್ತಿ ಸಮಸ್ತ ಪ್ರಶಸ್ತಿಸಹಿತಂ ಶ್ರೀ-
ಮನ್ಮಹಾಮಂಡಳೇಶ್ವರಂ ।ಉ
೪೨. ಜ್ಜಯಿನೀಪುರವರಾಧೀಶ್ವರಂ ವ-
ಟಕಲ್ಪವೃ(ವೃ)ಕ್ಷಲಾಂಛಿತವಿಜಯಧ್ವ-
ಜಂ । ಭುವನರಕ್ಷಣೈಕದಕ್ಷಿಣಭುಜಂ
ಚಂದ್ರಗು

41b-46a. King Vīra Vikramāditya, known for his celebrity, mahāmaṃḍaḷeśvara of paṃca mahāśabda,[1] lord of Ujjayinī, who has a *vaṭakalpavṛkṣa* or banyan tree as an emblem on his victorious banner, unique right arm in protecting the earth,

---

[1] Five great instruments for the glorification of royal families. See the introduction of *South Indian Inscriptions* vol. XVIII.

೪೩. ಪ್ತಾನ್ವಯಸುಧಾರ್ಣ್ಣವಪೂರ್ಣ್ಣ-
ಚಂದ್ರಂ । ವಿಭವಾಮರೇಂದ್ರಂ ಹರ-
ಚರಣನಖಕಿರಣಸಾಂದ್ರಚಂದ್ರಿಕಾಚ-
ಕೋರಂ ಶ್ರೀ ಗು
೪೪. ರುಪದಪಯೋಧರಧ್ವಾನಾನನ್ದಿತ-
ಮಯೂರಂ। ಮಾನಿನೀಮಾನಸರ್ವ್ವಸ್ವ
ಸೂಱೆಕಾಱಂ ರಣದೊಳು ನೀಱಂ
ಮಂ
೪೫. ಡಳಿಕಭಯಿರವಂ । ಆನಂದಿತ-
ಯುವತೀನಯನ[1] ಕಯಿರವಂ ಪಂ-
ನ್ನಿರ್ಬ್ಬರಗಂಡಂ । ಶ(ಸ)ಮರ
ಕಾಂಡಂ ಸ(ಶ)ರಣಾಗತವಜ್ರಪಂ
೪೬. ಜರಂ ಆಹವಾದಿತ್ಯಂ । ವೀರ-
ವಿಕ್ರಮಾದಿತ್ಯಂ । ಆತಂಗನುನಯ-
ದಿಂ ಸಂಜಾತ ಗುರ್ತಜೋಯಿವಿಕ್ರ-
ಮಾದಿತ್ಯರ್ವ್ವಿಖ್ಯಾತರ್ನ್ನಿಜಭುಜ ವಿಜ
೪೭.ಯೋಪೇತರ್ಪ್ಪಂನೆರಡು ಮಂಡಳಿ-
ಕರಗಂಡರು ॥೨೫॥

full moon to the ocean of nectar, the family of Caṃdragupta, lord of gods in magnanimity, *cakōra* to the moonlight which shoots off from the nails of the toes of Hara's feet, like a peacock enjoying the sound of clouds, the words of Guru, plunderer of the whole proud property of women (husband), brave in battles, Bhairava to vassals, white nenuphar to the eyes of joyful young damsels, overlord of twelve, passionately fond of fighting, diamond paws to those who are submissive, sun in wars; to him were born Gut(t)a, and Jōyivikramāditya known for the might of the arms, lord of twelve vassals. (25)

ಆವಿಕ್ರಮಂಗ[ಂ]ಮೈಳಲದೇವಿಗವುದಿಸಿ
ದ ಕುಮಾರಕಂಠೀರವ ಮತ್ತಾ ವಿಕ್ರ-
ಮಾನುಜಾತಂ ಶ್ರೀ
೪೮.ಗುತ್ತಂ ನಿಜಭುಜೈಕವಿಕ್ರಮನಾದಂ
॥೨೬॥

47b-48a. Śrī Gutta, lion like son , was born to such Vikrama and Maiḷaladēvi; born of Vikrama he became unique in *vikrama* (heroism) (26).

ಅನ್ತಾ ಗುತ್ತನೃಪನ ವಿಶಾಳವಕ್ಷಸ್ಥಳ-
ದೊಳನವರತಂ ಸಿರಿನಿಜಭುಜಾಸಿಧಾ
ರೆಯೊಳು ವಿಜ
೪೯.ಯಶ್ರೀಯೊಲಿದಿಪ್ಪುದಱಿಂ ವೀರವಿ-
ತರಣ ತ್ಯಾಗಭೋಗಂ ಗೆಯ್ಯುತ್ತಂ
ನಿಜರಾಜಧಾನಿ ಗುತ್ತವೊಳಲ ನೆಲೆ
ವೀಡಿನೊಳ್ಸುಖರಾಜ್ಯಂಗೆ
೫೦.ಯ್ಯುತಿರ್ದ್ದು ಶ್ರೀ ಶಿವದೇವರ ಕಾ
ರುಣ್ಯಮಂ ಪಡೆದು ಶ್ರೀ ಸೋಮನಾ
ಥಲಿಂಗಲಬ್ಧವರಪ್ರಸಾದನಾಗಿರ್ದ್ದವಸ
ರದೊಳು ಮನೋತ್ಸಾಹದಿಂ ಬರಸಿದ
೫೧. ಶಾಸನಕ್ರಮವೆನ್ತೆಂದೆಡೆ ।

48b-51. At the time when king Gutta, on the wide chest of whom resides the Goddess of fortune, on the sharp edge of the sword of whom is Vijayalakṣmī, who is always engaged in endowing grants to the brave, ruled with joy in his capital, Guttavoḷal, having obtained the compassion of Śrī Śivadēva, at the time of getting the grace of Śrī Sōmanāthaliṅga, he had a chart written delightfully thus :

---

1 The last letter ನ *na* is written above the line.

ಮುಂನ ಹಿರಿಯಜೋಯಿದೇವರ್ಸ್ಸರು
ಚಿಕ್ಕಕುಱುವತ್ತಿನಗ್ರಹಾರ ಮಾಡುವಂ
ದು ಶ್ರೀ ತ್ರಿಭುವನಮಲ್ಲದೇವನ ಪ-
ರಮವಿಶ್ವಾಸಿ ಮಣಂ
೫೨. ಬೆನಾಯಕನ ಪ್ರೇರಣೆಯಿಂ
ಆಗಾಮಿ ಯಕ್ಷಿಣಿಸಹಿತ ತಾಂಬ್ರಶಾ
ಸನದಲ್ಲಿ ಬರಸಿ ಕುಳವ ಕಡಿದು
ಕಲ್ಲ ನಟ್ಟು ಸರ್ವ್ವನಮಸ್ಯಂ ಮಾಡಿ
ಶಿವದೇವರ ಶಿವ
೫೩. ಕಾರ್ಯಕ್ಕಾರಾಧಿಸಿದ ವೃತ್ತಿ ೨
ಕ್ಕಂ । ಮನೆ ೨ ತುಡಿಕೆ ೨ ಮಳವ
೨ ಹಡಹುಗೆಯ ಹಳ್ಳದಿಂ ಮೂಡ
ಏಕಸ್ಥಲದಲಿ ಎರೆ ಮತ್ತರು ಎಂಟು॥

51b-53a. On the occasion of Hiriya Jōyidēva making Cikka Kuṟuvatti as an *agrahāra*, at the instigation of Maṇambenāyaka, a trustworthy minister of Tribhuvanamalla, having made an exemption of taxes, such as *akṣīṇi, āgāmi*, having had the order engraved on copper-plate and installed the stone, he (Gutta) endowed *vṛttis* to Śivadēva for his religious activities : for 2 *vṛttis* 8 *mattaru* of black soil in one piece, 2 houses, 2 *maḷava*, 2 *tuḍike*, to the east of Haḍahugehaḷḷa;

ಮತ್ತಂ
೫೪. ಕಾಳಯುಕ್ತ ಸಂವತ್ಸರದ ಕಾ-
ರ್ತ್ತಿಕ ಶುದ್ಧ ೮ ಸೋಮವಾರದಂ
ದು ಶ್ರೀ ಶಿವದೇವರ(ರು) ಗೋ(ಗೊ)-
ಪೆ ಕುಱುವತ್ತಿಯ ಪ್ರತಿ ಗೃಹಸ್ಥರ
ಕಯ್ಯಲು ಕ್ರಯಗೊಂ
೫೫. ಡ ಕ್ಷೇತ್ರ ಗೋ(ಗೊ)ಪೆಯಲ್ಲಿ
ಆಲಕೊಳನಿಂ ಮೂಡಲು ಎರೆಮತ್ತರು
೪ ಕಂ ೫೦ ಚಿಕ್ಕಕಱುವತ್ತಿಯಲಿ
ಹಿರಿಯ ಕೆಯಿಂ ತೆಂಕ ಹೆಡಹುಗೆ
ಹಳ್ಳದಿಂ
೫೬. ಮೂಡಲು ಎರೆಮತ್ತರು ೨ ಕಂ
೫೦ ॥ ಗೋ(ಗೊ)ಪೆಯಲ್ಲಿ ಮನೆ ೨
ತುಡಿಕೆ ೨ ಇಂತಿವಯಿಕ್ಕಂ ಅಶೇಷ
ಮಹಾಜನಂಗಳು ಅರ್ತ್ಥವ ಕೊಂಡು
ಕುಳವ ಕ
೫೭. ಡಿದು ಕಲ್ಲ ನಟ್ಟು ಸರ್ವ್ವ-
ನಮಸ್ಯಂ ಮಾಡಿ ಶಿವದೇವರಿಗೆ
ಆರಾಧನೆಯ ಮಾಡಿದರು ॥

53b-57. And, on Monday 8th day of the bright fortnight of Kārtika, in the year Kāḷayukta, lands were bought by Śivadēva at the hands of every gṛhastha at Kuṟuvatti and Gope :

50 *kaṃ* and 4 *eremattaru* of a field east of Ālakoḷa at Gope; 2 *eremattaru* and 50 *kaṃ* of black soil of a field to the east of Haḍahugehaḷḷa which is to the south of the big tank at Cikka Kuṟuvatti; at Gope 2 houses and 2 *tuḍike*; for all this, the Aśēṣamahājanas having taken an amount, having had a pit dug and the stone installed, made a service to Śivadēva, granting a tax exemption.

ಮತ್ತಂ ಶ್ರೀ ಶಿವದೇವರು ಮಹಾಜ-
ನಂಗಳ ಕಯ್ಯಲು
೫೮. ಕ್ರಯಗೊಂಡ ಸ್ಥಳವಿವರ ॥

57b-58a. And the details of the lands bought by Śivadēva at the hands of Mahājanas are :

ಗೋ(ಗೊ)ಪೆಯಲಿ ಬಂನ್ನಿ(ಯ
ಕೆಱೆ)ಯೊಳಗೆ ಹೊಂನ್ನವತ್ತಿಗೆ ಹೋದ
ನಡುವಣ ದಾರಿಯಿಂ ತೆಂಕಲೆರೆ
ಮತ್ತರು ೧ ಕಂ ೫೦ ಬಂ
೫೯. ನ್ನಿಯಿಂ ತೆಂಕಲೆರೆ ಕಂಬ ೬೦
। ಅಲ್ಲಿಂ ಮೂಡಮಕ್ಕ ಕಂಬ ೫೦ ।
ಹೊಂನ್ನವತ್ತಿಯಿಂ ಬಂದ ದೇವಿಯ
ದಾರಿಯಿಂ ಮೂಡ ಕೆಂಗಾಡು ಕಂಬ
೫೦ ಬಿಲ್ಲವತ್ತದೆ
೬೦. ರೆ ಮ ೧ ದಾರಿಯಿಂ ಬಡಗಲೆರೆ
ಕಂಬ ೬೦ । ಕುಱುವತ್ತಿಯಲ್ಲಿ
ಕೊಂಡಗೆಱೆಯಿಂ ತೆಂಕ
ಪ್ರಥಮಸ್ಥಳದಲ್ಲಿ ಕಂಬ ೬೦ ।
ಆಲಕೊಳನಿಂ ಮೂಡಲೆ
೬೧. ರೆ ಮ ೧ ಕಂ ೭೦

58b-61a. 1 *mattaru* and 50 *kamba* of black soil land to the south of the road between Baṃnikere tank at Gope and Honnavatti; 60 *kaṃba* of black soil land south of Baṃni; from there to the east a ricefield of 50 *kaṃba*; 50 *kaṃba* of red forest to the east of Dēviya dāri (Goddess' road) coming from Honnavatti; 1 *mattaru* of black soil land at Billavatta; to the north of that road a field of 60 *kaṃba*; 60 *kaṃba* in the beginning at Koṇḍagere in Kuruvatti; 1 *mattaru* and 70 *kaṃba* of black soil field to the East at Āladere;

ಅನ್ತು ಮತ್ತರು ೭ ಗೋ(ಗೊ)ಪೆ
ಮನೆ ೨ ಕುಱುವತ್ತಿಯಲ್ಲಿ ಮತ್ತರು
೧ ನಾಲ್ವತ್ತರ ಹೊಡದಲಿ ಯೆರೆಕಂಬ
೮೫ ಮೂಡಮಾನ್ಯ ಭೂಮಿಯಲಿ ಮ
೬೨. ತ್ತರು ೧ ಗೋ(ಗೊ)ಪೆಯ
ಕೊಂಟಬಂನ್ನಿಯೆರೆ ಕಂಬ ೫೦

61b-62a. total : 7 *mattaru* and 2 houses at Gope; 1 *mattaru* at Kuruvatti; 85 *yerekaṃba* at Nālvattara Haḍa(?); 1 *mattaru* in the eastern tax-free land; 50 *yerekaṃba* at Koṇṭabanni belonging to Gōpe;

ಅನ್ತು ಮತ್ತರು ೩ ಕಂ ೩೫ ಮನೆ
ಗೋ(ಗೊ)ಪೆಯಲ್ಲಿ ೧ ಕುಱುವತ್ತಿಯ
ಲಿ ಮನೆ ೨ ಅನ್ತು ಮತ್ತರು ೧೦ಕಂ
೬೩. ಬ ೩೫ ಮನೆ ೫ ಆ ಕುಳವ ಕ-
ಡಿವದಕೆ ಶ್ರೀಗುತ್ತರ್ಸದೇವನು ಅಶೇಷ-
ಮಹಾಜನಂಗಳಿಗೆ ಅರ್ತ್ಥವ ಕೊಟ್ಟು
ಕುಳವ ಕಡಿಸಿ ಕಲ್ಲನಟ್ಟು ಸರ್ವ್ವ-
ನಮಸ್ಯಂ ಮಾ
೬೪. ಡಿ ಶ್ರೀ ಶಿವದೇವರಿಗೆ ಆರಾಧಿಸಿ
ದನು ॥ ಮತ್ತಂ ಬೆಳುವೊಳಲ ಬೊ-
ಮ್ಮಗವುಡನ ಕಯ್ಯ[ಲು] ಕ್ರಯ-
ಗೊಂಡ ಕೆಯ್ಯ ಸ್ಥಳ ಬಡಗವೊಲನಲಿ
ತನ್ನ

62b-64a. total 3 *mattaru* and 35 *kaṃba*, one house at Gope 2 houses at Kuruvatti; total : 10 *mattaru* and 35 *kaṃba* and 5 houses. Guttarasa after giving money to the Aśēṣamahājana, having had a pit dug and the stone installed, made a service to Śivadēva, granting a tax exemption.

64b. The lands purchased from Boṃmagauḍa at Beḷuvoḷalu are :

64c-66. near his own northern fields

೬೫. ಬಳಿಯಿಂ ಪಡುವಲೆರೆ ಮತ್ತರು
೪ ಬಡಗ ಮ ೪ ಅನ್ತು ಮತ್ತರೆಂಟು
ಮನೆ ೧

to the west 4 *mattaru* of black soil lands; 4 *mattaru* to the north; total 8 *mattaru*, 1 house;

ಎಂದೆಂದು ಸರ್ವ್ವಬಾಧೆ ಪರಿಹಾರಮಾಡಿ ಮಕ್ಕಳು ಮಕ್ಕಳ...	removing all obstacles, promising that this will be observed from generation to generation, having the stone
೬೬. ದೆ ಸಲಿಸುವ ಬಾಸೆ(ಭಾಷೆ)ಯಿಂ ಕುಳವ ಕಡಿದು ಕಲ್ಲ ನಟ್ಟು ಬೊಂಮಗವುಡ ಶಿವದೇವರಿಗೆ ... ಆರಾಧಿಸಿ ‖ ಗುತ್ತರ್ಸದೇವನಾರಾಧಿಸಿದನು ...	installed, Boṃmagauḍa made a service ... to Śivadēva. Guttarsa made a service to...
೬೭. ಳಲ ಕಯಿ ಮ ೮ ಮನೆ ೧ ಕುಱುವತ್ತಿಯ ಕೆಯಿ ಮ ೨ ಕಂ೮೫ ಮನೆ ೨ ಗೋ(ಗೊ)ಪೆಯಲ್ಲಿ ಕೆಯಿ ಕಂ ೫೦... ಶಿವದೇವರು ಬಸವಯ...	67-68. Śivadēva granted these *vṛtti* to Basavaya : a field of 8 *mattaru* at ...and 1 house; 2 *mattaru* and 85 *kaṃ* of field and 2 houses at Kuṟuvatti; at Gope a field of 50 kaṃba ....
೬೮. ಣ್ಯ ಮಾಡಿಕೊಟ್ಟ ವೃ(ವೃತ್ತಿ) ‖ ಮತ್ತಂ ಸಿಂಘಣವರ್ಷ ಶುಭಕೃ(ಕೃತು) ಸಂವತ್ಸರ ಪುಷ್ಯ ಸು... ದೇವರ ಕಯಿ ...	68b. Then, in the regnal year of Siṅghaṇa, cyclic year Śubhakṛtu, in the bright half of the month of Puṣya, lands belonging to the god ...
೬೯. ವತ್ತಿಯಶೇಷಮಹಾಜಬನಂಗಳು ಹೊಂಗೆ ತಿಂಗಳಿಂಗೆ ಹಾಗ ವೊ ...	69. Aśēṣamahājana of (Hoṃge) ... vṛtti per month ...
೭೦. ಆ ಬಡ್ಡಿಯಿಂದಾದ ಗ ೧೫ ವಂ ಆ ಶಿವದೇವರು ಮಾಡುವ ಲಿಂಗಜಂಗಮ ...[1]	70. 15 *ga*(*dyāṇa*) of interest for food offerings to Liṅga and Jaṅgama by Śivadēva ...
[2]೭೧ (೧) ಶ್ರೀ ಕನ್ನರದೇವವರ್ಷದ ಸಿದ್ಧಾರ್ತಿ(ರ್ಥಿ) ಸಂವತ್ಸರದ ಚೈತ್ರ ಬಹುಳ ೧೫ ಸೋ ಸೂರ್ಯಗ್ರಹಣದ ಸಮಯದಲ್ಲಿ ಚವುಡಿಸೆಟ್ಟಿಯರ ಕರಣದ ನಾಗರ್ಸನ ತಂಮ ಭಾನುದೇವನು ಕೊಟ್ಟ ತೋಟ ಗದ್ದೆಯ ಕೆಳಗೆ	71-72a (1-2a) In the reign of Kanharadēva, on Monday, 15th day of the dark fortnight of Caitra, year Siddhārthi, at the time of a solar eclipse, Bhānudēva younger brother of Nāgarasa, secretary of Cauḍiseṭṭi, granted an orchard (situated) below a wet
೭೨ (೨). ಗಂಗನ ಕಂಬ ೫	land of 5 *gaṃgana kaṃba*;
ಆ ಸ್ಥಳದಲಿ ಜೋಗಿಸೆಟ್ಟಿ ಕೊಟ್ಟ ತೋಟ ಕಂಬ ೫	72b (2b). in the same place 5 *kaṃba* of grove was given by Jōgiseṭṭi.
ಮತ್ತಂ ಗುತ್ತರ್ಸದೇವನು ಕೊಟ್ಟ ತೋಟಕಂಬ ೬	72c (2c). An orchard of 6 *kaṃba* was granted by king Guttarsadēva.

1 The rest of the inscription is worn out. On the base of the stele the usual stanza "svadattāṃ paradattāṃ vā ..." has been engraved with the words "maṃgala mahā śrī".

2 The following text is carved on the semi-circular band at the top. Elliot gives it separately on fol. 237 recto of his collection. The line begins with a beautiful carving of a *śaṃkha* or conch.

ಅದಯಿಸಱ ಕುಳವ ಕಡಿಸಿ ಕಲ್ಲ ನಟ್ಟುಸರ್ವನಮಸ್ಯಂ ಮಾಡಿ ಶ್ರೀ ೭೩ (೩). ಶಿವದೇವರಿಗೆ ಗುತ್ತರ್ಸದೇ-ವನೆಯಾರಾಧಿಸಿದನು||	72d-73a (2d-3a). Adding to all these Śrī Guttadēvarasa made a service to Śivadēva, granting a tax exemption, having had a pit dug and the stone installed.
ಮುಂನ ಹೊಂನಬೊಮಿಸೆಟ್ಟಿಯರು ಶಿವದೇವರಿಗೆ ಆರಾಧಿಸಿದ ಗದ್ದೆ ಮತ್ತರು ೧೦ ... (ಹಡುವಲು)[1] ....ಹೂದೋಟ ಕಂಬ ೫	73b (3b). Earlier, 10 *mattaru* of wet land were donated to Śivadēva by Honnabomiseṭṭi, ...to the east flowergarden
೭೪ (೪). ಹೊಂನವತ್ತಿಯ ಲ್ಲಿ ಗೋ-(ಗೊ)ಪೆಯ ದಾರಿಯಿಂ ಬಡಗಲು ಗಂಗನ ಕಂಬ ೫	73c (3c). 5 *kaṃba* of flower garden. 74 (4). At Hoṃnavatti to the north of Gōpe road (a land of) 5 *gaṃgana kaṃbha* (was granted).
೭೫ (೧). ಯೀ ಶಾಸನಮಂ ಪೇಳ್ದ ಬ	75 (1). This Chart was recited (read)
೭೬ (೨). ರೆದ ಗುತ್ತವೊಳಲ [ಮೇವ]	76 (2). and written by Guttavoḷala
೭೭ (೩). ಣಂಗಳು.	77 (3). Mēvaṇa (Mēvaṇa of Guttavoḷal).

---

[1] It looks as if it is written "haḍuvalu" ಹಡುವಲು. for ಪಡುವಲು East.

[2] The following text is engraved on the pedestal of the figure of Nandin.

Inscription No. IV. (*Cauḍadānapura Monograph* No. III, p. 83 ff. No. 246 in S.I.I. vol. XVIII, p.327-328. In Elliot's collection : vol II, p. 243 ff. Mahādēvaru 3. It is photograph No. XXXVII in *The Inscriptions of Dharwar and Mysore* by Pigou and Biggs, edited by T. C. Hope.)

This stele containing the text of the fourth chart is now kept under the special pendal along with the other inscriptions.The text running into one hundred and seven lines occupies 7'.7" x 2'.5" of the surface of the slab which measures 10'.5" x 2'.5". As in the other steles the top is formed in a semicircle and is decorated with the usual conventional motifs from the universe such as the sun, the moon, to represent eternity, a temple, a couchant bull, a devotee etc. A replica of the Śiva temple occupies the central place and in style it resembles that of Muktēśvara shrine. The devotee inside the temple is engaged in worshipping the Liṅga. He is in the seated posture. The Liṅga is enveloped by multiple circles of garland of *rudrākṣas*.

The inscription is in a well preserved state. It is written in Kannaḍa characters of 13th century and the language, though, mainly Kannaḍa, is interspersed with Sanskrit verses specially the invocatory and the imprecatory parts. The *praśasti* or eulogy part of the text is full of Sanskrit terms; for example, from lines 4 to 12,is the praise of Śiva by his Gaṇas, which is nothing but a garland of epithets in Sanskrit. "There are totally twenty nine verses of which two are in *anuṣṭubh*, four in *mattēbha*, one in *utpala*, two in *campaka*, one in *śārdūla* and the remaining nineteen in *kanda*.". (*Cauḍadānapura Monograph* p.84)

The present chart begins with an invocation to Śiva and Muktīśa. Śiva is praised by his Gaṇas. He asks them the reason for their praise and they answer that in the world *dharma* is disappearing and *kalikāla* is occupying the place. So, they request Him to protect the earth. Śiva says : "where the river Tuṃgabhadrā flows westwards, on its south bank there is a place called Muktikṣētra. With Umā I shall be present there to protect the people". Then Śivadēva was born along with Śivagaṇas and settled down at Muktikṣētra where there was a temple to Śiva worshipped under the name of Muktīśa.

The date mentioned in l. 79-80 as Śaka 1185, Dundubhi saṃ, vaiśākha śu. 15, Sōmavāra, Sōmagrahaṇa is the same as in Ins. III, l. 40-41. It corresponds to Friday, 26th December 1262. Similarly in l. 99 an event is recorded which is dated Siṅgaṇa varṣa Śubhakṛtu, Puṣya śu.3, Śukravāra. The same date also occurs in ins. III l. 68 mentioning the same fact, but due to the damage caused to the stele there full reading is not possible. With the help of the present inscription it can be restituted.

When king Mahādēva of Dēvagiri was ruling the earth many gifts were made to the god Muktīśa on different dates and Śivadēva was the recipient In the cyclic year Rudhirōdgāri Jyēṣṭha bahuḷa 5, Ādivāra, which corresponds to 27th May 1263, Toragale Dēvarasa endowed a couple of grants to Śivadēva and to the deity under the orders of king Mādēvarāya. In the 16th year of Yādava Rāmacandra of Devagiri, Byaya (Vyaya) saṃvatsara another grant was made, but unfortunately further details of the astronomical data are lost owing to a damage to the stele. The cyclic year coincides with 1286-1287. One more grant was also made to the temple on the same date.

The inscription informs us of two important facts :

1) In Duṃdubhi saṃvatsara Gutta king Vikramāditya came to Muktikṣētra to have the *darśana* of the lotus feet of Śrī Śivadēva. On reckoning the saint's supreme ascetic powers the king decided to render visits to the saint every year.

2) Muktikṣētra was renamed as Śivapura by Śivadēva after God Śiva which was also his name.

There are a few more noteworthy points in the inscription. There is an echo of thoughts of Basavēśvara, founder of Vīraśaivism, who lived a century earlier than Śivadēva. Not only his name is mentioned as Saṃgana Basava, but also the institutions of Liṅga and Jaṅgama *pūje, dāsōha* etc are recalled. However, Śivadēva says that he will follow the example of Saṅgana Basava and worship Liṅga and Jaṅgama but he himself had a temple built for Śiva and also encouraged the temple construction. Though Basava encouraged the worship of Iṣṭaliṅga, he was not against the idea of temple.building and worshipping the image there. Śivadēva followed Basava in his true spirit.

೧. ಓಂ ನಮಃ ಶಿವಾಯ । ನಮ- ಸ್ತುಂಗಶಿರಶ್ಚುಂಬಿಚಂದ್ರಚಾಮರಚಾ- ರವೇ । ತ್ರೈಲೋಕ್ಯನಗರಾರಂಭಮೂ- ಲಸ್ಥ(ಸ್ತಂ)ಭಾ ೨. ಯ ಶಂಭವೇ ॥ ೧ ॥	1-2a. Homage to Śaṃbhu, lovely with a *cauri*, the moon kissing his lofty head, foundation column of the construction of a city, the three worlds.(1)
ಶಬ್ದಾದಯೋಪಿ ಗ್ರು(ಗೃ)ಹ್ಯಂತೇ ಕ್ರಿ- ಯ(ಂ)ತೇ ವಚನಾದಯಃ ॥ ಅಖಿಲಂ- ಘ್ಯಾ ಹಿ ಸರ್ವೇಷಾಮಾಜ್ಞಾ ಶಂ ೩. ಭೋರ್ಗ್ಗರೀಯಸೀ ||| ೨ ॥	2b-3a. Indeed his command is inviolable and the mightiest of all. His very words are received and his rules too are obeyed. (2)

(ಕಂ) ಶ್ರೀ ಮುಕ್ತೀಶ್ವರನತುಳ ಪ್ರೇ-
ಮದಿ ರಕ್ಷಿಸುಗೆ ಜಗಮನನುಪಮ
ಲಕ್ಷ್ಮೀಧಾಮನಗಣ್ಯಮಹೋ
೪. ದಯ ನಾಮಂ ಶೃತಿಮೌಳಿರಂಜಿತ
ಶ್ರೀಚರಣನು||೩||
ಸ್ವಸ್ತಿ ಸಮಸ್ತಸುರಾಸುರಗಣಕಿಂನ್ನರ
ಕಿಂಪುರುಷಗ
೫.ರುಡಗಂಧರ್ವ್ವಸಿದ್ಧವಿದ್ಯಾಧರಪನ್ನ
ಗಪ್ರಮುಖನಾಕಿನಿಕಾಯವಿನಿಮಿತಪ್ರೋ
ದ್ಯದುತ್ತುಂಗಮಕುಟತಟಪಟುಘಟಿತ
೬.ಚಂಚಚ್ಚಟಚಟುಳಮಣಿಮಾಣಿಕ್ಯಶ್ರೇ-
ಣಿಕಿರಣಾರುಣಮರೀಚಿಮಂಜರೀರಂಜಿ
ತ ಶ್ರೀಪಾದಪದ್ಮ ಸತ್ಯಸಮುದಿ
೭.ತಸತ್ಕ್ರಿಯೋಪಕ್ರೃತಕ್ರಿಯಾಕಾಂಡಫ-
ಲಾನಪೇಕ್ಷಿತನಿರಸ್ತಾತಿಶಯನಿತ್ಯೋತ್ಸ
ವೋದಗ್ರಪ್ರತ್ಯಗ್ರೀಕೃತಹರಾಮಳಚರಣ
೮. ಧ್ಯಾನನಿರ್ದ್ದಿಷ್ಟಾಪರೋಕ್ಷಜ್ಞಾನಸಿ-
ದ್ಧಶಿವಯೋಗಾರೂಢ ಗೂಢನಿವಾಸನಿ
ಜ ಸದ್ಮ ।

3b-4a. May Muktīśa protect the world with love, abode of incomparable splendour, whose name is one of inexhaustible glory, whose lovely feet are pleased by the crests of *vēdas*.(3)

4b-12a. Be it well. O! God, you reside in a secret resort accessible only by Śivayōga achieved through direct experience of Hara's sacred feet always refreshed at daily festivals celebrated with unsurpassed pomp, without expectation of a fruit, according to scriptures of rites assisted with good customs rising from truth, beautiful lotus feet of Śiva illuminated with a cluster of radiance reddened by the rays of rows of rubies, gems ever scintillating on edges of high diadems deposited by all troops of celestials, Suras, Asuras, Gaṇas, Kinnaras, Kimpuruṣas, Garuḍa, Gaṃdharvas, Siddhas, Vidyādharas, Serpents.

ಪೃಥುಳಕಟೀತಟೋಪಶೋಭಿತಮ
೯. ಹಾಪದ್ಮ । ಕಪರ್ದ್ದಬಂಧಾಂತ-
ರಂಗ ರಂಗನರ್ತ್ತಿತಮಂದಾಕಿನೀ-
ತುಂಗತರಂಗಾಕುಳೋಚ್ಚಳದ್ವಿಶದವಿ-
ಶುದಕೀರ್ತ್ತಿ
೧೦.ಕರಪಲ್ಲವೇವ ಚೂಡಾಗ್ರಖಚಿತಚಾ-
ರುಚಂದ್ರಕಳಾವತಂಸ ।

Your large waist is bedecked with big lotuses. You are adorned with a fine moon crescent set on your leading crest, resembling the new shoot like hand of Fame, pure and white, rising up, agitated by the huge waves of Mandākinī dancing on a stage, the interior of Your matted hair.

ಅಭೀಳಬಾ(ಭಾ)ಳಭುಜಂಗಯುಗಕುಂಡ
ಳ ಮಂಡಿತಕರ್ಣ್ನಾ
೧೧. ವತಂಸ ।

You are adorned with a pair of earrings, fearful, young serpents[1].

---

[1] Lord Śiva pleased with the excellent music of Aśvatha and Kambala, the two Yakṣa-s requested them to be always near him and sing for him.So, He metamorphosed them

ಮಹಾವಿಷ್ಣುಕಂಕಾಣಭೃತವಾಮಾಂಸ।
ಅತಿಮಥನಸಂಭೂತಾಖಿಳಹಾಳಾಹಳ
ಕಾಳಕೂಟಕಪಿಶನೀಲಗ್ರೀ
೧೨. ವ । ಅಚಿಂತ್ಯಪ್ರಭಾವ ॥ ಶ್ರೀ
ಮಹಾದೇವ ।

You hold the kaṅkāla of Mahāviṣṇu[1] in your hand; Your throat has turned a brown-blue colour by the deadly poison produced at the time of excessive churning of the ocean[2]; Your power is inconceivable, O! Great God.

ಯೆಂದಸಂಖ್ಯಾತಾಮರಗಣಂಗಳು
ಸ್ತೋತ್ರಂಗೆಯ್ಯುತ್ತಮಿರೆ ಶ್ರೀ ಕೈಳಾಸ
೧೩.ನಿವಾಸಿಯಿಂತೆಂದಂ

12b-13a While innumerable gaṇas were praising Him thus, the resident of Kailāsa asked them the reason for their laudation.

॥ ವ್ರಿ ॥ ಸ್ತುತಿಗೇಂ ಕಾರಣ ಪೇಳಿ-
ಮೆಂದೊಡೆ ಗಣಂಗಳು ಬಿಂನ್ನಪಂ
ದೇವದೇವ ದು:ಕ್ರು(ಕೃ)ತದಿಂ ಧರ್ಮ-
ವಡಂಗಿ
೧೪. ಪೋಯ್ತು ಕಲಿಕಾಲಂ ಪೆರ್ಚ್ಚ
ಚಾರ್ಬ್ಬಾ(ರ್ವಾ)ಕ ಸಾ(ಸೌ)ಗತಬೌ
ದ್ಧಾಗಮವರ್ತ್ತಿಸುತ್ತಮಿದೆ

13b-15a. The Gaṇas replied respectfully : "O Lord, owing to people's bad actions *dharma* is vanishing, Kali age is in spate, the influence of Cārvāka, Saugata, Bauddhāgama is cumulating in the world;

ಲೋಕಾಲೋಕಮಂಪಾಳಿಪೊಳ್ಕೃತಿಯಂ
೧೫.ಮಾಳ್ಪುದೆ ಕಜ್ಜಮೆಂದು ನುಡಿಯ-
ಲು ಶ್ರೀ ಪಾರ್ವ್ವತೀವಲ್ಲಭಂ ॥೪॥

it behoves on your part to turn your favourable mind to the task of protecting the world and beyond. Immediately Pārvatī's husband said : (4)

---

into coiled serpents and wore them as his ear-rings. It is believed that they always sing for Him in His ears.

[1] Here the text is not very clear. If we read *mahāviṣṇukaṃkāṇabhṛtavāmāṃsa*, it can be translated as: whose left shoulder was taken as a support by Viṣṇu. In that case kaṃkāṇa does not take any sense. If we correct it in *kaṃkāḷa*, *bhṛta* becomes meaningless. In either case we are sure that it refers to one of the twenty-five *līlā*s of Mahēśvara. Either it is an allusion to Śiva in His sixteenth *līlā* when he holds the bone (*kaṅkāla*) of the god after punishing him in his Vāmanāvatāra (*vide Śivapurāṇa, Liṅgapurāṇa, Vātulaśuddhāgama* I.133, p. 53). Or in the 22nd *līlā* Viṣṇu emanates from Mahēśvara's left shoulder, when He stands on one foot (*ibid.* I.136, p. 54).

[2] At the time of feuds between Gods and Demons the strength of the army of the latter remained ever the same owing to the recitation of magic hymns by their Guru Śukrācārya, whereas the former was diminishing. Gods desired to drink the elixir of immortality which was stored at the bottom of the milky ocean. The churning of the ocean was necessary. The snake Vāsuki became a rope put around the mount Mandara used as churning stick. Owing to the pressure during the churning the snake spat out a deadly poison called *hālāhala* or *kālakūṭa*. To save the world from this calamity Śiva consumed it and held it in his throat. That is why his throat turned reddish-blue. So he became Nīlagrīva, Nīlagarala etc. (18th *līlā*, ibid. I.134, p. 53).

ಅಕ್ಷಯನಿಧಾನ ಮುಕ್ತಿಯ ದಿಕ್ಷಾ-
ಸ್ಥಳ ತುಂಗಭದ್ರೆ ಪ
೧೬. ಶ್ಚಿಮ ಮುಖದಿನಘಕ್ಷಯಮಂ
ಮಾಡಲು ತದ್ದಕ್ಷಿಣ ತಟದಲ್ಲಿ ಮೆರ-
ಗು ಮುಕ್ತಿಕ್ಷೇತ್ರಂ ||೫||

15b-16a. "Inexhaustible treasure, place of initiation to liberation, on Tuṅgabhadrā who washes off the sins, while it runs westwards, on its southern bank shines Muktikṣetra; (5)

ಅಲ್ಲಿದ್ದು ಮೂಱು ಲೋಕದ
೧೭.ರೆಲ್ಲರ ಪಾವನವ ಮಾಳ್ಪೆನೆನುತ-
ಗಜಾತಾವಲ್ಲಭನವತರಿಸಿದಭೂವಲ್ಲಭೆ-
ಗನುರಾಗಮಪ್ಪಿನಂ ಮುಕ್ತೀಶನು||೬||

16b-17a. staying there I shall purify all in the three worlds" saying thus the beloved of mountain's daughter appeared as Muktīśa and aroused love in the Lord of the Earth. (6)

ಲಿಂ
೧೮. ಗವವತರಿಸಿತಾ ಹಾ ಹಿಂಗದೆ
ನಾವಿಪ್ಪೆವೆಂದಸಂಖ್ಯಾತಭ್ಯೂರ್ಬ| ರಂ-
ಗಕ್ಕೆ ಬರಲಿಕಮರಗಣಂಗಳಮೋಘಾ-
ಜ್ಞೆ
೧೯. ಯಿಂದ ಶ್ರೀ ಶಿವದೇವನು ||೭||

17b-19a. "Liṅga has already appeared on the Earth; why should we lag behind" saying thus Asaṃkhyāta Gaṇas[1] descended on the earth under the unerring order of Amaragaṇas. (7)

ಉದಯಿಸಿದನಗ್ರಜನ್ಮದಪದದೊಳ್ತನು-
ಗುಣವನೊಂದದೆಲ್ಲಾಗಮದೊಳ್ಮದನವಿ
ರೋ
೨೦. ಧಿಯೆ ಶ್ರೌತೋದಿತ ದೇವನೆನುತ್ತ
ತಿಳಿದು ಶ್ರೀ ಶಿವದೇವನು ||೮||

19b-20a. Śrī Śivadēva appeared in the highest rank of birth, without falling prey to temptations of flesh and also realised that the only God eulogised in all Āgamas and scriptures is the Enemy of Cupid[2]. (8)

ಆಶ್ರಮ ನಾಲ್ಕುಂ ತಿಳಿಯಲನಾಶ್ರಮ-
ವಾಶ್ರಮಮೆನೆ
೨೧. ಯ್ದದಶ್ರಮದಿನ್ದ ಶಿವಾಶ್ರಮವಿನಿ-
ಹಿತವೆಂದತ್ಯಾಶ್ರಮಮಂ ಧರಿಸಿ
ಮೆರೆದ ಶ್ರೀ ಶಿವದೇವನು ||೯||

20b-21a. While trying to understand the value of the four āśramas, seeing that in reality they are pointless, he shunned the labour of seeking them, playfully Śrī Śivadēva entered Śivāśrama and became secure in a state beyond the four āśramas. (9)

---

1 *Karnataka University Journal*, vol. II, No. 2, p.155 :"Asaṃkhyātaru" by P.B. Desai.

2 Here is an allusion to the seventh *līlā* of Śiva according to *Vātulaśuddhāgama*. Śiva burnt and reduced to ashes the God of love to show the world that though He is in the company of Śakti He is not affected by desires (I.131).

ಲಿಂಗವನಪ್ಪಿದ ತೋ
೨೨.ಳ್ಗಳಿನಂಗನೆಯರನಪ್ಪೆನಳಿಪಿ
ನೋಡೆಂ ಕೂಡೆ ಮನಂಗೊಡೆನವ
ಧಾರ್ರೆನುತವಭಂಗಬ್ರತಿ ಶಂಕರಂಗೆ
ಭಾಸೆ (ಷೆ)ಯ ಕೊಟ್ಟನು ||೧೦||

21b-22. "I will not embrace women with the arms which embrace the Liṅga, nor will I cast a greedy look on them, nor unite with them, nor give place to them in my thoughts, nor give attention to them" (thus) Śivadēva, the undisturbed saint gave pledges to Śaṅkara.(10)

೨೩. ವ || ಮತ್ತಮನೇಕಭಾಸೆ(ಷೆ)ಯ
ನೀಶಂಗೆ ಕೊಟ್ಟು ||ಕಂ|| ತಲೆದಂಡ
ಸ್ವರ್ಗ್ಗಮುಕ್ತಿಯಫಲವನಪೇಕ್ಷಿಸಿದೆ-
ನಾದಡೆ ಶಂಕರ ಕೇಳ್ || ಸ
೨೪. ಲೆ ಪುಂಣ್ಯಪಾಪವೆರಡರ ಫಲವ-
ಲ್ಲದ ನಿತ್ಯಪೂಜೆಯಂ ಮಾಡಿದಪೆಂ
||೧೧||

23-24. Also he gave many other pledges to Īśa : "capital punishment (may be inflicted) upon me if I desire the fruits, *svarga* and *mukti*. Śaṅkara, listen, only this is true : daily I shall perform *pūjā* without hankering after any fruit good or bad." (11)

ಎನ್ದು ಧ್ರು(ಧೃ)ಢಸಂಕಲ್ಪನಾಗಿ ||
ಆಸೆ(ಶೆ)ಯ ಪಾಸ(ಶ)
೨೫. ಮಂ ಪಱಿದು ರೋಸ(ಷ)ದ
ಮೀಸೆಯ ಕಿತ್ತು ಕಾಮ ಬಿಡೋಸರಿ-
ಸೆಂದು ಲೋಭಮದಮಂ ಬೆದಱಿಟ್ಟುತ
ಮಾನಮೋಹತೃಷ್ಣಾಸೆ
೨೬. ಬಲಂಗಳಂ ಜಱಿದು ಬಗ್ಗಿಸಿ ಗೆ-
ಲ್ದುಱಿ ತೊತ್ತು ಮಾಡಿದಂ ದೂಸಕ
ಧೂಮಕೇತು ಶಿವದೇವನತರ್ಕ್ಕಗುಣ-
ಪ್ರಭಾವನಂ ||೧೨||

24b-26. Having determined thus, he tore off the loops of desire, pulled out the moustaches of anger, chased away lust, greed and pride, frightened and pushed off, enslaved haughtiness, bewilderment, thirst, might by conquering them; Śivadēva, comet to vices, was endowed with wise qualities. (12)

೨೭. ಮೆಟ್ಟಿದ ಕಲಿಕಿಯ ನೊರೆಯ
ಕಟ್ಟಿದ ನೂರೆಂಟು ಬ್ಯಾ(ವ್ಯಾ)ಧಿಗೋಂ
ನಮಶಿವಯೆಂದಿಟ್ಟಂ ವಿಭೂತಿತಿಲಕವ-
ಕಟ್ಟಾಳ್ದ
೨೮.ಲದಂಕ ಮನದೊಳತಿ ನಿ:ಸಂ-
(ಶಂ)ಕನು ||೧೩||

27-28b. He crushed the evil cause of hundred and eight varieties of maladies by saluting Śiva; the great warrior, unwavering Śivadēva decorated his forehead with *vibhūti*[1]. (13)

---

[1] Cf. *Śaivaratnākara* by Jyotirnātha, VII.121-2, p. 158: bhasmasarvāṅgadigdhāṅgo bhasmadīptatripuṇḍrakaḥ । bhasmaśāyī ca puruṣo bhasmaniṣṭha iti smṛtaḥ ॥ bhūtapretapiśācādyā rogāś cātīva dussahāḥ । bhasmaniṣṭhasya sānnidhyāt vidravanti na saṃśayaḥ ॥ "A man who has anointed the whole of his body with ashes, who wears shining ashes as treble frontal mark, who lies down on ashes, is taught as Bhasmaniṣṭha. In the presence of a Bhasmaniṣṭha, Bhūtas, Piśācas, etc., and unbearable maladies run away, no doubt."

ಜಳ(ಲ)ಮೊದಲಾಗಿರೆ ಪತ್ತುಜ್ವಳವೆನಿಪ
ಸ್ನಾನಮೆಂಟು ಪತ್ತಱೊಳಿದೆ ನಿ ।
ರ್ಮ್ಮಳ(ಲ)ಮೆನಿ
೨೯. ಪುದೆಂದು ಭಸ್ಮದಿ ತೊಳೆದಂ ಕ-
ರ್ಮಾದಿಮುವನೀ ಶಿವದೇವನು ||೧೪||

28b-29a. "Water etc. are the eight varieties of best baths[1]; amongst them this is the holiest" saying thus Śivadēva washed off the *mala* of *karman* etc. on the earth by using ashes. (14)

ಝುಂಕೆಗೆ ಮನದೊಳ್ಸ(ಳ್ಯ)ಂಕಿಸಿದಡೆ
ನಿಂನ ಭ
೩೦. ಕ್ತರಾಣೆಲೆ ಪಶುಪತಿ । ಶಂಕರ-
ನೊಳಾದೊಡಂ ಬೇಡೆಂ ಕೇಳ್ ಬೇಡಿ-
ದಡೆ ಯೆಂನತಲೆಯ ದಂಡವು ||೧೫||

29b-30a. I swear Thee upon Thy devotees, Lo! Paśupati, that I shall not chide or desire for anything even in my heart. I shall not beg even Śiva. If there be any rupture in this pledge, my head be the penalty. (15)

ಅಣಕದಣೆ
೩೧. ಕಲಿಗೆ ಮುಂಕಣೆ ನೆಣಸುವರಾ-
ದಿಗಳ್ಗ ಬಾಯಸಣೆ ಜಗವರಿಯಲ್
ಗುಣೆ ಸಕಳವೇದಶಾಸ್ತ್ರದ ಕಣೆ ಶಿವ-
ತತ್ವಾನುಭಾವ
೩೨. ನೀ ಶಿವದೇವನು ||೧೬||

30b-32a. A pin-point to mockery, an obstacle stone to Kali, a mouth lock to contestants, renowned in the world for all good merits, mine of all Vēda and Śāstra, Śivadēva experiences Śivatattvānubhāva. (16)

ಶಿವಸದ್ವಿದ್ಯೆ[2]ಯೇ ವಿದ್ಯೆಯೆಂದು ಶಿವ-
ಭಾವಂ[3] ಭಾವವೆಂದುವಾ ಶಿವ-
ಮಂತ್ರಗಳೆ ಮಂತ್ರವೆಂದು ಶಿವಮೂ-
ರ್ತಿ್ಧ್ಯಾ

32b. Śivadēva took heroic vows saying : "the true knowledge of Śiva is the only knowledge, the state of Śiva is the only state, the *mantra* of Śiva is the only *mantra*, the meditation of Śivamūrti is the only meditation,

---

[1] Cf. ibidem VII.113, p. 157. In his *Dīkṣābōdhe* Kereya Padmarasa quotes this verse and a few others indicating the importance of *bhasmasnāna* : भस्मस्नानं जलस्नानादसंख्येयगुणाधिकं । तस्माद्वारुणमुत्सृज्य स्नानमाग्नेयमाचरेत् ॥ सर्वतीर्थेषु यत्पण्यं सर्वयज्ञेषु यत्फलं । तत्फलं कोटिगुणितं भस्मस्नान्न संशयः ॥ भस्मस्नानं परं तीर्थम् गङ्गास्नानाद्दिनेदिने । भस्मरूपी शिवस्साक्षात् भस्म त्रैलोक्यसाधनम् ॥ "Bath with *bhasma* (ashes) is countless times superior to bath with water; that is why having given up water bath one must bathe in *bhasma*. The quantity of merit acquired in holy centres, the fruits of all yajñas are multiplied by crores of times by the bath with *bhasma*, there is no doubt about it. Bath with *bhasma* is much superior to the daily bath in Gaṅgā; he who is smeared with *bhasma* is Śiva in person; *bhasma* is the best medieum in the three worlds." (Karnatak University, Dharwar, 1973, p. 76, verses 50-53)

[2] The letter ದೈ *dai* is written above the line.

[3] The two letters ಭಾವಂ *bhāvaṃ* are written above the line.

೩೩. ನವೇ ಧ್ಯಾನವೀ ಶಿವನಿತ್ಯೋತ್ಸವ-
ವುತ್ಸವಂ ಶಿವಕಥಾಳಾಪಂಗಳಾಳಾಪ
ಮಿಕ್ಕವನೇಬ್ಯಂಗಳೆನುತ್ತ ವೀರಶಿವದೇ-
ವನು ತಾಳ್ದ
೩೪. ವೀರಬ್ರತಂ ||೧೭||
ಶಿವನಂ ತೋರುವ ಮಾರ್ಗ್ಗ ಮಾ-
ರ್ಗ್ಗ ಶಿವನದಾಚಾರಂಗಳಾಚಾರವೀ
ಶಿವಸಂಯೋಗವೇ ಯೋಗ[1] ನಿತ್ಯಶಿ-
ವಪೂಜಾ ಕ
೩೫. ರ್ಮ್ಮವೆ ಕರ್ಮ್ಮವೀ ಶಿವನೆ ದೇವ-
ನು ದೇವನನ್ಯ ವಿಷಯಂ ಬೇಡಲ್ಲ
ಹೊಲ್ಲೆಂದು ಶ್ರೀಶಿವದೇವಪ್ರಭುವೆತ್ತಿದಂ
ಧ್ವಜಪತಾಕೋದ್ದಂ
೩೬. ಡಮಂ ದಂಡಮಂ ||೧೮||
ಎಲಗಳ ವಾದಿಗೀದಿ ಪಡವೈಷ್ಣವಗೀ-
ಷ್ಣವ ಸೌರಗಿವುರ ಮಾಣೆಲಗಳ
ಬೊಂಮಿಗಿಂಮಿ ನಿಗಮಾರ್ತ್ಥ
೩೭. ವನಱಿಯದ ಯಜ್ವಿಗಿಜ್ವಿ ಬೇಡೆ-
ಲಗಳ ಬೌದ್ಧಗಿದ್ಧ ಬಱಿಯಾಗಮಿ-
ಗೀಗಮಿ ಮಂತ್ರವಾದಿ ಸಾಕುಲಿಯದಿ
೩೮. ರೆಂದು ಬಗ್ಗಿವುದು ಶ್ರೀ ಶಿವದೇ-
ವನ ಕಾಲಹೊಂದೊಡರು ||೧೯||
ಬೆರಳಂ ಕರ್ಚ್ಚಿ ಕರಂಗಳಂ ಮುಗಿ-
ದು ಬಾಯಂ ಪಾ
೩೯. ಯುವಂ ತಂಮೆರಡ್ಕರದಿಂ ಮು-
ಚ್ಚುತ ಬಾಯಿಬಿಟ್ಟು ಕುಸಿದೊ ಮೆ
ಯ್ಯಿಕ್ಕುತಂ ಪಲ್ಗಳಂ ಕಿರಿದಂಬೇ ಶ-
ರಣಾರ್ತ್ಥಿ
೪೦. ಯೆಂದನುದಿನಂ ಷಡ್ದರ್ಶನಂ
ಬಾಹುಲಿ ಭರದೊಳ್ತಳ್ತೆಳಲುತ್ತವಿದ್ರ್ದ-
ವನಿಶಂ ಶಿವದೇವ[2] ವಾಮಾಂಘ್ರಿಯೊ
೪೧. ಳು || ವ[3] |

33-34a. the daily festivals of Siva are the only festivals, telling Śiva's stories is the only story-telling, the rest is unworthy; (17)

34b-36a. the path shown by Śiva is the only Path, the religious traditions of Śiva are the only traditions; union with Śiva is the only *yōga*; the daily worship of Śiva is the only rite; Śiva is the unique God; the rest neither will I beg nor long for it" saying thus Śivadēva lifted up a high staff with a lofty flag flying high. (18)

36b-38a. The golden anklet in the left foot of Śivadēva seems to be crying out : "Oh! you fanatical followers of Viṣṇu, Sun, Brahma, sacrificial priests ignorant of the meaning of Vēdas, buddhists, all followers of *tantra* and *mantra*, stop your practices, it is enough, don't speak." (19)

38-41a. The six *darśanas* themselves having taken the form of the golden anklet in the left foot of Śivadēva were resounding, as though exhibiting all teeth to say "I seek your grace" (by) rendering service like a slave, joining hands, fully covering the mouth with both hands. (20)

---

1 These two letters are written above the line.

2 ವ *va* is written above the line.

3 ವ *va* is written above the line.

ಮತ್ತಂ ದುಟ್ಟರಘರಟ್ಟ ಲಿಂಗಕ್ಕೆ
ಕಟ್ಟದೊರೆ ಕೊಟ್ಟ ಬಾಸ(ಭಾಷೆ)
ದಿಟ್ಟೆವಾರಿಯ ಕಟ್ಟಾಳು ಶಿವದೇವಂ
ಶ್ರೀ ಜ್ಯೋತಿನಾಥ
೪೨. ನೆ ಮುಕ್ತನಾಥನೆಂದರಿದು
ಕಾಲಕಲ್ಕಿಯಂ ಜಱಿದು । ತನುಗು-
ಣಂಗಳಂ ಮೆಱೆದು। ಆವರಣಂಗಳಂ
ತೊ
೪೩. ಱದು । ಉಭಯಕರ್ಮ್ಮದ ಬೇರ-
ಕೊರದು । ಮದನಶರಂಗಳಂ ಮು-
ಱಿದು। ಮಾಯಾಪಾಶಮಂ ಪರಿದೂ
೪೪. ।।ಕಂ।। ಮಾನಸ ವಾಚಿಕ ಕಾಯ-
ಕವೇನುಂಟುಡ [ಗಿ] ನಿಂನ್ನಭಕ್ತರೊ-
ಳನಿಶಂ ಸಾನಂದದಿಂದ ಮಾಳ್ಪೆಂ
ನಾನನ್ಯವನೆನೆ
೪೫.ಯೆ ನುಡಿಯೆ ಮಾಡೆಂ ಕೂಡೆಂ
।।೨೦।।
ಇಂತೆನುತ್ತ ದೇವಲೋಕದಲ್ಲಿ ಕೊಟ್ಟ
ಪ್ರತಿಜ್ಞೆಯಂ ತಿಳಿದು।। ನಿಷ್ಕೆಸಿ
೪೬. ನೋಡುತ ವುಳಿದಾನುಷ್ಠಾನಂ
ಪೊಲ್ಲವೆಂದು ಕಂಡಾ ಶಿವಪದ ನಿಷ್ಠೆ
ನೆಲೆಗೊಳಲು ಶ್ರೇಷ್ಠಾನುಷ್ಠಾನವ ಮಾ
೪೭. ಳ್ಪನನುದಿನಂ ಶಿವದೇವನು।।೨೧।।
ಲಿಙ್ಗಕ್ಕೆ ಜಂಗಮಕ್ಕಂ ಹಿಂಗದೆ ದಾ-
ಸಿತ್ವ ಮಾಳ್ಪುದೇ ಬೆಸನೆನ್ನಾ ಸಂ
೪೮. ಗನಬಸವಂ ಬೆಸನೆ ಮನಗೊಂ-
ಡರ್ಚ್ಚಿಸುವನುಭಯಲಿಂಗವ ಮುದದಿಂ
।।೨೨।।

41b-42a. A grinding stone in destroying wickeds, not winking the eyes, Śivadēva having understood that the Lord of the Light (Jyōtinātha) is Muktinātha,

42b-43. humiliated the evil of the time, displaying physical excellences, broke away from the bonds, cut off the roots of both *karmas*, severed the arrows of Cupid, tore off the loops of illusion.

44-45a. "Whatever of mine there will be in mind, speech and body, I shall join and serve Thy devotees with great pleasure; I shall not speak, nor do otherwise, nor unite (with heretics)", (20 *bis*)

45b-47a. saying thus, recalling pledges and promises he made in God's abode, looking without batting the eyes, seeing that other rites are of no use, and for the firm establishment of worship, Śivadēva practised daily the best worship. (21)

47b-48a. As said by Saṃgana Basava, "serving Liṅga and Jaṅgama[1] is the best of religious duties"; having understood this fully well, Sivadēva with great pleasure engaged himself in offering honours to both. (22)

---

[1] The promulgator of Jaṅgama worship was Basava, founder of the Vīraśaiva community. Though he met with opposition in his time, his ideas received recognition after his death. An inscription from Raṭṭihaḷḷi (Hirekerūr tk, Dharwar dt), dated 1238 A.D. speaks highly about Jaṅgama-s. (*Karnātaka Inscriptions* VI, 44, l. 24-25, p.135)

ಮೃಡಗಣವರಪ್ರಸ(ಸಾ)ದವಂಪಡೆದಂ
೪೯. ಜಗವರಿಯಲಂದು ಸಂಗನ ಬ-
ಸವಂ ಪಡೆದಾ ಪ್ರಸಾದಸಿದ್ಧಿಯ। ಕ-
ಡುವೀರಬ್ರತದಿಂ ಪಡೆದನೀ ಶಿವದೇ-
ವನು॥೨೩॥

48b-49. As was understood by the world that Basava obtained Śivagaṇa's grace, the same was achieved by Śivadēva through heroic vows, (23)

೫೦. ॥ವ॥ ಮತ್ತಂ ಸತ್ಯಗಣಂಗಳ
ನಿತ್ಯ ಪ್ರಸಾದಸಂಪನ್ನನಾಗಿ ಹಿಂಗದೆ
ಲಿಂಗಾರ್ಚ್ಚನಙ್ಗಯ್ಯುತ್ತಮಿರೆ ಯಿರೆ॥

50. and (thus) he attained the everlasting grace of Satyagaṇa, while he was engaged in performing *Liṅgārcana.*

೫೧. ಸ್ವಸ್ತಿ ಶ್ರೀಮತು ಯಾದವರಾಯ
ನಾರಾಯಣಂ ಭುಜಬಳ ಪ್ರೌಢಪ್ರತಾಪ
ಚಕ್ರವರ್ತ್ತಿ ಶ್ರೀ ವೀರ[ಮ]ಹ
೫೨. ದೇವರಾಯ ವಿಜಯರಾಜ್ಯಪ್ರವ-
ರ್ದ್ಧಮಾನಮಾಚಂದ್ರಾರ್ಕ್ಕತಾರಾಂ-
ಬರಂ ವುದಿತೋದಿತ ಬರುತ್ತಮಿರೆ

51-52. Be it well. In the reign of Mahādēvarāya, the emperor of mighty kings, Yādavanārāyaṇa, ruling over the victorious, progressing kingdom lasting as long as moon, sun and stars endure.

೫೩. ಸ್ವಸ್ತಿ ಸಮಸ್ತ ಪ್ರಶಸ್ತಿಸಹಿತಂ
ಶ್ರೀಮನ್ಮಹಾಮಂಡಳೇಶ್ವರಂಉಜ್ಜಯ-
ನೀಪುರವರಾಧೀಶ್ವರಂ ಚಂ
೫೪. ದ್ರಗುಪ್ತಾನ್ವಯಂ ಗುತ್ತಕುಳಕ
ಮಳಮಾರ್ತ್ತಂಡ ಕದನಪ್ರಚಂಡ
ಹಂನ್ನಿಬ್ಬರಗಂಡ ಮಂಡಳಿಕಭೈರವಂ
ಶರಣಾ
೫೫. ಗತ ವಜ್ರಪಂಜರಂ ಶ್ರೀ ಸ್ಪ-
ರ್ಶಲಿಂಗ ಗೆ(ಗ)ಳಗನಾಥದೇವರ ದಿ-
ಬ್ಯ ಶ್ರೀಪಾದಪದ್ಮಾರಾಧಕನಪ್ಪ ಶ್ರೀ
ವೀರ ವಿಕ್ರಮಂಗಂ ಮ
೫೬. ಹಾದೇವಿಯರಿಗಂ ಪುಟ್ಟಿದ ವಿಕ್ರ-
ಮಾಂಕನ ಪ್ರಭಾವಮೆಂತೆಂದೊಡೆ ॥

53-56a. Be it well. To tell the *prabhāva* of Vīra Vikramāṃka born to Mahādēvi and king Vikrama with all the *praśasti*s : Śrīmanmahāmaṃḍalēśvara, Lord of the town of Ujjayinī, pertaining to the family of Candragupta, sun to the lotus family of Gutta, fierce in battle, Lord of twelve, Bhairava to vassals, diamond cage to those who surrender, worshipper of the holy lotus feet of Sparśaliṅga at Gaḷaganātha;

ಧರ್ಮ್ಮದ ಪೆರ್ಮ್ಮನೆ ಸತ್ಯದನಿರ್ಮ್ಮ
ಳತೆಯ
೫೭.ಗೊತ್ತು ಕವಿಜನಂಗಳ ಕಡವರ॥
ಕೂರ್ಮ್ಮೆಯ ತಾಯ್ಮನೆ ಜಾಣಿನ ನಿ-
ರ್ಮ್ಮಾಣದ ರತ್ನಕಳಶ ವಿಕ್ರಮಭೂ-
ವನು

56b-57. a major mansion to dharma, a pure symbol of verity, a resort to poets, maternal house of love, a *ratnakaḷaśa* in involving skilled works, is the king Vikrama.

೫೮. ಆ ವಿಕ್ರಮನೃಪಂಗಂ ಮಯಿಳ-
ಲದೇವಿಯರಿಗಂ ಪುಟ್ಟಿದ ಗುತ್ತನೃಪನ
ಪ್ರಭಾವಮಂ ಪೊಗಳ್ವಡೆ

58. To make the eulogy of Guttabhūpāla born to the king Vikrama and Mayiḷaladēvi :

೫೯. ದಿಕ್ಕಾಂತಾಜನತಾಲಲಾಟಪಟಳ-
ಮೊದ್ಭಾಸಿರತ್ನೋಜ್ವಳಾದರ್ಶ್ಯಂ ಸಜ್ಜ-
ನಚಿತ್ತವೃತ್ತಿವಿಭವಪ್ರಖ್ಯಾತಕೀರ್ತ್ತಿರ್ಧ್ವ
೬೦.ಜ:। ಸತ್ಯೋತ್ಸಾಹಸುಖಾಬ್ಧಿವರ್ದ್ಧ-
ನಯಶ: ಕೌಮೋದಿನೀವಲ್ಲಭ: ಶ್ರೀ-
ಮಾನ್ಭೂಪತಿವಿಕ್ರಮಾಂಕತನುಜಂ
೬೧. ಶ್ರೀಗುತ್ತಭೂಪಾಳಕ: ||೨೪||

59-61a. mirror radiant with gems illuminating the foreheads of the goddesses of directions, banner of fame praised with abundance of thoughts in good people's mind, Lord of blue lotuses swelling the ocean of pleasure, enthousiasm and truth, this is King Gutta, son of Vikramāṅka.(24)

ಕಂ|| ಆ ವಿಕ್ರಮನ ಪರಾಕ್ರಮವಾ
ವಿಕ್ರಮ...[1]ನೊಲವದಾರತನಗೊಗೆಯ
೬೨.ಭುದಗ್ಗ್ರೀವಡೆಯೊಳು ಶರಣೆಂದರ
ಕಾವಡೆಯೊಳು ಭೂಮಿಪಂಗಾರ್ಸ್ವರಿ-
ಯೆ ||೨೫||

61b-62a. The bravery of that brave (Vikrama) … Who is equal to this king in making endowments to brahmins, in protecting those who solicit refuge ?(25)

ಮಲಪವಿರೋಧಿ ವೈರಿಗ
೬೩. ಳ ಗಂಡ ರಣಾಂಗಣದೊಡದ್ದ್ರ
ಬೆಂ । ಬಲವನೆ ಪೊದ್ದ್ರ ಬರತದಿ-
ಯ ನಿಡ್ವರ ಗಣ್ಣನಿದಿರ್ಚ್ಚ ಬೆರ್ಚ್ಚ
ಕಕ್ಕುಲತೆಯ ಮಾ
೬೪. ಡುವಗ್ಗಳದ ವೀರರ ಗಂಡನಾ
ಸಾಹಸಕ್ಕೆ ಮೆಯ್ಗಲಿಯೆನಿಸಿಪ್ಪ ತೊ-
ಣ್ಡರೊಳು ಗಂಡರಗಂಡನು
೬೫. ಗುತ್ತಭೂಭುಜನು ||೨೬||

62b-65a. King Gutta is an enemy to those who oppose heroes, pouncing in the battle-fields, takes up the responsiblity of protecting, frightening and questioning the bravery of those who go backward steps in the battlefield, master of boasting heroes overbearing amongst heroes. (26)

||ವ|| ಮತ್ತಂ [ದಶ]ದಿಗ್ವಳಯಂಗಳ
[ಯೆ]ಂಗಳಂ ಪರ್ಬ್ಬಿದಕೀರ್ತ್ತಿಕಾಂ-
ತೆಯಂ ವೀರವಿ
೬೬. ತರಣಂಗಳಂ ಪೊಗಳಿಸಿಕೊಳುತ್ತ
ನಿಜರಾಜಧಾನಿ ಗುತ್ತವೊಳಲೊಳ್ಸುಖ
ರಾಜ್ಯಂಗೆಯಿವುತ್ತಮಿರ್ದೂ

65b-66. And while protecting the kingdom in pleasure and amusements from his capital, Guttavoḷal, with all eulogies of gifted bravery, in the company of his consort, Fame, his fame spread in ten directions,

೬೭. ||ಕಂ|| ಚಂಡಾಸಿಯಿಂ ಪಂನ್ನಿ-
ರ್ಬ್ಬರ್ಮ್ಮಂಡಳಿಕರ ಗಂಡನೆಂಬ ಜ-
ನನಸಯಿತು ಭೂ । ಮಂಡಳವರಿಯ-
ಲು ಶಿವನೆ
೬೮. ಗಂಡನೆನಿಪ್ಪೊಂದು ಕೀರ್ತಿಯಂ
ಪಡೆದಿಪ್ಪನು ||೨೭||

67-68a. having obtained the title of subduer of twelve vassals through the sharp edge of his sword, and, as is known on the orb of the earth that "Siva is the only Lord", he acquired this same fame. (27)

---

1 Some letters have been effaced purposely.

ವ|| ಯಿಂತೆನುತ್ತ ತಂನ್ನೊಳು ಪರಿ-
ಭಾವಿಸಿನೋಡಿ ||ಕಂ|| ಧಾರಿಣಿಯೊಱು
೬೯. ಗ್ರ ತಪದಿಂ ವೀರೇಶ್ವರನೊಲವ
ಪಡೆದ ಶಿವದೇವಯ್ಯನ | ಕಾರುಣ್ಯ-
ವೆನಗೆ ಜೀವನ ಬೇಱಿಲ್ಲೆಂದರಿದು ತ-
ತ್ಪ್ರಸಾದ
೭೦. ವ ಪಡೆದನು ||೨೮||
ಅಂತಂ ಶಿವಗಣಪ್ರಸಾದದಿಂ ಶಿವದೇ-
ವರ ಕಾರುಣ್ಯವಂ ಪಡೆದು
ಶ್ರೀ ಸೋಮನಾಥಲಿಂಗ
೭೧. ವನವಧರಿಸಿಕೊಂಬ ಸಮಯದಲಿ
ಗುತ್ತರ್ಸರು ಶ್ರೀ ಶಿವದೇವರ ಶಿವಪಾ-
ದಂಗಳಿಗೆಯಾರಾಧನೆಯ ಮಾ
೭೨. ಡಿದ ಶಿವಪುರಕ್ಕ ಬೆವೊಳಲ
ರಾಮಗವುಂಡನ ಮಗ ಬೊಂಮಗ-
ವುಂಡನಂ ಕರಿಸಿ ಬೆವೊಳಲ ಬಡಗ
೭೩. ಣ ಹೊಲದಲ್ಲಿ ಗಂಗನಾಱು ಮ-
ತ್ತರುಯೆರೆಯ ಕೆಯ್ಯನಿಕ್ಕೆಂದಡ
ಬೊಂಮಗವುಂಡ ಬರೊಳ್ಳಿತಂ ಮ
೭೪. ಹಾಪ್ರಸಾದ ಜೀಯ ಯಂದು |
ಗುತ್ತೊಳಲ್ನಾಡ ಪ್ರಭುಗಳ ಮುಂದೆ
ಕೈ ಕಯಿಕೊಂಡು ತಂನ್ನಸ್ಥಳದ ಹೆ
೭೫. ಗ್ಗಡೆ ಮುದ್ದಯ್ಯ ಮುಖ್ಯ
ಸಮಸ್ತ ಪ್ರಜೆಪ್ರಕ್ರುತಿ ಯೆಂಟುಹಿಟ್ಟು
ಪಂಚಮಠ ನಖರ ಮುಂಮುರಿದಂ
೭೬. ಣ್ಡ ಸಹಿತ ಬಂದು | ತನ್ನ ಗ-
ವುಡಗೆಯಿಂ ಬಡಗಣ ಬಸಯ್ಯನ
ಕೆಯಿಂ ಮೂಡಲು | ಚಿ
೭೭. ಕ್ಕ ಕುಱುವತ್ತಿಯ ಹೊಲ ಮೇ-
ರೆಯ ಸಾಲಬೆಳನಿಂ ತೆಂಕಲು |
ಯೆಣ್ನೆಗೊಳಕಡದ ಕೊಳದಿಂ ಪ
೭೮. ಡುವಲು | ಕಲಿದೇವರ | ಕಂ
ಮಱಗೆಯಿಂ ಬಡಗಲೇಕಸ್ಥಳದಲಿ
ಯಿಕ್ಕಿದ ಯೆರೆಯ ಭೂಮಿ ಗಂಗನ

68b-70a. Saying and reasoning in himself "my life is only (to earn) the compassion of Śivadēva who has obtained the grace of Vīrēśvara and none else", saying thus (the king) obtained his (the saint's) grace. (28)

70b. Having obtained Śivadēva's compassion by Śivagaṇa's grace,

70c-73a. at the time of offerings made to God Sōmanāthaliṅga (in the capital), Guttarasa called Bommagavuṇḍa, son of Rāmagavuṇḍa of Bevoḷala to Śivapura, which was already offered to the holy feet of Śivadēva, ordered him to donate 6 *gaṃga mattaru* of land of black soil to the North of Bevoḷala,

73b-74a. Boṃmagavuṃḍa answered : "Yes My Lord, Your honour's prasāda[1] (shall be carried out)".

74b-79a. Having come with *muridaṃḍa* the chief Heggaḍe Muddayya and other members of the assembly of *eṃṭu hiṭṭu*, *paṃcamaṭha* and *nakhara* in the presence of the Nāḍaprabhu of Gottaḷal (Guttavaḷal), granted six *gaṃga mattaru* of black soil land in the (territory) of his own *gauḍike* : (the limits are) the field of Baḍagaṇa Basayya to the east; the fields rich with crops at Chikka Kuṟuvatti to the south; Yeṃṇekoḷa to the west; Kammagere of Kalidēva to the north;

1 An order given either by a king or by an official or a religious head is considered as *prasāda.*

೭೯. ಮತ್ತರಾಱು ॥ ಆ ಭೂಮಿಯ
ಫಲ ಬೆವೊಳಲ ಕಾರಣವಿಲ್ಲ ॥

the crops of this land are not subject to (taxes (?) of) Bevoḷala.

ಶಕವರ್ಷ ೧೧೮೫ ನೆಯ ದುನ್ದು
೮೦. ಭಿ ಸಂವತ್ಸರದ ವಯಿಶಾಖ ಶು-
ದ್ಧ ೧೫ ಸೋಮವಾರ ಸೋಮಗ್ರ-
ಹಣದಂದು ಶ್ರೀಮದಮರಂಗಣಂ
೮೧.ಗಳ ನಿಜಸಿಂಹಾಸನವಪ್ಪ ಮುಕ್ತಿ-
ಕ್ಶೇತ್ರ ಭೂಕಯಿಳಾ(ಲಾ)ಸವಿದೆಂದು ।
ಶ್ರೀ ಶಿವದೇವರು ಜಗದ್ಧಿತಾ
೮೨. ರ್ತ್ಥವಾಗಿ ರಚಿಸಿದ । ಶಿವದೇ-
ವಪುರಕ್ಕೆ ವರ್ಷಂಪ್ರತಿ ಬರುತ್ತಬಹುದು
। ಅದು ಸರ್ವ್ವಮಾನ್ಯ ಶ್ರೀಮಾನ್ಯ
೮೩. ಜಯಮಾನ್ಯ । ವಿಜಯಮಾನ್ಯ ॥

79b-83a. At the time of a lunar eclipse on Monday, 15th day of the bright fortnight of Vaiśākha, in the year Dundubhi, Śaka 1185, for the welfare of the world, Śrī Śivadēva created Śivadēvapura, real seat of Amaragaṇas, heaven on the earth.

That every year we must come to Muktikṣētra, this was accepted fully, accepted by Śrī, accepted victoriously.

ಮತ್ತಂ ಸ್ವಸ್ತಿ ಸಮಧಿಗತ ಪಂಚ-
ಮಹಾಶಬ್ದ ದ್ವಾರಾವತೀಪುರವರಾ
೮೪. ಧೀಶ್ವರ ಸುವರ್ಣ್ನಗರುಡಧ್ವಜಂ
ವೃಷ್ಣಿವಂಶೋದ್ಭವಂ ಯಾದವಕುಳಕ
ಮಳಕಳಿಕಾವಿಕಾಸಭಾಸ್ಕರಂ ಅರಿರಾ
೮೫. ಯ ಜಗಝಂಪ ಮಾಳವರಾಯ
ಕದನತ್ರಿನೇತ್ರಂ ಗೌರ್ಜ್ಜರಭಯಜ್ವ
ರಂಚೋಳರಾಯದಿಸಾ(ಶಾ)ಪಟ್ಟ(ಟ)ಂ
ತೆಲು
೮೬.ಗರಾಯಸ್ಥಾಪನಾಚಾರ್ಯ್ಯ ಇತ್ಯಾ-
ದಿ ರಾಜಾವಳೀಸಮಾಳಂಕ್ರ(ಲಂಕೃ)ತ
ಶ್ರೀ ಮತ್ಪ್ರೌಢಪ್ರತಾಪಚಕ್ರವರ್ತಿ ಶ್ರೀ
೮೭. ಮಹಾದೇವರಾಯ ವಿಜಯರಾಜ್ಯ
ಪ್ರವರ್ದ್ಧಮಾನಮಾಚಂದ್ರಾರ್ಕ್ಕಂ
ಬರುತ್ತಮಿರೆ ।

83b-87a. And be it well, he, who uses five instruments of big sounds, lord of Dvārāvatipura, with a golden eagle on his flag, born in Vr̥ṣṇi dynasty, sun to the full blossomed lotus of the Yādava family, startler to the world of enemies, Three Eyed Śiva in fighting Mālavas, frightening fever to Gurjaras, disperser in all directions of the Coḷa army, establisher of Telugu kings etc., thus adorned with many royal titles, while the victorious reign of this king Yādava Mahādēvarāya was advancing in the course of ever-increasing prosperity, to endure as long as moon and sun;

ದಕ್ಷಿಣದಿಕುತಟ
೮೮.ವಿಳಸಿತ ಲಕ್ಷ್ಮಿಮಿಗೆ ನೀನಧಿಪ-
ನೆಂದು ಯಾದವಭೂಪ ನಿರೀಕ್ಷಿಸಿ
ಬೆಸಸಲು ಮುದದಿಂ ರಕ್ಷಿಪ ತೊಱ-
ಗಲೆಯ
೮೯. ದೇವರಸ ಜನಪದವ ॥೨೮॥

87b-89a. "Thou shalt be the Lord of shining Lakṣmī on the border of the southern direction", when the Yādava king ordered thus, after verification, with pleasure Dēvarasa engaged himself in protecting the subjects at Toṟagale. (28)

||ವ|| ಶ್ರೀ ಶಿವದೇವರು ಮಾಡುವ
ಲಿಂಗಜಂಗಮಸಮಾರಾಧನೆಗೆ ಸ-
ರ್ವ್ವಭಾವದಿಂ ಶುಶ್ರೂ
೯೦. ಸೆ(ಷೆ)ಯ ಮಾಮ್ಬ್ವದೆಂದು ಶ್ರೀ
ಮಹಾದೇವರಾಯ ನಿರೂಪಂಗೊಡೆ
ಸ್ವಸ್ತಿ ಸಮಸ್ತಪ್ರಶಸ್ತಿಸಹಿತಂ ಶ್ರೀಮ-
ನ್ಮಹಾ

89b-90a. As soon as Mahādēvarāya gave order (to Dēvarasa) "the services to Liṅga and Jaṅgama performed by Śrī Śivadēva should be protected wholeheartedly" –be it well– accompanied with all praises, the chief minister,

೯೧. ಪ್ರಧಾನಂ ಸರ್ವ್ವಾಧಿಕಾರಿ ತೊ-
ಱಗಲೆಯ ದೇವರಸರು ಶ್ರೀಮದ್ದಕ್ಷಿಣ-
ವಾರಣಾಸಿಯೆನಿಪ [ಪ]ಶ್ಚಿಮವಾಹಿನಿ
ತುಂ
೯೨.ಗಭದ್ರೆಯ ದಕ್ಷಿಣ ತೀರದೊಳೆಸೆವ
ಮುಕ್ತಿಕ್ಷೇತ್ರನಿವಾಸರಪ್ಪ ಶ್ರೀಶಿವದೇ-
ವರ ಲಿಂಗದರ್ಶನಾರ್ತ್ಥಂ ಬಂದು||
|| ರು

90b-92a. *sarvādhikāri*, Dēvarasa of Toṟagale, having come with the purpose of taking *darśana* of the Liṅga worshipped by Śrī Śivadēva at Muktikṣētra, southern Vārāṇasi shining on the southern bank of westward flowing Tuṅgabhadrā ,

೯೩. ಧಿರೋಧಾ(ದ್ಗಾ)ರಿ ಸಂವತ್ಸರದ
ಜ್ಯೇಷ್ಠ ಬಹುಳ ೫ ಆದಿವಾರ ಷಡಶೀ-
ತಿಮುಖಸಂಕ್ರಾನ್ತಿ ತಾತ್ಕಾಲದಲ್ಲಿ ಬೆ
೯೪. ಳುವೊಳಲ ಬಡಗಣ ಹೊಲದಲ್ಲಿ
ಮುಂನ ಕಲ್ಲುನಟ್ಟಿದ್ದ ಗಂಗನಯೆಂ-
ಟು ಮತ್ತರು ಭೂಮಿಯನು
೯೫. ಸರ್ವ್ವನಮಸ್ಯವಾಗಿ ಸಮಾರಾಧ-
ನೆಯ ಮಾಡಿದನು || ಮಂಗಳಮಹಾ
ಶ್ರೀ ಶ್ರೀ ಶಿವಮಸ್ತು ||

92b-95. (Dēvarasa of Toṟagale), on Sunday, the 5th day of Jyēṣṭha in the year Rudhirōdgāri on the occasion of *ṣaḍaśīti saṅkrāṃti*, offered a land of 8 *Gaṃganamattaru* in the field north of Beḷuvola where boundary stones were planted earlier, after making it tax free. There be good luck; there be Fortunate Śiva.

೯೬. ಮತ್ತಂ ಗುತ್ತರಸನು ಆ ಬೆಳ-
ವೊಳಲ ಪಡುವ ವೊಲನಲ್ಲಿ ಹೊಂನ-
ವತ್ತಿಗೆ ಹೋದ ದಾ
೯೭. ರಿಯ ಬಡಗಣ ಯೆರ್‍ರೆ(ರೆ)ಯಕೆ-
ಯ ಗಂಗನ ಕಂಬ ೫೦ ಮಂ
ವೊಡೆಯರ ಪಾದಕ್ಕೆ
೯೮. ಆರಾಧಿಸಿದನು । ಆ ಕೆಯ್ಯನು
ವೊಡೆಯರು ಬಸವಯ್ಯಂಗೆ ಸರ್ವ್ವ-
ನಮಸ್ಯವಾಗಿ ಕೊಟ್ಟ
೯೯. ರಂ || ಶ್ರೀಮತು ಸಿಂಘಣವಶ್ರ-
(ರ್ಷ) ಶುಭಕ್ರು(ಕೃ)ತ್ಸಂವತ್ಸರದ
ಪುಷ್ಯ ಸು(ಶು)ದ್ಧ ೩ ಸು(ಶು)ಕ್ರವಾರ

96-99. Then, in the field to the west of that Beḷuvoḷal, to the north of the road leading to Hoṃnavatti a black soil field of 50 *Gaṃgana kaṃba* was offered by Guttarasa to the holy feet of Oḍeyar; (in his turn) Oḍeyar granted that land to Basavayya after making it tax free. On Friday, 3rd day of the bright fortnight of Puṣya in the year Śubhakṛt in the years of Siṃghaṇa's rule,

೧೦೦. ದ ... ಸಿ(ಶಿ)ವದೇವರ ಕೆಯ್ಯ-
ಲು ಗೋ(ಗೊ)ವೆ ಕುಱುವತ್ತಿಯ
ಯ(ಅ)ಶೇಷ ಮಹಾಜನಂಗಳು ಹಾಗ
ತಿಂಗಳಿಂ

100. counting one *hāga* of interest per year, for 15 *gadyāṇa* levied on the field donated by the assembly of Asēṣa mahājana of Kuṟuvatti[1], from this money Śivadēva feeds one Liṅgajaṅgama.

೧೦೧. ಶ್ರೀರಾಮದೇವರಾಯವಿಜಯರಾ-
ಜ್ಯೋದಯದ ೧೬ನೆ
೧೦೨. ಯ ಬ್ಯಯ ಸಂವತ್ಸರದ ...
[ಯಂತರ] ಯಶೇಷಮಹಾಜನಂಗಳು
ಯೀ ಧರ್ಮ್ಮವ ನಡೆಯಿಸಿದಲ್ಲಿಂ

101- 102. On the 16th year of Yādava Rāmacandra in the year Byeya (Vyaya) ... these mahājanas should see that the order is executed ...

೧೦೩. ದಂ ಮೇಲೆ ... ಗಣಂಗಳ
ಸಮಕ್ಷದಲ್ಲಿ ಯಾ ಮುಕ್ತೇಶ್ವರ ದೇ-
ವರು ಸಿದ್ಧಾಯ
೧೦೪. ವ ತೆಱುವ ಯಾಟು ಮತ್ತರು
ಕೆಯ ... (ಯ್ಯ)ವತ್ತು ಹೊಂನ್ನಿಂ-
ಗೆವು ಬಡ್ಡಿಗೆವು ಸಲುವಾಗಿ ಯಾ ಭೂ

103-105. Offered to Muktīśvara after making tax free a land of … mattaru …[2].

೧೦೫. ಮಿಯನು ಕುಳವ ಕಡಿದು
ಯಾ ಮಹಾಜನಂಗಳು ಮುಕ್ತೇಶ್ವರ-
ದೇವರ್ಗ್ಗೆ ಸರ್ವ್ವಮಾನ್ಯವಾಗಿ
ಕೊಟ್ಟರು ॥ ಈ ಧರ್ಮ್ಮಕೆ

105. After making it tax free, the Mahājanas gave it to God Muktēśvara.

೧೦೬. ಯಾರು ಯಹುದಲ್ಲಿಂದರೆ ...
ಸಾಸಿರಕೆ ಹೊಱಗು ಹದಿನೆಂಟು ಸ-
ಮಯಕೆ ದ್ರೋಹಿಗಳು॥

106. Antagonists of this order will be considered as traitors of Eighteen Samayas.

೧೦೭.ಸ್ವದತ್ತಂ .ಸಹಸ್ರಾಣಿ ವಿಷ್ಟಾ-
ಯಾಂ ಜಾಯತೇ ಕ್ರಿಮಿ ॥ ೩೦ ॥

107. One who steals the land given by oneself or by others will become a worm in filth for sixty thousand years.[3]

---

[1] Ref. to l. 68 to 70 in the preceding inscription.
[2] Too many gaps hinder the comprehension of the text.
[3] From l. 100 onwards the inscription is badly damaged.

Inscription No. V.

(*Cauḍadānapura Monograph* No. V, p. 103-107. S I I XVIII no. 245. In Walter Elliot's collection, *South Indian Inscriptions*, vol II. No. 1, folio 239 recto to 240 recto. Also "A broken stone inscription from Chaudadanapura" in *Studies in indian History and Culture; Prof. P. B. Desai Felicitation Volume*, Karnatak University, Dharwar, 1971, p. 76ff)

Walter Elliot's copyist says that this stele was in the temple of Gōpadēvamuni. *Bombay Gazetteer* also mentions the same fact that the stele is in Gōmunidēva's shrine. But, now it is kept in the common shed where all the other inscriptions have been preserved in the temple complex.

Nandimath while editing this inscription writes that the stone is broken and the broken part is missing (*Cauḍadānapura Monograph* p. 103). Luckily, in the last century it was copied fully by Walter Elliot and the copy has been preserved in the India Office Library, London. Nandimath also says that the collection containing the copy of this inscription is kept in the Library of the Royal Asiatic Society, London. He could go through it, while he was there, and restore the full text for the publication. We could obtain xerox copies of the same from the Royal Asiatic Society, London (plate 7.). The stele must have been damaged recently, because in *South Indian Inscriptions* vol. XVIII, No. 245, p. 326 the text is complete up to the twenty-seventh line, whereas in the *Cauḍadānapura Monograph* right from the first line Nandimath has given the missing part of the text into brackets indicating that it has been restituted from Elliot's collection.

Altogether there are 46 lines of which the last four are not completely preserved. There are totally 15 verses. The language of the text is Kannaḍa, except the beginning and the imprecatory verses which are in Sanskrit. The whole text is written beautifully in Kannaḍa characters of the 13th century.

The importance of the inscription lies in the fact that it mentions the name of Rēvaṇasiddha, one of the most important Vīraśaiva saints. In this inscription we also come across with terms such as *kāruṇika*, *gaṇasukha*, Jaṅgama and Śivagaṇa which are very familiar to the Vīraśaivas of to-day.

Another important fact that we gather from this inscription is about the Śivaliṅgatattva. Almost all the *Śaivāgama*s speak about three *tattva*s or realities of Śiva at the time of the creation of the universe. Sadāśivatattva and Mahēśatattva can be represented in the form of Liṅga and images (*mūrti*). This idea is suggested in the verse 7.

The purport of the chart is that Kannādēvi, wife of Kallarasa from Toṟagale, built a temple to God Kal(l)idēva in memory of her deceased husband and Guttarasa of Guttavoḷal endowed some lands for the conduct of rituals perpetually. Kannādēvi, a pious lady, was always engaged in the service of Guru and Jaṅgamas. She wanted to commit *sati* when her husband went to the heavenly abode. Instead of allowing her to go on the funeral pyre, Guru Siddha Rēvaṇadēva counselled her to go to Muktēśvarakṣētra where an ascetic resides under the orders of Sirigiridēva (Lord of Śrīśailaṃ). Pleased with this advice she went to Muktikṣētra where she had a temple built in the name of her defunct husband Kalidēvarasa and spent the rest of her life in the service of Guru and Jaṅgama.

Places mentioned in this inscription can be identified : Sirigiri with Śrīśailam in Āndhra; Lokki with modern Lakkuṃḍi near Gadag; Ulihaḷḷi or Hūliyahaḷḷi with modern Hullaḷḷi in Byāḍgi tālūk, three kilometres from Kadaramaṇḍalagi known for its association with the saint poet Kanakadāsa in the 16th century. The date as given in Elliot's collection and the *Chauḍadānapura Monograph* is Śaka 1184, cyclic year Dundubhi, Kārtika Paurṇami, Sōmavāra, whereas in S.I.I. vol. XVIII the Śaka year is missing due to the damage caused to the slab. It corresponds to 1262 A. D. October 28.

We have followed here the text given in Walter Elliot's collection.

೧.ನಮಸ್ತುಂಗಶಿರಶ್ಚುಂಬಿಚಂದ್ರಚಾರ- ಚಾರವೇ । ತ್ರೈಲೋಕ್ಯನಗರಾರಂಭ ೨. ಮೂಲಸ್ತಂಭಾಯ ಶಂಭವೇ ॥೧॥	1-2a. Homage to Śambhu, lovely with a *cauri*, the moon kissing his lofty head, foundation column of the construction of a city, the three worlds.(1)
ಶಬ್ದಾದಯೋಪಿ ಗ್ರು(ಗೃ)ಹ್ಯಂತೇ ೩. ಕ್ರಿಯಂತೇ ವಚನಾದಯ: । ಅವಿ- ಲಂಘ್ಯಾ ಹಿ ಸರ್ವೇಷಾಮಾಜ್ಞಾ ಶಂ- ಭೋರ್ಗ್ಗರೀಯಸೀ ॥೨॥[1]	2b-3a. Indeed his command is inviolable and the mightiest of all. His very words are received and his rules too are obeyed. (2)
ಬಾಲೇಂದು ೪. ಕಳಾಭೂಷಿತ । ಮೌಳಿ ಶ್ರೀ ಕಲ್ಲಿ- ನಾಥನವನೀ ಜನಮಂ ಪಾಳಿಸುಗೆ ಶ- ರಧಿ ಶಶಿತಾ । ರಾಳಿ ಕುಲಂ ದಿಗ್ಗಜಂ ೫. ಂಗಳಿಪ್ಪಂನ್ನೆವರಂ ॥೩॥	3b-5a. May Śrī Kallinātha adorned with the young crescent moon as a diadem protect the inhabitants of the earth including the ocean, the moon, the rows of stars, mountains and white elephants of the directions. 3

---

[1] See p. 46, n. 1. Also *Vīraśaivamāhēśvarācārasaṃgraha* by Nīlakaṃṭhanāganāthācārya, vol. I, XII.14, p. 339; var. : *tasya* instead of *śambhor.*

ಸ್ವಸ್ತಿ ಸಮಸ್ತ ದಿವಿಜದನುಜಖಚರ-
ಖೇಚರಗಂಧರ್ವಕಿಂನರಕಿಂಪುರುಷ
೬. ಶಿ(ಸಿ)ದ್ಧ ಮುನೀಂದ್ರ ಫಣೀಂದ್ರ
ಗಣೇಂದ್ರ ಪ್ರಮಥ ಪ್ರಚಂಡ ಪ್ರಣಿತ
ವಿವಿಧ ನ್ರು(ನೃ)ತ್ಯ ಗೀತ ವಾದ್ಯ ವಿ
೭. ದ್ಯಾ ವೀಣಾವೇಣುನಾದವಿನೋದ-
ಪ್ರಸಂನ್ನವರದಾನಿ ಮಲ್ಲಿಕಾರ್ಜುನಂ
|| ಕಂದ || ಶಿರಿಗಿರಿ
೮. ಯೊಳಿರ್ದು ತಂನ್ನಯ ಭ(ಚ)-
ರಣವೆ ಶರಣೆಂಬ ವೀರ ಶಿವದೇವರಿ-
ಗಾ । ಶ್ಚರಿಯುವೆನಿಪ್ಪ ।
೯. ಪಶ್ಚಿಮ । ವರವಾಹಿನಿ ತುಂಗ-
ಭದ್ರೆಯಂ ತೋರುತ್ತಂ ||೪||
ಆದೇಶದಿಂದ (ಆದೇಶಿಸಿದಂ) ನಡೆ
ನೀನಾದೇಶ[1]
೧೦.ಕ್ಕಲ್ಲಿ ಮುಕ್ತನಾಥನೊಳೆಂದ್ದುಮು।
ಮಾದೇವಿಸಹಿತವಿಹೆನು । ಸಮಾಧಾನ-
ದೊಳರ್ಚಿಸು
೧೧. ವುದೆನಲ್ನಡೆತಂದು || ೫||
ಅನವರತ ಲಿಂಗ್ಗಸಂವುಜ ್ಞವನನುಕ-
ರಿಸಿದನಂನ್ಯಕಾಸಿ(ಶೆ) ಮಾಡದೆ
೧೨. ಮುಕ್ತೇ । ಶನನಪ್ರತಿಮನೆನಿಪೂ ।
ಜನೆಯಿಂದರ್ಚ್ಚಿಸಿ ಮೆಚ್ಚಿಸುವನೆನ-
ವಂತ್ತದೊ||೬|| ತೊ
೧೩.ನೆವಂ [ಮು]ತ್ತು ಕಂಗೊಳುವನು।
ಯನುಮಾನಿಪನಡಿಗಡಿಗೆ ಸ್ರು(ಶೃ)ತಿಗ-
ಳೊಳು ಪುಗಳಂ ।
೧೪. ನೆನೆನೆನೆದು ಮೂರ್ತಿಗೊಳಿಸುವ ।
ಘನತರ ಶಿವಲಿಂಗ್ಗತತ್ತ್ವವಂ ಶಿವದೇ-
ವಂ||೭||

5b-9a. Be it well. Mallikārjuna, bestower of boons to gods, demons, wanderers in sky and air, Gandharvas, Kinnaras, Kimpuruṣas, best of ascetics, Lord of serpents, master of Gaṇas, Pramathas, pleased with various dances, chants, the skillful play of instruments like vīṇā and flute, residing at Sirigiri, showing the westward running river Tuṅgabhadrā, said, to the great wonder of Śrī Vīra Śivadēva who believed that only His feet are the ultimate refuge : (4)

9b-11a. "Thou shalt go to that country where I reside in the company of Umādēvi in Muktanātha; fixing your mind intently worship (Him)". As soon as (He) said thus, (Śivadēva) walked down (to Muktiksētra); (5)

11b-12. and said (to himself) : "without desiring for anything else, following the *Liṅgasaṃvujña*[2] , I shall worship incomparable Muktēśa incessantly to please Him"[3] (6)

12b-14. (In devotion) he swings (his body), sees (Śiva's) image, honours (Him), so highly praised in the scriptures, at every step, Śivadēva meditates over Śivaliṅgatattva which he causes to take form. (7)

---

1 *Cauḍadānapura Monograph*:reads erroneously : ā dēśadiṃda naḍe nīnā dēśa (ಆದೇಶದಿಂದ ನಡೆ ನೀನಾದೇಶಕ್ಕ) Then the meaning will be "you go away from that country to that country". S.I.I. gives : ādēśisidaṃ naḍe nīnādēśake... The real meaning might be that God orders Śivadēva to obey Him and go to Muktikṣētra.

2 Liṃgasaṃga is one of the principles that a Vīraśaiva must observe.

3 "I shall please Him through the performance of rituals continuously" is the meaning according to S.I.I. XVIII reading.

೧೫. ಪರದೈವಮಾನಮರ್ದ ।ಪರದೈವ-
ರಘರಟ್ಟದಿಟ್ಟ ಪರದೈವಕುಭ್ರು । ದ್ವ-
ರವಜ್ರಪಾತನೆನಿ
೧೬. ಪಂ । ವೀರಗಣತೇಜ:ಪ್ರಭಾವದಿಂ
ಶಿವದೇವನು ॥೮॥

15-16a. With the magnanimous radiance of Ṡivagaṇas, Ṡivadēva came to be called destroyer of prestige of those who worship other gods, mocker at the sinful loud cries of other deities, *vajra* in destroying mountains, the other gods. (8)

॥ವಚನ॥ ಅಂತ್ತಾ ಶಿವದೇವರು ಶಿವ
೧೭.ಗಣಾಜ್ಞಾಸುಖದೊಳಿರುತ್ತಮಿರೆ
ಯಿರೆ। ಕಾರಣಿಕರೆನಿಪರೊಳು ತಾಂ ।
ಕಾರಣಿಕ
೧೮. ರೆನಿಪ ಶಿ(ಸಿ)ದ್ಧರೇವಣದೇವನ ।
ಕಾರುಣ್ಯಶಿಶ್ಯಾ ಭಕ್ತ್ಯಾ । ಚಾರದ
ಬೆಲ್ಲಾಳದೇವ^ ಲೊಕ್ಕಯೊ
೧೯. ಳೆಸೆದಂ ॥೯॥

16b-19a. Thus Ṡivadēva was pleased to live under the orders of Ṡivagaṇa. Cīlāḷa shining (governing) at Lokki, the compassionate child of Siddha Rēvaṇadēva who is said to be (more) compassionate amongst the compassionates; (9)

ಮಿಕ್ಕ ಶಿವಭಕ್ತಸುಖದಿಂ । ದುಕ್ಕಿ
ಮಹಾದೇವ ಭಾವಭರದಿಂ ಜಗಮಂ ।
ಲೆಕ್ಕಿ
೨೦.ಸದೆ ಗಣಸುಖದೊಳಿಹ ಲೊಕ್ಕಿಯ
ಚಿಲಾಳಾದೇವ ತೊಱಗಲೆ ನಾಡೊಳ್
॥೧೦ ॥

19b-20a. caring for nothing else in the world by the overflowing weight of devotion to Lord Ṡiva, Cīlāḷadēva of Lokki in Toṟagalenāḍu was engaged in pleasures like those of Gaṇas. (10)

ಅಂತ್ತಿರುತ್ತಮಿ
೨೧.ದ್ರು॥ ಪದಪಿದ ಶಿವಭಕ್ತಿಯ ಸಂ।
ಪದಮಂ ಕಲ್ಲರಸನರಸಿ ಕಂನಾದೇ-
ವಿಗೆ । ಮುದದಿಂದಪಿತ್ತ ಚಿ
೨೨. ಲ್ಲಾ । ಳದೇವ ಜಂಗಮಸುಖೈಕ-
ಗುಣಸದ್ಭಾವಂ॥೧೧ ॥

20b-22a. While it was like this, Cīlāḷadēva having the best of the intentions towards Jaṅgamas, with joy offered to Kannādēvi, queen of Kallarasa, the treasure of Ṡivabhakti. (11)

ಆ ಸತಿ ಕಂನಾದೇವಿಯ್ಯಾ । ಶ್ರೀ
ಸುಖಸಂಪದವಿಳಾ
೨೩. ಸವಿಭವಾದಿಗಳಂ । ಬಾಸಣಿಸಿ-
ಸಿ(ಶಿ)ವಗಣಂಗಳಿ । ಗೊ(ಗೋ)ಸರಿ-
ಸದೆ ಮಾಡಿ ಕೂಡಿ ಸುಖಿಸುತ್ತಿಪ್ಪ
೨೪. ಳ್ ॥ ೧೨ ॥

22b-24a. That loyal espouse Kannādēvi having shunned the (doors) to the pleasures of wealth, without getting tired was serving the Ṡivagaṇas and enjoying their company. (12)

---

[1] In *P.B. Desai Felicitation Volume* Dr. Nandimath thanks Dr. Kalburgi for drawing his attention on a verse in *Vīraśaivāmṛtapurāṇa* in which the name Cīlāḷa occurs. (*Ibid.* p. 84, n. 3).

ವಚನ॥ ತದನಂತ್ತರವು ॥ ಕರ್ಮಾ- ತಿಶಯದಿ ನಿಜಪತಿ ಧರ್ಮಧ್ವಜ ದೇವ- ಲೋಕವ । ನೆ ತಾನೆಯಿದಲ್ ೨೫. ಧರ್ಮಜ್ಞೆದೇವಿ ಕಂನ್ನರೆ(ಹ್ನಲೆ)। ಕರ್ಮ್ಮರಿಯಂ ಪಾಯಲುಜ್ಯುಗಂ ಗೆ- ಯಿವನ್ನಂ ॥೧೩॥	24b-25a. And then, when her lawful husband the banner of *dharma*, joined the world of Gods, Kahnale the follower of the laws of *dharma* said : "I shall do the duty of zealous action (I shall follow him)". (13)
ಪರಮಗುರು[1] ಶಿ(ಸಿ)ದ್ಧ ರೇ ೨೬. ವಣ । ಸಿರಿಗಿರಿಯ ನಿವಾಸನಾ- ಜ್ಞೆಯಂ ಬೆಸಸಿದನ । ಚ್ಚರಿಯ ಮು- ನಿಯಪ್ಪ ಮು ೨೭.ಕ್ತೇ । ಶ್ವರಲಿಂಗದೊಳಲ್ಲಿ ತುಂ- ಗ್ಗಭದ್ರೆಯ ತಡಿಯ್ಯೊಳ್ ॥೧೪॥	25b-27a. Paramaguru Siddha Rēvaṇadēva (advised her) : "on the orders of the Resident of Sirigiri a wonderful saint is living in the (presence of) Muktēśvaraliṅga on the bank of Tuṅgabhadrā". (14)
ಯಿಂತ್ತೆನೆ ॥ ಆನೆನನೆನದೇ ಸದ್ಗುರು ೨೮.ತಾನೇನಂ ತೋರಿ(ಚೆ)ದ ವಿಚಿತ್ರ- ವೆನುತ್ತಂ ॥ ಮಾನಿನಿ ಕಂನ್ನಾ(ಹ್ನಾ)- ದೇವಿಯರಾ । ನಂದದಿ ಬಂದು ೨೯. ಮುಕ್ತನಾಥನ ಕಂಡರು ॥೧೫॥	27b-29a. When said so by the noble Siddha Rēvaṇadēva, "What am I to become when, strangely enough, the best of the Gurus shows me this marvellous (way)", saying thus Kaṃhnādēvi with joy came and saw Muktanātha. 15
ಅನ್ತಾ ಮುಕ್ತಿಕ್ಷೇತ್ರದಲ್ಲಿರ್ದು ಹಿಂಗದೆ ಜಂಗಮಾರ್ಚ ೩೦. ನೆ [ತ]ತ್ಪರೆಯಾಗಿರೆ ಯಿರೆ ॥ ಶಿವಯೋಗಿಯ ಕೃಪೆಯಿಂದ ವೀರ ಕ ೩೧. ಂನ್ನಾದೇವಿ । ಭುವನವರಿಯಲ್ಕೆ ಕಲಿದೇವರ ಸ್ಥಾಪಿಸಿದಳ್ ॥	29b-31. Thus Kaṃnādēvi, while living at Muktikṣētra, engaged in the service of the devotees of Śiva, by the grace of Śivayōgi, to the best of the knowledge of the world, consecrated a Liṅga (called) Kalidēva. (15)
೩೨. ಸ್ವಸ್ತಿ ಶ್ರೀಮತು ಯಾದವನಾ- ರಾಯಣ ಪ್ರವುಢಪ್ರತಾಪ ಚ ೩೩. ಕೃವರ್ತ್ತಿ ಮಹಾದೇವರಾಯ ರಾಜ್ಯಪ್ರವರ್ಧಮಾನಮಾಚಂದ್ರಾರ್ಕ್ಕ- ತಾರಂಬರಂ ಸಲುತ್ತಮಿರೆ ಯಿರೆ ॥	32-33a. Let there be good luck. While emperor Mahādēva, Yādavanārāyaṇa, (is) advancing in the course of increasing his kingdom to endure as long as moon, sun and stars,
ಸ್ವಸ್ತಿ ಶ್ರೀ ೩೪. ಮಹಾಮಂಡಳೇ(ಲೇ)ಶ್ವರಂ ವು- ಜ್ಜಯನಿಪುರವರಾಧೀಶ್ವರಂ [ವಟಕ- ಲ್ಪವೃಕ್ಷಲಾಂಛಿತ ವಿಜಯಧ್ವಜಂ ಚಂದ್ರ]ಗುತ್ತಕುಲಕಮ	33b-37a. –be it well– Guttarasa son of Vikramāditya, mahāmaṇḍalēśvara, overlord of Ujjayanipura, having the banyan tree on his victorious banner, sun to the lotus of Candragupta's

1 *Ru* (ರು) is written above the line.

೩೫.ಳ(ಲ)ಮಾರ್ತ್ತಂಡಂ । ಕದನಪ್ರ-
ಚಂಡಂ । ಹಂನಿರ್ಬರಗಂಡಂ ಸ-
(ಶ)ರಣಾಗತವಜ್ರಪಂ
೩೬. ಜರಂ ವಿಕ್ರಮಾದಿತ್ಯಪುತ್ರ ವೀರ-
(ಗುತ್ತರಸದೇವರು ಶಿವದೇವರ ಕಾ-
ರು)[1]
೩೭. ಂಣ್ಯಮಂ ಪಡೆದು
ಲಿಂಗೋತ್ಸವಸಮಯದಲ್ಲಿ ಕಂನಾ-
ದೇವಿಯರು
೩೮. ಮುಕ್ತಿಕ್ಷೇತ್ರದಲ್ಲಿ ಪ್ರತಿಷ್ಠೆಯಂ
ಮಾಡಿಸಿದ ಕಲ್ಲಿದೇವರಿಗೆ ಸರ್ವ್ವಶ್ರೀ
ಕಾರ್ಯಾರ್ಥಮಾಗಿ
ಶ್ರೀಮನ್ಮ
೩೯.ಹಾಪ್ರಭು ವೂಲಿಯಹಳ್ಳಿಯ ಮು-
ದ್ದಗೌಡನಿಂ ಶಖ(ಕ)ವರುಷ ೧೧೮೪
ನೆಯ
೪೦.ದುಂದುಭಿ ಸಂವತ್ಸರದ ಕಾರ್ತಿಕ
ಶು ॥ ೧೫ ಸೋಮವಾರದಂದು
ವೊಡೆಯರ
೪೧. ಪಾದ ಸಮಕ್ಷಮದಲ್ಲಿ ಸರ್ವ್ವ-
ನಮಶ್ಯಮಾಗಿ ವೂಲಿಹಳಿಯ ಜೋಯಿ
ಗೌಡನ ಕೇಯಂ ಗು
೪೨. ತ್ತರಸದೇವಂ ಧಾರಾಪೂರ್ವ್ವಕ-
ಮಾಗಿ ಕೊಟ್ಟ॥
೪೩.ಗಂಗನ ಮತ್ತರು ೧ ಮನೆ ೧
ತುಡಿಕೆ ೧
೪೪. ಸರ್ವನಮಶ್ಯಮಾಗಿ ಕೊಟ್ಟ
ಯೆರೆ ಬಡಗಣ (ಪೊ)ಲನಲ್ಲಿ ಗಂಗನ
ಮತ್ತರು ೧ ಮನೆ ೧ ತುಡಿಕೆ ೧
೪೫. ಗೋಪೆಯಲ್ಲಿಯ ಬೈಲ ಮತ್ತರು
೧ ...ಮತ್ತರು ೧... ಯಿನ್ತೀ ಧರ್ಮವ
ಸಿ(ಶಿ)ವದೇವರ ಗಣಂಗ
೪೬. ಳು ಪಾಲಿಸುವರು. [2]

family, terrific in the battlefield, passionately fond of wars, diamond cage to those (who) are submissive, having obtained the grace of Śivadēva,

37b-38a. at the time of the Liṅga festival, for the fulfillment of all the purposes of the rituals of God Kalidēva installed by Kaṃnādēvi at Muktikṣētra,

38b-40a. from Mahāprabhu Śrīman Muddagauḍa of Ūlihaḷḷi (Hūliya haḷḷi), on Monday, full moon day of the bright fortnight of Kārtika in the year Dundubhi, Śaka 1184,

40b-42. in the presence of the (holy) feet of Voḍeyar, making tax free the field of Joyigauḍa of that village, Guttarasa gave it with libation of water.

43-45. House 1 … *ga* banyan tree … black soil field … etc.

45b-46. Thus the order should be protected by the Gaṇas of God Śiva.

---

1 Not in Elliot's text.

2 Towards the end the slab is badly damaged. So the reading is full of gaps and no meaning can be ascertained.

Inscription No. VI

(*Cauḍadānapura Monograph* No. VI, p. 107; .S.I.I. vol XVIII, No. 247; Elliot's collection No. 5, folio 247 verso and 248 recto, with the mention "On the back of No. 2, Mahādēvaru")

On the other side of this stele there is the text of inscription No. III. Nandimath writes : "This has a figure of Vīrabhadra in the front side and the inscription is on the back side. The slab is now lying in front of the temple of Vīrabhadra which is also situated along with other temples in the compound of the temple of Muktīśa" (p 107). But his statement is incorrect, because this inscription is not engraved on the back of the stele bearing the image of Vīrabhadra but on the back of the stele containing the text of the record No. III. (The inscription No. V is on the stele on the back of which is the image of Vīrabhadra). Judging from the old photographs, this stele was installed along with others in the temple complex. But now it is installed to the north in the same shed where the other inscriptions are and on the northern face is seen the present text of the record. For its measurements see Ins. No. III. A surface of 1.35 m has been polished and 1.11 m of it is covered by the text of the inscription. There are no figures at the top. As the slab is narrower towards the top some lines are shorter with a breadth of only 32 cms about. There are 44 lines in all. The number and the size of the letters in each line vary according to the shape of the slab. At the top the first line consists of only ten letters, a line in the centre has 32 and the one at the bottom 25 letters. "The biggest letter is 3/5'x3/2" and the smallest letter is 1/2"x1/2". The average size is 1'x1'. The letters are clear, round and legible. The whole inscription is preserved in good condition". (*Cauḍadānapura Monograph* p. 107)

The inscription begins with a salutation to Śiva. Then it proceeds to relate the events. On the orders of emperor Mahādēva, from Toṟagale Dēvarasa came specially to Muktikṣētra for the purpose of granting some villages to the temple of Muktanātha. At first, Śivadēva smilingly refused to accept the grant but after seeing the ambassador's agony, comforted the donor by saying : "after all, you are offering it to God Vīrēśa; it is His wish to accept the grant and I shall receive it on behalf of the Lord". Maiḷaladēvi, the queen mother of Gutta kings is mentioned as one from whom the lands were obtained. Dēvarasa then worshipped Śivadēva who was held in high reverence by kings of the north, south and west. Śivadēva blessed the king. The Guttas of Guttavoḷal namely Guttarasadēva, Hiriyadēva, Joyidēva and their mother

Maiḷaladēvi were the disciples of Śivadēva. Also they were worshippers of "Sparśaliṅga Gaḷaganātha" at Gaḷaganāth which is also on the bank of river Tuṅgabhadrā near Guttala. Dēvarasa made this endowment with the consent of officers such as Nāḷprabhus of Guttavaḷalnāḍu and Gāvuṇḍas after obtaining lands from the hands of the rulers with the ceremony of libation of water.

The inscription is dated Śaka 1187, cyclic year Raktākṣi, Puṣya b. 15 ādivāra, Śravaṇānakṣatra, Vyatīpāta Ardhōdaya, auspicious day. These details correspond to 1265 A. D. January 18. It is considered to be the most propitious moment for accomplishing pious deeds, if the new moon day of the month of Puṣya falls on a Sunday with śravaṇā constellation and vyatīpāta. If it is joined with solar eclipse, it is the most auspicious moment for religious ceremonies. The act bears the fruits of crores of meritorious charitable deeds made at the time of solar eclipse.

It is important to note that the Gutta chieftains have accepted Śivadēva as their Rājaguru, whereas in earlier inscriptions there are references to gurus belonging to Kiṭṭagāvisantati of Kāḷamukha school (in the years 1188-89 S.I.I. XVIII, Nos. 295-297). This is an indication that by now the Kāḷamukha movement was declining and Vīraśaivism was gradually.gaining terrain.

೧. ಓಂ ನಮ[:] ಶಿವಾಯ ।	1a. Salutation to Śiva.
[1]ಮುದದಿ ಪಾ ೨.ಲಿಸುಗುರ್ವ್ವೀಪದಮಂ ಚಂದ್ರಾರ್ಕ್ಕ ತಾರಕಂ ೩. ಬರ[೦] ಗಿರಿಜಾವದನಾಂಬುಜಾತ- ಮಿತ್ರಂ ತ್ರಿದಶೇಶ್ವರ ಮು ೪. ಕ್ತನಾಥ ದೇವರ ದೇವನು ॥	1b-4a. May He protect the earth in joy as long as the moon, the sun and the stars endure, the friend of the lotus faced lady born to the mountain, God of gods, Muktanātha, Lord of thirty-three deities[2]. (1)
ಸ್ವಸ್ತಿ ಶ್ರೀಮತು ಯಾದವ ೫. ರಾಯ ನಾರಾಯಣಂ ಪ್ರೌಢಪ್ರತಾ- ಪ ಚಕ್ರವರ್ತ್ತಿ ಶ್ರೀ ೬. ವೀರ ಮಹಾದೇವರಾಯನಬೆಸದಿಂ॥	4b-6a. Be it well. On the orders of Śrī Vīra Mahādēvarāya, emperor of great valour, Nārāyaṇa amongst the Yādavas,
ಸ್ವಸ್ತಿ ಶ್ರೀಮನು (ಶ್ರೀಮನ್) ೭. ಮಹಾಪ್ರಧಾನಂ ಸರ್ವ್ವಾಧಿಕಾರಿ ತೊಱಗಲೆಯ ಶ್ರೀ ದೇವರ್ಸ ೮. ರು ಕಟಕದಿಂ ಬಂದು ॥	6b-8a. –be it well–, Dēvarasa, chief minister, Sarvādhikāri, having come (to Muktikṣētra) from Toṟagale his capital,

[1] The symbol of a conch has been carved before the beginning of this verse in *kanda*.
[2] 11 Rudras, 12 Ādityas, 1 Dyaus, 1 Pṛthvī, 8 Vasus.

ಸ್ವಸ್ತಿ ಶ್ರೀಮದಾರೂಢ ವೀರಭ್ರ(ಬ್ರ)ತಿ
ಶಿವ
೯. ಯೋಗಸಿದ್ಧ ಶಿವದೇವರಿಗೆ ಸಾ-
ಷ್ಟಾಂಗಪ್ರಣಾಮಪೂರ್ವ್ವಕಂ
೧೦. ಬಿಂನಪಂಗೆಯಿದನಿಂತೆಂದಂ ॥
ವೊಂದು ಗ್ರಾಮವ ಕೊಡು ನೀನೆನ್ದಂ
೧೧. ಯದುಕುಲ ನ್ರು(ನೃ)ಪೋತ್ತಮಂ
ಮಹದೇವಂ । ಯಿಂದದ ಪತಿಕರಿಸಲು
೧೨. ಬೇಕೆನ್ದೊಡೆ ಶಿವಯೋಗಸಿದ್ಧ ನ-
ಗುತಿಂತೆನ್ದನು ॥
ತ್ರಿಭುವನವೆಂದು
೧೩. ದು ಪಟಿಯ ಪ್ರಭುತ್ವವೇಂ ಶ್ಲಾ-
ಘ್ಯವೆ ಯದಲ್ಲದು ಮಾಣೆನ್ದಭಯಕ
೧೪. ರಸಿದ್ಧನೆನಲಾ
ಶುಭಲಕ್ಷಣ ದೇವರಾಜ ಮರಳಿಂತೆಂ-
ದಂ ॥ವೃ॥ ದೇವರು ಕೊ
೧೫. ಟ್ಟದೊಲ್ಲದಿರಲಪ್ಪುದು ದೇವಣಿ
ಮಾಡಿ ಸಿದ್ಧಿಯಿಂ ಶ್ರೀ ವಿಭವಗಳಿಂ
ಮನು
೧೬. ಜ ಲೋಕದಧೀಶ್ವರರಿತ್ತಡೊಲ್ಲ-
ದೆಂದೆವಿರಲಪ್ಪುದುತ್ತಮ ಪದಾರ್ತ್ಥಚ-
ಯಂಗ
೧೭.ಳನಲ್ಲದಾತ್ಮಜರ್ಭಾವಕರಾರ್ತ್ತ್ರತ್ತ-
ಡದನೊಲ್ಲೆವೆನಿಪ್ಪುದು ಧರ್ಮ್ಮವಪ್ಪುದೆ
ಎಂ
೧೮. ದಮೃತೋದರ ಪ್ರಭವ ದೇವನೃ-
ಪಂ ನುಡಿದೊಂದು ವಾಕ್ಯದೊಳು
ಬಂದಖಿಳಾಗಮಾರ್ತ್ಥಂ
೧೯. ನೆಲಸಿದ್ದುದು ಶಾಸ್ತ್ರದ ಸರ್ವ್ವ-
ಸಂಪದಂ ಸಂದುದು ವೈದಿಕಾರ್ತ್ಥ-
ವೊಡನಿರ್ದ್ದ ಧ
೨೦.ರ್ಮ್ಮದ ಪೆರ್ಮ್ಮೆವೆತ್ತುದೆನೆನ್ದಪೆನೆಂ-
ದು ತಂನ್ನೊಳನುಮಾನಿಸುತಂ ಶಿವ-
ದೇವರ್ರ್ರಂ(ರೆಂ)
೨೧. ದಪರು ॥

8b-10a. –be it well–, after prostrating with eight limbs, stood up to make a respectful representation to the elevated saint Śivadēva, Vīrabrati, accomplished in Śivayōga and said :

10b-11a. "Give a village" said Mahādēva the best king in Yadu's line.

11b-12a. As soon as he said "treat this kindly", then Śivayōgasiddha answered smilingly, in this manner :

12b-14a. "When He is the lord of the three worlds, is it worthwhile to own one village? No, no it is not proper" said the Siddha giver of protection.

14b-17a. Then the handsome Dēvarāja said again : "When something is given by the Lord Himself, one may refrain from accepting it. But when a king of mortal beings of this world gives something after making it *dēvaṇi*[1], with the intention of uplifting his own *ātman*, is it right to say no ?"

17b-21a. On hearing the words uttered by Dēvarasa born of sacred womb, Śivadeva brooded over the matter and arguing within (himself) that in this one sentence there is the essence of all the *āgamas*, the treasure of all the *śāstras*, accompanied by the meanings of *Vēdas* and the grandeur of *dharma* is depicted, he said :

[1] *Dēvaṇi* probably means *dēvasva* i. e. that which belongs to God.

ಆರಾಧಿಸುವಂ ನೀನೊಲಿದಾರಾಧಿಸಿಕೊಂ
ಬನೀಶ್ವರನುವೇನಾನುಮನಾರಾಧಿಸು
೨೨. ಕಯಿಕೊಂಬಂ ವಿರೇಶ್ವರನೆನ್ದು
ಸಿದ್ಧನೇಮಿಸಲೊಲವಿಂ॥

21b-22a. "You do the service and Śiva is the receiver; worship (Him) the way you like; anyway the donee will be Vīrēśvara", thus when Siddha gave the permission with love,

ಆ ದೇವರಾಜಂ॥ ಉತ್ತರ ದಕ್ಷಿಣ
ಪಶ್ಚಿಮ
೨೩. ದತ್ತುಂಗಾಸನದ ರಾಯರಾರಾ
ಧಿಸೆ ವರವಿತ್ತಂ ಶಿವದೇವರಂ ಶ್ರೀ
ಗುತ್ತಾನ್ವಯ ರಾಜ
೨೪. ಗುರುವನಾರಾಧಿಸಿದಂ ಅದೆನ್ತೆಂ-
ದಡೆ ॥

22b-24a. Śivadēva, graced the kings who have adorned the lofty thrones in the north, south and west who rendered services, Dēvarāja rendered service to the royal preceptor of the family of Gutta kings, if asked in what manner :

ಸ್ವಸ್ತಿ ಶ್ರೀಮನ್ಮಹಾಮಂಡಳೇಶ್ವರಂ
೨೫.ಉಜ್ಜಯನಿಪುರವರಾಧೀಶ್ವರಂಚಂ-
ದ್ರಗಪ್ತಾನ್ವಯಂ ಗುತ್ತಕುಳಕಮ-
ಳಮಾರ್ತ್ತಂಡ ಕದನ
೨೬.ಪ್ರಚಂಡ ಪನ್ನಿಬ್ಬರಗಣ್ಡ ಮಂ
ಡ ಳಿಕಭಯಿರವಂ ಶರಣಾಗತವಜ್ರ-
ಪಂಜರಂ ಶ್ರೀ ಸ್ಪರ್ಶಲಿಂ
೨೭. ಗ ಗಳಗನಾಥದೇವ ಶ್ರೀ ಪಾದ-
ಪದ್ಮಾರಾಧಕರಪ್ಪ ಗುತ್ತರ್ಸದೇವ ।
ಹಿರಿಯದೇವ । ಜೋಯಿ
೨೮. ದೇವಂಗಳ । ಅವರ ತಾಯ್ವ-
ರಪ್ಪ ಮೈಳಾದೇವಿಯರ ಕಯ್ಯಲು
ಧಾರೆಯ ಕೊಣ್ಡು ಗೊತ್ತೊಳಲ್ನಾ
೨೯.ಡಪ್ರಭು ಗಾವುಂಡಗಳನೊಡಂಬ-
ಡಿಸಿ

24b-29a. –be it well– (land was) taken with libation of water from the hands of Maiḷādēvi the queen mother of Jōyidēva, Hiriya dēva and Guttarasadēva, Śrīman mahāmaṇḍaḷēśvara, Lord of Ujjayinīpura, descendant of Candragupta, sun to the lotus of the Gutta family, terrible in war, lord of twelve, Bhairava to the vassals, diamond cage to those who are subservient, adorer of the lotus feet of Gaḷaganatha Sparśaliṅga, after making the Prabhugāvuṇḍa of Gottoḷalnādu (Guttavaḷalnāḍu) to agree,

ಶಕವರ್ಷ ೧೧೮೭ ರಕ್ತಾಕ್ಷಿ ಸಂವ-
ತ್ಸರದ ಪುಷ್ಯ ಬ ೧೫
೩೦. ಆದಿವಾರ ಶ್ರವಣ ನಕ್ಷತ್ರ ಬ್ಯ-
(ವ್ಯ)ತೀಪಾತಂಗೂಡಿದಅರ್ದೋ(ರ್ಧೋ
)ದಯ[1] ಪುಂಣ್ಯತಿಥಿಯಲ್ಲಿ ದೇವರ್ಸರು
೩೧.ಮಾಡಿದಾರಾಧನೆಯಕ್ರಮವೆಂತ-
[ಂದ] ಡೆ ॥

29b-31a. in the Śaka year 1187, year Raktākṣi, on the 15th day of Puṣya, on Śravaṇa naksatra, vyatīpāta at the juncture of the moon rise, most auspicious occasion, the manner in which the service was made by Dēvarasa : details of the gifts :

---

[1] In *Cauḍadānapura Monograph* the two words *puṇyatithiyalli dēvarsaru* (ಪುಂಣ್ಯತಿಥಿಯಲ್ಲಿ ದೇವರ್ಸರು) are omitted.

[1]ಗೊತ್ತೊಳಲ ಬಡಗವೊಲದಲ್ಲಿ ಯೆರೆ ಗ ೩೨. ಂಗನ ಮತ್ತುರು ೧ ಹಿರಿಯ ಕೆಱೆಯ ಕೆಳಗೆ ಗದ್ದೆ ಗಂಗನ ಕಂಬ ೧೦ ಮನೆ ೧ ತು ೩೩. ಡಿಕೆ ೧ ಹೊಂನ್ನವತ್ತಿಯ ಮೂ- ಡವೊಲದಲ್ಲಿ ಯೆರೆ ಗಂಗನ ಮತ್ತರು ೧ । ಮನೆ ೧ । ೩೪. ತುಡಿಕೆ ೧ ॥ ಯಾಲೂರ ಕೆಱೆ ಯ ಬಡಗಲೆರೆ ಗಂಗನ ಮತ್ತರು ೧। ಮನೆ ೧ ೩೫. ತುಡಿಕೆ ೧।	31b-35a. 1 *mattaru* of *yeregaṃga* in the field north of Guttoḷal; 10 *gaṃganakaṃba* of wet land abutting the main tank, one house and one *tuḍike*; one *gaṃgana mattaru* in the field east of Honnavati with one house and one *tuḍike*; one house, one *tuḍike* and one *gaṃgana mattaru* of black soil land north of Yālūr tank.
ಉಲಿಹಳ್ಳಿಯಲ್ಲಿ ವೂರ ಮೂಡ [ದೆ]- ಸೆಯಲ್ಲಿ ಕಂಬ ೫೦ ತೆಂಕ[ದೆ] ಸೆಯಲಿ ಕಂಬ ೫೦ ೩೬. ಅಂತಲ್ಲಿ ಯೆರೆಗಂಗನ ಮತ್ತರು ೧ । ಮನೆ ೧ । ತುಡಿಕೆ ॥	35b-36a. At Ulihaḷḷi to the east of the agglomeration fifty *kaṃbas* in the east and fifty *kaṃbas* in the south[2]; total : one *yeregaṃgana mattaru*, one house and one *tuḍike*.
ಹಾಹನೂರ ಪಡುವ ವೊ ೩೭. ಲನಲ್ಲ ಯೆರೆಗಂಗನ ಮತ್ತರು ೧ । ಮನೆ ೧ । ತುಡಿಕೆ ೧ ॥	36b-37a. One house and one *yeregaṃgana mattaru* in a field west of Hāhanūru (Hāvanūru).
ನಗೆಯೂರ ವೊಲ ೩೮. ನಲ್ಲಿ ಯೆರೆ ಗಂಗನ ಮತ್ತರು ೧ ಮನೆ ೧ ತುಡಿಕೆ ೧ ॥	37b-38a. One *tuḍike*, one house with one *yeregaṃganamattaru* of land at Nageyūru.
ವೇಲಗುತ್ತೂರ ಮೂಡಲ ವೊಲ ೩೯. ನಲ್ಲಿ ಯೆರೆ ಗಂಗನ ಮತ್ತರು ೧ ಮನೆ ೧ ತುಡಿಕೆ ೧ ॥	38b-39a. One *tuḍike*, one house and one *yeregaṃgana mattaru* of land in a field to the east of Valaguttūru.
ಕಂನವಳ್ಳಿಯ ಬಡಗವೊಲನಲ್ಲಿಯೆ ೪೦. ರೆ ಗಂಗನ ಮತ್ತರು ೧ ಮನೆ ೧ ತುಡಿಕೆ ೧ ॥	39b-41. At Kannavaḷḷi to the north one field of one *yeregaṃgana mattaru*, one *tuḍike*, one house.
ಅಗಡಿಯ ಬಡಗ ಹೊಲದಲ್ಲಿ ಯರೆ (ಯೆರೆ) ಗಂಗನ ೪೧. ಮತ್ತರು ೧ ತುಡಿಕೆ ೧ ಮನೆ ೧॥	40b-41a. At Agaḍi one *yeregaṃgana mattaru* in the northern field, one *tuḍike*, one house.

---

[1] In *Cauḍadānapura Monograph* from the l. 31 onwards the text is full of reading and printing mistakes. We have read it with the help of S.I.I. vol. XVIII No. 247 and the photograph of the estampage published in *Śivadēva vijaya* (ಶಿವದೇವ ವಿಜಯಂ).

[2] From this account it appears that one *yeregaṃganamattaru* is equal to a hundred *kaṃba*.

ಹಾದರಗೇರಿಯ ಪೊಲನಲ್ಲಿ ಯೆರೆ- ಗಂಗನ ೪೨. ಮತ್ತರು ೧ ಮನೆ ೧ ತುಡಿಕೆ ೧ ॥	41b-42a. one house and one *tuḍike*, one *yeregaṃgana mattaru* of a field in the quarter of Hādaragēri.
ಇಂತೀ ಹತ್ತು ಗ್ರಾಮಂಗಳಲ್ಲಿ ದೇವ- ರ್ಸರು ಶ್ರೀ ಶಿ ೪೩. ವದೇವರಿಗೆ ಸಮಾರಾಧನೆಯ ಮಾಡಿದ ಧರ್ಮ್ಮವು ಆ ಚಂದ್ರಾರ್ಕ್ಕಪ- ರ್ಯ್ಯಂತಂ ೪೪. ಸರ್ವ್ವನಮಸ್ಯವಾಗಿ ಗುತ್ತೊಳ ಲ್ನಾಡ ಪ್ರಭುಗಾವುಂಡುಗಳು ಸಲಿಸು- ವರು.	42b-44. Thus these ten tax free agglomerations were made a service to Śrī Śivadēva by Dēvarasa. And Nāḷprabhu and Gāvuṇḍas of Guttoḷalnāḍu should see that this charitable act be protected as tax free, as long as the moon and the sun endure.

Inscription No. VII

(*Cauḍadānapura Monograph* No. VII, p. 111; S.I.I. XVII No. 265. This inscription does not figure in Elliot's collection)

It is engraved on one side of the stone pillar, about 45 ft in height and set up in the compound of the temple of Muktēśa to the right of the modern entrance. The portion on which the inscription is carved is roughly 55 x 65 cms at the bottom of the pillar.

Except the first line which contains the date in Kannaḍa, the language of the inscription is Sanskrit written in Kannaḍa characters. It is dated Śaka 1210, Sarvadhāri Sam, Srāvaṇa Su. 5 sōmavāra corresponding to 1288, July 5th, Monday. After the date and the name of the king the inscription is a little worn out, says Nandimath in *Cauḍadānapura Monograph* where his reading stops after the 8th line. In S.I.I. XVIII all the 34 lines are given but after the 15th line the gaps become bigger and bigger. From a few words here and there no meaning can be derived.

The inscription records the fact that on the given date the mast was installed at Muktikśetra by Sāḷiveya Siṃhadēva. Lines 11 and 12 reveal an important fact. Muktēśvara was called Śrī Śiddhaśivadēva. That means the saint was no longer alive. He had attained liberation and was united with Muktēśvara. Therefore his name was also given to Mukteśvara. The previous inscription which is dated 1265 records a grant made to Śivadēva. Probably his demise must have occured a few years after this date but prior to the date of the present record i. e. 1288 A.D.

It is interesting to note that this Muktikṣētra is expressly mentioned as being in Kannāḍadēśa. In Orissa, during the same period a temple to Śiva was built and was called Muktēśvara. May be that is the reason why the present temple has been qualified as Kannāḍadēśa Muktēśvara.in order to distinguish one from the other

೧. ಸ್ವಸ್ತಿ ಶ್ರೀ ಸ(ಶ)ಕವತ್ಸರ ೧೨೧೦ ನೆಯ ಸರ್ವ್ವಧಾರಿ ಸಂವತ್ಸರದ ಸ್ರಾ(ಶ್ರಾ)ವಣ ಸು(ಶು)ದ್ಧ ೫ ೨. ಸೋಮವಾರದಂದು	1-2a. Be it well. On monday, 5th day of the bright fortnight of Śrāvana, in the year Sarvadhāri, Śaka 1210,

ಸ್ವಸ್ತಿ ಶ್ರೀ ರಾಮುಪ್ರತಿಜ್ಞಾ ಪರಶು-
ರಾಮ ಯಾ
೩. ದವಕುಳ(ಲ)ಕಮಳ(ಲ) ಕಳಿಕಾ
ವಿಕಾಸ ಭಾಸ್ಕರ ದ್ವಾರಾವತೀಪುರವ-
ರಾಧೀಶ್ವರ ವಿಷ್ಣು ವಂ
೪. ಸೋ(ಶೋ)ದ್ಬವ ಮಾಳವಿಯ
ಮಲ್ಲಾಹಿತರಾಯಮದಂ ಗುರ್ಜ್ಜರ-
ರಾಯ ವಾರಣಾಂಕುಸ(ಶ) । ತೆ
೫.ಲುಂಗರಾಯಸಿರಕಮಳಪೂರ್ಣಸಂ-
ದೋಹಮರ್ದನ... ಭೋಜಭೂಪಾಳವ್ಯಾ
೬.ಳವಿದ್ರಾವಣ ಲಖುಮಿದೇವಕಂಸ ...
ಇತ್ಯಾದಿ ಸಮಸ್ತ ರಾಜಾವಳೀ
೭. ವಿರಾಜಮಾನ ಶ್ರೀಮತು ಯಾದವ
ನಾರಾಯಣ ಭುಜಬಳ ಪ್ರೌಢಪ್ರತಾಪ
ಚಕ್ರ
೮. ವರ್ತ್ತಿ ಶ್ರೀ ರಾಮಚಂದ್ರ ದೇವರಾ-
ಯ ರಾಜ್ಯ ವಿಜಯೋದಯದ
ಮಹಾಪ್ರಧಾನ [ಮಸಿನಾಸ್ತಿಹ?]

2b-8a. while in the victorious dawn of the reign of the king Yādava Śrī Rāmacandra, pratāpacakravartin, king of kings, obedient (like) Rāma, like Paraśurāma in vows, sun for the blooming of the group of lotuses, the family of Yādavas, lord of Dvārātipura, progeny of Viṣṇu, suppressor of the royal intoxication of kings warriors of Māḷavas, like a goad in warding off evils of Gurjara kings, destroyer of multitude of lotuses (which are) the heads of Telugu kings, ...

೯. ... ಶ್ರಿಮಂನಾ ... ನ ಕಾಳೇ
ಪ್ರವರ್ತ್ತಮಾನೇ ಕಂನ್ನಾಡದೇಸೇ ಗು-
ತ್ತೂಳಲದೇಸೇ

9. In the region of Guttaḷa (which is) in Kannāḍadeśa ...

೧೦. ತಂ ಮಧ್ಯೇ ಗೊಪನಾಮಗ್ರಾಮೇ
ತುಂಗಭದ್ರಾಯಾಂ ತಟ...[ಮಧ್ಯೆ]
ಮುಕ್ತಿಕ್ಷೇತ್ರೆ ಶ್ರೀ ಶಿದ್ಧಸಿ(ಶಿ)ವ
೧೧. ದೇವನಾಮ್ನಿ ಮುಕ್ತೇಸ್ವರದೇವ-
ಸಂನ್ನಿಧೌ

10-11. In the town Gope on the bank of Tungabhadrā in the sacred place called Muktikṣētra, in the presence of Muktēśvara called Śrī Siddhaśivadēva.

ಶ್ರೀಮಂಮಹಾ ಮಂಡಳೇಸ್ವರ ಅಂ-
ರಾ
೧೨. ಯ ವಿಭಾಡ ಕದನ [ಪ್ರಚಂಡ]
ಸ್ಥಾಪನಾಚಾರಿಯ......ಹೊಸಣರಾಯ-
ದಿಸಾಪಟ್ಟಣ.... ನಿರಾಯರಕ್ಷಪಾಳಕ
೧೩. ಸಕಳಸೈನ್ಯಾಧಿಪತಿ ರಾಣಕ ಶ್ರೀ
ಸಳಿವಾ ಆಖ್ಯೋ ದೇವಣ್ನಯ್ಯ ಪ್ರ-
ಪೌತ್ರಾಯ ಸಿಂಹದೇವಸೈ
೧೪. ನ್ಯಾಧಿಪತಿ ಪೌತ್ರಾಯ ಬಲ್ಲಾಳ-
ದೇವಸೈಂನ್ಯಾಧಿಪತಿ ಪುತ್ರಾಯ ಶ್ರೀ
ಸಾಳಿವ ಸಿಂಮದೇವಸೈಂ

12-14. Śri (Sāḷiveya) Mahāmaṇḍaleśvara, arirāya vibhāda, terrific in battles, establisher of..., who scattered away the army of Hoyisaṇa (Hoysaḷas), commander of entire army, great grandson of Devaṇṇaya, grandson of commander of the army Siṃha Deva, son of the general Ballāḷa, the general Sāḷiva Simma ...

೧೫. ನ್ಯಾಧಿಪತಿ [ನಾಮ] ...ನಾಳಿವೆ-ಯಾಖ್ಯ ಕೀರ್ತಿಸ್ತಂಭ ಪ್ರತಿಷ್ಠಾಧರ್ಮೋ ಯಾವತು
೧೬. ಚಂದ್ರಾರ್ಕ್ಕ ಮೇದಿನೌ ತಾವತು ಸ್ತಿರೋಭೂತ್ ಮಂಗಳ ಶ್ರೀ ಶ್ರೀ

performed the *dharma* of installing the Kīrtistambha (in the precincts of Muktēśvara temple at Gope) which will remain on the earth permanently as long as the sun and the moon endure

೧೭. ನೂರ... ಯಸ್ಯೋದ್ಧ ... ನೇನ ಮಹಾ ... ಸಿತದಂ ... ಕೇಣ । ... ನಾಳಾಯಿ
೧೮. ... ನರೋರುಹ ... ಪ್ರಭಾಂ ... ಕಳಾಪ ... ಕಾಂ ...
೧೯. ತಿಕ ಕಾಂತಿ ... ಹಂಸ ... ಕಾಳ ... ಗಳಿತ ...
೨೦. ... ಮತಾ । ಅವ್ಯಾದವ್ಯಾಹತ ಜಪಂ .... ಆರತಿ ಭಾನಯಂ
೨೧. ... ಭುಕಂ ಖಟ್ವಾಂಗ ಹಸ್ತ ನರ ...ಕೃತ್ತಿಸುಳವಾಳಂ ಖಡುಗಹ-ಸ್ತಂ ...
೨೨. ಗತಂ । ವಾಮಹಸ್ತಂ ದಿನಕರ ಚಂದ್ರಾಕೃತು ಮಾಳಾದಿ ಆವೃತಂ ಸಿರಂ ಸರ್ಪಯಜ್ನೋಪ
೨೩. ವೀತಂ । ಕಳಾಕೋವಿದಕಾರಂ ಮಹಾದೇವಂ ನಮೋಸ್ತುತೆ ||೩|| ಕೃಧಾ
೨೪. ದಪಿಂ ಮೇಸ್ತಿ ಘನಮೇದಿನೀ ಮಹಿಮಾಲಿಂಗ ಮಹತಾ ಮಹೇಂದ್ರ-ಮೇರೌಮಂದರಾದ್ರೌ ಮಳ್ಯಾಯ...
೨೫.ಮಗಿಳ ನೂಮವಕ್ತ್ಯಾ ಪ । ರತ್ವಂ ದವಪಕ್ಪಪದತ್ವಂ...
೨೬. ...ಮಹಾ ಕಂತುವಾಹನ ... ಜ್ಯಾಯಾ ಪ್ರೇರಿತಭ್ರ...ಕ್ಕಾರಹಂ ||೪||
೨೭....ತತ್ವಾದಿ ಸ್ಫುರತಿ ವಸುದೇವ-ಮಂ ಪ್ರಾಣಿಪ್ರಣಿತನರಸೀಕೃತ ಪದಂ
೨೮. ಮಂ ನ್ಯಸ್ತ ವೈವ ನಿಮಿತ್ಯಾಂ ವಿಕೃತಚಕ್ಷುಖ್ಯಾತವಲ್ಲಭ: ಕಾಮಿನೌ
೨೯. ಸ್ತತೆ ನಮಲತು ಸೀಮಾಯ ... ವಿಧಾನ್ಯಾ ... ಹಾಯಾವತ್ತಾ ...

೩೦.ಭೂಧರಾಭಯಭವ:...ಚಾಮರ-
ತೋಮರಂ।ಯಾವದ್ಗ್ರಾಮ ಕರಾಮ-
ರನ
೩೧. ರಾಂ। ರಾ..ಯಣಂ ಸಮುದ್ರ-
ಭೋಗಭುವನ ... ರಾಯ ನಿತ್ಯನ ...
೩೨ ಬ್ರಹಂ । ಕೃತಬ್ರರೋತಮ
....ಚ್ರಂದ್ರಮಸ್ತ:....ಸಮುದ್ರ
೩೩.ಹರ..ಮನ...ತೃಗಂ ...ಕ್ಷೆತ್ರತುರು
ವಿಮಲ...ಮುನಯೋ ಮ್ಯೋಮರಸ್ವಿನ:
೩೪. .....ವಸುಂ ಸಿವಾಯ....ಕ್ಷ್ಮ
ಭಗವಾನ್ಪಾರ್ವ್ವತೀಸ್ವರಪತೆ .....॥೭॥

Inscription No. VIII

(*Cauḍadānapura Monograph* No. VIII, p. 112-4; S.I.I. vol. XVIII, No. 268. In Walter Elliot's collection No. 9, folio 264)

This stele is set up in the same shed as the others in the compound of Muktēśa temple. It measures 2'7" in height and 1'4" in breadth. The writing covers a space of 1'9"x1'3". At the top there is an arc of a circle of about 6" in height at the centre and 1'3" in breadth at the base. There is a Linga in its centre. To the right of the Linga is carved a cow with a sucking calf. Above them there is the figure of the moon. To the left of the Linga there is the figure of Nandin in sitting posture. Above it is carved the image of the sun.

The inscription contains 27 lines, having about 15 letters in each line. The biggest letter measures about 1'x1', and the smallest about 1/2"x1/2". The language is Kannaḍa and it is in prose. An orthographical peculiarity is that often long letters (*dīrgha*) and *śa* have been omitted.

"The ruling king was Rāmacandra of Devagiri Yādava family. The date of the inscription is the 24th year of the reign of King Devagiri Yādava Rāmacandra, Khara Saṃvatsara, the auspicious day of Pauṣya Amāvāsyā, ādivāra, Sūryagrahaṇa, the day being Ardhōdaya. By the order of the *Mahāpradhāna, Sarvādhikāri* Paraśurāmadēva, the *Sarvādhikāri* Habbarasa, Dēvarasa, Suṅkada Sitāla Heggaḍe assigned as donation perpetually i. e. as long as the sun and moon would last, the income derived from tax on the artisans, oil men, weavers, shops, load on 25 bullocks, headload etc., in the presence of 120 leading men of Gope, the southern Vāraṇāsi situated on the river Tungabhadrā flowing towards west, to the God Muktesvara, the Prāṇaliṅga (titulary deity) of Siddha Śivadēva of Gope who was the Rājaguru, the Mahāvīravrati, and the observer of 108 vows." (*Cauḍadānapura Monograph*, p. 112)

A few names occur in l. 15-16. Both, the editor of S.I.I. XVIII and Nandimath have not noticed the construction of the phrase, which ends with the verb *koṭṭanu* i. e. "gave". The form of the verb indicates that the subject is singular. That casts a doubt on the interpretation that the donation was made by several persons. Moreover, there is also uncertainty in the reading of the word *sitāḷahegaḍe* in l. 16. After *sitāḷa* one letter is missing, only the superscribed sign of the vowel *e* is seen; and the next letter is an *anusvāra* followed by *gaḍe*. So, the reading may be *sitāḷa eṃgaḍe*. Sacred water is called *sitāḷa*. Probably it refers to a shop where sacred water was sold and probably taxes were levied on this shop. It may not be wrong to conjecture that Dēvarasa, an associate of Sarvādhikāri Habbarasa was in charge of this tax collection. Moreover, the word *aṅgaḍi* occurs again in the list of taxes levied upon various organisations such as *muktanāthadēvara staḷada purasuṅka, telligaru* "oilmen", *maggadeṛe* "tax on looms", *aṃgaḍistaḷasuṃka* "local tax on shops".

One more important fact comes to our notice. The chart begins with *śrī śivadēvaprabhu śaraṇu* which is an indication that Śivadēva was no longer in this world and his *ātman* had been united with the God. That is why the inscription begins with a salutation to Śivadēvaliṅga.

The inscription is dated in the 24th year of Rāmacandra, Khara saṃvatsara, Puṣya bahuḷa amavāse, ādivāra corresponding to January 21st, 1292. Here also the grant was made at the time of *ardhōdaya* the most auspicious occasion for meritorious acts.

೧. ಶ್ರೀ ಓಂ ನಮ: । ಸಿ(ಶಿ)ವಾಯ ।
ಸ್ರೀ (ಶ್ರೀ) ಸಿ(ಶಿ)ವದೇವಪ್ರಭು
೨. ವೇ ಸ(ಶ)ರಣು ।
ಸ್ವಸ್ತಿ ಶ್ರೀಮತು ಯಾದವರಾಯ
೩.ನಾರಾಯಣಂ ಭುಜಬಳಪ್ರವುಢಪ್ರ
ತಾಪ
೪. ಚಕ್ರವರ್ತ್ತಿ ಶ್ರೀ ವೀರ ರಾಮಚಂ-
ದ್ರದೇವ ವಿಜಯರಾ
೫. ಜ್ಯೋದಯದ ೨೪ನೆಯ ಖರಸಂ-
ವತ್ಸರದ ಪು
೬. ಸ್ಯ(ಷ್ಯ) ಬಹುಳ ಅಮವ(ವಾ)ಸೆ
ಆದಿವ(ವಾ)ರ ಯ(ಅ)ರ್ಧ್ದೋದ
೭. ಯ ಸೂರ್ಯಗ್ರಹಣದಲ್ಲಿ
ಸ್ವಸ್ತಿ ಶ್ರೀಮತು ರಾ
೮. ಯರಾಜಗುರು ಮಹಾವೀರಬ್ರತಿ
ನೂಱೆಂಟು
೯. ನವಬ್ರತನಿಷ್ಟರಹ ಗೋ(ಗೊ)ಪೆಯ
ಸಿದ್ಧ ಸಿ(ಶಿ)ವದೇವರ ಪ್ರ(ಪ್ರಾ)ಣ
೧೦. ಲಿಂಗ ಮುಕ್ತೇಸ್ವ(ಶ್ವ)ರದೇವರ
ತುಂಗಭದ್ರೆ ಪಶ್ಚಿಮವಾ
೧೧. ಹಿನಿ ದಕ್ಷಿಣವಾರಣಾಸಿಯ ಗೊ-
ಪೆಯ
೧೨. ನೂಱಿಪ್ಪತ್ತಿಂಬರ ಷ(ಸ)ಂನ್ನಿಧಿ-
ಯಲ್ಲಿ ಯಿ ಮುಕ್ತನಾ
೧೩. ಥ ದೇವರಿಗೆ ।

1. Salutation to Śiva.

1-2a. Śri Śivadēvaprabhu is the refuge.

2b-5a. Be it well. In the 24th year of victorious and expanding reign of King Rāmacaṃdradēva, Nārāyaṇa amongst Yādavas, emperor, puissant by the strength of his arms,

5b-7a. on sunday, new moon day of the dark fortnight of Puṣya, in the year Khara, at the time of solar eclipse,

7b-13a –be it well–, to god Muktanātha of Gope, prāṇalinga of Siddha Śivadēva, royal preceptor, ascetic of heroic vows, observer of hundred and eight vows, on the southern bank of westward running Tuṅgabhadrā, southern Vāraṇāsi, in the presence of hundred and twenty two (persons) of Gope,

ಸ್ವಸ್ತಿ ಶ್ರೀಮನು ಮಹಾಪ್ರಧಾನಂ ಸ ೧೪. ರ್ವ್ವಾಧಿಕಾರಿ ಪರಸು(ಶು)ರಾಮ- ದೇವರ ನಿರೂಪದಿಂ	13b-14a. –be it well–, on the orders of Sarvādhikāri, the great minister, Paraśurāmadēva,
ಸ ೧೫. ರ್ವಾಧಿಕಾರಿ ಹಬ್ಬರಸದೇವರ್ಸರು ಸುಂಕದ	14b-16a. Dēvarasa, associate of Sarvādhikāri Habbarasa, tax-collector (?)
೧೬. ಸಿತಾಳಹೆಗಡೆ ಆ ಮುಕ್ತನಾಥದೇ ವರ ಪುರದ ೧೭. ಸ್ಥಳಸುಂಕ ಕಾರುಕ ತೆಲ್ಲಿಗ- ರುಂ ಮಗ್ಗ ತೆಱ ಅಂಗಡಿ ೧೮. ಮುಖ್ಯವಾಗಿ ಅಷ್ಟಭೋಗತೇಜ- ಸಾಂಮ್ಯ ೨೫ ಎ ೧೯. ತ್ತಿನ ಸುಂಕ ಮೆಯಿದೆಱ ಮೂಲೆ ಸಂಕವನು ೨೦.ಸರ್ಬ್ಬ(ರ್ವ್ವ)ಮಾನ್ಯವನು ಆಚಂದ್ರಾರ್ಕ್ಕವಾಗಿ ಸೀ ೨೧. ಮೆಯಂ ಮುದ್ರೆಸಹಿತ ಧಾರಾಪೂ ೨೨. ರ್ವ್ವಕವಾಗಿ ಕೊಟ್ಟನು || ಮಂಗಳ ಮಹಾ ಶ್ರೀ	16b-22. granted the revenues of taxes on farm, local taxes, tax paid by the oil-men, tax on looms, shops etc., all *aṣṭabhōgatējasāmya*, tax on 25 oxen, *mayidere, mūlesuṅka* etc.; with the libation of water the tax-free grant was given , to last as long as the sun and the moon, with the installation of boundary marks of the limits, with the royal seal. There be goodluck.
೨೩. ಸ್ವದತ್ತಂ(ತ್ತಾಂ) ಪರದತ್ತ- (ತ್ತಾಂ) ವಾ ಯೋ ಹರೇ ೨೪. ತಿ(ತ) ವಸುಂಧರಾ(ಂ)|| ಷಷ್ಟಿ- ರ್ವರ್ಷಸಹಶ್ರಾ(ಸ್ರಾ) ೨೫. ಣಾಂ(ಣಿ) ವಿಷ್ಟಾಯಾಂ ಜಾಯ- ತೇ ಕ್ರಿ	22b-26a. One who steals the land given by himself or by another, will be born as a worm in filth during sixty thousand years.
೨೬. ಮಿ: || ಮಂಗಳ ಮಹಾ ಶ್ರೀ ಶ್ರೀ ಶ್ರೀ	Maṅgala Mahā Śri Śri Śri
೨೭. ಶ್ರೀ ಮುಕ್ತನಾಥ ಸ(ಶ)ರಣು ||	27. Salutation to Muktanātha.

Fragmentary Records.

I. There are a few records written on the steps of the ghat leading to the river Tuṃgabhadrā. Among them one is very important because it gives a date. A person named Paruvaṇanāyaka either made repairs or built a door gate in stone and rendered services to Muktiliṅgadēva. Effectively, there is a Nandikaṭṭe in Cauḍadānapura. The name of Paruvaṇanāyaka has also been written on the central tower (*vimāna*) in Kaḍaṃbēśvara temple at Raṭṭihaḷḷi. The date corresponds to 1565. This year is very important in the history of Karnāṭaka. Note the name of the god also. The deity is called here Muktiliṅgadēva. This is practically the last dated record at Cauḍadānapura.

On the 7th step from the river.

೧. ಸ್ವಸ್ತಿ ಶ್ರೀ ಜಯಾಭ್ಯುದಯ ಶಾಲಿವಾಹನಶಕವರ್ಷ ೧೪೮೬ನೆಯ ರಕ್ತಾಕ್ಷಿ ಸಂವಛರ ಕಾರ್ತಿಕ

೨. ಪರುವಣನಾಯ್ಕನು ನಂದಿಕಟ್ಟೆಯಲ್ಲಿ ಹೊಂದಿರುಸಿಹ ಕಲವಾಗಿಲ.....

೩. ಮುಕ್ತಲಿಂಗದೇವಸೇವೆ ... ಮಾಡಿದ ।

1. svasti śrī jayābhyudaya śālivāhanaśakavarṣa 1486neya raktākṣi saṃvachara kārtika

2. paruvaṇanāykanu naṃdikaṭeyalli hoṃdisiha kalavāgila …

3. muktiyalimgadēvasēve … māḍida ।

"Be it well. In the month of Kārtika in the cyclic year Raktākṣi, Śālivāhanaśaka 1486 Paruvaṇa Nāyaka [made] a stone gate near Nandikaṭṭe … and offered services to Muktiliṅgadēva."

II. On the 10th step.

೧. ವೀರಣರಸರ ಗವಿಯೊಳಗೆ ೧೨೦ ಲಿಂಗ ।

1. Vīraṇarasara gaviyoḷage 120 liṃga ।

"One hundred and twenty liṅga in the cave of Vīraṇa."

III. On the 11th step.

೧. ಗುರುದೇವಪ್ಪರ ಕುಮಾರ ಶ್ರೀ ವೀರಣ್ಣಗಳು ।

1. gurudēvappara kumāra śrī vīraṇṇagaḷu ।

"Vīraṇṇa son of Gurudēvappa."

IV. On a separate stele.

This stele with figures of devotees and their names has been placed at the foot of the great mast "kīrtistambha". Its original place is not known.

ತಿಂಮಕ। ನರಸಪ್ಪರಸರು। ಪದ್ಮಕ। ನರಸಣ।

Tiṃmaka । narasapparasaru । padmaka । narasaṇa ।

There are a series names such as : Liṅgakka, nāgakka, nīlaka, nilika, cennaka, siddhaka, giraka, gauraka, girika, kāmaka, paruvarasanāyaka, basavaka, tiṃmaka, tikkama, jāṃnaka, mallaka, dammaka, paruvaka, viruka, nilaka, mallaka, dabaka, somakka.

Most of these names seem to be of female pilgrims.

III

Architecture

The most appropriate technical vocabulary to describe Indian architecture is the Indian one, in Sanskrit or in a regional language, because it was used by the builders of the monuments themselves. Architectural and æsthetic concepts are enshrined in this technical language. Therefore it is particularly important to have recourse to it, as a way to approach the thinking and spirit of the authors of great artistic and religious creations. In the following description we use Sanskrit terms, as long as we have full confidence in having ourselves ascertained their precise meaning and relevancy to Cāḷukyan architecture. In this attempt we experience some limitations. We do not have a scriptural source which we may declare to have been known and used directly by the builders of that time. However, the type of monuments erected by them is structurally close to the type of temples built in Tamilnāḍu in later Cōḻa period. The latter are appropriately described with the language of *Mayamata* and *Śaivasiddhānta Tantras*, such as *Ajitāgama*, etc. Thanks to this similarity we can have recourse to these texts as a source for selecting technical words appropriate to the monument under study. Later Cāḷukyan architecture has several remarkable features, which are certainly more than local variants of a consecrated style, and which are not identifiable in our sources. This is an indication that the Cālukyan artists had also sources, written or oral, slightly different from their Cōḻa contemporaries. Therefore, our attempt at a reconstruction of the technical language and thought of the Cāḷukyan artist does not cover all details of their creations, does not pretend to be more than a reconstruction and claims only to be an approach to the culture of the creative artist.

General description.

The monument itself remains the principal source of this study. We consider only the ancient remains. Recent repairs and slight modifications have been conducted on the site and have obliterated the traces of some ancient elements. In 1926, Cousens published a general plan[1] which gives us information on a few elements no more visible now. Here we will refer to his plan in several occasions and make abstraction of the recent modifications. Among these the most prominent are the compound, the shed for the inscriptions which have been displaced (their original place is shown on Cousens' plan), the levelling and paving of the courtyard which has suppressed the foundations of some structures apparent on Cousens' plan, and the platforms of the two groups of secondary shrines.

The site is on the left bank of the Tuṅgabhadrā, on the convex and elevated bank of a meander of the river, which flows from east to west at this particular point. The westward direction of the river has a strong poetical, or even religious resonance in the minds of the people, as it is a feature repeatedly emphasized in the inscriptions. The religious site covers the highest ground, looking down towards the river and the flat cultivated plain on the opposite bank. The steep slope of the bank has been built into a flight of steps on a length of 40 metres approximately. The ancient built site must have been larger than the area delimited by the modern compound. The modern village is at a distance of about 500 metres from the temple site. Villagers recently excavated the ground to the south-west of the compound and found a few ancient sculptured slabs which were re-used by them when erecting a small shrine dedicated to the Goddess Honnamma.

The main ancient elements are : (see fig. 1 opp. p. and Plate 1)

1) on the northern side, the temple of Muktēśvara (No. 1), the largest and most beautiful monument on the site; to the east, in its east-west axis a later *maṇḍapa*[2];

2) on the eastern elevation of the ground three smaller shrines (2-4);

3) on the southern elevation four shrines in one row (6-9);

4) to the south a lofty monolithic stone mast (5);

5) six inscribed steles recently installed in a modern shed (10; their original place visible on old photographs is indicated in No. 11).

---

[1] COUSENS, H., *The Chalukyan Architecture of the Kanarese Districts*, Archæological Survey of India, Calcutta, 1926.

[2] This the common designation of many kinds of open, closed or partially closed pillared halls or pavilions used as meeting places for the devotees or as shelters for movable images of the deities and for rituals requiring a large space.

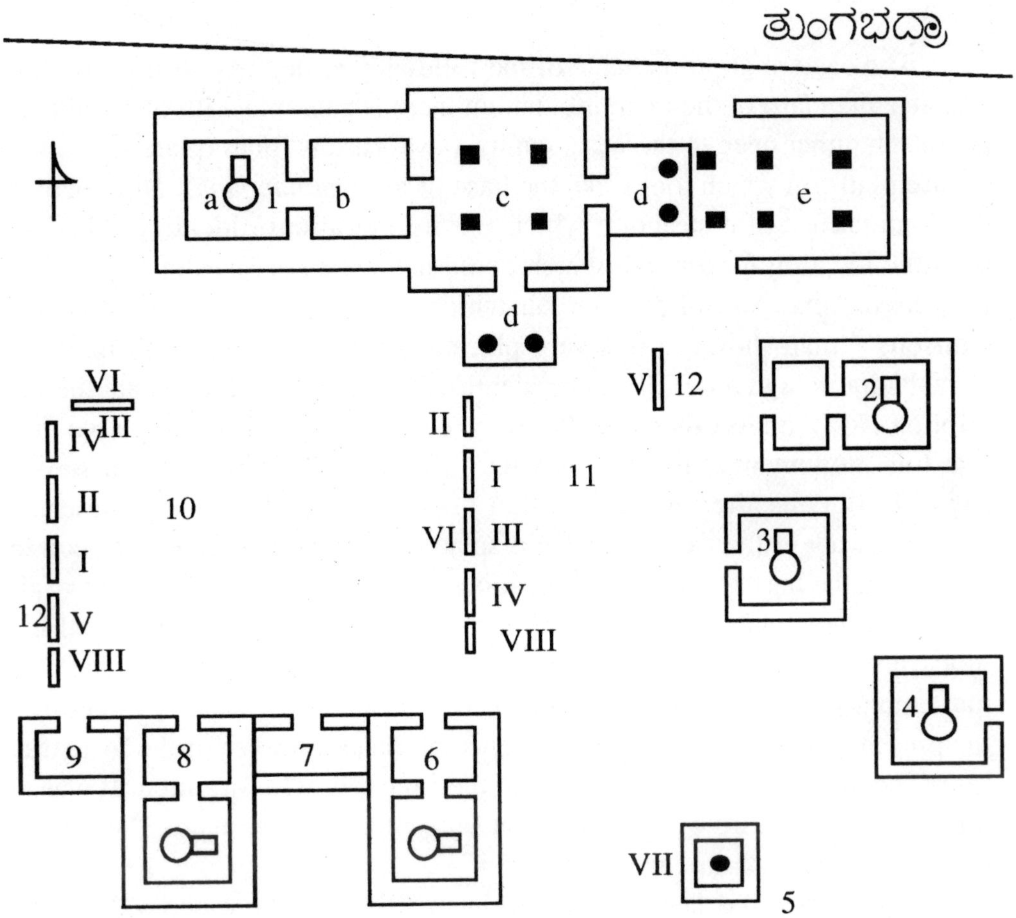

Fig. 1. A diagram of the site (not to scale)

1. Muktēśvara
2. Kallidēva
3. Liṅga
4. Liṅga
5. Kīrtistambha
6. Liṅga
7. Vīrabhadra
8. Liṅga
9. Goddess
10. Inscribed steles (new location in a modern shed; roman numbers refer to chp. II Epigraphy)
11. Inscribed steles (old location) from Cousens' plan
12. Vīrabhadra

a. garbhagṛha
b. śukanāsī
c. raṅga-maṇḍapa
d. mukhabhadra
e. maṇḍapa

A. The minor structures.

The eastern group is made of the following structures. To the south of the later *maṇḍapa* of the main monument there is a temple with one cella and an antechamber open to the west. On its axis Cousens' plan (plate I) shows a square platform which looks like the base of a *raṅgamaṇḍapa*[1], and traces of the foundations of a structure which we are not able to identify. This is a possible location for a porch which could have been erected in front of the *raṅgamaṇḍapa.* An old photograph which may be contemporaneous with Cousens'[2] plan shows in this very place a large stele bearing an image of Vīrabhadra in high relief. It can be identified as the stele which bears the inscription No. V on its other side. From the contents of the inscription we infer that this monument is the temple where Kaṃnādēvi had a Liṅga installed, called Kallinātha after the name of her defunct husband, Kal(l)idēvarasa, in 1262. Nowadays the stele has been displaced; its original place has been levelled and the traces of the old foundations have disappeared; the traces of the *raṅgamaṇḍapa* platform seen on Cousens' plan have also disappeared in a modern platform. On the west façade of the surviving building we see clear indications of the existence of an attached structure, i. e. pilasters and corbels the presence of which imply the existence of the architraves of the lost structure. The original name, Kallinātha, of the Liṅga, is also forgotten. It was already so in the time of Walter Elliot who recorded the name "temple of Gomuni" still in use among the villagers.

This shrine has kept its doorjambs and lintels. The outer walls of the cella have a double axial projection, but no other decoration. There is a tower above the cella and a projection, called *śukanāsī*[3], coming above the antechamber. The tower is made of seven low strata of gradually diminishing

---

1 This is the current designation in Karnāṭaka of the first closed *maṇḍapa* situated in the axis of the cella and antechambers. It generally has a slightly elevated platform in its centre, said to be a stage (*raṅga*) for the performance of ritualistic dance. This term is not known to Śaivasiddhānta Āgamas, but is attested in Kannaḍa inscriptions of that region (see V. Filliozat, *Le temple de Tirumaṅkaiyāḻvār à Hampi*, Pondichéry, 1976, p. 4, n. 1, p. 32).

2 Published in *Śivadeva Vijayaṃ*, Bangalore, 1949.

3 This is the designation current in Karnāṭaka of the antechamber adjacent to the cella. In *Śilpaśāstra* literature it is generally the name of a projection of the tower of a *vimāna*, visible on the terrace and covering the antechamber. In Karnāṭaka the name is extended to the antechamber covered by that type of projection. The name applied to the antechamber is attested in Kannaḍa inscriptions of the region (see V. Filliozat, *ibidem*).

size, with a small dome. The *śukanāsī* has six strata. Each strata has indentations in a regular spacing. We interpret this feature as a schematic representation of an eave with its attic windows and with turned up points at the angles. The small dome of square plan rests upon a flat moulding with a *padma*[1] moulding between two recesses. It has a double axial projection on each face. Its graceful curve turns up at the base with upward points at the angles. The crowning motif is a *padma* moulding of square plan supporting a double circular base for a bulb shaped moulding and a pointed flower bud. The *śukanāsī* is covered with a flat roof. Its west side is closed with a gable-end motif.

To the south of this structure, a shrine consisting of only one cella open to the west, the outward wall of which has no projection, nor any decoration, is what remains of a small temple. There is no visible trace of any other structure attached to it. There is no superstructure. On an old photograph[2] a post is seen in front of that shrine. It is a short post in stone, approximately 1.5 m high, with a lotus bud at the top, and on one side two mortices, at the bottom and towards the top.

To the south-east, there is a third structure consisting of only one cella of slightly larger size, open to the east. Only the inward facing of the wall remains. The outward facing, as well as the door frame, had already disappeared when Cousens drew his plan.

The southern group comprises four shrines. Cousens' plan shows two parallel temples, with cella and antechamber, open to the north-west. At the level of their antechamber they are connected by one single rectangular cella, open to the same direction. To the west extremity of the row there is one more single cella of equal size. Only the inward facings of the walls remain. The three first shrines have preserved their doorframe. The whole has been modified by recent renovations.

The monolithic mast has a double base. From bottom to top its section is successively square, octogonal, sixteen edged. It is topped by a large square abacus. On an old photograph[3] one sees three small pillarets on the

---

[1] As indicated by the common meaning of the word *padma*, i. e. 'lotus', this is the technical name of a moulding having the shape of a flower petal with two, convex and concave, curves, the centres of the curves being approximately on a same horizontal line.

[2] Published in *Śivadeva Vijayaṃ*, Bangalore, 1949.

[3] *Ibidem.*

abacus; this is what remains of the ancient superstructure. The mast bears a Sanskrit inscription recording its foundation and where it is called *kīrtis-tambha* "pillar of fame".

Cousens' plan also shows the original place of four huge inscribed steles, and in dotted lines the place of an excavated pit with steps, which is still existing, but may have been modified during the renovations.

B. The main monument.

This is a structure (Plate 2) comprising one cella (*garbhagṛha*[1]), one antechamber (*śukanāsī*) and a closed hypostyle hall (*raṅgamaṇḍapa*), all placed on the same east-west axis. All of them are open to the east. The *raṅgamaṇḍapa* has a second opening to the south, and a porch for each opening.

To the east one more *maṇḍapa* with four central pillars, of slightly larger size, has been added in later times. It has, in fact, no structural connection with the main monument. It is slightly out of its axis. It is closed on its south and north sides. Only the internal facings of these walls remain.

The main structure is a remarkably well-built monument. It is clearly the product of one well-thought architectural project. Though an inscription mentions a renovation made in the 13th century, in the construction, as we see it now, we do not observe any recast of an initial project, nor any later modification or important repair. The renovation may have been such an important reconstruction, that no earlier parts, nor any trace of an older stage have been left visible.

The theological concept.

It shelters a liṅga called Muktēśvara "Lord of the Released (Souls)". This dedication explains the general concept of the monument, which is a mere reflection of a theological concept. The deity is conceived as an abstract entity, which has numerous external manifestations. There are several degrees of manifestation of the supreme. The idea of manifestation is expressed in Sanskrit by the root *añju* and the preverb *vi* which indicates the idea of separation. The supreme Śiva is *a-vyakta* "non-manifested". It differentiates itself

---

1 The *garbhagṛha* is the closed cella where the main and unmovable object of worship (*mūla-vigraha*) is installed and consecrated. It is generally of small size and in south India only the officiating priest is allowed to enter it to conduct the service of the deity.

in a new entity called *vyakta-a-vyakta* "manifested and non-manifested", then in a third one called *vyakta* "manifested" fully. By "manifested" is understood the quality of being accessible to the senses. Manifestation is achieved by the Supreme God himself through parts (*kalā*) of its power (*śakti*). Therefore the supreme is also called niṣkala "without [manifesting] part [of power]". The second entity is *sakala-niṣkala*, the third *sakala*. Each entity has a name : the supreme is Śiva, the second Sadāśiva, the third Mahēśa. Śiva is one, the other two have subdivisions : Sadāśiva five, Mahēśa twenty-five. This is clearly stated in Śaivāgamas such as *Vātulaśuddha* :

शिवतत्त्वं महासेन निष्कलं त्विति कीर्तितम् । सकलो निष्कलश्चैव सदाशिव इहोच्यते ॥
महेशं सकलं विद्यात् त्रिविधास्ते भवन्ति वै । शिवमेकं विजानीयात् सादाख्यं पञ्चधा भवेत् ॥
महेशस्तु महासेन पञ्चविंशतिभेदकः ।

śivatattvaṃ mahāsēna niṣkalaṃ tv iti kīrtitam ।
sakalo niṣkalaś caiva sadāśiva ihocyate ॥
maheśaṃ sakalaṃ vidyāt trividhās te bhavanti vai ।
śivam ekaṃ vijānīyāt sādākhyaṃ pañcadhā bhavet ॥
maheśas tu mahāsena pañcaviṃśatibhedakaḥ ।

"The essence Śiva is well-kown as *niṣkala*, o Mahāsēna. In this [scripture] Sadāśiva is told to be *niṣkala* and *sakala*. One should know Mahēśa as *sakala*. Thus there are three aspects. One should know Śiva as one. Sadāśiva should be of five aspects. Mahēśa, o Mahāsena, has twenty-five divisions."[1]

The supreme Śiva is not the subject of any representation in the temple, because of its unmanifested nature. It is dealt with in rituals only through a *mantra*, called *mūla-mantra* "the root-*mantra*".

Sadāśiva appears in the temple in the form of the liṅga, which can be told to be manifested, since it is a visible object, and also non-manifested, since it is a purely geometrical shape, not revealing any particular aspect of the manifest God. The aspect which remains non-manifested in the Liṅga is properly called Sadāśiva or Sādākhya. There are five Sādākhyas or five heads which remain in the imagination of the worshipper. In rituals the visible *liṅga* is not the real object of worship. It is a support on which the worshipper superimposes the five heads by means of mental representation (*dhyāna*). The heads are not manifested. They remain in the mind of the worshipper. They are introduced in the rituals through *mantras* called *brahma-mantras*. This

---

[1] *Vātulaśuddhāgama* (with Kannaḍa translation), ed. by H. P. Malledevaru, Oriental Research Institute, Mysore, 1988, I.18-20a, p. 9-10.

concept is very important, for it is the very basis of the religious activity which integrates mental representations in pure ritualistic actions. It answers perfectly to the religious need of integration of mental and material actions.

ध्यानपूजानिमित्ताय सकलं निष्कलं भवेत् । तद्रूपं हि महासेन सादाख्यमिति कीर्तितम् ॥

dhyānapūjānimittāya sakalaṃ niṣkalaṃ bhavet ।
tad rūpaṃ hi sādākhyam iti kīrtitam ॥

"He should be *sakala* and *niṣkala* for the purpose of meditation and worship; this form is well-known as Sādākhya."[1]

The third Śaiva entity, Mahēśa, is the fully manifested form, with characteristic features and actions, detailed descriptions of which are given in mythological accounts of *Āgama*s and *Purāṇa*s. In general the diverse myths about Śiva depict him with the attributes of a king, with a benevolent attitude to submissive and loving subjects or with violent actions against enemies. Śiva is the Lord of the universe, chastising powerfully the evil forces and giving grace to devotees. He has a palace on a mountain, Kailāsa, and a court of other submissive gods, celestial beings, saints, sages, yogins, etc.

महेशं सकलं विद्यात् सृष्टिस्थितिलयावहम् ॥ पञ्चविंशतिभेदैस्तु तन्मूर्तिर्विविधा भवेत् । ...

mahēśaṃ sakalaṃ vidyāt sr̥ṣṭisthitilayāvaham ॥
pañcaviṃśatibhedais tu tanmūrtir vividhā bhavet । ...

"One sould know Mahēśa as *sakala*, conducting creation, maintenance and destruction [of the world]. This bodily form should be diverse through twenty-five varieties..."[2]

The inscriptions which contain a number of references to the liṅga called Muktēśvara and express the feelings and thoughts of the worshippers, in the form of refined literary eulogies of the god, reveal a noteworthy evolution in their attitude and conceptions. The two first inscriptions describe mostly the mythological aspect of Śiva. The following ones keep the same theme and introduce new concepts. In ins. III the foundation of a temple is told to be the bringing of Kailāsa on the earth (l. 33) :

ಹವಣಿಸಲಱಿಯದೆನಿಸುವ ಶಿವಕೈಲಾಸವನಖಿಳ ದೇವತಾಪದಸಹಿತಂ ಭುವನಕ್ಕೆ ತಂದು ಶಿವಸುಖಭವನವನೊಲಿದು ಶಿವಸುಖಭವನದ ನೆವದಿನ್ದ ರಚಿಸಿದಂ ಶಿವದೇವನು ॥

---

[1] *Ibidem* I.31, p. 14.
[2] *Ibidem* I.124b-125a, p. 48-9.

havaṇisalaṟiyadenisuva śivakaviḷāsavanakhiḷadēvatāsahitī bhuvanakke taṃdu śivasukhabhavanavanolidu śivasukhabhavanada nevadinda racisidaṃ śiva-dēvanu ॥

"Śivadēva having brought the Kailāsa, said to be beyond imagination, with the army of all gods, to the earth, had a pleasant abode built to Śiva, to produce Śiva's pleasure."

Similarly the temple of Śiva is declared to be a Mēru, Muktikṣētra being a Kailāsa (III l. 23-24).

The same ins. III introduces a new religious figure, Śivadēva. With him comes a new concept of the deity, which includes the mythological representation, but does not give to it the same emphasis. The emphasis is put on devotion. A larger place is given to the view of the worshipper. Śivadēva is told to be an incarnation of Nandin or Amara-Gaṇa, i. e. a courtier of Śiva in Kailāsa. He did a cult mostly in the form of heroic vows described in Ins. III. In fact he belongs to the class of saints and yogins practicing meditation and pursuing mystic experiences. He is turned more towards the unmanifested aspects of God. His attachment to the manifested aspect appears in his vow not to move out of Muktikṣētra. Maybe that was due to his belief in the sanctity of this place. His belief in the sacredness of Śrīśailam in Āndhra, where he resided before his coming to Muktikṣētra in 1225, is also recorded (III l. 15b-16a). The attachment to the Liṅgas of these two particular temples seems to be the main link maintained by him with the manifested.

The attitude of the worshipper who directs his mental representation towards a concrete object, who places the unmanifest on the manifest is directly expressed in III l. 16b-17a) :

ಅಭ್ಯ(ವ್ಯ)ಕ್ತಶಂಕರನನತಿಸುಭ್ಯ(ವ್ಯ)ಕ್ತಂ ಮಾಡಿತೋರ್ಪೆನೆನುತೀ ಜಗದೊಳ್ ।
ದಿಬ್ಯಧವಳೇಶಲಿಂಗನಬ್ಯಯ ಶಿವಮುದ್ದುಮುನಿ ವರಂ ಭಾವಿಸುವನು ॥

abhya(vya)ktaśaṃkarananatisubhya(vya)ktaṃ māḍitōrpenenutī jagadoḷ ।
divyadhavaḷēśaliṃganabyaya śivamuddumuni varaṃ bhāvisuvanu ॥

"Śivamuddudēva who says : "I shall show to this world that the invisible Śiva is manifested here in Dhavaḷaliṅga" believes in it firmly."

Later the emphasis is placed more on the practice of meditation, than on ritual practices. It goes upto the point to declare that the the mental representation creates the concrete form. In ins. No. V stanza 7 which describes the sage Śivadēva meditating on the Śivaliṅgatattva and causing it to take form :

ನೆನೆನೆನೆದು ಮೂರ್ತಿಗೊಳಿಸುವ ಘನತರ ಶಿವಲಿಂಗತತ್ವಮಾ ಶಿವದೇವನು

nene-nenedu mūrtigoḷisuva ghanatara śivaliṃgatatvam ā śivadēvanu
"This Śivadēva who caused the very rich essence Śivaliṅga to take form by meditating intensely over it".

The essence called Śivaliṅga is in Vīraśaiva doctrine the supreme entity, not accessible to the senses. The qualification *ghanatara* is often given to the supreme principle to indicate the plenitude of its essence (compare with the epithet *cidghana* "full of consciousness"). Śivadēva practices meditation over the supreme. The intensity of his meditation gives a concrete form to the abstract entity. By the force of meditation the yogin gets a direct perception. Thus the non-manifest and the manifest are linked by the religious practice.

The identification of the concrete liṅga with the abstract concept of God is also remarkably illustrated in ins. VIII l. 9-10 :

ಸಿದ್ಧ ಸಿ(ಶಿ)ವದೇವರ ಪ್ರ(ಪ್ರಾ)ಣಲಿಂಗ ಮುಕ್ತೇಸ್ವ(ಶ್ವ)ರದೇವಂ
siddha si(śi)vadēvara pra(prā)ṇaliṃga muktēsva(śva)radēvaṃ
"the god Muktēśvara who is the Liṅga-soul of the siddha Śivadēva."

Śivadēva is a siddha, i. e. one who has acquired supernatural powers by yōga, who has attained liberation in the form of union with the supreme Śiva. In Vīraśaiva vocabulary he has become the principle of Śiva Liṅga. His soul or livening power called *prāṇa* is a Liṅga, one with the supreme. The demise of the saint took place in Muktikṣētra. This is his *samādhi* or fusion with Liṅga. From that time the soul of the saint equated with God is placed on the Liṅga in the temple. The soul of the saint fused with God is the unmanifest placed in the manifest by the event of the demise and liberation of the saint. In ins. VII l. 10-11 the name of the saint is transferred to the *liṅga* :

ಶ್ರೀ ಶಿದ್ಧಸಿ(ಶಿ)ವದೇವನಾಮ್ನಿ ಮುಕ್ತೇಸ್ವರದೇವಸಂನ್ನಿಧೌ
śrī śi(si)ddha si(śi)vadēvanāmni muktēśvaradēvasaṃnidhau
"In the presence of the god Muktēśvara who has the name Śrī Siddha Śivadēva".

One more fact about the Liṅga Muktēśvara deserves to be recorded. Today the villagers declare that the deity of their temple is Muktēśvara in the form of an *udbhava liṅga.* This is the common designation in Kannaḍa of a liṅga which is believed to have come out spontaneously, by itself, in a particular place. The installation is not ascribed to men, but to the god himself, who is considered as having come to the earth in a particular place by his own will. In Sanskrit this type of temple image is called *svayaṃbhū-liṅga*. Nīlakaṇtha Śivācārya defines it in his *Kriyāsāra* :

देवर्षितपसा तुष्टः सांनिध्यार्थं तु तत्तु वै ॥
पृथिव्यन्तर्गतः शम्भुर्बीजं वै नादरूपतः । स्थावराङ्कुरवद्भूमिमुद्भिद्य व्यक्त एव सः ॥
स्वयं भूतं जातमिति स्वयम्भूरिति तं विदुः । तल्लिङ्गपूजया ज्ञानं स्वयमेव प्रवर्धते ॥

dēvarṣitapasā tuṣṭaḥ sāṃnidhyārthaṃ tu tat tu vai ॥
pṛthivyantargataḥ śambhur bījaṃ vai nādarūpataḥ ।
sthāvarāṅkuravad bhūmim udbhidya vyakta eva saḥ ॥
svayaṃ bhūtaṃ jātam iti svayambhūr iti taṃ viduḥ ।
talliṅgapūjayā jñānaṃ svayam eva pravardhate ॥

"Satisfied with the penance of gods and sages, in order to make himself present, Śambhu who is inside the earth as a seed in the form of *nāda*, like an immobile germ, breaks the ground and becomes manifest. Because he is *bhūta* i. e. born from himself, he is known as *svayambhū* "self-born". By the worship of this *liṅga*, knowledge grows by itself."[1]

The denomination of *svayambhū* or *udbhava* does not occur in the inscriptions, nor is it told in any of them that the *liṅga* was installed by any historical figure. References are to the construction of temples, not to the creation of a *liṅga*. However two passages give clear indications that the belief in the spontaneous presence of Śiva in Muktikṣētra was current in the times of Śivadēva. In ins. IV a myth of the descent of Śiva in Muktikṣētra is narrated with the words (l. 16b-18a) :

ಅಲ್ಲಿದ್ದು ಮೂಱು ಲೋಕದರೆಲ್ಲರ ಪಾವನವ ಮಾಳ್ಪೆನೆನುತಗಜಾತಾವಲ್ಲ-
ಭನವತರಿಸಿದ ಭೂವಲ್ಲಭೆಗನುರಾಗಮಪ್ಪಿನಂ ಮುಕ್ತೀಶನು ||೬||
ಲಿಂಗವತರಿಸಿತಾ ...

alliddu mūṟu lōkadarellara pāvanava māḷpenenutagajātāvallabhanavatarisida bhūvallabheganurāgamappinaṃ muktīśanu ॥ 6 ॥ liṃgavatarisitā ...

"Staying there I shall purify all in the three worlds" saying thus the beloved of mountain's daughter appeared as Muktīśa and aroused love in the Lord of the Earth. "Liṅga has already appeared on the Earth..."[2]

Therefore nothing goes against the local oral tradition which we record nowadays. And we may consider that Muktēśvara has been regarded as being a *svayambhū-liṅga* in the past also.

---

1 Nīlakaṇṭha Śivācārya, *Kriyāsāra*, vol. I, Oriental Research Institute, Mysore, 1954, III.347b-349, p. 159.

2 See also Ins. V l. 9b-11a.

The architectural concept.

This elaborate theological concept is well reflected in the architectural concept which comprises a general volume sheltering the *liṅga* and numerous secondary structures dedicated to the outward manifestations. The former is the *garbhagṛha*, the secluded cella, innermost centre of the monument. The latter have the form of the main temple in reduced size and are surperimposed on its external face (see Plate 4, III.1, IV.2, VII.1-3).

The monument as a whole, with its tower in pyramidal form can be taken as the representation of the Kailāsa montain. The interior and central cella sheltering the Liṅga is the private residence of the god-king in his palace. The court of that king is provided with architectural spaces, which are the miniature images of temples. The relation of manifested-cum-non-manifested with the fully manifested is transcribed in the architecture by the disposition which gives a secluded and hidden shelter to the Liṅga, and outward, fully exposed places to the manifested images.

The reduced representations of temples are frequently treated as decorative architectural motifs by historians of art. But they can also be understood as being something more than a decoration. They have a close connection with the main structure, and must have a theological dedication, as well as the main structure. The dedication of some of them to the external manifestations of the deity is shown through images of several *mūrti*s placed on their prominent face or even inside them in the case of niches.

In Cauḍadānapura most of the *mūrti*s were carved on steles placed in niches or fixed in different places. Unfortunately the temple has been plundered and deprived of most of its sculptures. Traces of mortices on the capitals of thin pilasters, under the eave etc. show the original places of those steles (Plate II.1-2); more than 100 can be seen, and that shows to which extent the monument was rich in sculptures and has been plundered. Only those which were carved in low-relief on non easily removable stones of the monument have remained *in situ.* Therefore, we can identify only a few dedications of the numerous secondary structures, and reconstruct only a very fragmentary iconographic scheme for this very elaborated architectural system. The images which have survived are those of Bhairava, terrifying form of Śiva, also the guardian of the temple compound, of Mahēśvara, manifestation of the supreme Śiva as a serene sovereign over the universe, of Pārvatī, the consort of Mahēśvara and a representation of supreme Śiva's *śakti* or power, of Vīrabhadra, a creation of the anger of the powerful god, chastiser of the wicked, who destroyed a sacrifice conducted by Dakṣa in defiance of his superiority over the other deities, of dancing Pārvatī, of several yogins and devotees, dancers and musicians as found in a human royal court or as described in Kailāsa, etc. On the Eastern side, topping the entrance and *śukanāsī* there is an image of Sūrya, the Sun God who is associated with Śiva because the worship of Śiva starts with a worship of the Sun.

The following diagram shows the location of the surviving images :

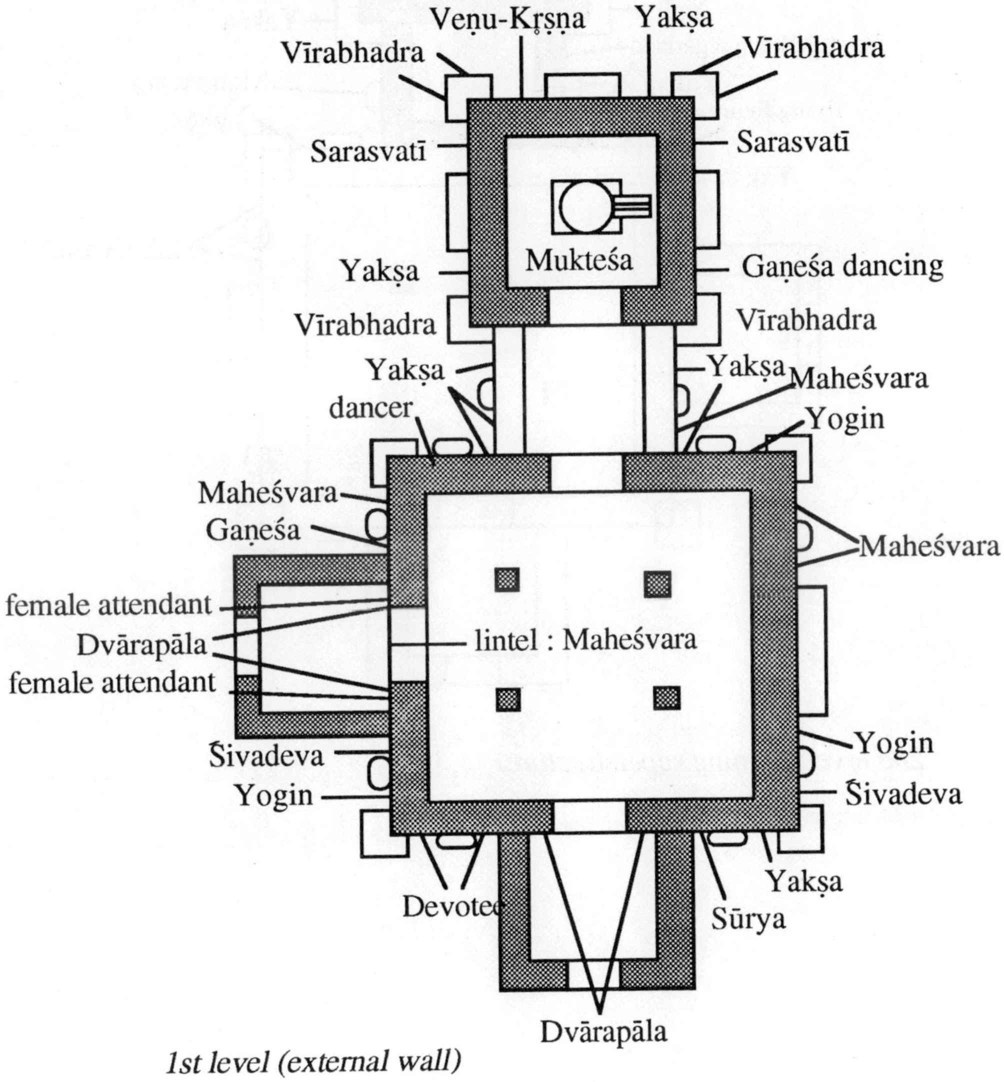

1st level (external wall)

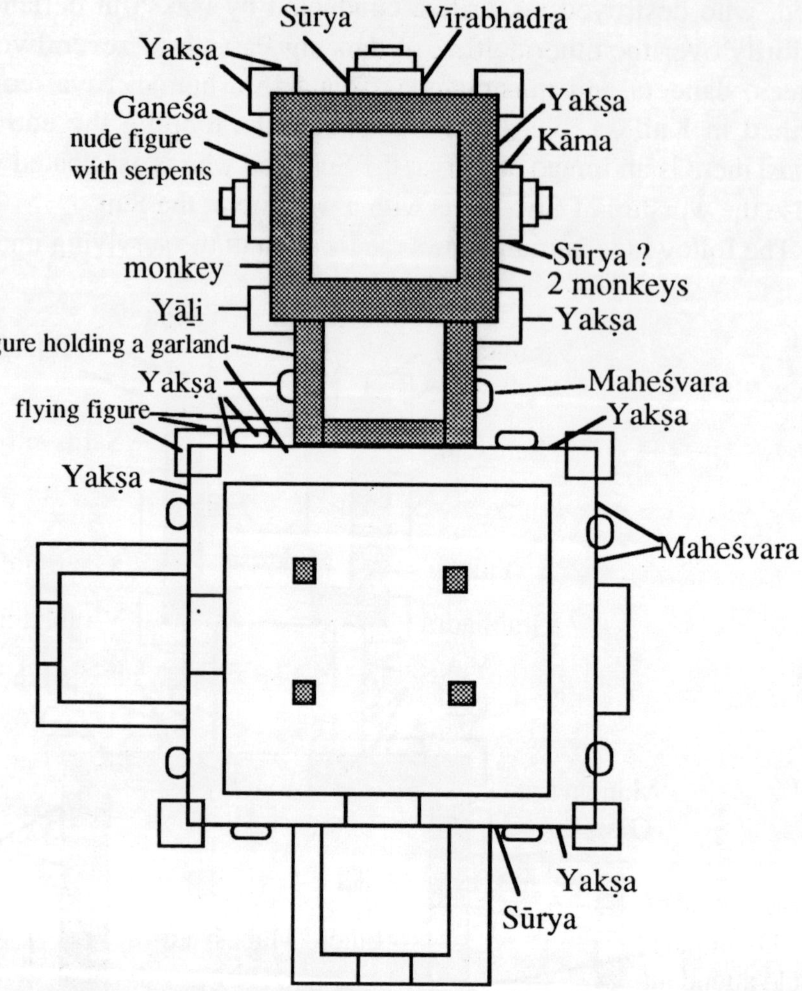

2nd level (running superstructure)

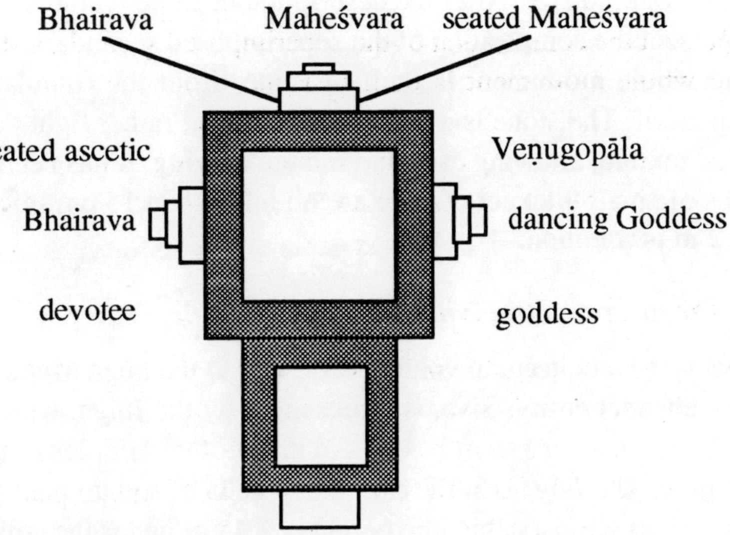

3rd level (Ist level of the tower)

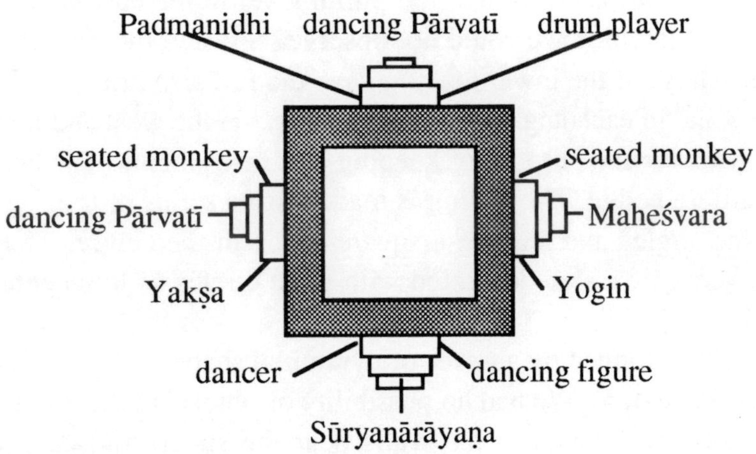

4th level (2nd level of the tower)

We will first describe the architectural features of the main volume, i.e. the structure sheltering the *liṅga*, without considering the secondary superimposed structures. These in fact bear exactly the same features and are made of the same architectural elements, as they are reproductions of the main structure in reduced size. After the description of these features and elements we will present the composition of the superimposed secondary structures.

The whole monument is built in stone, from the foundations to the crowning motif. The stone is a variety of schist, of rather light density (2.8), and of fine texture, allowing easy and minute carving. It has been quarried in long slabs of small thickness (some are no more than 15 cm thick); a length of about 2 m is common.

1) The main structure (vimāna).

This is the architectural volume dedicated to the liṅga Muktēśvara (Plate 2, 5). The abstract entity, Śiva, is represented by the *liṅga*, which is here of small size and on a very short base, as in many other temples of the same region and time. The *liṅga* is at the centre of a cella of square plan (2.20 x 2.20 m). This cella is almost cubic, the height is 2.45 m under the ceiling, 2.20 m under the architraves. It is called *garbhagṛha* as it is the innermost part of the monument. It has only one opening, a door on the eastern side. The walls of considerable thickness (1.50 m at the plinth level in the east-west axis) are made of a filling, which we could not observe, between two facings of long stone slabs. Those of the inward facing have the full size of the wall on each side of the cella. In each angle there is a pilaster. On the west and north walls there is a cyma for the purpose of keeping cult instruments. The architraves have a chamfered edge. The ceiling is made of two series of triangular slabs placed in the angles and leaving a square space in the centre. That square space is covered by a slab decorated with three circles of lotus petals and a flower bud.

The cella is topped by a tower of pyramidal shape with two steps and a small dome (Plate 4, 5). We had no possibility of observing the interior of it.

The outward facings of the walls bear the superimposed secondary structures, which will be described later. In the recesses between them parts of what may be considered as belonging to the main structure, are seen. The elements which it is made of are the same as those of the secondary shrines, so that there is agreement and continuity of both structures. For the cella they are a double base, a wall with pilasters, an eave; for each step of the tower there is a wall with pilasters and an eave. The dome of square plan rests upon a base and a recess. Its outward shape is that of lotus petals curved downwards and with turned up points at the base. It has three axial projections on each side. The last is the architectural motif of a square gable-end of a roof; it is now a flat stone; it may have been the support for a sculptured stele. There is one more crowning motif : three rows of lotus petals and a lotus bud on a double base.

The whole, cella and tower, bears the name of *vimāna* or *prāsāda.* These two terms are used for the dwellings of gods or kings, or more technically refer to buildings having a superstructure. The word *vimāna* is sometimes used in reference to the superstructure alone (*Mayamata* XVIII 195) and this use which seems to be rare in ancient times, seems to become more current in modern times.

Thus the facings of the walls are of a totally different nature. The inward facing is made of seemingly thin stone slabs placed on edges and devoid of decoration; it is a pure stone architecture. The outward facing is made of thicker stone slabs bearing a sculptured representation of wooden architectural models. The ground level is the same for the cella and the courtyard outside, so that the two facings have the same height.

a) The base (*upapīṭha*). (Plate 5, IV.4-5)

We have not been able to observe the foundations. The last layer, the top of which is apparent at the level of the paving of the courtyard, is made of long stone slabs. That may be understood as the component called *upānah* in *Śilpaśāstra.* It is the basic layer, the strength and horizontality of which ensures the tightness of the construction. The plinth is a few centimetres in recess. Following the most common prescriptions of *Śilpaśāstra* the base is to be considered as made of two parts, lower and upper, called *upapīṭha* and *adhiṣṭhāna.* The former comprises three major protruding mouldings : a flat plinth (*jagatī* or *pāduka*) repeated in slight recess and topped by a lotiform moulding (*padma*), a chamfered band (*kumuda*), a terminal moulding (*kapota*) in the shape of an eave, i. e. a sloping roof with jutting out attic windows called *nāsikā* or *nīḍa.* In between these three mouldings there are two deep recesses (*kaṇṭha*). A finer square moulding, which may be called *kampa,* together with small *padmas* provide graceful transitions between them. There are deep hollow joints at the base and between the plinths. This series of mouldings forms a unit, as shown by the *upānah* which is a lower element and by the *kapota* which is an upper and terminal element. That is why it bears the distinctive name : *upapīṭha.* It is the proper base of the building.

All the three major mouldings bear a refined decoration sculptured in very low relief : a creeper motif on the first plinth, a frieze of *haṃsa* on the second one, a geometrical jewellery motif on the outward edge of the *kumuda*, a series of *nāsikā*, symmetrically disposed, with the lion-head motif on the *kapota* (Plate IV.4-5).

b) The wall (*pāda*).

The upper part of the base, or *adhiṣṭhāna*, is a base for the pillars of the wall. Therefore it may be considered more properly as a part of the wall itself. It consists of two protruding mouldings separated by low recesses (Plate IV.5). The first moulding above the *kapota* of the *upapīṭha* is an original feature, which is proper to this type of temple in Karnāṭaka; it is the representation of a series of extremities of beams with connecting bands. Their number and disposition depend upon the representations of secondary structures and will be described later with them (p. 115). The last moulding is a square band supported by a large inverted *padma*. It may be called *prati* which in *Śilpaśāstra* is a common designation of the uppermost moulding of the *adhiṣṭhāna*. It supports directly the pilasters and is not cut by any of the niches.

All the protruding mouldings of both parts of the base are at the vertical of the duplicate plinth. That produces an impression of unity for the whole base. In spite of this we have to consider that there are two parts for this base. The *kapota* is a moulding which indicates the top part of an architectural structure and it is often a terminal moulding of what is called *upapīṭha*. Its presence indicates the composition of the base in the two succesive traditional elements, *upapīṭha* and *adhiṣṭhāna* (see *Mayamata* XIII, 1). In a few other temples of the same region and period, one sometimes sees the same series of mouldings, but with a slightly recessing position for the two upper ones; that makes more visible the difference between the two parts (see the elevation of a jaina temple in Lakkundi, of the temple of Mahādeva at Ittagi, Cousens pl. LXIII, CII).

This *adhiṣṭhāna* can be understood as the direct support of the pillars in a wooden construction. The crossed and radiating beams, the extremities of which are seen in the lower moulding, could be the representation of a tight wooden base for a superstructure. This feature can be seen in modern wooden temple cars (Plate III.4). The second band or *prati* can be a representation of a connecting beam passing through the pillars. Because it is continuous, it ensures the fixation of the pillars and the tightness of the building.

The wall (*pāda*) shows a series of small pilasters (*kuḍyastambha*) carved in the body of the massive stones (Plate 4, III.1-3, V.1-2). This is a representation of thin wooden pillars of an hypostyle pavillion, the space between the pillars being filled with some material. The other structures carved between the pilasters are secondary structures which will be described below. The represented pillar (Plate IV.1-2) consists of a base, a shaft of square section and an upper part made of three elements, a bulb slightly protruding, a chamfered band and a large abacus, with thin transition mouldings. The middle element and the upper one are much larger than the shaft. They are the most conspicuous elements and may be the *kalaśa* and *maṇḍi* (or *phalaka*) of *Śilpaśāstra*.

Between the abacus of the pilaster and the first architrave there seems to be an intermediary system of corbels (Plate IV.2). We call corbel the protruding element (*potikā* or *bodhikā*) which supports an architrave (*uttara*) and which is the usual intermediary between a pillar and any superstructure in Indian wooden or stone architecture. The corbel does not rest directly on the abacus. In the space between them appears a square element which has the breadth of the body of the pillar. That may be a representation of the square tenon engaged in the abacus and the corbel, visible in the space between them, and which is of square section to prevent the abacus and corbel to turn. In *Śilpaśāstra* it is called *vīrakaṇṭha* (or *vīrakaṇḍa*) and is given as the terminal part of the pillar below the *potikā*. In the angles of the monument, where orthogonal architraves are crossed, there is a system of crossed orthogonal corbels.

c) The entablature and eave (*prastara*).

The entablature is the representation of two superposed architraves (*uttara*). Where there is a representation of an angle, orthogonal architraves are crossed and their crossed extremities are shown. These extremities appear above the corbels, so that we see a series of three corbelling elements above the pilasters. Such a superposition of corbels and architraves is a feature of wooden architecture which can be still observed in recently built houses in North Karnataka.

The pair of architraves bears a long, non-curved eave. The angles have a turned up point. Occasionally there are attic windows called *nāsikās*. The eave is topped by one more protruding moulding, which is a *kapota* after a small recess. It has the shape of a shorter eave with *nāsikās*. This is not a duplication of the previous eave. The role of the *kapota* is to mark the termination of an architectural element. Here it indicates the termination of the first level of the building. It has also a functional role. The very long eave rests on the architraves in cantilever position and a strong counterweight must be placed above in order to prevent it to topple down.

Architraves, eave and *kapota* are given in Śilpaśāstra as one unit called *prastara.*

d) The superstructure.

The *prastara* described so far supports, not one superstructure, but a frieze of figured superstructures of reduced sizes (Plate 4, III.1, VII.2-3).

Each one comprises an *adhiṣṭhāna* similar to that of the wall, i. e. the moulding made of beam extremities and the upper band (*prati*), then, after a small recess, a dome-shaped roof (*śikhara*). Because of the division and composition of the façade into multiple representations of secondary structures, the frieze is made of several types of *śikharas*. Those which are placed in the angles are of square plan and called *karṇakūṭa.* Those which are in the axis are of oblong plan and called *madhyakoṣṭha* (or *bhadraśālā*). Those which are in the intermediary left spaces are square, are still more reduced in size and called *pañjara.*

With this frieze of *śikharas* we can consider that the first level (*tala*) of the monument is completed. It is topped by two more levels, the structure of which is quite similar to the first one. These two upper levels are of diminishing size and less elaborate than the first one. Because of their reduced sizes they look like attics. But we can recognize in their structure the wall (the *adhiṣṭhāna* of which is hidden in the terrace of the lower level behind the frieze of *śikharas*) with pilasters, the *prastara* (without the longer eave), the superstructure with its *adhiṣṭhāna* and frieze of *śikharas.*

We had no possibility to observe the interior of the tower. However, from the observation of the external construction, one can determine the different layers of stone (Plate 5). It is probable that the walls of the tower are made of corbelling stone slabs. We do not know whether there are internal reinforcing built walls, as found in other monuments of the same period and style (Raṭṭihaḷḷi, etc.). The height of the two upper *talas* taken together leaves an inner hollow volume approximately equal to the volume of the *garbhagṛha* of the first level. But there is no trace outside that any access to it had ever been provided.

e) The dome-shaped roof (*śikhara*). (Plate 4, VII.1-3)

The terminal shallow dome (*śikhara*) of the monument is borne by a very small drum (20 cm)called *gala.* Its section is square with two axial projections and an axial large *nāsikā* called *bhadranāsikā.* It is 2.20 m in its axis at the base, 1.10 at the top. Its height is 95 cm. Its double curve is comparable to the graceful one of the *padma* moulding. A rib marks the passage from the convex curve to the concave one which starts in slight recess below the fall of the first one. The topmost motif (*stūpī*) is made of three beautiful lotiform mouldings diminishing in size and a lotus bud with its base. The dome is hollow and is closed by the slabs of the *stūpī.*

2) The antechamber (śukanāsī)

Starting from the cella the plan of the main monument shows a succession of elements placed on the west-east axis. After the cella there is an antechamber of equal volume (Plate 2, 3). The dividing wall between the two is very thick (75 cm). The opening is arranged with two slabs placed obliquely. There is a doorframe with a threshold richly decorated on the side of the antechamber. The antechamber has the same construction and ceiling as the cella. Its outer walls are the prolongation of the *vimāna* wall. It is topped by a projection from the tower of small size (length 1.30 m, width 1.55 m) (Plate 3-5, VII.1). The term *śukanāsī* is employed for both the projection and the antechamber situated below.

3) The raṅgamaṇḍapa.

The antechamber is open to the east, through a richly decorated doorframe with a threshold, into a pillared hall of square plan, on the same east-west axis (Plate 2, 5). This hall is much more spacious (5.30 m). It has four central pillars forming a square. The height of the ceiling is the same as in the cella and the antechamber. The distance between two pillars is 1.85 m. Therefore they delimitate a cubic volume similar to that of the cella and the antechamber. The structure of the ceiling is also identical to that of the cella and antechamber but endowed with more ornamentation. This space is also marked by a very low platform.

This platform, in spite of its very low height (no more than 5 cm) is considered as a stage. It may have been the place of music and dance performances offered to the deity as a part of worship. This is especially reflected in the usual denomination of this pillared hall as *raṅgamaṇḍapa* "stage-pavillion".

The pillars (Plate 5) have a base, a shaft divided in three parts, two of square section and between them one which is itself divided in three parts, one of octagonal section between two of hexadecagonal section. The upper part of the pillar consists of three main elements with transition mouldings allowing the passage from the square section to a circular section : first a recessing curved moulding, an astragal in the recess, a band of circular section, a recess, then a large three faced band jutting out by 8 cm, a recess, finally a large abacus with a lower doucine, jutting out by 18 cm. Above the pillar, after the recess marked by the square *vīrakāṇḍa*, there is an intermediary system of corbels (*bodhikā*) carrying the architraves (*uttara*). *Śilpaśāstra* nomenclatures of pillars cannot be applied in this particular case with certitude. The middle and upper elements of the capital may be the *kumbha* and *maṇḍi* commonly mentioned in association in *Ajitāgama* for example. But the lower series of mouldings seems to be much more than the *tāṭi* given in that position, but appearing to be a simple astragal.

On the walls of the hall there are pilasters in alignment with the central pillars and in the angles. The distance from a pilaster to a central pillar is 1.20 m. The space around the central volume is therefore relatively narrow and it gives the impression of a gallery.

The hall is open on three sides : in the west the access to the antechamber of the cella, in the east an opening in the east-west axis, in the south an opening in the north-south axis. The two last openings are equipped with a very richly decorated doorframe and threshold and are preceded by a porch. The doorframes on their external façade are the parts which have received the most elaborated decoration in the whole monument (Plate VI.1-3).

The porch of square plan is made of two thick pilasters, one on each side of the door, and two pillars resting on a kind of high bench with a railing slanting towards the outside. The outer face of the bench (90 cm high) has a double plinth, which is the continuation of that of the monument, then a frieze of decorative small pilasters with architectural superstructure. The distance between the pillars is 1.80 m, and from the pilaster to a pillar 1.90 m in the eastern porch, 2.10 m in the southern one. The elaborately decorated ceiling of both porches is at the same height as in the central volume of the hall.. Therefore we have again a delimitation of a volume approximately equal to those already described.

The pillars belong to the type made of a square base, a series of mouldings of circular section, a bulb, a second set of circular mouldings and a large abacus supporting a corbel system. Even though they are of short size and relatively simple, they are good samples of the pillars which typically adorn later Cāḷukyan temples (compare with the porch pillars of the temple of Somēśvara in Haraḷahaḷḷi).

The architraves bear a long eave with a graceful curve carved in a solid mass of stone which on its inward face shows a figuration of a wooden carpentry work made of rafter ends with transversal connections (Plate V.4). The top of this long eave is at the same level as the short eave of the rest of the monument. The same mouldings and frieze of *śikharas* is continued above the porches. The ceiling inside the porch is elevated by doubling the architrave, as in the pillared hall. It is more decorated, with nine images of open lotuses.

The term *mukhabhadra* occurs in an inscription of the Kedārēśvara temple in Baḷḷigāve, where it seems to refer to the porches of the vast *maṇḍapa*[1]. *Mukha-* may refer to an opening and *bhadra* in southern *Śilpaśāstra* refers to a jutting out part of a *maṇḍapa*. The porches of Mukteśvara temple are quite similar to those at Baḷḷigāve. Therefore the designation of *mukhabhadra* seems appropriate for them.

With regard to the long double-curved eave with figurative carpentry work, we have to emphasize the fact it seems to be a specific feature of this Cāḷukyan style of temples. This feature is well-known as a conspicuous characteristic of Vijayanagara architecture. In fact it is already commonly seen in Cāḷukyan pre-Vijayanagara times in Karnāṭaka.

4) The miniature secondary structures.

The most simple of these structures has a square plan and consists of the following elements :

a) A double base, *upapīṭha* and *adhiṣṭhāna*. The top moulding of the *upapīṭha* has a large attic window (*nāsikā*) in its centre, one or several (according to its size) attic windows on each side symmetrically, at the extremities a small one in recess on the slope of the roof. The first moulding of the *adhiṣṭhāna* shows the ends of beams which seem to radiate from the centre of a square.

---

1 *Epigraphia Carnatica*, vol. vii, Sorab taluk, No. 89.

b) On the square base is a slender pilaster in each angle identical to the pilaster described above; it bears the same system of corbels, architrave and eave.

c) A roofing with its base. In the case of a structure with a square plan there is the shallow dome (*śikhara*) described above.

This structure is therefore a miniature reproduction of the structure of the main monument. A variant of this square structure is a miniature building made of the same elements in oblong plan. The only remarkable difference with the previous one is the cylindrical shape of its roof built on high hoops with gable-ends.

There are several scales of reduction for this structure. It is represented by one façade or by two in an angle. Several of these structures, being of diminishing scale, can be surperimposed one upon the other.

5) Composition of the miniature secondary structures.

a) The *vimāna.* (Plate 4, V.1)

On the external wall of the *vimāna*, on the two axis, on the north, west and east façadès there is a system of three projections of diminishing size superimposed onė upon the other. Each one is the representation of an architectural structure, at all the levels, base, wall and ṙoof; it has a pillar at each angle and a longitudinal cylindrical roof. The roof of the third and narrowest one is placed orthogonally so that only its gable-end is visible. A fourth miniature building is again superimposed on the wall of the third projection in the same axis; it differs from the previous ones by its smaller size and by the fact it has a real opening, so that it plays the role of a niche (Plate III.1). The opening is decorated with a representation of a doorframe sheltered under a long eave. Its roof is the miniature representation of a tower with double attic and dome, an exact copy of the *vimāna* tower of the main monument. There has been in the niche a statue which was worshipped; a small channel has been carved in the stone for the outflow of ablution waters. To-day the statue has disappeared and the absence of any other document hampers all attempt of identification.

At each angle of the square plan of the *vimāna*, on the outer wall, there is a superimposed representation of a square structure made of the same elements, in slight projection (Plate III.2). It has a pilaster in each of its visible angles and a dome. Each of its visible façades bears the representation of a miniature temple, with a double-storeyed tower, replica of the main monument, but without opening and not made into a niche like the axial one.

In the interval between the axial projections and the corner one there is a little space of wall which is not left undecorated, but bears one more type of architectural miniature representation (*pañjara*) consisting in the image of a short pillar supporting an architectural superstructure under a decorative arch (Plate IV.1, 3).

The two attics of the tower repeat the same sequence of miniature structures with the same elements, with the exception of the base, in diminishing sizes. Images of deities are carved on the gable-ends of the roofs. In the axial gable-ends there were separate small steles which have now disappeared, but mortices are stil there to show that a provision had been made for them.

It is thus clear that all these miniature architectural representations are not a mere ornamentation. With the main structure they form an architectural unit representing the theological concept of the supreme inward abstract form of God surrounded by a hierarchy of outward anthropomorphic manifestations.

b) The *śukanāsī*

The antechamber is a transition element. On the external façade the separation between the cella and the antechamber is marked by the position of the antechamber's wall in recess from the cella's wall (Plate III.2-3, V.2). The transitional character is shown by the representation of a thick pilaster which seems to be a transitional motif in this style of architecture. Here it is shown on a projection of the double base of the monument and topped by the eave and a separate superstructure motif. The shaft of square section is very short. The upper portion is very elaborate : an astragal between recesses, a large lotiform moulding, a lower parasol shaped moulding, a large recess, a bigger projecting chamfered band (*kumbha*), a new recess and a large abacus (*maṇḍi*) on a lotiform moulding. The whole pilaster is repeated in slenderer size in the form of axial projections surperimposed on itself.

The superstructure of the antechamber, i. e. the projection of the tower (Plate VI.5, VII.1), is made of the continuation of the tower motifs at the level of the first attic, one square architectural structure, without the base, in the east-west axis, two superimposed one on the other on the north and south façades. At the level of the second attic of the tower, there is the long roof of the *śukanāsī*, made of stone slabs dotted with many schematised *nāsikās*. On the eastern façade there is a large gable-end. It must have been decorated with a sculptured stele which has disappeared now.

c) The *raṅgamaṇḍapa*.

On the northern façade, in the north-south axis there is a system of three projections with a pilaster in the visible angles and longitudinal cylindrical roofs. A fourth projection has a cylindrical roof in orthogonal position showing only its gable-end. A fifth axial projection shows the representation of a temple with an opening, playing the role of a niche; it has a miniature doorframe, long eave and three double-storeyed towers, exact copies of the main *vimāna*. Here also, the image in the niche has disappeared. The figuration of three towers may be an indication that there were three images in the niche.

There is a structure with a square roof at each angle of the *raṅgamaṇḍapa*. Each visible face of these structures bears one more representation of a miniature temple with a double-storeyed tower.

On the northern façade the transition between the axial system of projections and the angle projections is made by the transitional thick pilaster in a slight recess (Plate V.2-3). On the other façades the transitional pilaster appears also between the angle projections and the implantation of the *śukanāsī* or the porches. The frieze of roofs of the main part of the monument is continued on the porches. On each visible side of the porch the frieze consists of a central cylindrical roof and square domes in the angles.

There is no space of wall which has been left blank. As the *raṅgamaṇḍapa* has a larger size, the space between the pilasters of the central projections is sufficiently large to be occupied by one more architectural motif, a small pilaster supporting a double-storeyed tower. On each side of the transitional thick pilaster there is the motif of the pilaster with simple superstructure under an arch.

The rule of composition of these miniature shrines is a common one in South India in the diverse styles of temples in all periods. It has also a base in Southern *Śilpaśāstra* which gives the names of *karṇakūṭa* to the figurations of square plan, *bhadraśālā* to those of oblong plan, *pañjara* to pilaster-superstructure motif, and prescribes the corner, axial and intermediary positions for them respectively.

V

ICONOGRAPHY

With regard to the iconography of the temple nothing much can be said owing to the vandalism of which this otherwise extremely rich temple has been the victim. A good number of statues have disappeared. Numerous empty mortices, obviously made for the tenons of sculptured steles, are testimonies to prove that the whole external wall of the temple was adorned with bracket figures. There must have been more than a hundred figures decorating the external walls. Adding the steles plundered in other parts of the monument, the total number of lost statues raises to some hundred and sixty. Now what is *in situ* is not of great interest. However we shall try to describe a few remarkable preserved iconographic representations.

Inside the temple.

Muktēśvaraliṅga.

The main shrine which goes by the name of Muktēśvara is literally on the river embankment. The Liṅga in the *sanctum sanctorum* is an *udbhava-mūrti*. It is a very small cylindrical stone with its *pāṇipīṭha.* almost at the ground level. By and large *liṅgas* of*udbhavamūrti* type are placed on low sockets whereas *liṅgas* installed by human beings are on an elevated *pīṭha.* Virūpākṣaliṅga at Hampi, Muktēśvara at Cauḍadānapura and Saṅgamēśvara at Kūḍalasaṅgama in Bijāpura district are a few among the best examples of *svayambhū* or *udbhava liṅgas*, whereas Bṛhadīśvara in Tanjāvur and Gaṅgaikoṇḍacōḷapuram are the best examples of man made *liṅgas*.

Saptamātṛkā panel.

Like in most of the temples built during this period, a panel of Saptamātrikās has been installed in a niche in the *raṅgamaṇḍapa.* By and large this panel is found to the left, when the devotee stands facing the main deity in the *sanctum sanctorum.* According to *Ajitāgama* and *Mayamata* the Mother goddesses should be installed in villages or in temples[1] *Mayamata* precises that the goddesses should be installed either facing north or east and should be near the main entrance[2] To the Śaivas the temple represents Kailāsa. According to *Rudrakōṭisaṃhitā* in *Śivapurāṇa* the fort gates of Kailāsa are guarded by Bhairavas. Each of the goddesses stands there as the Śakti of the guardian. As these Śaktis are none but the consorts of main gods such as Brahmā, Viṣṇu, Mahēśvara, Indra, Varāha and so on, they must have the same vehicles and attributes. As they are the Śaktis and their energy is primordial in the protection of the fort they must be worshipped first. This idea has been depicted on the stone in the form of a panel. On either side of the panel are seated, in the beginning Śiva as Vīṇādharamūrti playing on the *vīṇā*. and Gaṇēśa at the other end. These goddesses were highly revered in temples to Śiva built by Kālāmukha and Pāśupatas.

On entering the temple from the southern entrance the panel is found in a niche in south-western corner facing north. These goddesses are Brāhmī, Māhēśvarī, Kaumārī, Vaiṣṇavī, Vārāhī, Indrāṇī and Cāmuṃḍā. Images of their vehicles are carved at the foot of each one. All the goddesses are in seated position. The panel is in a very good state of preservation. Only it needs a good cleaning.

Texts and treatises on iconography prescribe the order of the goddesses as given above. On the panel Vaiṣṇavī should have the fifth place. In Muktēśvara temple Kaumārī is placed in the third position, i. e. Śiva-Vīṇādhara, Brāhmī, Kaumārī, Māhēśvarī, Vaiṣṇavī etc. The reason for this alteration is unknown.

Sūrya.

Facing south is an image of Sun god Sūrya placed on a pedestal on which seven horses have been represented. Sun, according to *Śivapurāṇa* is the disc of Śiva. So the worship of Sun god was very popular when the Lākuḷaśaiva movement was quite fervent. In many temples such as Brahmēśvara temple at Ablūru, Śiva temple at Mattihaḷḷi etc. a special *sanctum sanctorum* was built for the Sun god.

However, the statue of Sun god in the Muktēśvara temple at Cauḍadānapura is not original. It has been saved from further damage and decay from the neighbouring village Narasiṃhapura temple. Probably, there

---

1 *Ajitāgama* paṭala 48, verse 3, p. 145; *Mayamata* part II, adhyāya 36, śl. 235ff., p. 451.
2 *Ibid* , śl. 236, p. 451.

must have been a statue of Sūrya in Muktēśvara temple also. But, that statue had been lost. As the seat of the Sun god seems to be in its original place the statue must have been stolen, leaving the empty *pīṭha* (pedestal) *in situ.* The image of Sun god hailing from elsewhere has filled up the vacant seat. This is an interesting piece of sculpture. Sūrya is carved standing under snake hood (Plate VII.5).

Nandin.

There is a beautiful couchant Naṃdin facing west, placed near the eastern door. Nandin or bull is the vehicle of Śiva. According to Purāṇas and Āgamas.[1] "at the time of *pralaya* (deluge) when Dharma in distress went to see Śiva, the Lord assured him protection and advised him to be there as his mount. So, Dharma transformed itself into a Nandin or bull and stood there at His service. The four feet of Nandin represent : *tapas, jñāna, yajña* and *dāna* (*Citrasūtra of Viṣṇudharmottara*, ed. by C. Shivaramamurthy, p. 36).

In every temple dedicated to Śiva an image of Nandin is installed either at the entrance of the temple complex or in one of the *maṇḍapa*s which are contiguous to the main shrine. In Muktēśvara temple at Cauḍadānapura also there is a beautifully hewn image of Nandin exquisitely decorated with bells.

Outside the temple, walls and tower.

Dancing images of Śiva-Bhairava are prominent Three sides of the round domical tower namely west, south and east are adorned with the images of Śiva-Bhairava or Bhikṣātana in dancing poses with that of the goddesses on the fourth i. e. northern direction. The Eastern and Southern slanting railings of the porches contain images of pilasters and in the intervals figures of many female dancers and musicians. There are two bas-reliefs on each railing and about twelve figures in each one. Representations of Vīrabhadra are also numerous.

Facing east on the south side of the *vimāna* there is an interesting image of a male figure standing, holding a lotus in each hand. It can be identified with Sūrya but horses are missing. Apart from this there are a few images of dancers and yogis seated in yogic postures.

On each side of the *vimāna* in the centre are four gable-ends (*nāsika*) in vertical row, in which carved images were inserted. Unfortunately the hands of vandals have reached upto the first of the series. As a result on each side the one at the first level is missing.

---

[1] *Vātulaśuddhāgama*, ed. by Dr. H.P.Malledevaru, Tattvabhedapaṭala 1, śloka 130, p. 51;

On the south, in the second gable-end there is a standing image of Śiva holding in his upper and lower right hands *triśūla* and *khaḍga* or *daṇḍa*, then *ḍamaru* and *mātuluṅga* in his upper and lower left hands. A skull is hanging to his left hand carved just below the fruit. A dog is licking the blood dripping out of the skull. By the side of Śiva are carved two skeleton-like male *bhūtas* or vampires. When there is *khaḍga* there must be *khēṭaka*. In the absence of *khēṭaka* the attribute in the hands of Śiva here can be taken as *daṇḍa* or *laguḍa*. In Karnāṭaka images of Śiva with *laguḍa* are frequently met with in the temples of this period. The image of Śiva in Muktēśvara temple can be identfied with Śiva Laguḍīśvara. It is bedecked with all sorts of ornaments including *vaijayṃtihāra*.

On the third gable-end is seen an image of a dancing goddess holding *triśūla, akṣamālā, ḍamaru* and *mātuluṅga* fruit in upper and lower right and left hands respectively.

On the west side of the *vimāna*, as the first gable-end is empty, we go to the second. In its panel an image of seated Śiva has been represented. He holds in the right upper and lower hands *triśūla* with skull, and *akṣamālā* in *abhayahasta*; in the left hands upper and lower *ḍamaru* with skull and *mātuluṅga* fruit. Ḥere the image is adorned with *kirīṭamakuṭa* and all kinds of ornaments. Below his seat is seated Naṃdin with profile facing north. Can this image be identified with Sadyojātamūrti ? There are *cauri* bearers on either side of the main image.

In the superior gable-end again the dancing goddess has been carved holding the same attributes as in the previous one. Here she is standing in *dvibhaṅga* pose. She is adorned with *ruṇḍamālā* along with other ornaments. The animal carved on the pedestal looks like a jackal. Or is it a dog ? By the side of the goddess are two lady-accompanyists, one on the right playing an instrument of percussion resembling a *mṛdaṅga* and the other to the left playing on cymbals. It is also interesting to note that a skull is fixed on both *triśūla* and *ḍamaru*. The head on the *triśūla* can be identified with the head of Viśvaksēna but what about the one on ḍamaru ?

In the north, the goddess is represented on the second panel and the god on the last. The goddess, being the Śakti of Śiva, occupies the left or *vāma* part of his body. Śiva is omnipresent and He occupies the whole universe. The temple represents Śiva. So the left part is reserved to his Śakti. In almost all the temples of Kāḷāmukhas and Pāśupatas the goddess is represented in the northern gable-ends, e. g. in the Kadaṃbēśvara temple in Raṭṭihaḷḷi,

Kēdārēśvara in Baḷḷigāve, Sōmanāthēśvara at Haraḷahaḷḷi etc. So in Muktēśvara temple also the godddess is shown on the north.

In the panel above it is represented seated Śiva Mahēśvara. This seated figure of Śiva comes repeatedly in this monument. It is also on the lintels of the southern and eastern doors. His attributes are : *triśūla* and *akṣamālā* in the right upper and lower hands; *ḍamaru* and *mātulaṃga* in upper and lower left hands respectively.

A word about the fruit *mātulaṃga* may not be out of place here. In Karnāṭaka this fruit occurs frequently in the sculptures of monuments of this period. It is also seen, but rarely in other places outside Karnāṭaka. *Mātuluṅga* or *mādal* in Tamil means "pomegranate". So Gopinatha Rao identifies it thus. But the fruit we see on the sculptures does not have the smooth skin of a pomegranate. On the contrary it is uneven. Seeing stylised image of this fruit, some other modern scholars are of the opinion that it is maize. But maize entered India with its colonisation by Europeans. So, this identification also does not hold good. Others think that it represents the *sītāphala.* Here also is a problem. According to B. G. L. Svami one of the renowned botanists of Karnāṭaka, in his book *Namma hoṭṭeyalli dakṣiṇa amērike* this fruit is foreign to India. According to him it was also brought from South America and introduced to the Indian soil by westerners. Can it be taken literally as *muktāphala* a fruit with pearls ?

Images of a figure holding *khaḍga, kheṭaka,* bow and arrow in upper and lower right and left hands have been carved on three sides of the *vimāna* on its wall or *pāda* Taking into consideration these attributes these images can be identified with Vīrabhadra. But the personnage is adorned with a kind of *dhoti* draped in the fashion of pants called in Kannaḍa *callaṇa.* Fine designs of checks and other decorative motifs have been shown clearly on the dress. In his *Elements of Hindu Iconography* Gopinatha Rao writes that Śrīkaṇṭha has the same attributes as Vīrabhadra, but distinguishes them on the basis of their dresses. Śrīkaṇṭha wears a *dhoti* with *citra* on it. *Citra* may be interpreted as "design, embroidery (*kasūti*), coloured" On the basis of this the images of Muktēśvara temple can be identified with Śrīkaṇṭha and not with Vīrabhadra. (See below for the image of Vīrabhadra).

Another feature of these temples is about an image of Viṣṇu-Kṛṣṇa. When Śiva stood on one foot as Ekapādamūrti, Viṣṇu emanated from his left side. An image of Vēṇugōpālakṛṣṇa proves that this belief was deeply rooted in the minds of the people. This representation of Viṣṇu-Kṛṣṇa is, by and large, depicted on the northern façade of the temple. An image of Vēṇugōpālakṛṣṇa shines on the tower of Muktēśvara too.

According to Āgamas and Purāṇas, Kubēra, the treasurer of Gods, is supposed to be the friend of Śiva. Kubēra is known for his invaluable nine kinds of treasures. Amongst them are two, Śankhanidhi and Padmanidhi, which are most important. They decorate the external walls of the shrine. They are represented in the form of seated human figures with big stomach, holding either a *śankha* (conch) or *padma* (lotus). Their big belly is the sign of prosperity.

In the case of Gajalakṣmī, these two *nidhis* transform themselves into elephants and pour water on the goddess who is seated on a lotus, with *pūrṇakuṃbha* or pots of abundance.

In the temple enclosure there is a set of four shrines built contiguously one to another in the south western angle. All the four face the river, i. e. north. Two of them are double celled whereas the other two are single celled. A newly built common open pillared pavilion serves the purpose of *mahāmaṃṭapa* to all four of them. Starting from the east the first shrine has a *sanctum sanctorum* and an antechamber. There is a Liṅga in the *sanctum* and its *praṇāḷa* or outlet for the ablution water is to the right instead of the left. A statue of Naṃdin adorns the ante-chamber or *śukanāsi.*

Second shrine. This is a single sanctum with the image of Vīrabhadra which is still under worship (as a consequence we could not take the measurements of the statue). The fact that his right foot is turned towards west and the left faces north shows that the god is set to bring miscreants to heel. Both the legs are bending with protruding knees. Sword, arrow, bow and shield are held in his four hands from lower right to lower left hand respectively. His anklets are in the form of snakes. The *vaijayantihāra* is so long that it almost touches the pedestal. *Yajñōpavīta* hangs to the right side. Many bracelets and necklaces adorn the deity. A high *kirīṭamukuṭa* embellishes the head. On the pedestal are the images of devotees and warriors.

A liṅgāyat priest is in charge of conducting the rituals and *pūjā* in the temple. He always keeps a wooden stick by the side of the statue. He told us that it is a tradition to place it by the side of the god. During the course of our survey of temples of 10th to 12th centuries in this region[1]. often we came

---

[1] There is a place called Mattihaḷḷi in Hirekērur tāluk where in a triple celled shrine God Śiva in the form of a Liṅga adorns the central cella. A stick is placed by the side of the

across with this custom of placing a stick by the side of Śiva liṅga or Vīrabhadra. This may be one of the last lingering influences of Lākula-śaivism.

The third sanctum is identical to the first one as having a cella and an antechamber. Like in the first, here too there is Liṅga in the cella and Nandin in the *śukanāsi.* The only difference is that by the side of the door-jambs there are perforated windows with beautiful scrolls in the centre of which are dancing figures, blowing wind instruments etc.

The last shrine which is single-celled houses a seated goddess with eight hands of which the two front ones are mutilated. Her left foot rests on the seat folded in acute angle whereas the hanging right leg rests on a skull. In fact four skulls have been carved on the pedestal. Her right hands from lower to upper hold sword, arrow and *ḍamaru.* In the same way, the left lower to upper have been adorned with shield, bow and *triśūla.* She wears a high *kirīṭa*, ear-rings, *ruṇḍamālā* (garland of skulls), various necklaces, bracelets and anklets. She is bare chest. The lower part of her body is clad in a *sari* but draped in the fashion of a *dhoti.* Foliage motifs with the lion in the centre decorate the pedestal.

Liṃga. "It is a tradition" was always the answer of local people to our question about its significance.

Appendix 1

Transliteration in nāgarī script

Italics indicate the Kannaḍa short *e* and *o*, the consonants *ṟ* and *ḻ*.

Inscription no. I

१. नमस्तुङ्गशिरश्चुंबिचंद्रचामरचारवे । त्रैळोक्यनगरारंभमूलस्तंभाय सं(शं)भवे ॥ (१) त्रिणानि कोटिवर्षाणि म्रिणा(ण्)मयं

२. दशकोटिभिः दारेष्टशतं कोटिशहश्र (सहस्र) कोटि शिळा(ला)मयं ॥ २

३. स्वस्ति समश्त(स्त) ॥ भुवनाश्रयं श्री प्रिथ्वीवल्लभं महाराजाधिराज परमेश्वर परमभट्टारक श(स)त्याश्रय कुळतिलकं

४. चाळुक्याभरणं श्रीमत्त्रिभुवनमल्लदेवर विजयराज्यमुत्तरोत्तराभिवृद्धिप्रवर्द्धनमाचंद्रार्क्कता

५. रंबरं सलुत्तमिरे ॥ कन्द ॥ पडुवलु पडुवण वारिधि गडि मूडलु मूडणब्धि गडि बडगलु हिमं । गडि *तें*क से

६. तु*वे*रेगं । गडियागिरे विक्रमांकनाळ्वं धरेयं ॥ ३ ॥ जळनिधि परिव्रि(वृ)त धात्रीतळ*मेल्ल*मं तन्न हस्ततळ*मेने* पें*पं* । त*ळ्दे*दी चाळुक्यान्वय

७. कुळतिळकं विक्रमांकनाळ्वं धरेय ॥ ४ ॥ व ॥ आ परमेश्वरन श्री पादपद्मोपजीवि श(स)मधिगतपंचमहाशब्द महासामन्ताधिपति महा

८. महाप्रचंड दंडनायक वैरिगिरिवज्रसायक सुभटसेनानाथ सि(शि)खामणि स(श)रणागतरक्षामणि श्रीमन्महाप्रधानं गोविंदरसरा

९. जं बनवासि पन्निच्छ्रासिरमुमं सुखदिमाळुत्तमिरे ॥ [एर]गदवरं *कोदुं* सलेतन । *गेर*गि-दरं कादु दक्षिणापथ*मेल्लने* बेस*केय्*वंतागिरे *मेर*दं श्री

१०. कीर्तिलक्ष्मियं गोविंद ॥ (५) व ॥ स्वस्ति समस्तभुवनविन्यस्तमस्तकसंस्तूयमान-चारुचरणारविंद वैरिबळविळय गोविंदनुज्जनीमहाकाळ

११. देवतालब्धवरप्रशा(सा)द समस्तविद्याविनोद । पाटळीपुरवराधीश्वर । कीर्त्यंगनाधीश्वर वटव्रि(वृ)क्षध्वज । धैर्यगरुडध्वज । सोम

१२. वंशललाटलोचन । मृगराजलांछन । गुत्तर भीमं । छलदंक राम । अरिकुमरमकुट-घट्टितचरण । गुत्तराभर
१३. ण । रिपुबळतिमिरमार्त्तंड । वैरिकुळकाळदंड । हयवत्सराज । रूपमनोज । भ्रित्यचिंतामणि । सुभटचूडामणि वंदिजन कळ्प(ल्प)व्रि (वृ)क्ष
१४. शरणागत रक्ष । चंद्रगुप्त महाराजाधिराज कुळ(ल)संपूर्ण्ण । नन्नियलु कर्ण्न । मनु-मार्ग्गमानि । सनुमानदानि । शौचांजनेय संपंन्न । नुडिदु म
१५. त्तेन्न । अय्यन चक्र । भूचक्रशक्र विक्रमादित्यवंशोद्भवरप्प श्रीमत् गुत्तान्वयर महिमेयं पेळ्वेडे ।। कन्दं ।।
१६. अल्लिगे मन्नेय लक्ष्मी । वल्लभ रेंनिसिर्द्द गुत्तभूपान्वय रोळ् ।। बल्लिदनजयनप्रतिमल्लं मागुत्तभूपनेंबं नेगळ्द ।। ६ ।। (कं) अंता
१७. न्रिप(नृप)तिगे सुत विक्रांतधनं राजवंस(श) चूडामणि मा । रांतरिगंतक वंदिगे चिंता-मणि गुत्तभूपनंगजरूप ।। (७) व्रित्त ।। तंदेय तं
१८. देयिंद मेवगाळुव महीतळवज्जपज्जरिं बंदुदे सालुगु वेंदिर दे विक्रमदिंदिरांत भूपरं कोंदु ।। धरित्रियं पडेदनर्त्तिगे बेर्पुदनित्तु
१९. कीर्तियं मंदिरविर्पिनं पडेद गुत्तन्रि(नृ)पाळिसिदें क्रि(कृ)तार्थनो ।। ८ ।। कंद ।। गुत्तान्वय वंशाग्रणि । गुत्तान्वय राजभवनमंगळ कळशं ।। गुत्तान्वय
२०. चूडामणि । गुत्तान्वय तिळकनेंनिसिदं गुत्तन्रि(नृ)पाळक।। ९ ।। आतन तनयं जगदोळु नीतिपरं रिपुकरींद्र कंठीरव ।। भूतळ क्षत्रियरोळजा
२१. तभयं मल्लिदेवनदटं देव ।। १० ।। व्रित्त ।। एणिसलु भूपाळरींगळु पलबरुमोळरा भूपवर्ग्गंगळिळ्देगणिदें पूर्वाद्रियोळु चंद्रमनेसे
२२. व सरोमध्यदोळु पंकजं केवणदोळु माणिक्यविर्पंतिरे भुवनजनक्काश्रयं राजचूडा । म-णयिप्पं मल्लिदेवं त्रिभुवनतिळ
२३. कं राजमान्धातभूपं ।। ११ ।। भंडणदोळु रिपुभूपर । तंडमनवयवदे गेल्दु जयलक्ष्मिय दो । र्दंडदोळिरिसिद धीरद ।। गंडं केवळ
२४. मे मेरुगिरि नम्म मल्लन्रि(नृ)पाळ ।। १२ ।। कंद ।। नुडियेदडे नुडियदि क्केमे कुडु वें निमगेंदु नुडिदनप्पडे म्रि(मृ)डनोळु । पडेद बर
२५. मेरुगिरियोळु । कडेदक्कर मल्लभूप नुडिदिं बळिकं (१३) ।। व्रि ।। पदपिं न्रि(नृ)पाळ(ल) निन्न रणकेळीलीळे(ले)यं पक्षपातदि नां पेळदोडे नो पोदप
२६. लवुं सुग्रामदोळ् पुत्तने । त्तिद पुल्गर्चिद कय्दुवं बिसुटि नीरं पोक्कि निग्रन्थमो । डिद निंदाडिद केय्गळं मुगिदरातिब्रात

२७. वें पेळवे ॥ १४ ॥ कंद ॥ आजियं धरणियनेरिद । वाजिय खुरदिंद मुर्त्तुरिपुसिरमेंबी बीजमने बित्ति बेळेवं राजि

२८. क विख्यात कीर्त्तियं मल्लन्रिप ॥ १५ ॥ व्रित्त ॥ देसेवोस(वुण्न)दिं देसेव नेत्त र सुट्टुरेयिं नभस्थळं पसरिसि बिळ्द वीर भट्टरट्टेगळिं हय

२९. खंडखंडियिं कुसुरिवोलागे वैरिबलमं तरेदोड्डिडदगुर्वु तानुगु । विंसिदुदु मल्लिदेवनिरे-दाहवरंगद वैरिसेने

३०. य ॥ १६ ॥ वचन ॥ आ गुत्तान्वयर हि(ह्र)दयाळ[व]ळंबिगळप्प जटाचोळान्वयरु माडिसिद शिवालयद मुक्तितीर्थद व्यावर्णन ॥ क ॥

३१. हरन जटाग्रदि नेलसिद सुरनदिगं वेदशैळ(ल)सि(शि)खराग्रदि नी । धरेगेळिद तुंग-भद्रावरनदिगं दोरेये जगद नदमुं नदियुं (१७) ॥

३२. व्रि ॥ सुदतीकुंकुमपंकितारुणजळंदाभिदानाजळं विदळतु पंकजप्पुररंजित जळं वेदाचळेंद्रोपकण्ठदिनेतं सुरि

३३. दिंदुकान्तद जळं पेरर्व्व संदोहदिं पु। दिदेत्तं लहरीदिशाबधिरितं श्रीतुंगभद्रा जळं ॥ १८ ॥ क ॥ गंगेसमान दक्षिणगंगान

३४. दि मिंद मर्त्यरघसंकुळमं पिंगिसुव गंगेयुं तिरिपिंगिपळघकुळम नम्म दक्षिण गंगे ॥ १९ ॥ पावनवेंनिसिद गंगादेविगे

३५. सरिदोरे समान दक्षिणगंगादेवियने तुंगभद्रादेवियनिनेरये पोगळ लावं नेरवं ॥ २० ॥ व्रित्त ॥ सुरसै

३६. ळें(लें)द्रद हिम्या(मा)चळ(ल)द महिमेगं तारशैळ(ल)क्कं नोडलु दोरेवेत्तिवेदशैळे-ंद्रदलमरनदिसंनिभं मेघब्रिंदोत्करदिंदं

३७. भत्तथिदण्डद बहळतेयेंबंददिं बंदु ता निकरद पापक्षय माडुव विमळ जळं तुंगभद्रा प्रवाह ॥ २१ ॥ गद्य ॥ अदेंतें

३८. दोडैररावतगंडमंडळभित्तियंते दानोचितस्थानमुं हरजटाग्रदंते नदीविराजितमुं । पाताळ-लोकदंते नाग

३९. सहितमुं । सुरेंद्रसयनदंते रंभायतमुं । देवलोकदंते सुमनाभिराममुं शयन संगीतकदंते ताळ

४०. सहितमुं ब्रह्मसभेयंते द्विजविराजितमुं । अंतल्लि मूरुं कालमुं । आरुं रि(ऋ)तुगळुं । सर्वर्त्तुकमप्प मु

४१. क्तितीर्त्त(र्थ)दस्थानदोळु सु(शु)कसारिकारमणमुं मत्तमधुकरगीतारमणमुं । पुगलपुगलेंब कोकिळ(ल)स्वनारमणमुं

४२. नमेरु मंदार पा[रि]जातादि सकळपुर्प(ष्प)राजितमुं सामवेद सप्तस्वर मंत्राक्षरंगळिं होमं गैय्व द्विजोत्तमर

४३. होमधूमस्तोममुं । देवतातर्प्पण रि(ऋ)षितर्प्पण दिक्तर्प्पण गायत्री श(ष)डक्षर जपंगळं मार्प्प सद्ब्राह्मणरिं व

४४. ज्रासन पद्मासन स्वस्तिकासनंगळिं । नादभेद । बिंदुभेद । स(श)क्तिभेद । आत्मभेदमेंब नाल्कुतेर(र)द योगलक्षणलक्षितरप्प योगिग

४५. ळिं । मुक्तिमार्ग्गमे मूर्त्तिगोंडिर्द्द मुक्तितीर्थद बहुविध लिंगाश्रयंगळोप्पुगुमल्लि ॥ २२ ॥ कंद ॥ अजसभेयंते

४६. सदा द्विजपरिवित(वृत)मिंद्रनंते सुमनाश्रयवा त्रिजसगजदंते दानब्रजमयमा मुक्तितीर्थमदु केवळमे ॥ २३ ॥

४७. ॥ व्रित्त ॥ (चंपक) कुसुमित मल्लिकाभिनव पाटळसंकुळदिं कोनर्तु तळ्तसदळमागि बंद पोस मावुगळिं मोरेवुन्मदाळियिं मस

४८. गित [म]ष्ट बग्गिप पिकाळिगळिं नयदिंद तेंकणिंदेसपलरिंदवी मुक्तितीर्त्त(र्थ)-वदोप्पुगुमेंतु नोर्पड ॥ २४ ॥ वंसा(शा)वतार

४९. कंद ॥ श्रीगेनेले दानधर्म्मकागर वेने नेगळ्दनी जटान्वय कुलदोळु भोगपुरंदर नेयविद सागर परिवि(वृ)त

५०. धरित्रियोळ(ळे) जोम्मन्रिपं (नृपं)॥ २५ ॥ कंद ॥ आतंगे पुट्टिद विख्यातिपरं राजसु-तरोळमळचरित्र भूतळदलर्त्थिगम

५१. रकुजातं केवलमे दास वीरविळासं ॥ २६ ॥ सरसीरुहवदने चंदब्बरसिरु गुणनिळय नेमिप दासन्रि(नृ)पंगं परहित चरितं

५२. पुट्टिद हरचरणपयोज भ्रिं(भृं)गनत्तिन्रि(नृ)पाळं ॥ २७ ॥ आतन तम्म ॥ चंदग-वज्ज(ब्ज)नाभन कंदंगे सेतुगट्टि लंकेश्वरन कोंदंगे सुरनदि

५३. यं तंदंगे दोरेये मनुजरवनीतळदोळु ॥ २८ ॥ (वचन) मावं महामंडलेस्व(श्व)रं । वीरारातिमदनमहेस्व(श्व)र । मूरुराय

५४. मंडळिकमदगजेंद्रकण्ठीरवं रायन महिमेय पेळ्विडे ॥ कंद ॥ मरवट्टिवुदु सुरतरु परळागिये कुडुतमि

५५. [र्क्कु] चिंतामणिया मरनुं कल्लुं प्रियदिं करदेनिप्पुवे रायनंतिरे जगदोळु ॥ २९ ॥ व्रित्त ॥ परमार्त्थक्किष्टदेय्वंते

५६. नगखिळजगत्स्वामिसंदादि देवगिरिजाळ्वंगानुसंगं शिवनेगड कुलस्वामि कारुण्यदिंदु पोरेदाळ्वं विक्रमांकान्वय

५७. कुळतिळकं मल्लभूपं गडिंती *धरेयोळु* धन्यं जटाचोळरोळु मळयसो(शो)राजनीयत्त(ति)राजं ॥ ३० ॥ कंद ॥ *धरेयोळगे* वारणा

५८. सिय *दोरेयेनिसुव* पुण्यनदिय तीरद समदं हरनिळयमनघकुळ(ल)संहारनिळ(ल)-यमनर्त्तियिंदमत्तिन्निपाळं ॥ ३१ ॥ उत्तमर

५९. *केलदोळं* भूपोत्तमरास्थानरंगदोळु सुजनकवित्वोत्तमरस*मेयोळ*मत्युत्तमनी यत्तिराजनं पो-गळदरारो ॥ ३२ ॥ *धरेयो*

६०. ळनेकरिल्ल सुजनर्क्कलिकालदोळं*ते* भद्रसिंधुरघटियिल्लदं*ते* सुजनोत्तमनक्षर पक्षपाति नंटर *बेळेगेयि* धरामरर कव्विडि

६१. सिष्टनिधाननिर्द्दपं वरगुणियत्तिराज *नेळेगोर्वने* कळ्प(ल्प)कुजातनिर्प्प*वोल्* ॥ ३३ ॥ स्वस्ति श्रीमन्महासामंत वीरलक्ष्मीकान्तं जटान्वय चो

६२. ळ वंशाग्रणि शिष्टचिंतामणि गोत्रपवित्र सबळ त्रिणेत्र वीरविळा(ला)सं गुत्तर चंद्रहासं हरचरण सरसीरुह

६३. मधुकर विनयरत्नाकरं ...

Inscription No. II

१. श्री मुक्तेषं(शं) । नमो यस्य जटाजूटे विधोः कळा । तुंगगंगानदीतीरचा

२. रे हंसीव राजते ॥ १ ॥ पदपिं मुक्तेश्वरं माळ्कभिमत सुखमं भक्त

३. लोकक्के भक्तयास्पदचंद्रोपेंद्रवृंदारकनिकरनुत श्री पदद्वंद्वनुद्दामदषा(शा)सं

४. भूतभूतिप्रदनखिळजगत्स्वामि संबद्धगौरीहृदयानंदैककं

५. दं विषदतरयशःप्राप्तसच्छांसनाकं (व्रि) ॥ २ ॥ विषदतरेश्वरा*ज्ञेयोदविं*

६. द*मे* संभविसिर्द्दवी चतुर्द्दष(श)भुवनंगळष्टतनुधर्म्मदनेर्मदल्लियुं मनःकुष(श)

७. लमनित्तु भूभुवनामाभुवनंगळ*नेळि*कुं रमावषरभिवांच्छेयं सलिप स

८. तुक्रि(कृ)तियं *सले* तोर्प्पनेर्प्पिनिं ॥ ३ ॥ कं ॥ सप्तसमुद्रद बळसिं सप्तद्वीपप्रदेशदिं भुवनं

९. गळव्याप्तियनुळिदीरेळुमवाप्तसुखावळिगळिर्द्द *केनलिळेयेसगुं* ॥ ४ ॥ द्वीपावळि*यो*

१०. ळ्जंबूद्वीप*वे* सोगयिक्कुवल्लदेंदुळिदारुं द्वीपगळुमं *पोरगण* कां

११. पिंगिरिसिद विधात्रनेन*रियदनेम* ॥ ५ ॥ इवि जंबूद्वीपलक्ष्मीविळसित लाव

१२. ण्य*मेंबन्ते* देवद्दपूर्विं चन्दनोर्व्वीरुहद सोवडिनिं रत्नभूपाळियिं फेनविनिविबद्धमा

१३. दा *तेरेगळ* निरेयुं सन्महामच्छयपुंच्छात्तविचित्रोरुपत्रदिं राजिसि बळसिद लावण्य

१४. वारासि तोर्क्कुं ॥ ६ ॥ वारिधि तिळिगोळनदरे ॥ कं ॥

रो / ळ्नीरजद वोलेसगुमल्ते जंबूद्वीपं । मेरुवे क

१५. र्णिके देसेयेसळारेये बलवर्प्प राशिचक्रं भ्रमरं ॥ ७ ॥ (कं) सुरगिरियिळावित्तं(तं) किंपुरु

१६. शं(षं) हरिवर्षंमेसेव हिमवद्गिरियं भरतोर्व्वी षट्खंडं तरतरदिं तेंकलल्लि माळवमेस

१७. गुं ॥ ८ ॥ तावरेयेंदेंनिप्प कमळंगेळसाल्केम जातिसंकरं पूविनोळक्के नूतन करग्रहणं

१८. विवाहदल्लितोक्कविर क्वेंगदल्सुरभियंक रेयेंबदेंनिप्पलक्ष्मीकामाळि राजनीतिहि(हृ)दय स्थिति

१९. माळवदोळ् विराजिकुं ॥ ९ ॥ ॥ क ॥ माळवदोळगुज्जयनिये पाळिसुगुं कर्ण्नपुण्यमं कण्णेळगिंबाळेवो

२०. सरिसे चंद्रशिळा(ला)लयमं मळेयनुळिदु बळेये बनंगळुं ॥ १० ॥ अमर्दं तत्पुरदोळ्नृपोत्तमनेंनिप्पा विक्रमा

२१. दित्यन । प्प महासिद्धियनेय्दे साधिसि जगक्कानन्दमागित्तभीष्टम निंशक(ंशंक)नागि मूजगमुमं सत्कीर्तियिं मुच्चि

२२. भूरमेगिं तंनेय तोळबाळे मरुवाळिल्लेंबिनंताळ्दु(ळ्वु)तुं ॥ ११ ॥ उगुगुं रत्नाळिगळ्कांथेयिनेसगिक्कुमिष्टान्न

२३. मं खर्परं पाहगेवोय्युं पेळ्द ताणक्के सपुदसुवनंटंटु चित्रक्के बेत्तं । बगेदागळ्तीर्चुगुं शतृवनसिरस

२४. धिं पोगंळक्कु पटं दिट्टगद्रिश्यवक्केयक्कुं घुटिकेय सदळं विक्रमादित्यपुण्यं ॥ १२ ॥ कं ॥ एनलेसेद विक्रमादि

२५. त्यनेंनित्तंल्चंद्रगुप्तवंष(श)दो[ळं]न्यज्जनियसतिनिपिद नोडिसि जनियिसिदं वीरविक्रमादित्य न्रि(नृ)पं ॥ १३ ॥

२६. चरितंगं नीतिगळां घनमेंनिसुपुवाप्तर्थिगिष्ठार्थदिंदं पिरिदुंदच्छौर्य्यमुर्बी(र्वी)वळयद बळसिंद

२७. ग्गळं लक्ष्मीसाम्राज्यरमाविस्तारदिंदत्यधिक मनुविनोदं मनोजंगमाय्तुब्बरमा स

२८. तुकीर्त्ति(र्ति) लोकक्कतुळमेंनिसिदं विक्रमादित्यदेवं ॥ १४ ॥ कं॥ आ वीरविक्रमादि । त्यावनिपंगुदयगिरि

२९. योळुदयिसुवंदिन श्रीवरनेने जोम्मन्रि(नृ)पं । भूवधुकण्देरेये पुट्टिदं कमळे(ले)शं ॥ १५ ॥ विनतानंदन सं

३०. गतं सजनितोद्यत्कामवर्षप्रवर्ध्दमानहर्षं विबुधाश्रयस्तुत पदं श्री मण्डळा(ला)ग्रवळो(लो)कनरागोदय

३१. ना सुदर्ष(र्श)नकरंगाश्चर्य्यरूपं सुजोम्मं नृपं राजिसुतिर्प्पनिंद्रदिवसेंद्रोपेंद्र वों दंददिं ॥ १६ ॥ अर

३२. सग्गिल्लरसप्रशक्ति रसिकत्वं कूडे कूर्प्पिल्ल कूर्प्पिरे विद्यावळियिल्ल विद्येयिरे नेर्प्पिल्लागे नेर्प्पिल्ल सच्चरितं पोदळ्दि

३३. रे विळा(ला)स प्रीतियिल्ल गुणोत्कर केल्लं नेरेदिर्द्द वेंदेनिसिदं श्री जोयि दे वोर्ब्बे(र्वि)पं ॥ १७ ॥ ॥ कंद ॥ आ जोम्मननुज

३४. गुत्तं राजाचारप्रशस्तियं कुवळेयलक्ष्मीजाप्यमंत्रविळसद्बीजाक्षरमं बुधाळियिंदोदिसुवं ॥ १८ ॥ मनसि

३५. जनोलगिप्पेसकदिं पडेदं । नेरे केट्ट मेय्यनीतनिनिवुद्धकीर्त्तियने पोर्द्दि हिमद्युति तत्कळंकवर्त्तनमनिदिर्प्पिदं

३६. यमनुमीतन खळ्गदोळिप्पनल्ते भोजनसुखदिंद मेंदेनिपुदुत्तम गुत्तनृपाळवृत्तकं ॥ १९ ॥ एनिसिद गुत्त

३७. भूमिपन वल्लभे पद्मलदेवि जाति पद्मिनियेने लक्ष्मियंतळदिनंगनुरागिसि राजहं-सवर्त्तनदेडेयागि सेब्य(व्य)

३८. कविचक्रदेसंस्तुतेयागि कामराजन जलदुर्ग्ग रसविशेषविनोददि माडिरूढिपळु ॥ २० ॥ । कं ॥ पद्मेय नि

३९. र्मळनोदर पद्मदिनी वीरविक्रममं पुट्टिदना पद्मभवनन्ते क्रिष्ण(कृष्ण)न पद्मोदरदल्लि पुट्टे नयविनुतुंटे ॥ २१ ॥ विन

४०. यं विक्रमशक्ति पुण्यवेंनिपी मूरुं गुणं राज्यमंडन देहंशुगळेन्तनल्सिरिगे पुण्यचेत

४१. नं बल्पु मेय्विनयं भूषणमेंदु षा(शा)स्त्रं रुचि शस्त्राभ्यासधर्मप्रवर्त्तनमेंदिंतिवु वीर विक्रमनोळिर्क्कुं

४२. प्राज्यसाम्राज्यनोळ्ळु ॥ २२ ॥ मोनेयोळ्खळ्गसहायवित्ति तनगाब्रिं(वृं)दं नरेंद्रायतेयेनेस-ल्सेनेम्मनं सततवमे

४३. यथारूपं तथा शीलं मेंदेनिसल्काव सुखं याविळने तां तेजःफळं राज्य मेंदेने निसल्विक्रम-शक्ति राजिसु

४४. गुमिंती विक्रमादित्यनोळ्ळु ॥ २३ ॥ जयवधुवुं वोर्मेयुं बयसुतिर्प्पदटंगनेयर्व्विळासदिं । बयसु

४५. वचेल्वु नीतितितिगळ्नडेयल्सुपथ प्रपंचमं बयसुव मार्ग्गवर्त्तिगळपेक्षगळं बयसुत्तवि-र्प्पतिप्रिय

४६. वेंनिपार्प्प राजिसुदिनं मिसुपं विभु वीर विक्रमं ॥ २४ ॥ स्वस्ति समधिगतपंचमहाशब्द म

४७. हामंडळे(लेश्व)रं उज्जयनीपुरवराधीश्वरं वटकल्पवि(वृ)क्षलांछितविजयध्वजं भुवन[र]क्ष

४८. णैकदक्षदक्षिणभुजं चंद्रगुप्तान्वय सुधार्ण्णवपूर्ण्नचंद्रं विभवामरेंद्रं

४९. हरणचरणनखकिरणसांद्रचंद्रिकाचकोरं गुरुपदपयोधरध्वानानंदित म

५०. यूरं मानिनी मानसर्ब(र्व)स्वसूरेकारं रण*दोळ्वी*रं मंडलि*कभै*रवं आनंदित युवतीन

५१ यनकैरवं पन्निर्ब्बर गण्डं समरषौं(शौं)डं आहवादित्यं वीर विक्रमादित्यं । बनवा*से*नाडं

५२. दुष्ट निग्रह शिष्टप्रतिपाळनदि पाळिसुत्तं गुत्त*वोळल नेलेवीडि नोळ्*सुखसंकथाविनो

५३. ददिं राज्यं*गेयु*त्तमिरे ॥ आ भूपाळपदाब्जभ्रंग*नेंनि*पं सद्भक्तियिं युक्तियिंदा भूपा

५४. ळनमंत्रयोग्य*नेंनि*सिपं तंन्नुद्ध वीरत्वदिंदा भूपाळन दक्ष दक्षिणभुजादंड निजं

५५. ता*नें*नल्का भूपाळन नायकाग्रणि जगद्विख्यातनी का*मेय* ॥ २५ ॥ वचन ॥ तदन्वय-*मेंतेने* । अत्य

५६. रसं चंडरसं सत्यद क*णेयें*निसि मिसुप धर्म्मद धुरमं नित्योत्सवदिं धरियिप क्रि(कृ)त्यौचित्य

५७. *मे* समस्त गुण*वे* नलेसेदरु ॥ २६ ॥ तत्सु*ते* माचलदेविय हि(हृ)त्सरसीरुह*दोळे*सेव रसमधुलहरी

५८. प्रोत्सुक*नेंनि*सि करग्रहसत्सुखमं पडेदनंदु नायक मारं ॥ २७ ॥ मारेयनायकं*गे*युत मा

५९. चलेगं जनिसिद्दों शंकरोदारपदाब्जभृंगनतिमंगळचेष्टितनंगनाजनक्की रतिवल्लभं जनित*नें*बिनविंबिन

६०. सद्गुणंगळिंदारुसमानविंदमम *नोळ्पडे* का*मेय*नायकाग्रयेय*नोळु* ॥ २८ ॥

६१. भीमन बल्पिं *नेग*ळ्दा । रामन साहसदिनणुवनि । न सद्भक्ति प्रेमदिनाद्य*नेंनि*प्पं । का*मेय*

६२. नुदात्तचित्रचरित्र ॥ २९ ॥ जवदिं श्री विक्रमांकस्थि(क्षि)तिपतितिळकं शतृसेनांगमं

६३. [तां] तविपुल्कुद्योगमं माळ्प*नेगे*वतिमदोच्चंड*वे* दंडषंडं नववेगब्राजि

६४. वाजिव्रजपतिबळपादतवन्ने ॥ क्रि(कृ)पाणाहव*दोळ्*मुंतिर्दविन्ने*के* निन*गे* भर *वें*दें बनाळ्दं*गे*

६५. कामं ॥ ३० ॥ कंद ॥ आ नरनाथन विश(ष)यद दानजळं कूडि परिदु*वें*ब*वो* लुर्ब्बीमानिनिय हारदंतिरे

६६. ता*नें*दुं तुंगभद्रे तद्देशदोळं ॥ ३१ ॥ भूरमणीतरळद *वोलीरे*ळुं भुवनंग*ळूळगे* सविततमहि

६७. माधारं मुक्तेश्वरनामारंभ*नेसे*पुतिर्प्पनीशनुमेशं ॥ ३२ ॥ स्वस्ति समस्त प्रशस्तिसहितं

६८. श्रीमनुमहामंडळेश्वरं वीर विक्रमादित्यदेवरसरु गुत्त*वोळल नेलेवीडि नोळु*

६९. सुखसंकथाविनोदिं राज्यं *गेय्यु*त्तमिरे ॥ तत्पादपदोपजीवि*येंनि*प खंडेय

७०. कार कामेयनायकं तंन स्वामिय चित्तवनुपार्ज्जिसि पारितोषिकमागि पडेद *होन्नव*

७१. तिय *होलदोळु* चामेश्वरदेवर *केय्यिं* मूडलु गो(*गो*)प्पेय ओणियिं *तें*कलु चतुराघाट

७२. शुद्दमागिरला रु मत्तरुमं स(श)कवर्षं १११३नेय विरोधिक्रि(कृ)तु संवत्सरद मा
७३. र्गशिरदमावासे सूर्य्यग्रहणदंदु श्रीमनु मुक्तेश्वरदेवर अंगरं
७४. गभोगक्के जीन्नोर्द्धार क्केन्दु मुक्तजीयर कालं कर्च्चि धा
७५. रापूर्व्वकं माडि कोट्ट ।। ।। श्री विश्वनाथाय नमः ।। श्री मुक्तेश्वराय नमः ।।
७६. ।। ।। ईंतीधर्म्मव प्रतिपाळिस(सि)दवरु प्रयागेयलग्घ्यतीर्थ
७७. कविलेयं कोंडु कोळगमं पोन्नलु कट्टिसि सासिर्ब्ब(र्व्व)रु वेदपारगरिगे कोट्ट फल ।। इ(ई) धर्म्मव
७८. नावनानुं कि(के)डिसिदनाब्राह्मणरुमं कविलेयं कोन्द महापातकनक्कु ।। स्वदत्तं(त्तां) परद
७९. त्तं(त्तां) वा यो हरेति(त) वशुं(सुं)धरा(राम्) ।। षष्टिर्व्वर्षसहस्राणि विष्टायां जायते क्रिमिः ।। ३३ ।। ...कब्ब
८०. विरोधिकृतु संवत्सरद पुश्य(ष्य)दमावासे ब्रि(बृ)हस्पति ... संक्रमण ... कूडिदल्लि श्री मुक्तेश्वरदेवर त्रिकाल
८१. दुपहारके श्रीमन्महामंडळेश्वरं वीर ... विक्रमादित्यदेवर ... महाजनंगळ संनिधान
८२. दलु कोट्ट गद्दे श्रीमदग्रहारं हेंनवतिय हाळ श्री कलिदेवर गद्देय तेंक आ देवरिं मूड बिट्ट गद्देकंब ।। २०।। इन्ती धर्मवं
८३. तप्पदे प्रतिपाळिसुवदु ।। [क]लुहंदरादियागि होरथर सहित रेओजन केलस ।। मुक्तेश्वराय नमः ।।

Inscription No. III

१. ॐ नमः शिवाय । नमस्तुंगशिरश्चुंबिचंद्रचामरचारवे । त्रैलोक्यनगरारंभमू
२. लस्तंभाय शंभवे ।। १ ।। शब्दादयोऽपि गृह्यंते क्रियंते वचनादयः ।। अविलंघ्या हि सर्वे
३. षामाज्ञा शंभोर्ग्गरीयसी ।। २ ।। स्वस्ति श्री जयमंगळप्रदमहादेवशृ(श्रु)तिव्रातदिं प्रस्तुत्य प्रभु सं
४. स्थिरायवनखंडानन्दसंप्रीतियं वस्तुसोमनुडुघ कीर्तियनुदारैश्वर्य्यमं शौर्य्यमं
५. विस्तीर्णावनिमंडळक्कनुदिनं कूर्त्तीगे मुक्तेश्वरनुं ।। ३ ।। स्वस्ति समस्तसुरासुरकिरीट-कोटिखचितमणिमरीचिरेचिधाम
६. विराजितचरणं । अचिंत्यगुणाभरणं । अनंतब्रह्मांडषंडनिवासनिजभवनं । इच्छामात्रकृतच-तुर्द्दशभुवनं

७.रु(ऋ)ग्यजुःसामाथर्ववेदार्थस्रु(स्मृ)तिपुराणधर्म्मशास्रोपगीयमानशुभचरितं । निजशक्तिकळा-
मात्रविमोहित

८. लीलाचरितं । प्रमथगणमनःसरोजराजहंसं । समुत्तुंगजटाजूटविभूषितचंद्रकळावतंसं । श्री
पार्वती

९. वदनपम्कजराजमित्रं । शरणागततापत्रितयरौद्रविद्रावणकारुण्यछ्छत्रनप्प श्रीमन्महादेवं
दिव्यसिंहासनारू

१०. ढनागि पार्वतीसहितमिरे नंदि नंदिनाथ वीरभद्र भद्रकाळ महाकाळ भृंगीश प्रमुखासंख्यात
गणंगळिं संसेव्यमा

११. ननागि श्री कयिळासदल्लि वइडोलगंगोट्टु सुखसंकथाविनोददिंदिर्द्द संप्रस्थानवसमयदोळु
आ उमामहेश्वरं ग

१२. णंगळिगे प्रसन्ननागि यिंतेंदं ॥कंद॥ इदे नाल्कुं वेदपारं बगेवडे दिटदिं
सर्व्वशास्रार्त्थपारं पदपिं स्रु(स्मृ)त्यर्त्थपारं त्रिभुवनभुव

१३. नज्ञानविज्ञानपारं । सद्वाक्यार्त्थैकपारं । प्रणवसमुदितं ध्यानभावैकपारं विदितं श्री
ज्योतिर्लिंगामरगणकरुणोत्पंन्नभक्तिप्र

१४. सादवु एने केळ्ददद्रिजे बिन्नपं शिव जगक्की मार्गमन्तोरबेळ्केनलन्दा प्रभु नंदिनाथन
मोगन्नोडल्के श्री संगमेशनपुत्रं

१५. बसवय्य बंकनदरें (देरं) शिवमुद्दुदेवं जनक्कनिमित्तं शिवदेवनागियु गण श्रीपादमन्तो-
रुवों। ५ ॥ अदेंतेंदडे ॥ कं ॥ अवन

१६. तकंधररागियें दिविजर्शिवरात्रि माडिदा तत्पददोळ् धवळेश्वराख्य लिंगदोळविरळ शिव-
मुद्दुदेवमुनिपतियिप्पनं ॥ ६ ॥ अ

१७. भ्य(व्य)क्तशंकरननतिसुभ्य(व्य)क्तं माडितोर्पेन्नेनुती जगदोळ् । दिव्यधवळेशलिंगनब्यय
शिवमुद्दुमुनि वरं भाविसुवनु ॥ ७ ॥ शिवमुद्दु

१८. ब्रतिपतिगीदिविजेंद्रपदगळेंबिवें पासटियो भवने कलिकालकलुषव ताविसुवंवेवदिंद
मूर्त्तियन्ताळ्दिर्द्दनु ॥ ८ ॥ केशव जिन

१९. बौद्धादिगळीशन किंकररु बेरे देवतेयल्लेंदा शिवमुद्दुब्रतिप महेशनोलिदालिसिदं जगत्रय-
वरियलु ॥ ९ ॥ अम

२०.रगणचरणकोमळविमळदळोत्फुल्लकमळयुगळपरागप्रमोदितमनद्विरेफोपमेयिं शिवमुद्दुदेव-
मुनिपतियिप्पं ॥ १० ॥

२१. अनंतरवु श्रीगिरिनिवासनाज्ञेयिं बंद वीरब्रतियं नोडि ॥ वृ ॥ हवणिसभारद-
ग्रजकुलोद्भवनागि विधात्रि(तृ)निं

२२. द संभविसिद नाल्कु सृष्टियोळु पुट्टिदनेंबडे जायतेस्तियेंबवु मोदलाद षड्विकृति-
योळसले कूडिदनल्ल भावि
२३. सद्भवनोलविन्द वीर शिवदेव गणेश्वरनागि तोरिदन् ॥ ११ ॥ ॥व ॥ एन्दु तन्नोळपरि-
भाविसि मिंतेन्दं ॥ सुरनदिये तुंग
२४. भद्रावरनदि सुरसमिति विप्रगणनिकरवु आ सुरगिरि महेशभवनवु धरेयोळ्ळकविळास-
वेनिप मुक्तिक्षेत्रवु ॥ १२ ॥
२५. आ मुक्तिक्षेत्रदोळिर्द्दी मैमेयमेरेयबेकेनुत गुरु नुडियल् । स्वामि मुकुतेशने परंधाम श्री
ज्योतिर्नेदोल
२६. विन्दं ॥ १३ ॥ शकवर्ष ११४८नेय पार्थिवसंवत्सरद भाद्रपद शुद्ध १५ सोमवार चंद्रो-
पराग पुण्यति
२७. थिय मध्याह्न समयदोळु बंदु पोक्कु ॥ कं ॥ विरचिसिदं कैळा(ला)सद चरित्रमं
वीरभद्रन श्री
२८. पदमं । स्मरिसुत वीरव्रतमं धरिसिदनतुळविक्रमं शिवदेवं ॥ १४ ॥ सी-
मेयनुल्लंगि(घि)सदुदे नेम धरेगोरगदिप्पु
२९. दे सले नियमुवु । कामिसदिप्पुदे नेमं स्वामि महादेवनित्तोडल्लद नेमं ॥ (१५) ॥
अदरटिद भूतंगळ चेदरिसि बेन्न
३०. ट्टिकुट्टिदं भैरवं । केदरुव भंतरदैववनोदेदं वीरेशनात्मजं शिवदेवनु ॥ १६ ॥ मारिदो-
रेयागि लिंगद सलेवरंब
३१. रलु तुंगभद्रेय पडे होसान्तु जरेदु नूकिद वीरगणंगळ कुमारनी शिवदेवनु ॥ १७ ॥
शिवपदमन्देदु
३२. वडे मार्गविदेयेमुत्तखिळजगके तोरुव नेवदिन्दविरळवागिरे नलविं शिवकट्टेयकट्टि तोरिदं
शिवदेवनु ॥ १८ ॥
३३. हवणिसलरियदेनिसुव शिवकविळासवनखिळ देवतापदसहिती भुवनक्के तंदु शिव-
सुखभवनद नेवदिन्द रचिसिदं शिवदेवनु ॥ १९ ॥
३४. त्रयियंनेलेगोळिसद वोल्त्रयंगदिं मूरु भुवनमं निलिसिद वोल्त्रयिभुवनिकेयिं रुद्रप्रियभवनव-
नोलिदु
३५. माडिसिद शिवदेवनु ॥ २० ॥ आ कळशांतंबरे मूलोकवरियॆ जीर्णवाद
शिवभवनवमत्ता कळसंबरे शिलेयिं लोकोत्तमवागि मा
३६. डिसिद शिवदेवनु ॥ २१ ॥ शिवदेवव्रतींद्रस्य लिंगार्च्चने कळालवं । अचिंत्य सर्वशास्त्रा-
द्यैरनौपम्यमगोचरं ॥ (२२) ॥ अळख्खळख्खयरू

३७. णैकळद्द दिडभक्तिभावसंपण्णा कळिबळकुळणिम्महणो भळसग्गुणसायरोभवेवोल्खु शिवदेव ।। २३ ।।आरुं दर्शनमं

३८. सले मीरि शिवगणाज्ञाचिंतामणि कयिसारे शिवदेवमुनिपति तोरिमेरद लिंगजंगम-वैक्यक्रमवं ।। २४ ।। मत्तं पुरात

३९. नर चरित्रक्कतिविचित्रमागि लिंगार्च्चनंगेय्युतमिरियिरे ।। स्वस्ति श्रीमतु यादवनारायणं भु

४०. जबळप्रतापचक्रवर्ति श्रीवीरमहादेवराय विजयराज्योदयद (मू)रनेय दुंदुभि संवत्सरद वयिशा

४१. ख सु(शु)ध्द १५ सोमवार सोमग्रहणदल्लि स्वस्ति समस्त प्रशस्तिसहितं श्रीमन्महामंडळेश्वरं । उ

४२. ज्जयिनीपुरवराधीश्वरं वटकल्पवृक्षलांछितविजयध्वजं । भुवनरक्षणैकदक्षिणभुजं चंद्रगु

४३. प्तान्वयसुधार्ण्णवपूर्ण्नचंद्रं । विभवामरेंद्रं हरचरणनखकिरणसांद्रचंद्रिकाचकोरं श्री गु

४४. रुपदपयधरध्वानानन्दितमयूरं । मानिनीमानसर्वस्वसूरेकारं रणदोळु नीरं मं

४५. डळिकभयिरवं । आनंदितयुवतीनयन कयिरवं पंन्निर्ब्बरगंडं । श(स)मरकांडं शर-णागतवज्रपं

४६. जरं आहवादित्यं । वीरविक्रमादित्यं । आतंगनुनयदिं संजातर्गुतजोयिविक्रमादित्य-व्विख्यातर्न्निजभुज विज

४७. योपेतर्प्पन्नेरडु मंडळिकरगंडरु ।। २५ ।। आ विक्रमंग(म्) मैळलदेविगवुदिसिद कुमारकंठीरव मत्ता विक्रमानुजातं श्री

४८. गुत्तं निजभुजैकनादं ।। २६ ।। अन्ता गुत्तनृपन विशाळवक्षस्थळदोळनवरतं सिरि निज-भुजासिधारेयोळु विज

४९. यश्रीयोलिदिप्पुदरं वीरवितरण त्यागभोगं गेय्वुत्तं निजराजधानि गुत्तवोळलनेलेवीडिनो ळसुखराज्यंगे

५०. य्वुत्तिर्द्दु श्री शिवदेवरकारुण्यमं पडेदु श्री सोमनाथलिंगलब्धवरप्रसादनागिर्द्दवसरदोळु मनोत्साहदिं बरसिद

५१. शासनक्रमवेन्तेंदेडे । मुंन हिरियजोयिदेवर्सरु चिक्ककुरुवत्तिनग्रहार माडुवम्दु श्री त्रि-भुवनमल्ल देवन परमविश्वासि मणं

५२. बेनायकन प्रेरणेयिं आगामि यक्षिणिसहित तांब्रशासनदल्लि बरसि कुळव कडिदु कल्ल नट्टु सर्व्वनमस्यं माडि शिवदेवर शिव

५३. कार्यक्काराधिसिद व्रति २ ककं । मने २ तुडिके २ मळव २ हडहुगेय हळ्ळदिं मूड एकस्थलदलि एरे मत्तरु एंटु ।। मत्तं

५४. काळयुक्त संवत्सरद कार्त्तिक शुद्ध ८ सोमवारदंदु श्री शिवदेवर(रु)गो(गो)पे कुरुवत्तिय प्रति गृहस्थर कय्यलु क्रयगों

५५. ड क्षेत्र गो(गो)पेयल्लि आलकोळनिं मूडलु एरेमत्तरु ४ कं ५० चिक्ककरुवत्तियलि हिरिय केयिं तेंक हेडहुगे हळ्ळदिं

५६. मूडलु एरेमत्तरु २ कं ५० ॥ गो(गो)पेयल्लि मने २ तुडिके २ इंतिवयिक्कुं अशेष महाजनंगळु अर्त्थव कोंडु कुळव क

५७. डिदु कल्ल नट्टु सर्व्वनमस्यं माडि शिवदेवरिगे आराधनेय माडिदरु ॥ मत्तं श्री शिव-देवरु महाजनंगळ कय्यलु

५८. क्रयगोंड स्थळविवर ॥ गो(गो)पेयलि बंन्नि(य केरे)योळगे होंन्नवत्तिगे होद नडुवण दारियिं तेंकलेरे मत्तरु १ कं ५० बं

५९. न्नियिं तेंकलेरे कंब ६० । अल्लिं मूडमक्किककंब ५० । होंन्नवत्तियिं बंद देविय दारियिं मूड केंगाडु कंब ५० बिल्लवत्तदे

६०. रें म १ दारियिंबडगलेरे कंब ६० । कुरुवत्तियल्लि कोंडगेरेयिं तेंक प्रथमस्थळदल्लि कंब ६० । आलकोळनिं मूडले

६१. रे म १ कं ७० अन्तु मत्तरु ७ गो(गो)पेमने २ कुरुवत्तियल्लि मत्तरु १ नाल्वत्तर होडदलि येरेकंब ८५ मूडमान्य भूमियलि म

६२. त्तरु १ गो(गो)पेय कोंटबंन्नियेरे कंब ५० अन्तु मत्तरु ३ कं ३५ मने गो(गो)पेयल्लि १ कुरुवत्तियलि मने २ अन्तु मत्तरु १० कं

६३. ब ३५ मने ५ र कुळव कडिवदके श्रीगुत्तर्सदेवनु अशेषमहाजनंगळिगे अर्त्थव कोट्टु कुळव कडिसि कल्लनट्टु सर्व्वनमस्यं मा

६४. डि श्री शिवदेवरिगे आराधिसिदनु ॥ मत्तं बेळुवोळल बोम्मगवुडन कय्य[लु] क्रयगोंड केय्य स्थळ बडगवोलनलि तन्न

६५. बळियिं पडुवलेरे मत्तरु ४ बडग म ४ अन्तु मत्तरेंटु मने १ व एंदेंदु सर्वबाधे प-रिहारमाडि मक्कळु मक्कळ ...

६६. दे सलिसुव बासे(भाषे)यिं कुळव कडिदु कल्ल नट्टु बोंमगवुड शिवदेवरिगे ... आराधिसि ॥ गुत्तर्सदेवनाराधिसिदनु ...

६७. ळल कयि म ८ मने १ कुरुवत्तिय केयि म २ कं ८५ मने २ गो(गो)पेयल्लि केयि कं ५० ... शिवदेवरु बसवय ...

६८. ण्य माडि कोट्टु व्रुत्ति ॥ मत्तं सिंघणवर्ष शुभकु(कृ)तु संवत्सर पुष्य सु... देवर कये ...

६९. वात्तियशेषमहाजनंगळु होंगे तिंगळींगे हाग वो ...

७०. आ बड्डियिंदाद ग १५ वं आ शिवदेवरु माडुव लिंगजंगम ...
७१ (१). श्री कन्हरदेववर्षद सिद्धार्ति(र्थि) संवत्सरद चैत्र बहुळ १५ सो सूर्यग्रहणद समयदल्लि चवुडि सेट्टियर करणद नागर्सन तंम भानुदेवनु *कोट्ट* तोट गद्देय *केळगे*
७२ (२). गंगन कंब ५ आ स्थळदलि *जोगिसेट्ट कोट्ट* तोट कंब ५ मत्तं गुत्तर्सदेवनु *कोट्ट* तोट कंब ६ अदयिसर कुळव कडिसि कल्ल नट्टु सर्वनमस्यं माडि श्री
७३ (३). शिवदेवरि*गे* गुत्तर्सदेव*नेया*राधिसिदनु ॥ मुंन *होंन* बोमिसेट्टियरु शिवदेवारि*गे* आराधिसिद गद्दे मत्तरु १० ... (हडुवलु) ... हूदोट कंब ५
७४ (४). *होंन*वत्तियल्लि गो(*गो*)पेय दारियिं बडगलु गंगन कंब ५
७५ (१). यी शासनमं पेळ्दु ब
७६ (२). रेद गुत्तवोळल [मेव]
७७ (३). णंगळु

Inscription No. IV

१. ॐ नमः शिवाय । नमस्तुंगशिरश्चुंबिचंद्रचामरचार वे । त्रैलोक्यनगरारंभमूलस्थं(स्तं)भा
२. य शंभवे ॥ १ ॥ शब्दादयोऽपि गु(ग)ह्यंते क्रिय[ं]ते वचनादयः ॥ अविलंघ्या हि सर्वेषामाज्ञा शं
३. भोर्ग्गरीयसी ॥ २ ॥ (कं) श्री मुक्तेश्वरनतुळप्रेमदि रक्षिसु*गे* जगमननुपम लक्ष्मीधामनगण्यमहो
४. दय नामं शृतिमौळिरंजित श्रीचरणनु ॥ ३ ॥ स्वस्ति समस्तसुरासुरगण किंन्नरकिंपुरुष ग
५. रुडगंधर्व्वसिद्धविद्याधरपन्नगप्रमुखनाकिनिकायविनिमितप्रोद्यदुत्तुंगमकुटतटपट्टघटित
६. चंचच्चटचटुळमणिमाणिक्यश्रेणिकिरणारुणमरीचिमंजरीरंजितश्रीपादपद्म सत्यसमुदि
७. तसत्क्रियोपकृतक्क्रियाकांडफलानपेक्षितनिरस्तातिशयनित्योत्सवोदग्रप्रत्यग्रीकृत हरामळचरण
८. ध्याननिर्द्दिष्टापरोक्षज्ञानसिद्धशिवयोगारूढगूढनिवासनिजसद्म । पृथुळकटीतटोपशोभितम
९. हापद्म कपर्द्दबंधांतरंगरंगनर्तितमंदाकिनीतुंगतरंगाकुळोच्चळ द्विशदविशुदकीर्त्ति
१०. करपल्लवेव चूडाग्रखचितचारुचंद्रकळावतंस । अभीळबा(भा)ळभुजंगयुगकुंडळमंडित-कर्ण्णा
११. वतंस । महाविष्णुकंकाणब्रतवामांस । अतिमथनसंभूताखिळहाळाहळकाळकूटकपिश-नीलग्री
१२. व । अचिंत्यप्रभाव ॥ श्री महादेव । येंद्रसंख्यातामरगणंगळु स्तोत्रं*गेय्*युत्तमिरे श्री कैळास

१३. निवासियिंतेदं ॥ व्रि ॥ स्तुतिगें कारण पेळिमेंदोडे गणंगळु बिंन्नपं देवदेव दुःक्रु(कृ)तदिं धर्म्मवडंगि

१४. पोय्तु कलिकालं पेर्च्चे चार्ब्बा(र्वा)क सा(सौ)गतबौद्धागमवर्त्तिसुत्तमिदे लोकालोकमं पाळिपोळ्मतियं

१५.माळ्पुदे कज्जमेंदु नुडियलु श्री पार्व्वतीवल्लभं ॥ ४ ॥ अक्षयनिधान मुक्तिय दिक्षास्थळ तुंगभद्रे प

१६. श्चिम मुखदिनघक्षयमं माडलु तद्दक्षिण तटदल्लि मेरगु मुक्तिक्षेत्रं ॥ ५ ॥ अल्लिद्दु मूरु लोकद

१७. रेल्लर पावनव माळ्पेनेनुतगजातावल्लभनवतरिसिद भूवल्लभेगनुरागमप्पिनं मुक्तीशनु ॥ ६ ॥ लिं

१८. गववतरिसिता हा हिंगदे नाविप्पेवेंदंसंख्यातर्भू। रंगक्के बरलिकमरगणंगळमोघाज्ञे

१९. यिंद श्री शिवदेवनु ॥ ७ ॥ उदयिसिदनग्रजन्मदपददोळ्तनुगुणवनोंददेल्लागम-दोळ्मदनविरो

२०. धिये श्रौतोदित देवनेनुत्त तिळिदु श्री शिवदेवनु ॥ ८ ॥ आश्रम नाल्कुं तिळियलना-श्रमवाश्रममेने

२१. यदश्रमदिन्द शिवाश्रमविनिहितवेंदत्याश्रममं धरिसि मेरेद श्री शिवदेवनु ॥ ९ ॥ लिंगवनप्पिद तो

२२. ळ्गाळिनंगनेयरनप्पेनळिपि नोडें कूडे मनंगोडेनवधारेंनुतवभंगव्रति शंकरंगे भासे(षे)य कोट्टनु ॥ १० ॥

२३. व ॥ मत्तमनेकभासे(षे)य नीशंगे कोट्टु ॥ कं ॥ तलेदंड स्वर्ग्गमुक्तियफलव-नपेक्षिसिदेनादडे शंकर केळ् ॥ स

२४. ले पुंण्यपापवेरडर फलवल्लद नित्यपूजेयं माडिदपें॥ ११ ॥ एन्दु धु(ट्ट)ढसंकल्पनागि ॥ आसे (शे)य पास(श)

२५. मं परेदु रोसद मीसेय कित्तु काम बिडोसरिसेंदु लोभमदमं बेदरट्टुत मानमोहतृष्णासे

२६. बलंगळं जरदु बगिसि गेल्दु रे तोत्तु माडिदं दूसक धूमकेतु शिवदेवनतर्कगुणप्रभावनं ॥ १२ ॥

२७. मेट्टिद कलिकिय नोरेय कट्टिद नूरेंटु ब्या(व्या)धिगोंनमशिवयेंदिट्टं विभूतितिलक-वकट्टाळ्द

२८. लदंक मनदोळतिनिःसं(शं)कनु ॥ १३ ॥ जळमोदलागिरे पत्तुज्वळवेनिप स्नानमेंटु पत्तरोळिदे नि। र्म्मळमेंनि

२९. पुदेंदु भस्मदि *तोळेदं* कर्मादिमवनीशिवदेवनु ।। १४ ।। झंकेगे मनदोळ्सं(ळ्शं)किसिदडे निंन्न भ

३०. क्कराणेले पशुपति । शंकरोळादूडं बेडें केळ् बेडिदेडे येंन्नतलेयदंडवु ।। १५ ।। अणकदणि

३१. कलिगे मुंकणि सेणसुवरादिगळ्गे बायसणि जगवरियल् गुणि सकळवेदशास्त्रद कणि शिवतत्वानुभाव

३२. नी शिवदेवनु ।। १६ ।। शिवसद्विद्येये विद्येयेंदु शिवभावं भावक्केंदुवा शिवमंत्रगळे मंत्रक्केंदु शिवमूर्त्तिध्या

३३. नवे ध्यानवी शिवनित्योत्सव वुत्सवं शिवकथाळापंगळाळाप मिक्कवसेब्यंगळेसुत्त वीरशिवदेवनु ताळ्द

३४. वीरव्रतं ।। १७ ।। शिवनं तोरुव मार्ग्ग मार्ग्ग शिवसदाचारंगळाचारवी शिवसंयोगवे योग नित्यशिवपूजा क

३५. र्म्मवे कर्म्मवी शिवने देवनु देवनन्य विषयं बेडल्ल होल्लेंदु श्री शिवदेवप्रभुवेत्तिदं ध्वजपताकोद्दं

३६. डमं दंडमं ।। १८ ।। एलगळ वादिगीदि पडवैष्णवगीष्णव सौरगिवुर माणे लगळ बोमिगिंमि निगमार्त्थ

३७. वन रियद यज्जिगिज्जि बेडेलगळ बौद्धगिद्द बरि यागमिगीगमि मंत्रवादि साकुलियदि

३८. रें दुबग्गिपुदु शिवदेवन कालहोंदोडरु ।। १९ ।। बेरळं कर्च्चि करंगळं मुगिदु बायं पा

३९. युवं तंमेरड्करदिं मुच्चुत बायिविट्टु कुसिदो मेय्यिक्कुतं पल्गळं किरिदं बे शरणार्त्थि

४०. येंदनुदिनं षड्दर्शनं बाहुलि भरदोळ्तळ्तेळलुत्तविर्द्दुवनिशं शिवदेव वामांघ्रियो

४१. ळु ।। व ।। मत्तं दुट्टरघरट्ट लिंगक्के कट्टिदोरे कोट्टबास(भाषे)दिट्टेवारिय कट्टाळु शिवदेवं श्री ज्योतिनाथ

४२. ने मुक्तनाथनेंदरिदु कालकल्कियं जरेदु । तनुगुणंगळं मेरेदु । आवरणंगळं तो

४३. रदु । उभयकर्मद बेरकोरदु । मदनशरंगळं मुरिदु । माया पाशमं परिदो

४४. ।। कं ।। मानसवाचिकायकवेनुंटुड [गि] निंन्नभक्तरोळनिशं सानंददिंद माळ्पें नानन्यवनेने

४५. येनुडिये माडें कूडें ।। २० ।। इंतेनुत्तदेवलोकदल्लि कोट्ट प्रतिज्ञेयं तिळिदु ।। निष्ठिसि

४६. नोडुत वुळिदानुष्ठानं पोल्लक्केंदु कोडा शिवपदनिष्ठेनेलेगोळु श्रेष्ठानुष्ठानव मा

४७. ळ्पननुदिनं शिवदेवनु ।। २१ ।। लिङ्गक्के जंगमक्कं हिंगदे दासित्व माळ्पुदे बेसनेन्दा सं

४८. गनबसवं *बेससे* मन*गों*डच्चिर्सुवनुभयलिंगव मुददिं ॥ २२ ॥ मृडगणवरप्रस(सा)दवं पडेदं

४९. जगवरियलंदु संगनबसवं पडेदा प्रसादसिद्धिय । कडुवीरव्रतदिं पडेदनी शिवदेवनु ॥ २३ ॥

५०. ॥ व ॥ मत्तं सत्यगणंगळ नित्यप्रसादसंपन्ननागि हिंग*दे* लिंगार्च्चनङ्ग्य्वुत्तमि*रे* यि*रे* ॥

५१. स्वस्ति श्रीमतु यादवरायनारायणं भुजबळ प्रौढप्रताप चक्रवर्त्ति श्री वीर[म]ह

५२. देवराय विजयराज्यप्रवर्ध्धमानमाचंद्राक्र्कतारांबरं वुदितोदित बरुत्तमिरे

५३. स्वस्ति समस्त प्रशस्तिसहितं श्रीमन्महामंडळेश्वरं उज्जयनीपुरवराधीश्वरं चं

५४. द्रगुप्तान्वयं गुत्तकुळकमळमार्त्तंड कदनप्रचंड हंन्निब्बरगंड मंडळिकभैरवं शरणा

५५. गत वज्रपम्जरं श्री स्पर्शलिंग *गे*(ग)ळगनाथदेवर दिब्यश्रीपादपद्माराधकनप्प श्रीवीर विक्रमंगं म

५६. हादेवियरिगं पुट्टिद विक्रमांकन प्रभाव*मेंतेंदोडे* ॥ धर्म्मद *पे*र्म्मने सत्यद निर्म्मळ*तेय*

५७. *गो*तु कविजनंगळकडवर ॥ कूर्म्म*य* ताय्व*ने* जाणिन निर्म्माणद रत्नकळश विक्रमभूपनं

५८. आ विक्रमनृपंगं मयिळलदेवियरिगं पुट्टिद गुत्तनृपन प्रभाववं *पोग*ळ्वडे

५९. दिक्कांताजनताललाटपटलप्रोद्भासिरत्नोज्वळादर्शं सज्जनचित्तवृत्तिविभवप्रख्यात कीर्त्तिध्व

६०. जः । सत्योत्साहसुखाब्धिवर्द्धनयशः कौमोदिनीवल्लभः श्रीमान्भूपतिविक्रमांकतनुजं(जः)

६१. श्री गुत्तभूपाळकः ॥ २४ ॥ कं ॥ आ विक्रमन पराक्रमवा विक्रम ... *नो*लवदारतन-*गोगेय*

६२. भुदर्ग्गीव*डेयो*ळु शर*णें*दर काव*डेयो*ळु भूमिपंगार्स्सरि*ये* ॥ २५ ॥ मलपविरोधि वैरिग

६३. ळ गंड रणांगणदोडर्द्दु *बे*। बलव*ने पो*र्द्दु बरतदिय निड्डर गण्डनिदिर्च्चि*बे*र्च्चिकक्कुल*तेय* मा

६४. डुवग्गळद वीरर गंडना साहसक्के *मेय्*गलि*ये*निसिप्प *तो*ण्ड*रो*ळु गंडरगंडनु

६५. गुत्तभूभुजनु ॥२६ ॥ ॥ व ॥ मत्तं [दश]दिग्वळयंगळ [यें]गळं पर्ब्बिदकीर्त्तिकां*ते*यं वीरवि

६६. तरणंगळं पोगळिसिकोळुत्त निजराजधानि गुत्त*वोळ*ल*लो*ळ्सुख राज्यं गेयिवुत्तमिर्द्दू

६७. ॥ कं ॥ चंडासियिं पंन्निर्ब्बर्मंडळिकर गंडनेंब जससयितु भू । मंडळवरियलु शिवने

६८. गण्ड*नें*निप्पोंदु कीर्तियं पडेदिप्पनु ॥ २७ ॥ व ॥ यिं*ते*नुत्त तं*न्नो*ळु परिभाविसि नोडि ॥ क ॥ धारिणि*योळु*

६९. ग्र तपदिं वीरेश्वर*नो*लवपडेद शिवदेवय्यन । कारुण्य*के*न*गे* जीवन बेरिल्लेंदेंरिदु तत्प्रसाद

७०. व पडेदनु ॥ २८ ॥ अंतं शिवगणप्रसाददिं शिवदेवर कारुण्यवं पडेदु श्री सोमनाथलिंग

७१. वनवधरिसि*को*ंब समयदलि गुत्तर्सरु श्री शिवदेवर शिवपादंगळि*गेया*राध*ने*य मा

७२. डिद शिवपुरक्के बेवोळल रामगवुंडन मग बोंमगवुंडनं करिसि बेवोळल बडग
७३. ण होलदल्लि गंगनारु मत्तरुयेरेय केय्य निक्केंदड बोंमगवुंड बरोळ्लितं म
७४. हाप्रसाद जीय यंदु । गुत्तोळल्नाड प्रभुगळ मुंदे कै कयिकोंडु तंन्नस्थळद हे
७५. ग्गडे मुद्दय्य मुख्य समस्त प्रजेप्रकुति येंटुहिट्टु पंचमठ नखर मुंमुरिदं
७६. ण्ड सहित बंदु । तन्न गवुडगेयिं बडगण बसय्यन केयिं मूडलु । चि
७७. क्क कुरुवतिय होल मेरेय सालबेळनिं तेंकलु । येण्नेगोळकडद कोळदिं प
७८. डुवलु । कलिदेवर । कंमरगेयिं बडगलेकस्थळदलि यिक्किद येरेय भूमि गंगन
७९. मत्तरारु । आ भूमिय फल बेवोळल कारणमिल्ल ।।शकवर्ष ११८५नेय दुन्दु
८०. भि संवत्सरद वयिशाख शुद्द १५ सोमवार सोमग्रहणदंदु श्रीमदमरंगणं
८१. गळ निजसिंहासनवप्प मुक्तिक्षेत्र भूकयिळासविदेंदु । श्री शिवदेवरु जगद्धिता
८२. र्त्थवागि रचिसिद शिवदेवपुरक्के वर्षंप्रति बरुत्तबहुदु । अदु संर्व्वमान्य श्रीमान्य
८३. जयमान्य । विजयमान्य ।। मत्तं स्वस्ति समधिगत पंचमहाशब्द द्वारावतीपुरवरा
८४.धीश्वर सुवर्ण्न गरुडध्वजं वृष्णिवंशोद्भवं यादवकुळ कमळकळिकाविकासभास्करं अरिरा
८५. य जगझंप माळवराय कदनत्रिनेत्रं गौर्ज्जरभयज्वरं चोळरायदिसा(शा)पट्टं(टं) तेलु
८६. गरायस्थापनाचार्य्य इत्यादि राजावळीसमाळंक्र(कृ)त श्रीमत्प्रौढप्रतापचक्रवर्ति श्री
८७. महादेवराय विजयराज्य प्रवर्द्धमानमाचंद्रार्क्कं बरुत्तमिरे । दक्षिणदिकुतट
८८. विळसितलक्ष्मिगे नीनधिपनेंदु यादवभूप निरीक्षिसि बेससलु मुददिं रक्षिप तोरगलेय
८९. देवरस जनपदव ।। २८ ।। ।। व ।। श्री शिवदेवरु माडुव लिंगजंगमसमाराधनेगे सर्व्वभावदिं शुश्रू
९०. से(षे)य मार्प्पुदेंदु श्री महादेवराय निरूपंगोडे स्वस्ति समस्तप्रशस्तिसहितं श्रीमन्महा
९१. प्रधानं सर्व्वाधिकारि तोरगलेय देवरसरु श्रीमद्दक्षिणवारणासियेनिप [प]श्चिमवाहिनि तुं
९२. गभद्रेय दक्षिण तीरदोळेसेव मुक्तिक्षेत्रनिवासरप्प श्री शिवदेवरलिंगदर्शनार्त्थं बंदु ।। रु
९३. धिरोधा(द्गा)रि संवत्सरद ज्येष्ठ बहुळ ५ आदिवार षडशीतिमुखसंक्रान्ति तत्कालदल्लि बे
९४. ळुवोळल बडगण होलदल्लि मुंन कल्लुनट्टिद्द गंगनयेंटु मत्तरु भूमियनु
९५. सर्व्वनमस्यवागि समाराधनेय माडिदनु ।। मंगळमहा श्री श्री शिवमस्तु ।।
९६. मत्तं गुत्तरसनु आ बेळवोळल पडुव वोलनल्लि होंनवत्तिगे होददा
९७. रिय बडगण येरें(रे)यकेय गंगन कंब ५० मं वोडेयर पादक्के
९८. आराधिसिदनु । आ केय्यनु वोडेयरु बसवय्यंगे सर्व्वनमस्यवागि कोट्ट
९९. रं ।। श्रीमतु सिंघणवश्र(र्ष) शुभकु(कृ)त्संवत्सरद पुष्य सु(शु)द्ध ३ सु(शु)क्रवार

१००. द ... सि(शि)वदेवर केय्यलु गो(*गो*)*पे* कुरुवत्तिय य(अ)शेष महाजनंगळु होंगे
तिंगळिं

१०१. श्रीरामदेवरायविजयराज्योदयद १६*ने*

१०२. य ब्यय संवत्सरद ... [यंतर] यशेषमहाजनंगळु यी धर्म्मव नडेयिसिदल्लिं

१०३. दं मेले ... गणंगळ समक्षदल्लि या मुक्तेश्वर देवरु सिद्धाय

१०४. व *तेरु*व या*ळु* मत्तरु *के*य ... (यै)वत्तु *होन्निंगे*वु बड्डिड*गे*वु सलुवागि या भू

१०५. मियनु कुळव कडिदु या महाजनंगळु मुक्तेश्वरदेव*र्गे* सर्व्वमान्यवागि कोट्टरु ॥ ई
धर्म्मकि

१०६. यारु यहुदल्लंदरे ... सासिर होरागु हदिनेंटु समय*के* द्रोहिगळु ॥

१०७. स्वदत्तं ... सहस्राणि विष्टायां जायते क्रिमि ॥

Inscription No. V

१. नमस्तुंगशिरश्चुंबिचंद्रचामरचारवे । त्रैलोक्यनगरारंभ

२. मूलस्तंभाय शंभवे ॥ १ ॥ शब्दादयोऽपि ग्र(गृ)ह्यंते

३. क्रियंते वचनादयः ॥ अविलंघ्या हि सर्वेषामाज्ञा शंभोर्ग्गरीयसी ॥ २ ॥ बालेंदु

४. कळाभूषित मौळि श्री कल्लिनाथनवनीजनमं पाळिसुगे शरधि शशिता । राळि कुलं दिग्गजं

५. गळिप्पंनेवरं ॥ ३ ॥ स्वस्ति समस्तदिविजदनुजखचरखेचरगंधर्वकिंपुरुष

६. प्रशि(सि)द्ध मुनींद्र फणींद्र गणेंद्र प्रमथ प्रचंड प्रणित विविध नृत्य गीत वाद्य वि

७. द्या वीणावेणुनादविनोदसंगवरदानि मल्लिकार्ज्जुनं ॥ कंद ॥ सिरिगिरि

८. *यो*ळिर्दु तंन्नय भ(च)रण*वे* शर*णें*ब वीर शिवदेवरिगाश्चरिय *मे*निसिप्प

९. पश्चिमवरवाहिनि तुंगभद्रेयं तोरुत्त ॥ ४ ॥ आदेशदिंद(आदेशिसिदं) नडे नीनादेश

१०. क्कल्लि मुक्तनाथ*नो*ळें द्दुमु । मादेविसहितविह्नेनु । समाधान*दो*ळच्चिर्सु

११. वुदेनल्नडेतंदु ॥ ५ ॥ अनवरतलिंगसंवुज्ञवननुकरिसिदनंन्यकासि(शे) माड*दे*

१२. मुक्ते । शननप्रतिम*ने* नि[प्प]पू । ज*ने* यिंदच्चिर्सि *मे*र्चसुवनेनवंत्तदो ॥ ६ ॥ *तो*

१३. नेवं [न्तू] कं*गो*ळुवनु । यनुमानिपनडिगडिगे स्रु(श्रु)तिगळोळु पुगळं

१४. *ने* नेने नेदु मूर्त्तिगोळिसुव घनतर शिवलिंगतत्ववं शिवदेवं॥ ७ ॥

१५. परदैवमानमर्दन । परदैवरघरट्टदिट्ट परदैवकुभृद्वरवज्रपात*नें*नि

१६. पं । वीरगणतेजप्रभावदिं शिवदेवनु ॥ ८ ॥ ॥ वचन ॥ अंत्ता सि(शि)वदेवरु शिव

१७. गणाज्ञासुख*दो*ळिरुत्तमिरे यिरे । कारणिकरेनिप*रो*ळु तां कारणिक

१८. रेनिप शि(सि)द्धरेवणदेवन कारुंण्यद शिश्या भक्त्याचारद चीलाळदेव *लो*क्किक*यो*

१९. *ळेसेदं* ।। ९ ।। मिक्क शिवभक्तिसुखदिं । दुक्कि महादेव भावभरदिं जगमं *लेक्कि*
२०. सदे गणसुखद*ोळि*ह लोक्किय चीलाळादेव *तोर*गले नाड*ोळु* ।। १० ।। अन्तिरुत्तमि
२१. र्दु ।। वदविद शिवभक्तिय सं । पदमं कल्लरसनरसि कंनादेवि*गे* मुददिंदवित्त चि
२२. ला । ळदेव जंगमसुखैकगुणसद्भावं ।। ११ ।। आ सति कंनादेवियया । श्री सुखसंपद-विळा
२३. सविभवादिगळं । बासणिसि सि(शि)वगणंगळि*गो*(गो)सरिस*दे* माडि कूडि सुखिसुत्तिप्प
२४. ळ् ।। १२ ।। वचन ।। तदनंतरवु ।। कर्मातिशयदि निजपति धर्मध्रुज देवलोकव*ने* ताने यिदल्
२५. धर्मज्ञेदेवि कंन्हरे(ह्ले)कर्म्मारियं पायलुज्जुगं *गे* यिवनं ।। १३ ।। परमगुरु शि(सि)द्ध रे
२६. वण । सिरिगिरिय निवासनाज्ञे यं बेससिदन । च्चरिय मुनियप्प मु
२७. क्ते । श्वरलिंग*दो*ळल्लि तुंगभद्रेय तडि *यय्योळ्* ।। १४ ।। यिं*तोने* आ*न्ने*सनदे सद्गुरु
२८. तानेनं तोरिद विचित्र*वे* नुत्तं ।। मानिनि कंह्लादेवियरा । नंददि बंदु
२९. मुक्तनाथन कंडरु ।। १५ ।। अन्त्ता मुक्तिक्षेत्रदल्लिर्द्दु हिंगदे जंगमार्च
३०. ने तत्परेयागिरे यिरे ।। शिवयोगिय कृपेयिंद वीर कं
३१. नादेवि भुवनवरियल्के कलिदेवर स्थापिसिदळ् ।
३२. स्वस्ति श्रीमतु यादवनारायण प्रवुढप्रताप च
३३. क्रवर्ति महादेवराय राज्यप्रवर्धमानमाचंद्रार्क्कतारंबरं सलुत्तमिरे यिरे ।। स्वस्ति श्री
३४. महामंडळे(ले)श्वरं वुज्जयनिपुरवराधीश्वरं वटकल्पवृक्षलांछित विजयध्वजं चंद्रगुप्तकुल-कम
३५. ळ(ल)मार्त्तंड कदनप्रचंडं । हंनिर्बर गंडं स(श)रणागतवज्रपं
३६. जरं विक्रमादित्यपुत्र (वीरगुत्तरसदेवरु शिवदेवर कारुं)
३७. ण्यमं पडेदु लिंगोत्सवसमयदल्लि कंनादेवियरु
३८. मुक्तिक्षेत्रदल्लि प्रतिष्ठेयं माडिसिद कल्लिदेवरिगे सर्व्वश्री कार्यार्थमागि श्रीमन्
३९. महाप्रभु वूलियहळ्ळिय मुद्दगौडनिं शख(क)वरुष ११८४*नेय*
४०. दुंदुभि संवत्सरद कार्त्तीक शु ।। १५ सोमवारदंदु *वोडेयर*
४१. पाद समक्षमदल्लि सर्व्वनमस्यवागि वूलिहळिय जोयिगौडन केयं गु
४२. त्तरसदेवं धारापूर्वकमागि *कोट्ट* ।।
४३. गंगन मत्तरु १ मने १ ... तुडिके १
४४. सर्वनमश्यमागि*कोट्ट येरे* बडगण (वो)लनल्लि गंगन मत्तरु १ मने १ तुडिके १
४५. गोपेयल्लिय बैल मत्तरु १ ...मत्तरु १ .. इन्ती धर्मव सि(शि)वदेवर गणंग

४६. ळु पालिसुवरु

Inscription No. VI

१. ॐ नम[ः] शिवाय । मुददि पा
२. लिसुगुर्व्वीपदमं चंद्रार्क्कतारकं
३. बरं गिरिजावदनांबुजातमित्रं त्रिदशेश्वर मु
४. क्तनाथ देवर देवनु ।। स्वस्ति श्रीमतु यादव
५. राय नारायणं प्रौढप्रताप चक्रवर्त्ति श्री
६. वीर महादेवरायनबेसदिं ।। स्वस्ति श्रीमनु (श्रीमन्)
७. महाप्रधानं सर्वाधिकारि *तो*रगले य श्री देवर्स
८. रु कटकदिं बंदु ।। स्वस्ति श्रीमदारूढ वीरभ्र(ब्र)ति शिव
९. योगसिद्ध शिवदेवरि*गे* साष्टांगप्रणामपूर्व्वकं
१०. बिंनपं*गे*यिदनिं*ते*ंदं ।। *वे*ंदु ग्रामव *को*ड्डु नी*ने*न्दं
११. यदुकुल न्रु(नृ)पोत्तमं महदेवं । यिंदद पतिकरिसलु
१२. बे*के*न्*दो*ड*े* शिवयोगसिद्ध नगुतिं*ते*न्दनु ।। त्रिभुवनवेंदु
१३. दु प*ळ्ळि* य प्रभुत्ववें श्लाघ्यवे यदल्लदु माणेन्दभयक
१४. रसिद्द*ने*नला शुभलक्षण देवराज मरळिं*ते*ंदं ।। वृ ।। देवरु *को*
१५. ट्टदोल्लदिरलप्पुदु देवणि माडि सिद्धियिं श्री विभवगळिं मनु
१६. ज लोकदधीश्वररित्तड*ो*ल्लदें*दे*ंविरलप्पुदुत्तम पदार्त्थचयंग
१७. ळनल्लदात्मजर्भावकरार्त्तत्तडद*नो*ल्ले*वे* निप्पुदु धर्म्मवप्पुदे एं
१८. दमृतोदर प्रभव देवनृपं नुडि*दो*ंदु वाक्य*दो*ळु बंदखिळागमार्त्थ
१९. नेलसिद्दुदु शास्त्रद सर्व्वसंपदं संदुदु वैदिकार्त्थवोडनिर्दु ध
२०. र्म्मद *पे*र्म *के*तुदे*ने*न्द *पे*ने*ं*दु तंन्नोळनुमानिसुतं शिवदेवर्र *(रें)*
२१. दपरु ।। आराधिसुवं नीनोलिदाराधिसिकोंबनीश्वरनुवेनानुवनाराधिसु
२२. कयि*को*बं विरेश्वर*ने*न्दुसिद्धनेमिस*लो*लविं ।। आ देवराजं ।। उत्तर दक्षिण पश्चिम
२३. दत्तुंगासनद रायराराधिसे वरवित्तं शिवदेवरं श्री गुत्तान्वय राज
२४. गुरुवनाराधिसिदं अ*दे*न्*ते*ंदडे ।। स्वस्ति श्रीमन्महामंडळेश्वरं
२५. उज्जयनिपुरवराधीश्वरं चंद्रगुप्तान्वयं गुत्तकुळकमळमार्त्तंड कदन
२६. प्रचंड पन्निर्बरगण्ड मौडळिकभयिरवं शरणागत वज्रपञ्जरं श्री स्पर्शलिं
२७. ग गळगनाथदेव श्री पादपद्माराधकरप्प गुत्तर्सदेव । हिरियदेव । जोयि

२८. देवंगळ । अवर ताय्वरप्प मैळादेवियर कय्यलु धारेय कोण्डु *गोतोळल्ना*
२९. डप्रभु गावुंडगळनोडंबडिसि शकवर्ष ११८७ रक्ताक्षि संवत्सरद पुष्य ब १५
३०. आदिवार श्रवण नक्षत्र ब्य(व्य)तीपातंगूडिदर्दो(र्धो)दय पुंण्यतिथियल्लि देवर्सरु
३१. माडिदाराधनेयक्रमवेंतं[द]डे ।। *गोत्तोळल* बडग*वोलदल्लि येरे* गं
३२. गन मत्तरु १ हिरिय *केरेय केळगे* गद्दे गंगन कंब १० मने १ तु
३३. डिके १ होंन्नवत्तिय मूड *वोलदल्लि येरे* गंगन मत्तरु १ । मने १ ।
३४. तुडिके १ ।। यालूर *केरेय* बडगलेरे गंगन मत्तरु १ । मने १
३५. तुडिके १ । उलिहळ्ळियल्लि वूर मूड[दे]सेयल्लि कंब ५० तेंक[दे] सेयल्लि कंब ५०
३६. अंतल्लि *येरे*गंगन मत्तरु १ । मने १ । तुडिके ।। हाहनूर पडुव *वो*
३७. लनल्लि *येरे*गंगन मत्तरु १ । मने १ । तुडिके १ ।। *नगेयूर वोल*
३८. नल्लि *येरे* गंगन मत्तरु १ मने १ तुडिके १ ।। वोलगुत्तूर मूडल *वोल*
३९. नल्लि *येरे* गंगन मत्तरु १ मने १ तुडिके १ ।। कंनवळ्ळिय बडग*वोलनल्लि ये*
४०. रे गंगन मत्तरु १ मने १ तुडिके १ ।। अगडिय बडग *होलदल्लि* यरे (*येरे*)गंगन
४१. मत्तरु १ तुडिके १ मने १ ।। हादरगेरिय *वोलनल्लि येरे* गंगन
४२. मत्तरु १ मने १ तुडिके १ ।। इंती हत्तु ग्रामंगळल्लि देवर्सरु श्री शि
४३. वदेवरिगे समाराधनेयं माडिद धर्मवु आ चंद्रार्क्कपर्य्यंतं
४४. सर्व्वनमस्यवागि गु*तोळल्ना*ड प्रभुगावुंडुगळु सलिसुवरु

Inscription No. VII

१. स्वस्ति श्री स(श)कवत्सर १२१०नेय सर्व्वधारि संवत्सरद स्रा(श्रा)वण सु(शु)द्ध ५
२. सोमवारदंदु स्वस्ति श्री रामप्रतिज्ञा परशुराम या
३. दवकुळ(ल) कळिका विकास भास्कर द्वारावतीपुरवराधीश्वर विष्णु वं
४. सो(शो)द्भव माळविय मल्लाहितरायमदं गुर्ज्जरराय वारणांकुस(श) । ते
५. लुंगरायसिरकमळपूर्ण संदोहमर्दन ... भोजभूपाळव्या
६. ळ विद्रावण लखुमिदेवकंस ... इत्यादि समस्त राजावळी
७. विराजमान श्रीमतु यादव नारायण भुजबळ प्रउढ प्रताप चक्र
८. वर्ति श्री रामचंद्र देवराय राज्य विजयोद्ध्यद महाप्रधान [मसिनास्तिह?]
९. ... श्रीमंना ... न काळे प्रवर्त्तमाने कंन्नाडदेसे गुत्तोळलदेसे
१०. तं मध्येगोपनामग्रामे तुंगभद्रायां तट...[मध्ये] मुक्तिक्षेत्रे श्री शि(सि)द्धसि(शि)व

११. देवनाम्नि मुक्तेस्वरदेवसंन्निधौ श्रीमंमहामंडळेस्वर अरिरा
१२. य विभाड कदन [प्रचंड] स्थापनाचारिय होसणरायदिसापट्टण ......निरायरक्षपाळक
१३. सकळसैन्याधिपति राणक श्री सळिवा आख्यो देवण्णय्य प्रपौत्राय सिंहदेवसै
१४. न्याधिपति पौत्राय बल्लाळदेवसैंन्याधिपतिपुत्राय श्री साळिवेसिंमदेवसैं
१५. न्याधिपति [नाम] ... साळिवेयाख्य कीर्तिस्तंभ प्रतिष्ठाधर्मो यावतु
१६. चंद्रार्क्क मेदिनौ तावतु स्तिरोभूत् मंगळ श्री श्री
१७. नूर ... यस्योद्द ... नेन महा ... सितदं ... केण । ... नाळामि
१८. ... सरोरुह ... प्रभां ... कळाप ... कां
१९. तिक कांति ... हंस ... काळ ... गळित ...
२०. ... मता । अव्यादव्याहतजपं ... आरति भासयं
२१. ... भुकं खट्वांग हस्त सर ... कृतिसुळवाळं खड्गहस्तं ...
२२. गतं । वामहस्तं दिनकर चंद्राकृतु.माळादि आवृतं सिरं सर्पयज्ञोप
२३. वीतं । कळाकोविदकारं महादेवं नमोस्तु ते ॥ ३ ॥ कृधा
२४. दर्पिस्तघनमहिमालिंग महितोत्सव .मेरौमंदरादौ मल्याय..
२५. मगिळ सोमवक्ष्या..परत्वं ...दवपक्षपादत्वं....
२६. ... महा कंतुवाहन ... ज्याया प्रेरितभृ ... क्षारहं ॥ ४ ॥
२७. ... तत्वादि स्फुरति वसूदेवमं प्राणिप्रणितसरसीकृत पदं
२८. मं न्यस्त वैव निमित्यां विकृतचक्षुख्यातवल्लभः कामिनौ
२९. स्तते समलतु सीमाय ... विधान्या ... हायवत्ता ...
३०. भूधराभयभवः चामरतोमरं । यावद्ग्राम करामरन
३१. रां । रा..यणं समुद्रभोगभुवन ... राय नित्यस ...
३२. ब्रहं । कृतोबृरोतम...चंदमस्त..समुद
३३. हर..मन...तृगं ... क्षेत्रतुरु विमिल ... मुनयो व्योमरस्विनः
३४. ... वसुं सिवाय ... क्षम भगवान् पार्वतीस्वरपते ... ॥ ७ ॥

Inscription No. VIII

१. श्री ॐ नमः । सि(शि)वाय । स्रि(श्री) सि(शि)वदेवप्रभु
२. वे स(श)रणु । स्वस्ति श्रीमतु यादवराय
३. नारायणं भुजबळप्रवुढप्रताप
४. चक्रवर्त्ति श्री वीर रामचंद्रदेव विजयरा

५. ज्योदयद २४नेय खरसंवत्सरद पु
६. स्य(ष्य) बहुळ अमव(वा)से आदिव(वा)र य(अ)र्ध्दोद
७. य सूर्यग्रहणदल्लि स्वस्ति श्रीमतु रा
८. यराजगुरु महावीरव्रति नूरेंटु
९. नवव्रतनिष्ठरह गो*(गो)*पेय सिद्ध सि(शि)वदेवर प्र(प्रा)ण
१०. लिंग मुक्तेस्व(श्व)रदेवर तुंगभद्रे पश्चिम वा
११. हिनि दक्षिणवारणासियगो*(गो)*पेय
१२. नूरिप्पत्तिंबर षं(सं)न्निधियल्लि यि मुक्तना
१३. थदेवरिगे । स्वस्ति श्रीमनु महाप्रधानं स
१४. र्व्वाधिकारि परसु(शु)रामदेवर निरूपदिं स
१५. र्बाधिकारि हब्बरसदेवर्सरु सुंकद
१६. सिताळहेगडे आ मुक्तनाथदेवर पुरद
१७. स्तळसुंक कारुक तेल्लिगरुं मग्ग तेरे अंगडि
१८. मुख्यवागि अष्टभोगतेजसांम्य २५ ए
१९. त्तिन सुंक मेयिदेरे मूले संकवनु
२०. सर्ब्बमान्यवनु आचंद्रार्क्कवागि सी
२१. मेयं मुद्रेसहित धारापू
२२. र्व्वकवागि कोट्टनु ॥ मंगळ महा श्री
२३. स्वदत्तं(त्तां) परदत्तं(त्तां) वा यो हरे
२४. ति(त) वसुंधरा(रां) ॥ षष्टिर्वर्षसहश्रा(स्रा)
२५. णां(णि) विष्टायां जायते क्रि
२६. मिः ॥ मंगळ महा श्री श्री श्री
२७. श्री मुक्तनाथ स(श)रणु ॥

APPENDIX 2

Transliteration in latin script

Inscription no. I

1. namas tuṅgaśiraścumbicaṃdracāmaracāravē । trailōkyanagarārambhamūla-stambhāya sa(śa)mbhavē ॥ triṇāni kōṭivarṣāṇi mriṇā(ṇ)mayaṃ
2. daśakōṭibhiḥ dāreṣṭaśataṃkōṭi śahaśra(sahasra)kōṭi śiḷā(lā)mayaṃ ॥ 2 ॥
3. svasti samaśta(sta) ॥ bhuvanāśrayaṃ śrī prithvīvallabhaṃ mahārājādhirāja-paramēśvara paramabhaṭṭāraka śa(sa)tyāśraya kuḷatilakaṃ
4. cāḷukyābharaṇaṃ śrīmattribhuvanamalladēvara vijayarājyam uttarōttarābhi-vṛddhipravardhamānam ācaṃdrārkkatā
5. raṃbaraṃ saluttamire ॥ kanda ॥ paḍuvalu paḍuvaṇa vāridhi gaḍi mūḍalu mūḍaṇabdhi gaḍi baḍagalu himaṃ । gaḍi teṃka sē
6. tuveregaṃ । gaḍiyāgire vikramāṃkanāḷvaṃ dhareya ॥ 3 ॥ jaḷanidhi pari-vri(vṛ)ta dhātrītaḷamellamaṃ tanna hastataḷamene peṃpaṃ । taḷedī cāḷukyānvaya
7. kuḷatiḷakaṃ vikramāṃkanāḷvaṃ dhareya ॥ 4 ॥ va ॥ ā paramēśvarana śrī pādapadmōpajīvi śa(sa)madhigatapaṃcamahāśabda mahāsāmantādhipati mahā
8. mahāpracaṃḍa daṃḍanāyaka vairigirivajrasāyaka subhaṭasēnānātha si(śi)khāmaṇi sa(śa)raṇāgatarakṣāmaṇi śrīmanmahāpradhānaṃ gōviṃdara-sarā
9. jaṃ banavāsi pannircchāsiramumaṃ sukhadimāḷuttamire ॥ [eṟa]gadavaraṃ koṃdu sale tana । geragidaraṃ kādu dakṣiṇāpathamellane besakeyvaṃtāgire meṟadaṃ śrī
10. kīrtilakṣmiyaṃ gōviṃdaṃ ॥ (5) va ॥ svasti samastabhuvanajanavinyasta-mastakasaṃstūyamānacārucaraṇāraviṃda vairibaḷaviḷaya gōviṃdanuj-janīmahākāḷa
11. dēvatālabhdavarapraśā(sā)da samastavidyāvinōda । pāṭalīpuravarādhīśvara । kirttyaṃganādhīśvara vaṭavri(vṛ)kṣadhvaja । dhairyagaruḍadhvaja । sōma
12. vaṃśalalāṭalōcana । mri(mṛ)garājalāṃchana । guttara bhīmaṃ । chala-daṃkarāma । arikumaramakuṭaghaṭṭitacaraṇa । guttarābhara

13. ṇa I ripubaḷatimiramārttaṃḍa I vairikuḷakāḷadaṃḍa I hayavatsarāja I rūpamanōja I bhriciṃtāmaṇi vaṃdijanakalpa(lpa)vri(vr̥)kṣa
14. śaraṇāgatarakṣa I caṃdragupta mahārājādhirāja kuḷa(la)saṃpūrṇna I nanniyalu karṇna I manumārggadāni I sanumānadāni I sau(śau)cāṃjanēya sampanna I nuḍidu ma
15. ttenna I ayyana cakra I bhūcakraśakra vikramādityavaṃśōdbhavarappa śrīmat guttānvayara mahimeye pēlvaḍe II
16. allige manneya lakṣmīvallabharenisirdda guttabhūpānvayaroḷ II ballidana jayanapratimallaṃ māguttabhūpaneṃba negaḷda II6II (kaṃ) aṃtā
17. nripa(nr̥pa)tige suta vikrāṃtadhanaṃ rājavaṃsa(śa)cūḍāmaṇi mā II rāṃtarigaṃtaka vaṃdige ciṃtāmaṇi guttabhūpanaṃgajarūpa II 7 II vr̥tta II taṃdeya taṃ
18. deyiṃdamevagāḷuva mahītaḷavajjapajjariṃ baṃdude sālugaveṃdirade vikramadiṃdirāṃta bhūparaṃ koṃdu II dharitriyaṃ paḍedanarttige bērpudanittu
19. kīrtiyaṃ maṃdiravirpinaṃ paḍeda guttanri(nr̥)pāḷisidēṃ kri(kr̥)tārthanō II 8 II kanda II guttānvaya vaṃśāgraṇi guttānvaya rājabhavanamaṃgaḷa kaḷaśaṃ II guttānvaya
20. cūḍāmaṇi I guttānvaya tiḷakanenisidaṃ guttanri(nr̥)pāḷaka II 9 II Ātana tanayaṃ jagadoḷu I nītiparaṃ ripukarīṃdra kaṃṭhīrava II bhūtaḷakṣatriyaroḷajā I
21. tabhayaṃ mallidēvanadaṭaṃ dēva II 10 II vr̥ttaII eṇisalu bhūpāḷarīgaḷu palabarumoḷarā bhūpavarggaṃgaḷiḷdēgaṇidēṃ pūrvādriyoḷu caṃdramanese
22. va sarōmadhyadoḷu paṃkajaṃ kēvaṇḍoḷu I māṇikyavirppaṃtire bhuvanajanakkāśrayaṃ rājacūḍāmaṇi yippaṃ mallidēvaṃ tribhuvana tiḷa
23. kaṃ rājamāndhātabhūpaṃ II 11 II bhaṃḍaṇadoḷu ripubhūpara I taṃḍamanavayavade geldu jayalakṣmiya dō I rddaṃḍadoḷirisida dhīrada I gaṃḍaṃ I kēvaḷa
24. me mērugiri naṃma mallanri(nr̥)pāḷa II 12 II kanda II nuḍiyedaḍe nuḍyadikkeme kuḍuveṃ nimageṃdu nuḍidanappaḍe mri(mr̥)ḍanoḷu I paḍeda bara
25. mērugiriyoḷu I kaḍedakkara mallabhūpa nuḍidiṃ baḷikaṃ II 13 II vr̥tta II padapiṃ nri(nr̥)pāḷa(la) ninna raṇakēḷilīḷe(le)yaṃ pakṣapā I tadi nāṃ pē I ḷadoḍēn pōdapa
26. lavuṃ sugrāmadoḷu puttane I ttida pulgarcida kayduvaṃ bisuṭi nīraṃ pokki nigranthamō I ḍida niṃdāḍida keygaḷaṃ mugida rātibrāta
27. veṃ pēḷavē II 14 II kanda II ājiyaṃ dharaṇiyanērida I vājiya khuradiṃda murtturipusirameṃbī bijavane bitti beḷevaṃ rāji

28. ka vikhyāta kīrttiyaṃ mallanri(nṛ)pa ॥ 15 ॥ vṛtta ॥ deseposa(vuṇn)-dimdesevana nettara suṭṭureyiṃ nabhasthaḷaṃ pasarisi biḷda bhaṭaraṭṭegaḷiṃ haya
29. kandakhaṃḍiyiṃ kusurivolāge vairibalamaṃ taṟedoḍḍidagurvu tānugu । rvisidudu mallidēvaniṟedāhavaraṃgada vairisēne
30. ya ॥ 16 ॥ vacana ॥ ā guttānvayara hri(hṛ)dayāḷa (va)ḷaṃbigaḷappa jaṭācēḷānvayaru māḍisida śivālayada muktitīrtthada vyāvarṇana ॥ ka ॥
31. harana jaṭāgradi nelasida suranadigaṃ vēdaśaiḷa(la)si(śi)kharāgradinī । dharegiḷida tuṃgabhadrā । varanadigaṃ doreye jagada nadamuṃ nadiyuṃ ॥ 17 ॥
32. ॥ vri ॥ sudatīkuṃkumpaṃkitāruṇajaḷaṃdābhidānājaḷaṃ vi । daḷatu paṃkajappuṟaṃjita jaḷaṃ vēdācaḷēṃdrōpakaṃṭhadinettaṃ suri
33. diṃdukāṃtada jaḷaṃ pērarvva saṃdōhadiṃ pu । didettaṃ laharīdiśābha-ritaṃ śrītuṃgabhadrā jaḷaṃ ॥ 18 ॥ ka ॥ gaṃgesamāna dakṣiṇa gaṃgāna
34. di miṃda martyaraghasaṃkuḷamaṃ piṃgisuva gaṃgeyuṃ tiripiṃgipaḷa-ghakuḷam naṃṃa dakṣiṇa gaṃge ॥ 19 ॥ pāvanavenisida gaṃgādēvige
35. saridore samāna dakṣiṇa gaṃgādēviyane tuṅgabhadrādēviyanineṟevaṃ ॥ 20 ॥ vṛtta ॥ surasai
36. ḷē(lē)ṃdrada himyā(mā)caḷ(la)ada mahimegaṃ tāraśaiḷa(la)kkaṃ nōḍalu doṟvetti vēdaśaiḷē(lē)ṃdradalamaranadisaṃnibhaṃ mēghabriṃdōtkara-diṃdaṃ
37.bhattathidaṃḍada bahaḷateyeṃbaṃdadiṃ baṃdu tā nikarada pāpakṣya māḍuva vimaḷajaḷ(la)aṃ tuṃgabhadrā pravāha ॥ 21 ॥ gadya ॥ adeṃteṃ
38. doḍairāvatagaṃḍamaṃḍāḷābhittiyaṃte dānōcitasthānamuṃ harajaṭāgra-daṃte nadīvirājitamuṃ । pātāḷalōkadaṃte nāga
39. sahitamuṃ । surēṃdra sa(śa)yanadaṃte raṃbhāyatamuṃ । dēvalōkadaṃte sumanābhirāmamuṃ saṃgītakadaṃte tāḷa
40. sahitamuṃ brahmasabheyaṃte dvijavirājitamuṃ । aṃtalli mūṟu kālamuṃ āruṃ ri(ṛ)tugaḷuṃ । sarvvarttukamappa mu
41. ktitīrtta(rtha)da sthānadoḷu su(śu)kasārikāramaṇamuṃ । pugalpugaleṃba kōkiḷa(la)svaranāramaṇamuṃ
42. namēru maṃdāra pā[ri]jāt^di puṟpa(ṣpa)rājitamuṃ sāmavēda saptasvara maṃtrākṣaraṃgaḷiṃ hōmaṃ gaiyva dvijōttamara
43.hōmadhūpastōmamuṃ । dēvatātarppaṇa ri(ṛ)ṣitarppaṇa diktarppaṇa gāyatrī śa(ṣa)ḍakṣara japaṃgaḷaṃ mārppa । sabrāhmaṇarim va

44. jrāsana । padmāsana । svastikāsanaṃgaḷiṃ । nādabhēda । biṃdubhēda । sa(śa)ktibhēda । ātmabhēdameṃba । nālku teṟa(ra)da । yōgalakṣaṇalakṣitarappa yōgiga
45. ḷiṃ । muktimārggame mūrttigoṃḍirḋda muktitīrtthada bahuvidha liṅgāśrayaṃgaḷoppugumalli ॥ 22 ॥ kaṃda ॥ ajasabheyaṃte
46. sadā dvijaparivrita(vr̥ta)miṃdranaṃte sumanāśrayavā trijadasagajadaṃte dānabrajamayamu muktitīrtthamadu kēvaḷamē ॥ 23 ॥
47. vr̥tta ॥ kusumita mallikābhinavapāṭaḷasaṃkuḷadiṃ konarttu taḷtasadaḷamāgi baṃda posamāvugaḷiṃ morevunmadāḷiyiṃ masa
48. gita[ma]ṣṭa baggipa pikāḷigaḷiṃ nayadiṃda teṃkaṇiṃdesepalariṃdavī muktitīrtta(rtha)vadoppugumeṃtu norpaḍa ॥ 24 ॥ vaṃsā(ṃśā)vatāra
49. kanda ॥ śrīgenele dānadharmakāgaravene negeḷdanī jaṭānvayakuladoḷu bhōgapuraṃdara neyavida sāgaraparivri(vr̥)ta
50. dharitriyoḷa(ḷe)joṃmanripapaṃ ॥ 25 ॥ kaṃda ॥ ātaṃge puṭṭida vikhyātiparaṃ rājasutaroḷamaḷacaritra bhūtaḷadalartthigama
51. rakujātaṃ kēvaḷamē dāsa vīraviḷāsaṃ ॥ 26 ॥ sarasīruhavadane caṃdabbarasiru guṇaniḷayanenipa dāsanri(nr̥)paṃgaṃ parahitacaritaṃ
52. puṭṭida haracraṇapayōja bhri(bhr̥)ṃganattinri(nr̥)pāḷaṃ ॥ 27 ॥ ātana tamma ॥ caṃdaṃgavajja(bja)nābhana kandaṃge sētugaṭṭi laṃkēśvarana koṃdaṃge suranadi
53. yaṃ taṃdaṃge doreye manujaravanītaḷadoḷu ॥ 28 ॥ vacana ॥ māvaṃ mahāmaṃḍaḷēsva(śva)raṃ । vīrārāti madanamahēsva(śva)ra । mūṟurāya
54. maṃḍaḷika madagajēṃdrakaṃṭhīravaṃ rāyana mahimeya pēḷvaḍe ॥ kaṃda ॥ maṟavaṭṭīvudu surataru paraḷāgiye kuḍutami
55. rkku ciṃtāmaṇiyā maranuṃ kalluṃ priyadiṃ karedanippuve rāyanaṃtire jagadoḷu ॥ 29 ॥ vr̥tta ।: paramārthakkiṣṭadeyvaṃte
56. nagakhiḷa jagatsvāmi saṃdādi dēvagirijāḷvaṃgānusaṃgaṃ śivane gaḍa kulasvāmi kāruṇyadiṃdu poredāḷvaṃ vikramāṃkānvaya
57. kuḷatiḷkaṃ (kulatilakaṃ) mallabhūpaṃ gadiṃtī dhareyoḷu dhanyaṃ jaṭācōḷaroḷu maḷayasō(śō)rājanīyatta(tti)rājaṃ ॥ 30 ॥
58. siya doreyenisuva puṇyanadiya tīrada samadaṃ haraniḷa(la)yamanarghakuḷa(la) saṃhāraniḷa(la)ya manartt iyiṃdamattinri(nr̥)pāḷaṃ ॥ 31 ॥ uttamara
59. keledoḷaṃ bhūpōttamarāsthānaraṃgadoḷu sujanakavittvōttamara sabheyoḷamatyuttamanī yattirājanaṃ pogaḷaḋarārō ॥ 32 ॥ dhareyo
60. ḷanēkarilla sujanarkkalikāladoḷaṃte bhadrasiṃdhura ghaṭiyilladaṃte sujanōttamanakṣara pakṣapāti neṃṭara beḷegayi dharāmarara kayviḍi

61.siṣṭanidhānanirddapaṃ varaguṇiyattirājaneḷegōrvane kaḷpa(lpa) kujātanirppa vol ॥ 33 ॥ svasti śrīmanmahā sāmaṃta vīralakṣmīkāṃtaṃ jaṭānvaya cō
62. ḷa vaṃśāgraṇi śiṣṭaciṃtāmaṇi gōtrapavitra sabaḷa triṇētra vīra viḷā(lā)saṃ guttara caṃdrahāsaṃ haracaraṇasarasīruha
63. madhukara vinayaratnākaraṃ ...

Inscription No. II

1. Śrī muktēṣa(śa)ṃ । namō yasya jaṭājūṭē vidhōḥ kaḷā । tuṃgagaṃgānadītīracā
2. rīru haṃsīva rājatē ॥ 1 ॥ padapiṃ muktēśvaraṃ māḷkabhimatasukhamaṃ bhakta
3.lōkakke bhaktyāspadacaṃdrōpēṃdravṛṃdārakanikaranuta śrī padadvaṃdvanuddāmadaṣā(śā)saṃ
4. bhūtabhūtipradanakhiḷa jagatsvāmisaṃbaddha gaurīhṛdayānaṃdaikakaṃ
5. daṃ viṣadatarayaśaḥ prāpta sacchāṃsanākaṃ ॥ 2 ॥ vri ॥ viṣadatarēśvarājñeyodavim
6. dame saṃbhavisirddavī caturdaṣa(śa) bhuvanaṃgaḷaṣṭatanudharmmadanērmadalliyuṃ manaḥkuṣa(śa)
7. lamanittu bhūbhuvanaṃgaḷanēḷikuṃ ramāvaṣarabhivāṃccheyaṃ salipa
8. satukri(kṛ)tiyaṃ sale torppanerppiniṃ ॥ 3 ॥ kaṃ ॥ saptasadvīpapradēśadim bhuvanaṃ
9. galvyāptiyimdīrēḷumavāptasukhāvaḷigaḷirddavenalīḷeyesaguṃ ॥ 4 ॥ dvīpāvaḷiyo
10. ljaṃbūdvīpave sogayikkuvalladeṃduḷidāṟuṃ dvīpagaḷumaṃpōṟgaṇa kā
11. ṃpiṃgirisida vidhātranēnaṟiyada nēma ॥ 5 ॥ ivi jaṃbūdvīpa lakṣmīviḷasita lāva
12. ṇyamemḅante dēvadṛpūviṃ caṃdanōrvvīruhada sovaḍiniṃ ratnabhūpāḷiyiṃ phēnavinibaddhamā
13. dā teregaḷa niṟeyuṃ sanmhāmacchyapuṃcchāttavicitrōruputradiṃ rājisi baḷasida lāvaṇya
14. vārāsi tōrkkuṃ ॥ 6 ॥ vāridhi tiḷigoḷanadaṟe । ḷnīrajadavolesagumalte jaṃbūdvīpaṃ mēruve ka
15. ṛnikaideseyesaḷāraye balavarppa rāśicakraṃ bhramaraṃ ॥ 7 ॥ kaṃ ॥। suragiriyiḷāvṛtta(ta)ṃ kiṃpuru
16. ṣa(ṣa)ṃ harivarṣameseva himavadgiriyaṃ bharatōrvvī ṣaṭkhaṃḍaṃ taratataradiṃ teṃklalli māḷavamesa

17. guṃ ॥ 8 ॥ tāvareyeṃdenippa kamaḷaṃgḷesālkema jātisaṃkaraṃ pūvinoḷakke nūtana karagrahaṇaṃ
18. vivāhadaḻḻi tōrkkāvaraveṃgadalsurabhiyaṃ kaṟe yeṃbadenippa lakṣmīkāmāvaḷi rājanītihri(hṛ)dayasthiti
19. māḷavadoḷu virājikuṃ ॥ 9 ॥ kaṃ ॥ māḷavadoḷgujjayaniye । pāḷisuguṃ karṇṇapuṇyamaṃ kaṇṇeḷagiṃ bāḷe vō
20.sarise caṃdraśiḷā(lā)layamaṃ maḷeyanuḷidu baḷeye banaṃgaḷuṃ ॥ 10 ॥ amardaṃ tatpuradōḷnṛpōttamanenippā vikramā
21. dityana । ṣṭamahāsiddhiyaneyde sādhisijagakkānaṃda māgittabhīṣṭam niṃśa (ṃ)kanāgi mūjagamuṃ satkīrtiyiṃ mucci
22. bhūramegiṃ taṃneya tōḷabāḷe maṟevāḷkilleṃbinaṃ tāḷdu(ḷvu)tum ॥ 11 ।: uguguṃ ratnāḷigaḷkaṃtheyinesagikku miṣṭānna
23. maṃ kharparaṃ pāhage voyguṃ pēḷda tāṇakke sapuda suvanaṃṭaṃṭu citrakke bettaṃ । bagedāḷtūrccuguṃ śatṛvanaśirasa
24. diṃ poṃgaḷakku paṭaṃ diṭṭagadriśyavakkeyakkuṃ ghuṭikeya sadaḷaṃ vikramāditya puṇyaṃ ॥ 12 ॥ kaṃ ॥ enaleseda vikramādi
25. tyanenittalcaṃdraguptavaṃṣa(śa)doda(ḷa)ṃnyarjjaniyasatinipida nōḍisi janiyisidaṃ vīra vikramāditya nri(nṛ)paṃ ॥ 13 ॥
26. caritaṃgaṃ nītigaḷgaṃ ghanamenisupuvāptartthigiṣṭhārtthadiṃdaṃ piridiṃducchauryyamurbbī(rvī)vaḷayada baḷasiṃda
27. ggaḷaṃ lakṣmīsāmrājyaramāvistāradiṃdatyadhika manuvinōdaṃ manōjaṃgamāytubbaramā sa
28. tukkīrtti(rti) lōkakkatuḷamenisidaṃ vikramādityadēvaṃ ॥ 14 ॥ kaṃ ॥ ā vīra vikramādi । tyāvanipaṃgudayagiri
29. yoḷudayisuvaṃdina śrīvaranene jommanri(nṛ)paṃ । bhūvadhu kaṇḍeṟeye puṭṭidaṃ kamaḷē(lē)śaṃ ॥ 15 ॥ vinatānaṃdana saṃ
30. gataṃ sajanitōdyatkāmavarṣapravarddhamānaharṣaṃ vibudhāśrayastuta padaṃ śrī maṃḍaḷā(lā)gravaḷō (lō)kanarāgōdaya
31. nā sudarṣa(rśa)nakaraṃgāścaryyarūpaṃ sujommaṃ nṛpaṃ rājisutirppaniṃdradivasēṃdrōpēṃdravoṃdaṃdadiṃ ॥ 16 ॥ ara
32. sarggilla rasapraśakti rasikatvaṃ kūḍe kūrppilla kūrppire vidyāvaḷiyill vidyeyire nērppillāge nērppilla saccaritaṃ । podaḷdi
33. re viḷā(lā)sa prītiyilla guṇōtkaravellaṃ neredirddaveṃdenisidaṃ śrī jōyidēvorbbi(rvi)paṃ ॥ 17 ॥ kaṃ ॥ ā joṃmananuja
34. guttaṃ rājācārapraśastiyaṃ kuvaḷeyalakṣmījāpyamaṃtraviḷasadbījākṣaramaṃ budhāḷiyiṃdōdisuvaṃ ॥ 18 ॥ manasi

35.janolagippesakadiṃ paḍedaṃ neṟekeṭṭameyyanītaninivudgha kirttiyane-porddi himadyuti tatkaḷ(la)aṃkavarttanamanidirppida ṃ
36. yamanumītana khaḷgadoḷippanalte bhōjanasukhadiṃdameṃdenipuduttama guttanṛpāḷavṛttakaṃ ॥ 19 ।: enisida gutta
37. bhūmipana vallabhe padmaladēvi jāti padminiyene lakṣmiyaṃtaḷadi-naṃganurāgisi rājahaṃsavarttanadeḍeyāgi sēbya (sēvya)
38. kavicakrade saṃstuteyāgi kāmarājana jaladurggamaṃ rasaviśēṣavinōdadi māḍirūḍhipaḷu ॥ 20 ॥ kaṃ ॥ padmeya ni
39. rmaḷanōdarapadmadinī vīra vikramaṃ puṭṭidanā padmabhavanaṃte kriṣṇa(kṛṣṇa)na padmōdaradalli puṭṭe nayavinutuṃṭe ॥ 21 ॥ vina
40. yaṃ vikramaśakti puṇyavenipī mūṟuṃ guṇaṃ rājyamaṃḍanadē-hāṃśugaḷeṃte nalsirige puṇyacēta
41. naṃ balpu mēyvinayaṃ bhūṣaṇameṃdu ṣā(śā)straṃ ruciśastrābhyāsa-dharmmapravarttanameṃdiṃtivu vīra vikramanoḷirkkum
42. prājyasāmrājyanoḷu ॥ 22 ॥ moneyoḷkhaḷgasahāyavrittitanagābriṃ(vṛṃ)daṃ narēṃdrāyatē yenesal sēnemanaṃ satatvame
43. yathārūpaṃ tathā śīlaṃmeṃdenisalkāva sukhaṃ yāviḷane tāṃ tējaḥphaḷaṃ rājyameṃdenenisalvikramaśakti rājisu
44. gumiṃtī vikramādityanoḷu ॥ 23 ॥ jayavadhuvuṃ vormeyuṃ bayasutirppa-daṭaṃganeyurvviḷāsadiṃ । bayasu
45. va celvu nītitatigaḷnaḍeyalsupatha prapaṃcamaṃ bayasuva mārggavartti-gaḷapēkṣagaḷaṃ bayasuttavirppatipriya
46. venivārpparājisudinaṃ misupaṃ vibhu vīra vikramaṃ ॥ 24 ॥ svasti sa-madhigatapaṃcamahāśabdam
47. hāmaṃḍaḷēśvaraṃ ujjayanīpuravarādhīśvaraṃ vaṭakalpavri(vṛ)kṣalāṃchi-tavijayadhvajaṃ bhuvana[ra]kṣa
48. ṇaikadakṣadakṣiṇabhujaṃ caṃdraguptānvayasudhārṇnava pūrṇnacaṃ-draṃ vibhavāmarēṃdraṃ
49. haracaraṇanakhakiraṇasāṃdracaṃdrikācakōraṃ gurupadapayōdharadhvā-nānaṃdita ma
50. yūraṃ māninīmānasarbba(rvva)svasūṟekāraṃ raṇadoḷvīraṃ maṃḍaḷikab-hairavaṃ ānaṃdita yuvatīna
51. nayanakairavaṃ pannirbbara gaṃḍaṃ samaraṣau(śau)ṃḍaṃ āhavādityaṃ vīra vikramādityaṃ । banavāsenāḍaṃ
52. duṣṭanigraha śiṣṭapratipāḷanadi pāḷisuttam guttavoḷala nelevīḍinoḷsukha-saṃkathāvinō

53.dadiṃ rājyaṃgeyuttamire ॥ ā bhūpāḷapadābjabhriṃganenipaṃ sadbhakti-yiṃ yuktiyiṃdā bhūpā

54. ḷana maṃtrayōgyanenipaṃ taṃnnudghavīratvadiṃdā bhūpāḷana dakṣa dakṣiṇabhujādaṃḍaṃ nijaṃ

55. tānenalkā bhūpāḷana nāyakāgraṇi jagadvikhyātanī kāmeya ॥ 25 ॥ ॥ vacana ॥ tadanvayameṃtene । attya

56.rasaṃ caṃḍarasaṃ satyada kaṇeyenisi misupa dharmmada dhuramaṃ nityōtsavadiṃ dhariyipa । kri(kṛ)ttyaucitya

57. me samasta guṇavenalesedaru ॥ 26 ॥ tatsute mācaḷadēviya hri(hṛ)tsarasīru-hadoḷeseva rasamadhulaharī

58.prōtsukanenisi karagrahasatsukhamaṃ paḍedanaṃdu nāyaka māraṃ ॥ 27 ॥ māreyanāyakaṃgenuta mā

59. calegaṃ janisirddā śaṃkarōdārapadābjabhṛṃganatimaṃgaḷa cēṣṭinaṃga-nājanakkī rativallabhaṃ janitaneṃbinaviṃbina

60. sadguṇagaḷiṃdāru samānaviṃdamama nōḷpaḍe kāmeyanāyakāgryēyanoḷu ॥ 28 ॥

61. bhīmana balpiṃ negaḷdā । rāmana sāhasadinaṇuvani । na sadbhak-tiprēmadinādyanenippaṃ । kāmeya

62. nudāttacitracaritra ॥ 29 ॥ javadiṃ śrī vikramāṃka sthi(kṣi)tipatitiḷakaṃ śatṛsēnāṃgamaṃ

63. [tāṃ] tavipulkudyōgamaṃ māḷpinegevatimadōccaṃḍavērdaṃḍaṣaṃḍaṃ navavēgabrāji

64. vājibrajavatibaḷapādatavanne ॥ kri(kṛ)pāṇāhavadoḷmuṃtirdavinnēke ni-nage bharaveṃdeṃbanāḷdaṃge

65. kāmaṃ ॥ 30 ॥ kanda ॥ ā naranāthana viśa(ṣa)yada dānajaḷaṃ kūḍi pari-duveṃbavolurbbīmāniniya hāradaṃtire

66. tāneṃduṃ tuṃgabhadre taddēśadoḷaṃ ॥ 31 ॥ bhūramaṇītaraḷadavolīrēḷuṃ bhuvanaṃgaḷoḷage savitatamahi

67. mādhāraṃ muktēśvaranāmāraṃbhanesevutirppanīśanumēśaṃ ॥ 32 ॥ svasti samasta praśastisahitaṃ

68. śrīmanumahāmaṃḍaḷēśvaraṃ vīravikramādityādēvarasaru guttavoḷalanele-vīḍinoḷu

69. sukhasaṃkathāvinōdiṃ rājyaṃgeyyuttamire ॥ tatpādapadmōpajīviyenipa khaṃḍeya

70. kāṟa kāmeyanāyakaṃ taṃna svāmiya cittavanupārjjisi pāritōṣikamāgi paḍeda honnava

71. ttiya holadaḷu cāmēśvaradēvara keyyiṃ mūḍalu go(gō)peya ōṇiyiṃ teṃkalu caturāghāṭa
72. śuddhamāgiralāṟu mattaramaṃ śakavarṣaṃ 1113neya virōdhikri(kṛ)tu saṃvatsarada mā
73. rggaśiradamāvāse sūryyagrahaṇadaṃdu śrīmanu muktēśvaradēvara aṃgaraṃ
74. gabhōgakke jīrnnōddhārakkeṃdu muktajīyara kālaṃ karcci dhā
75. rāpūrvvakaṃ māḍi koṭṭa ॥ ॥ śrī viśvanāthāya namaḥ ॥ śrī muktēśvarāya namaḥ ॥
76. ॥ ॥ ī(i)ṃtī dharmmava pratipāḷi(li)sa(si)davaru prayāgeyalargghyatīrttha
77. kavileyaṃ koṃḍu koḷagamuṃ ponnalu kaṭṭisi sāsirbba(rvva)ru vēdapāragarige koṭṭa phala ॥ i (ī) dharmmava
78. nāvanānuṃ ki(ke)ḍisidanābrāhmaṇarumaṃ kavileyaṃ [konda] mahāpātakanakku ॥ svadatta(ttāṃ) paradat
79. ttaṃ(ttāṃ) vā yō harēti(ta) vaṣu(su)ṃdharā(ṃ) ॥ ṣaṣṭirvvarṣasahasrāṇi viṣṭāyāṃ (jāyate krimiḥ) krimiḥ ॥ 33 ॥.....kabba
80. Virōdhikṛtu saṃvatsarada puśya(ṣya)damavāse bri(bṛ)haspati... saṃkramaṇa kūḍidalli śrī muktēśvaradēvara trikāla
81.dupahārake srīmanmahāmaṃḍaḷēśvaraṃ vīra vikramādityadēvara ... mahājanaṃgaḷa saṃnidhāna
82.dalu koṭṭa gadde śrīmadagrahāraṃ hoṃnavatiya hāḷa śrī kalidēvara gaddeya teṃka ā dēvariṃ mūḍa biṭṭa gadde kaṃba ॥ 20॥ iṃtī dharmavaṃ
83. tappade pratipāḷisuvadu ॥ [ka]lu haṃdarādiyāgi hoṟathara sahita rēōjana kelasa ॥ muktēśvarāya namaḥ ॥

Inscription No. III

1.Oṃ namaḥ śivāya । namastuṃgaśiraścuṃbicaṃdracāmaracāravē । trailōkyanagarāraṃbhamūla
2. staṃbhāya śaṃbhavē ॥ 1 ॥ śabdādayōpi gṛhyaṃtē kri(kṛ)yaṃtē vacanādayaḥ ॥ avilaṃghyāhi sarvē
3.ṣāmājñā śaṃbhōrggarīyasī ॥ 2 ॥ svasti śrī jayamaṃgaḷaprada mahādēva śṛ(śru)tibrātadiṃ prastutya prabhu saṃ
4.sthirāyuvanakhaṃḍānandasaṃprītiyaṃ vastustōmanaḍughakīrtiyanudāraiśvaryyamaṃ śauryyamaṃ
5. vistīrṇāvanimaṃḍaḷakkanudinaṃ kūrttīge muktīśvaranuṃ ॥ 3 ॥ svasti samastasurāsurakirīṭakōṭikhacitamaṇimarīcirōcidhāma

6. virājitacaraṇaṃ । aciṃtyaguṇābharaṇaṃ । anaṃtabrahmāṃḍaṣaṃḍanivāsanijabhavanaṃ । icchāmātrakṛtacaturddaśabhavanaṃ
7. ru(ṛ)gyajuḥsāmātharvavēdārtthasmru(smṛ)tipurāṇadharmmaśāstrōpagīyamānaśubhacaritaṃ । nijaśaktikaḷāmātravimōhita
8. līlācaritaṃ । pramathagaṇamanaḥsarōjarājahaṃsaṃ । samuttuṃgajaṭājūṭavibhūṣitacaṃdrakaḷāvataṃsaṃ śrī pārvatī
9. vadanapaṃkajarājamitraṃ । śaraṇāgatatāpatritayaraudravidrāvaṇakāruṇyacchatranappa śrīmanmahādēvaṃ divyasiṃhāsanārū
10. ḍhanāgi pārvatīsahitamire naṃdi naṃdinātha vīrabhadra bhadrakāḷa mahākāḷa bhṛṃgīśa pramukhāsaṃkhyātagaṇaṃgaḷiṃ saṃsēvyamā
11. nanāgi śrī kayiḷāsadalli vaḍḍōlagaṃgoṭṭu sukhasaṃkathāvinōdadiṃdirdda saṃprasthāvasamayadoḷu । ā umāmahēśvaraṃ ga
12. ṇaṃgaḷige prasannanāgi yiṃteṃdaṃ ॥ kaṃ ॥ ide nālku vēdapāraṃ bagevaḍe diṭadiṃ sarvvaśāstrārtthapāraṃ padapiṃ smru(smṛ)tyarthapāraṃ tribhuvanabhuva
13. najñānavijñānapāraṃ । sadvākyārthaikapāraṃ । praṇavasamuditaṃ dhyānabhāvaikapāraṃ viditaṃ śrī jyōtirliṅgāmaragaṇakaruṇōtpannabhaktipra
14. sādavu ene kēḷadrije binnapaṃ śiva jagakkīmārgamantōṟabēḷkenalaṃdā prabhu naṃdināthana moga nōḍalke śrī saṃgamēśana putraṃ
15. basavayya baṃkanadeṟeṃ (deṟaṃ) śivamuddudēvaṃ janakkanimittaṃ śivadēvanāgiyu gaṇaśrīpādamantōṟuveṃ॥ 5 ॥: ademṭeṃdeḍ ॥ kaṃ ॥ avana
16. takaṃdhararāgiye divijarśivarātri māḍidā tatpadadoḷ dhavaḷēśvarākhya liṅgadoḷavirala śivamuddudēvamunipatiyippanaṃ ॥ 6 ॥ a
17 bhya(vya)kta śaṃkarananatisubhy(vya)ktaṃ māḍitōrppenenutījagadoḷ । dibya(vya)dhavaḷēśaliṅganabya(vya)ya śivamuddumunivaraṃ bhāvisuvanu ॥ 7 ॥ śivamuddu
18. bratipatigī divijēṃdrapadagaḷeṃbivēṃ pāsaṭiyō bhavane kalikālakaluṣava tavisuva nevadiṃda mūrttiyantāḷdirddanu ॥ 8 ॥ kēśava jina
19. bauddhādigaḷīśana kiṃkarau bēṟe dēvateyalleṃdā śivamuddubratipa mahēśanolidālisidaṃ jagatrayavaṟiyalu ॥ 9 ॥ ama
20. ragaṇacaraṇakōmaḷavimaḷadaḷōtphullakamaḷayugaḷaparāgapramōditamanadvirēphōpameyiṃ śivamuddudēvamunipatiyippaṃ ॥ 10 ॥
21. ॥ va ॥ anaṃtaravu śrīgirinivāsanājñeyiṃ baṃda vīrabratiyaṃ nōḍi ॥ vṛ ॥ havaṇisabāradagraja kulōdbhavanāgi vidhātri(tṛ)niṃ
22. da saṃbhavisida nālku sṛṣṭiyoḷu puṭṭidaneṃbaḍe jāyatēsti yeṃbavu modalāda ṣḍvikṛtiyoḷsale kūḍidanalla bhāvi

23. sadbhavanolavinda vīra śivadēva gaṇēśvaranāgi tōridan ॥ 11 ॥ ॥ va ॥ endu tannoḷparibhāvisi yiṃtendaṃ ॥ suranadiye tuṃga
24. bhadrāvaranadi surasamiti vipragaṇanikaravu ā suragiri mahēśabhavanavu dhareyoḷkaviḷāsa(kailāsa)venipa muktikṣētravu
25. ā muktikṣētradoḷirddī maimeya meṟeyabēkenuta gurunuḍiyal । svāmi mukutēśane paraṃdhām śrījyōtineṃdola
26. viṃdaṃ ॥ 13 ॥ śakavarṣa 1148neya pārtthiva saṃvatsarada bhādrapada śuddha 15 caṃdrōparāga puṇyati
27. thiya madhyāhna samayadoḷu baṃdu pokku ॥ kaṃ ॥ viracisidaṃ kaiḷā(lā)sada caritramaṃ śrī vīrabhadrana śrī
28. padamaṃ । smarisuta vīrabratamaṃ dharisidanatuḷabaḷavikramaṃ śivadēvaṃ ॥ 14 ॥ sīmeyanullaṃgi(ṃghi)sadude nēmaṃ dharegoṟagadippu
29. de sale niyamavu । kāmisadippude nēmaṃ svāmi mahādēvanittoḍallada nēmaṃ ॥ 15 ॥ adaṟaṭida bhūtaṃgaḷa cedaṟisi benna
30. ṭṭi kuṭṭidaṃ bhairavaṃ । kedaṟuva bhaṃtaṟadaivavanodedaṃ vīrēśanātmajaṃ śivadēvanu ॥ 16 ॥ māṟidoṟeyāgi liṅgada salevaraṃ ba
31. ralu tuṃgabhadreya paḍe hosāntu jaṟedu nūkida vīragaṇaṃgaḷa kumāranī śivadēvanu ॥ 17 ॥ śivapadamaneydu
32. vaḍe mārgavideyenuttakhiḷajagake tōruva nevadindaviraḷavāgire nalaviṃ śivakaṭṭeya kaṭṭi tōridaṃ śivadēvanu ॥ 18 ॥
33. havaṇisalaṟiyadenisuva śivakaviḷāsanakhiḷa dēvatāpadasahitī bhuvanakke taṃdu śivasukhabhavanada nevadiṃda racisidaṃ śivadēvanu ॥ 19 ॥
34. trayiyaṃ nelegoḷsidavoltrayaṃgadiṃ mūṟu bhuvanamaṃ nilisidavoltrayi bhuvanikeyiṃ rudrapriya bhavanavanolidu
35. māḍisida śivadēvanu ॥ 20 ॥ ā kaḷaśāṃtaṃbare mūlōkavaṟiye jīrṇnavāda śivabhavanavamattā kaḷasaṃbare śileyiṃ lōkōttamavāgi mā
36. ḍisida śivadēvanu ॥ 21 ॥ śivadēvabratīṃdrasya liṅgārcanekaḷālavaṃ । aciṃtya sarvaśāstrādyairanaupamyamagōcaraṃ ॥ 22 ॥ aḷakhkhaḷakhkhayarū
37. ṇaikaḷadda diḍabhaktibhāvasaṃpaṇṇā kaḷibaḷakuḷaṇimma haṇābhaḷa sagguṇasāyarōbhavavokhkhu śivadēva ॥ 23 ॥ āṟuṃ darśanamaṃ
38. sale mīṟe śivagaṇājñāciṃtāmaṇi kayisāre śivadēvamunipati tōṟimeṟada liṅgajaṃgavaikyakramavaṃ ॥ 24 ॥ mattam purāta
39. nara caritrakkativicitramāgi liṅgārcanaṃgeyyuttamire yire ॥ svasti śrīmatu yādavanārāyaṇaṃ bhu
40. jabaḷapratāpacakravarti śrīvīra mahadēvarāya vijayarājyōdayada (mū)ṟaneya duṃdubhi saṃvatsarada vayiśā

41. kha su(śu)ddha 15 sōmavāra sōmagrahaṇadalli svasti samasta praśasti-sahitaṃ śrīmanmahāmaṃḍaḷēśvaraṃ
42.ujjayanīpuravarādhīśvaraṃ vaṭakalpavru(vr̥)kṣalāmchita vijayadhvajaṃ । bhuvanarakṣaṇaikadakṣiṇabhujaṃ caṃdragu
43. ptānvayasudhārṇnavapūrṇnacaṃdraṃ । vibhavāmarēṃdraṃ । haracaraṇa-nakhakiraṇasāṃdracaṃdrikācakōraṃ śrī gu
44. rupadapayōdharadhvānānaṃdita mayūraṃ । māninī mānasarvasva sūṟrekāṟaṃ । raṇadoḷu niṟaṃ maṃ
45. ḍaḷikabhayiravaṃ । ānaṃdita yuvatīnayanakayiravaṃ paṃnnirbbara gaṃḍaṃ । śa(sa)marakāṃḍaṃ sa(śa)raṇāgatavajrapaṃ
46. jaraṃ āhavādityaṃ । vīra vikramādityaṃ । ātaṃganunayadiṃ saṃjātarguta(tta) jōyivikramādityarvvikhyātarnnijabhuja vija
47. yōpētar ppaṃneraḍu maṃḍaḷikara gaṃḍaru ॥ 25 ॥ ā vikramaṃga[ṃ] maiḷaladēvigudisida kumārakaṃṭhīrava mattā vikramānujātaṃ śrī
48. guttaṃ nijabhujaikavikramanādaṃ ॥ 26 ॥ antā guttanr̥pana viśālavakṣas-thaḷadoḷanavarataṃ sirinijabhujāsidhāreyoḷu vija
49.yaśrīyolidippudaṟaṃ vīravitaraṇa tyāgabhōgaṃ geyvuttaṃ nijarājadhāni guttavoḷala nelevīḍinoḷsukharājyaṃge
50. yvutirddu śrī śivadēvara kāruṇyamaṃ paḍedu śrī sōmanātha liṅgalabdha-varaprasādanāgirddavasaradoḷu manōtsāhadiṃ barasida
51. śāsanakramavemtemdaḍe । muṃna hiriya jōyidēvarsaru cikka kuṟuvattina-grahāra māḍuvaṃdu śrī tribhuvanamalladēvana paramaviśvāsi maṇaṃ
52. benāyakana prēraṇeyiṃ āgāmi yakṣiṇisahita tāṃbraśāśanadalli barasi kuḷava kaḍidu kalla naṭṭu sarvvanamasyaṃ māḍi śivadēvara śiva
53. kāryakkārādhisida vra(vr̥)tti 2 kkaṃ । mane 2 tuḍike 2 maḷava 2 haḍahugeya haḷḷadim mūḍa ēkasthaḷadali eremattaru eṃṭu ॥ mattam
54. kāḷayukta saṃvatsarada kārttika śuddha 8 sōmavāradaṃdu śrī śivadēvara(ru) gō(o)pe kuṟuvattiya prati gr̥hasthara kayyalu krayagoṃ
55. ḍa kṣētra gō(o)peyalli ālakoḷaniṃ mūḍalu eremattaru 4 kaṃ 50 cik-kakuṟuvattiyali hiriya keyiṃ teṃka hoḍahuge haḷḷadiṃ
56. mūḍalu eremattaru 2 kaṃ 50 ॥ gō(o)peyalli mane 2 tuḍike 2 iṃtiveyikkuṃ aśēṣamahājanaṃgaḷu artthava koṃḍu kuḷava ka
57. ḍidu kallanaṭṭu sarvvanamasyaṃ māḍi śivadēvarige ārādhaneyamāḍidaru ॥ mattaṃ śrī śivadēvaru mahājanaṃgaḷa kayyalu
58. krayagoṃḍa sthaḷa vivara ॥ gō(o)peyali baṃni(ya keṟe)yoḷage hoṃnavattige hōda naḍuvaṇa dāriyiṃ teṃkalere mattaru 1 kaṃ 50 baṃ

59. nniyiṃ teṃkalere kaṃba 60 । alliṃ mūḍamakki kaṃba 50 । hoṃnavattiyiṃ baṃda dēviya dāriyiṃ mūḍa keṃgāḍu kaṃba 50 billavattade
60. rre ma 1 dāriyiṃ baḍagalere kaṃba 60 । kuṟuvattiyalli koṃḍageṟeyiṃ teṃka prathama sthaḷadalli kaṃba 60. । ālakoḷaniṃ mūḍale
61. re mattaru 1 kaṃ 70 antu mattaru 7 gō(o)pe mane 2 kuṟuvattiyalli mattaru 1 nālvattara hoḍadali yerekaṃba 85 mūḍamānya bhūmiyali ma
62. ttaru 1 gō(o)peya koṃtabaṃniyere kaṃba 50 antu mattaru 3 kaṃ 35 mane gō(o)peyalli 1 kuṟuvattiyali mane 2 antu mattaru 10 kaṃ
63. ba 35 mane 5 ṟa kuḷava kaḍivadake śrī guttarsadēvanu aśēṣamahājanaṃgaḷige artthava koṭṭu kuḷava kaḍisi kalla naṭṭu sarvvanamasyaṃ mā
64. ḍi śrīśivadēvarige ārādhisidanu ॥ mattaṃ beḷuvoḷala boṃmagavuḍana kayya [lu] krayagoṃḍa keyya sthaḷa baḍagavolanali tanna
65. baḷiyiṃ paḍuvalere mattaru 4 baḍaga ma 4 antu mattareṃṭu mane 1 va eṃdeṃdu sarvabādhe parihāra māḍi makkaḷu makkaḷa ...
66. de salisuva bāsa(bhāṣe)yiṃ kuḷava kaḍidu kalla naṭṭu boṃmagavuḍa śivadēvarige guttarsadēvanārādhisidanu ॥........
67. ḷala keyi ma 8 mane 1 kuṟuvattiya keyi ma 2 kaṃ 85 mane 2 gō(o)peyalli keyi kaṃ 50 ... śivadēvaru basavaya ...
68. ṇya māḍikoṭṭa vru(vr̥)tti ॥ mattaṃ siṃghaṇavarṣa śubhakru(kr̥)tu saṃvatsara puṣya su ... dēvara keyi ...
69. ... vattiyaśēṣamahājanaṃgaḷu hoṃge tiṃgaḷiṃge hāga vo ...
70. ā baḍḍiyiṃdāda ga 15 vaṃ ā śivadēvaru māḍuva liṅgajaṅgama ...
71. (1). śrī kanharadēvavarṣada siddhārtti(tthi) saṃvatsarada caitra bahuḷa 15 sō sūryagrahaṇada samyadalli cavuḍiseṭṭiyara karaṇada nāgarsana taṃmma bhānudēvanu koṭṭa tōṭa gaddeya keḷage
72. (2) gaṃgana kaṃba 5. ā sthaḷadali jōgiseṭṭi koṭta tōṭa kaṃba 5 mattaṃ guttarsadēvanu koṭṭa tōṭa kaṃba 6 adayisaṟava kuḷava kaḍisi kalla naṭṭu sarvanamasyaṃ māḍi śrī
73. (3) śivadēvarige guttarsadēvaneyārādhisidanu ॥ muṃna honnabommisṭṭyaru śivadēvarige ārādhisida gadde ma 10...(haḍuvalu)...hūdōta kaṃba 5
74. homnavattiyalli gō(o)peya dāriyiṃ baḍagalu gaṃgana kaṃba 5.
75. (1) yī śāsanamaṃ pēḷdu ba
76. (2) rada guttavoḷala [mēva]
77. (3). ṇaṃgaḷu.

Inscription No. IV

1. Oṃ namaḥ śivāya । namastuṃgaśiraścuṃbicaṃdracāmaracāravē । trailōkya-nagarāraṃbhamūlastha(sta)ṃbhāya
2. śaṃbhavē ॥ 1 ॥ śabdādayōpi gru(gṛ)hyaṃte kriya(ṃ)tē vacanādayaḥ ॥ avilaṃghyāhi sarvēṣāmājñā śaṃ
3.bhōrggarīyasī ॥ 2 ॥ (kam) śrī muktīśvaranatuḷaprēamadi rakṣisuge jagananupama lakṣmīdhāmanagaṇyamahō
4. daya nāmaṃ śṛ(śru)timauḷiraṃjita śrī caraṇanu ॥ 3 ॥ svasti samastasurāsuragaṇakiṃnarakiṃpuruṣaga
5.ruḍagaṃdharvvasiddhavidyādharapannagapramukhanākinikāyavinimitaprōdyaduttuṃgamakuṭataṭapaṭughaṭita
6. caṃcaccaṭacaṭuḷamaṇimāṇikyaśrēṇikiraṇāruṇamarīcimañjarīraṃjita śrīpādapadma satyasamudi
7. tasatkriyōpakṛtakkriyākāṃḍaphalānapēkṣitanirastātiśaya nityōtsavōdagrapratyagrīkṛtaharāmaḷacaraṇa
8. dhyānanirddiṣṭāparōkṣajñānasiddhaśivayōgārūḍha gūḍhanivāsanijasadma । prathuḷakaṭītaṭōpaśōbhitama
9. hāpadma । kaparddabaṃdhāṃtaraṃgaraṃganarttita maṃdākinītuṃgataraṃgākuḷōccaḷadviśadaviśudakīrtti
10. karapallavēva cūḍāgrakhacita cārucaṃdrakaḷāvataṃsa । abhīḷabā(bhā)ḷabhujaṃgayugakuṃḍaḷamaṃḍitakarṇnā
11. vataṃsa । mahāviṣṇukaṃkāṇabhratavāmāṃsa । atimathanasaṃbhūtākhiḷahāḷāhaḷakāḷakūṭakapiśanīlagrī
12. va । aciṃtyaprabhāva ॥ śrī mahādēva । yeṃdasaṃkhyātamaragaṇaṃgaḷu stōtraṃgeyyuttamire śrī kaiḷāsa
13. nivāsi yiṃteṃdaṃ ॥ vri ॥ stutigēṃ kāraṇa pēḷimēmdoḍe gaṇaṃgaḷu biṃnapaṃ dēvadēva duḥkru(kṛ)tadiṃ dharmmavaḍaṃgi
14. pōytu kalikālaṃ percce cārbbā(rvā)ka sā(sau)gatabauddhāgamavarttisuttamide lōkālōkamaṃ pāḷipoḷmatiyaṃ
15. māḷpude kajjameṃdu nuḍiyalu śrī pārvvatīvallabhaṃ ॥ 4 ॥ akṣayanidhāna muktiya dīkṣāsthaḷa tuṃgabhadre pa
16.ścima mukhadinaghakṣayamaṃ māḍalu taddakṣiṇataṭadalli meragu muktikṣētraṃ ॥ 5 ॥ alliddu mūṛu lōkada
17. rellara pāvanava māḷpenenutagajāvallabhanavatarisida bhūvallabheganurāgamappinaṃ muktīśanu ॥ 6 ॥ liṃ

18. gavavatarisitā hā hiṃgade nāvippeveṃdasaṃkhyātarbbhū ı raṃgakke baralikamaraganaṃgaḷamōghājñe
19. yiṃda śrī śivadēvanu ॥ 7 ॥ udisidangrajanmadapadadoḷtanu - guṇavanoṃdadellāgamadoḷmadanavirō
20. dhiye śrautōdita dēvanenutta tiḷidu śrī śivadēvanu ॥ 8 ॥ āśrama nālkuṃ tiḷiyalanāśramavāśramamene
21. ydadaśramadinda śivāśrama vinihitaveṃdatyāśramaṃ dharisi mereda śrī śivadēvanu ॥ 9 ॥ liṅgavanappida tō
22. ḷgaḷinaṃganeyaranappenaḷipi nōḍeṃ kūḍe manaṃgoḍenavadhārrenutavabhaṃgabrati śaṃkaraṃge bhāse(ṣe)ya koṭṭanu ॥ 10 ॥
23.॥ va ॥ mattamanēkabhāse(ṣe)yanīśaṃge koṭṭu ॥ kaṃ ॥ taledaṃḍa svarggamuktiya phalavanapēkṣisidenādeḍele śaṃkara kēḷ ı sa
24. le puṃṇypāpaveraḍara phalavallada nityapūjeyaṃ māḍidapēṃ ॥ 11 ॥ endu dhru(dhṛ)ḍasaṃkalpanāgi āse(śe)ya pāsa(śa)
25. maṃ paṟidu rōsa(ṣa)da mīseya kittu kāma biḍōsariseṃdu lōbhamadamaṃ bedaṟaṭṭuta mānamōhatṛṣṇāse
26. balaṃgaḷaṃ jaṟadu baggisi gelduṟe totta māḍidaṃ dūsaka dhūmakētu śivadēvanatarkyaguṇaprabhāvanaṃ ॥ 12 ॥
27. meṭṭida kalikiya noreya kaṭṭida nūreṃṭu byā(vyā)dhigōṃnamaśivayeṃdiṭṭaṃ vibhūtitilakava kaṭṭāḷda
28. ladaṃka manadoḷatinisa(śa)ṃkanu ॥ 13 ॥ jaḷamodalāgire pattujvaḷavenipa snānameṃṭu pattaṟoḷide nirmmaḷameni
29. pudeṃdu bhasmadi toḷedaṃ karmādimavanī śivadēvanu ॥ 14 ॥ jhaṃkege manadoḷs(ḷśa)aṃkisidaḍe niṃna bha
30. ktarāṇele paśupati ı śaṃkaranoḷādoḍaṃ bēḍeṃ kēḷbēḍidaḍe yeṃna taleya daṃḍavu ॥ 15 ॥ aṇakadaṇi
31. kalige muṃkaṇi seṇasuvarādigaḷge bāyasaṇi jagavariyal guṇi sakaḷavēdaśāstrada kaṇi śivatatvānubhāva
32. nī śivadēvanu ॥ 16 ॥ śivasadvidyeyē vidyeyeṃdu śivabhāvaṃ bhāvaveṃduvā śivamaṃtragaḷe maṃtraveṃdu śivamūrttidhyā
33. navē dhyānavī śivanityōtsava vutsavam śivakathāḷāpaṃgaḷāḷāpa mikkavasēbyaṃgaḷenutta vīraśivadēvanu tāḷda
34. vīrabrataṃ ॥ 17 ॥ śivanaṃ tōruva mārgga mārgga śivasadācāraṃgaḷācāravī śivasaṃyōgavē yōga nitya śivapūjā ka
35. karmmave karmmvī śivane dēvanu dēvananya viṣaya bēḍalla holleṃdu śrī śivadēvaprabhuvettidaṃ dhvajapatākōddaṃ

36. ḍamaṃ daṃḍamaṃ ॥ 18 ॥ elgaḷa vādigīdi paḍavaiṣṇavagīṣṇava sauragi-vura māṇelagaḷa boṃmigiṃmi nigamārththa
37. vanaṟiyada yajjigijji bēḍelagaḷa bauddhagiddha baṟiyāgamigīgami maṃtra-vādi sākuliyadi
38. reṃdu baggipudu śrī śivadēvana kālahoṃdoḍaru ॥ 19 ॥ beraḷaṃ karcci karaṃgaḷaṃ mugidu bāyaṃ pā
39. yuvaṃ taṃmerḍkaradiṃ muccuta bāyiviṭṭu kusido meyyikkutaṃ palgaḷaṃ kiridembē śaraṇārtthi
40. yeṃdanudinaṃ ṣaḍdarśanaṃ bāhuli bharadoḷtḷteḷaluttavirdduvaniśaṃ śivadēva vāmāṃghriyo
41. ḷu ॥ va ॥ mattaṃ duṭṭaragharaṭṭa liṅgakke kaṭṭidore koṭṭa bāse(bhāṣe) diṭṭavāriya kaṭṭāḷu śivadēvaṃ śrī jyōtinātha
42. ne muktanāthaneṃdaridu kālakalkiyaṃ jaṟedu । tanuguṇaṃgaḷaṃ maṟedu । āvaraṇaṃgaḷaṃ to
43. ṟadu । ubhaya karmada bēraṃ koradu । madana śaraṃgaḷaṃ muṟedu । māyāpāśamaṃ parido
44. ॥ kaṃ ॥ mānasa vācika kāyikvēnuṃtuḍa [gi] niṃna bhaktaroḷaniśam sānaṃdadiṃda māḷpeṃ nānanyava nene
45. ye nuḍiye māḍeṃ kūḍeṃ ॥ 20 ॥ iṃtenutta dēvalōkadalli koṭṭa pratijñeyaṃ tiḷidu ॥ niṣṭhisi
46. nōḍuta vuḷidanuṣṭhānaṃ pollaveṃdu kaṃḍā śivapada niṣṭhe nelegoḷalu śrēṣṭhānuṣṭhānava mā
47. ḷpananudinaṃ śivadēvanu ॥ 21 ॥ liṅgakke jaṅgamakke hiṃgade dāsitva māḷpudē besanendā saṃ
48. ganabasavaṃ besase managoṃḍarccisuvanubhayaliṃgava mudadiṃ ॥ 22 ॥ mṛḍagaṇavaraprasa(sā)davaṃ paḍedaṃ
49. jagavariyalaṃdu saṃgana basavaṃ prasādasiddhiya । kaḍuvīrabratadi paḍedanī śivadēvanu ॥ 23 ॥
50. ॥ va ॥ mattaṃ satyagaṇaṃgaḷa nitya prasādasaṃpannanāgi hiṃgade liṅgārccanangeyvuttamire yire ॥
51. svasti śrīmatu yādavarāyanārāyaṇaṃ bhujabaḷa prauḍhapratāpacakravartti śrī vīra [ma]ha
52. dēvarāya vijayarājyapravarddhamānamācaṃdrārkkatārāṃbaraṃ vuditōdita baruttamire
53. svasti samasta praśastisahitaṃ śrīmanmahāmaṃḍaḷēśvaraṃ ujjayanīpura-varādhīśvaraṃ caṃ

54. draguptānvayaṃ guttakuḷakamaḷamārttaṃḍa kadanapracaṃḍa haṃnnibba-ragaṃḍa maṃḍaḷikabhairavaṃ śaraṇā
55. gata vajrapaṃjaraṃ śrī sparśaliṅga ge(ga)ḷaganāthadēvara dibya śrīpādapadmārādhakanappa śrī vīra vikramaṃgaṃ ma
56. hādēviyarigaṃ puṭṭida vikramāṃkana prabhāvameṃteṃdoḍe ॥ dharmma-da permmane satyada nirmmaḷateya
57. gottu kavijanaṃgaḷa kaḍavara ॥ kūrmmeya tāyvane jāṇina nirmmāṇada ratnakaḷaśa vikramabhūpanu ॥ 23 ॥
58. ā vikramanṛpaṃgaṃ mayiḷaladēviyarigaṃ puṭṭida guttanṛpana prabhā-vamaṃ pogaḷvaḍe
59. dikkāṃtājanatālalāṭapaṭaḷaprodbhāsiratnōjvaḷādarśaṃ sajjanacittavṛttivib-havaprakhyātakīrttidhva
60. jaḥ। satyōtsāhasukhābdhivarddhanayaśaḥ kaumōdinīvallabhaḥ śrīmān-bhūpati vikramāṃkatanujaṃ(ḥ)
61. śrī guttabhūpāḷakaḥ ॥ 24 ॥ kaṃ ॥ ā vikramana parākramavā vikrama .... nolavadāratanagogeya
62. bhudarggīvaḍeyoḷu śaraṇeṃdara kāvaḍeyoḷu bhūmipaṃgārssariye ॥ 25 ॥ malapavirōdhi vairiga
63. ḷa gaṃḍa raṇāṃgaṇadoḍarddu beṃ । balavane porddu baratadiya nidva-ragaṃḍanidircci bercci kakkulateya mā
64. ḍuvaggaḷada vīrara gaṃḍanāsāhasakke meygaliyenisippa toṃḍaroḷu gaṃḍaragaṃḍanu
65. guttabhūbhujanu ॥ 26 ॥ va ॥ mattaṃ [daśa]digvaḷayaṃgaḷayaṃgaḷaṃ parbbida kīrttikāmteyaṃ vīrav
66. taraṇaṃgaḷaṃ pogaḷisikoḷutta nijarājadhāni guttavoḷalsukharājyaṃ geyivu-ttamirdū
67. ॥ kaṃ ॥ caṃḍāsiyiṃ paṃnirbbarmaṃḍaḷikara gaṃḍaneṃba jasasayitu bhū । maṃḍaḷavariyalu śivane
68. gaṃḍanenippoṃdu kīrttiyaṃ paḍedippanu ॥ 27 ॥ va ॥ yiṃtenutta taṃnoḷu paribhāvisi nōḍi ॥ kaṃ ॥ dhāriṇiyoḷu
69. gra tapadiṃ vīrēśvaranolava paḍeda śivadēvayyana । kāruṇyavenage jīvana bēṟilleṃdaridu tatprasāda
70. va paḍedanu ॥ 28 ॥ aṃtaṃ śivagaṇaprasādadiṃ śivadēvara kāruṇyavaṃ paḍedu śrī sōmanāthaliṅga
71. vanavadharisikoṃba samayadali guttarsaru śrī śivadēvara śivapādaṃgaḷi-geyārādhaneya mā

72. ḍida śivapurakke bevoḷala rāmagavuṃḍana maga boṃmagavuṃḍanaṃ karisi bevoḷala baḍaga
73. ṇa holadalli gaṃganāṟu mattaru yeṟeya keyyanikkeṃdaḍa boṃmagavuṃḍa baroḻḻitaṃ ma
74. hāprasāda jīya yaṃdu । guttoḷalnāḍa prabhugaḷa muṃde kayi kaikoṃḍu taṃnna sthaḷada he
75. ggaḍe muddayya mukhya samasta prajeprakruti yeṃṭuhiṭṭu paṃcamaṭha nakhara muṃmuridaṃ
76. ṃḍa sahita baṃdu । tanna gavuḍugeyiṃ baḍagaṇa basayyana keyiṃ mūḍalu । ci
77. kka kuṟuvattiya hola mēreya sālabeḷaniṃ teṃkalu । yeṇnegoḷakaḍada koḷadiṃ pa
78. ḍuvalu । kalidēvara । kaṃmaṟageyiṃ baḍagalēkasthaḷadali yikkida yereya bhūmi gaṃgana
79. mattarāṟu ॥ ā bhūmiya phala bevoḷala kāraṇavilla ॥ śakavarṣa 1185 neya duṃdu
80. bhi saṃvatsarada vayiśākha śuddha 15 sōmavāra sōmagrahaṇadaṃdu śrīmadamaragaṇaṃ
81. gaḷa nijasiṃhāsanavappa muktikṣētra bhūkayiḻā(lā)savideṃdu śrī śivadēvaru jagaddhitā
82. rtthavāgi racisida । śivadēvapurakke varṣaṃprati baruttabahudu । adu sarvvamānya śrīmānya
83. jayamānya । vijayamānya ॥ mattaṃ svasti samadhigata paṃcamahāśabda dvārāvatīpuravarā
84. dhīśvara suvarṇnagaruḍadhvajaṃ vṟṣṇivaṃśōdbhavaṃ yādavakuḷakamaḷakaḷikāvikāsabhāskaraṃ arirā
85. ya jagajhaṃpa māḷavarāyakadanatrinētraṃ gaurjjarabhayajvaraṃ cōḷarāyadisā(śā)paṭṭa(ṭa)ṃ telu
86. garāyasthāpanācāryya ityādi rājāvaḷīsamāḷaṃkra(laṃkṟ)ta śrīmatprauḍhapratāpacakravrti śrī
87. mahādēvarāya vijayarājyapravarddhamānamācaṃdrārkkaṃ baruttamire dakṣiṇadikutaṭa
88. viḷasita lakṣumige nīnadhipaneṃdu yādavabhūpa nirīkṣisi besasalu mudadiṃ rakṣipa toṟagaleya
89. dēvarasa janapadava ॥ 28 ॥ ॥ va ॥ śrī śivadēvaru māḍuva liṅgajaṅgamasamārādhanege sarvvabhāvadiṃ śuśrū

90. se(ṣe)ya mārppudeṃdu śrī mahādēvarāya nirūpaṃgoḍe svasti samasta-praśastisahitaṃ śrīmanmahā
91. pradhānaṃ sarvvādhikāri toṟagaleya dēvarasaru śrīmaddakṣiṇavāraṇāsi-yenipa [pa]ścimavāhini tuṃ
92. gabhadreya dakṣiṇa tīradoḷeseva muktikṣētranivāsarappa śrī śivadēvara l iṃgadarśanārtthaṃ baṃdu ॥ ru
93. dhirōdhā(dgā)ri saṃvatsarada jyēṣṭha bahuḷa 5 ādivāra ṣaḍaśītimukhasaṃ-krāṃti tatkāladalli be
94. ḻuvoḷala baḍagaṇa holadalli muṃna kallunaṭṭidda gaṃgana yeṃṭu mattaru bhūmiyanu
95. sarvvanamasyavāgi samārādhaneya māḍidanu ॥ maṃgaḷa mahā śrī śrī śivamastu ॥
96. mattaṃ guttarasanu ā beḷavoḷala paḍuva volanalli hoṃnavattige hōda dā
97. riy baḍagaṇa yerre(re)yakeya gaṃgana kaṃba 50 maṃ voḍeyara pādakke
98. ārādhisidanu । ā keyyanu voḍeyaru basavayyaṃge sarvvanamasyavāgi koṭṭa
99. raṃ ॥ śrīmatu siṃghaṇavaśra(rṣa) śubhakrua(kr̥)tsaṃvatsarada puṣya su(śu)ddha 3 su(śu)kravāra
100. da ... si(śi)vadēvara keyyalu gō(go)pe kuṟuvattiya ya(a)śēṣa mahāja-naṃgaḷa hoṃge tiṃgaḷiṃ
101. śrī rāmadēvarāyavijayarājyōdayada 16 ne
102. ya byaya saṃvatsarada ... [yaṃtara]yaśēṣamahājanaṃgaḷu
yī dharmmava naḍeyisidalliṃ
103. daṃ mēle ... gaṇaṃgaḷa samakṣadalli yā muktēśvara dēvaru .. siddhāya
104. va teruva yāḻu mattaru keya ... y(ai).vattu hoṃniṃgevu baḍḍigevu sa-luvāgi yā bhū
105 miyanu kuḷava kaḍidu yā mahājanaṃgaḷu muktēśvaradēvargge sarvva-manyavāgi koṭṭaru ॥ ī dharmmake
106. yāru yahudallaṃdara... sāsirake hoṟagu .. hadineṃṭu samayake drōhigaḷu ॥
107. svadattaṃ ... sahasrāṇi viṣṭāyāṃ jāyate krimiḥ ॥ 30 ॥

Inscription No. V

1. namastuṃgaśiarscuṃbicaṃdracāmaracāravē । trailōkyanagarāraṃbha
2. mūlastaṃbhāya śaṃbhavē ॥ 1 ॥ śabdādayōpi gru(gr̥)hyaṃtē
3. kriyaṃtē vacanādayaḥ । avilaṃghyā hi sarvēṣāmājñā śaṃbhōrgarīyasī ॥ 2 ॥ bālēṃdu

4 kaḷābhūṣita । mauḷi śrī kallināthanavanījanamaṃ pāḷisuge sa(śa)radhi śaśitārāḷi kubhṛddiggaja ।
5.ṃgaḷippaṃnevaraṃ ॥ 3 ॥ svasti samasta divijadanujakhacarakhēcaragaṃdharvakiṃnarakiṃpuruṣa
6. śi(si)ddha munīṃdra phaṇīṃdra gaṇēṃdra pramatha pracaṃḍa praṇita vividha nru(nṛ)tyagītavādya vi
7. dyā vīṇāvēṇunādavinōdaprasaṃnnavaradāni mallikārjunaṃ ॥ kanda ॥ śirigiri
8. yoḷirdu taṃnnaya bha(ca)raṇave śaraṇemba vīra śivadēvarigā । ścariyavenippa ।
9. paścima । varavāhini tuṃgabhadreyaṃ tōruttaṃ ॥ 4 ॥ ā dēśadiṃda (ādēśisidaṃ) naḍe nīnādēśa
10. kkalli muktanāthnoḷeṃddumu । mādēvisahitavihenu । samādhānadoḷarccisu
11. vudenalnaḍetaṃdu ॥ 5 ॥ anavarata liṅggasaṃvujñananukarisidanaṃnyakāsi(śe) māḍade
12. muktē । śananapratimanenipū । janeyiṃdarcisi mercisuvanenaveṃttado ॥ 6 ॥ to
13. nevaṃ [ma]ttu kaṃgoḷuvanu । yanumānipanaḍigaḍige sru(śru)tigaḷoḷu pugaḷaṃ
14. nenanenadu mūrtigoḷisuva । ghanatara śivaliṅggatattvavaṃ śivadēvaṃ ॥ 7 ॥
15. paradaivamānamardda । paradaivaragharaṭṭadiṭṭa paradaivakubhru । dvaravajrapātaneni
16. paṃ । vīragaṇatējaḥprabhāvadiṃ śivadēvanu ॥ 8 ॥ ॥ vacana ॥ aṃttā śivadēvaru śiva
17. gaṇājñāsukhadoḷiruttamire yire । kāraṇikareniparoḷu tāṃ kāraṇika
18. renipa śi(si)ddharēvaṇadēvana । kāruṇya śisyā bhaktyā । cārada be(ci) llāḷadēva lokkiyyo
19. ḷesedaṃ ॥ 9 ॥ mikka śivabhaktisukhadiṃ । dukki mahādēva bhāvabharadiṃ jagamaṃ ॥ lekki
20. sade gaṇasukhadoḷiha lokkiya celāḷadēva toṟagale nāḍoḷ ॥ 10 ॥ aṃttiruttami
21. rd(d)u ॥ vadavida śivabhaktiya saṃpadamaṃ kallarasanarasi kaṃnādēvige । mudadiṃdavitta ci
22. llā । ḷadēva jaṅgamasukhaikaguṇasadbhāvaṃ ॥ 11 ॥ ā sati kaṃnādēviyu । śrī sukhasaṃpadaviḷā
23. sa vibhavādigaḷaṃ । bāsaṇisi si(śi)vagaṇaṃgaḷi । go(ō)sarisade māḍi kūḍi sukhisutirppa

24. ḷu ॥ vacana ॥ tadanaṃṭṭaravu ॥ karmātiśayadi nijapati dharmadhvaja dēvalōkava । tāneyidal
25. dharmajñedēvi kaṃnhare(hnale) karmmariyaṃ pāyalujjugaṃ geyivannaṃ ॥ 13 ॥ paramaguru śi(si)ddha rē
26. vaṇa । sirigiriya nivāsanājñeyaṃ besasidana । ccariya muniyappa mu
27. ktē । śvaraliṅgadoḷalli tuṃggabhadreya taḍiyyoḷ ॥ 14 ॥ yiṃttene ॥ ānenase-nadē sadguru
28. tānēnaṃ tōri(ṟi)da vicitravenuttaṃ ॥ mānini kaṃnnā(hnā)dēviyarā । naṃdadi baṃdu
29. muktanāthana kaṃḍaru ॥ 15 ॥ aṃttā muktikṣētradallird(d)u hiṃgade jaṃgārca
30. ne [ta]tpareyāgire yire śivayōgiya kr̥peyiṃda vīra ka
31. ṃnnādēvi । bhuvanavariyalke kalidēvara sthāpisidaḷ ॥
32. svasti śrīmatu yādavanārāyaṇa pravuḍhapratāpa ca
33. kravart(t)i mahādēvarāya rājyapravardhamānamācaṃdrārkkatārāṃbaraṃ saluttamire yire ॥ svasti śrī
34. mahāmaṃḍaḷē(lē)śvaraṃ vujjayanipuravarādhīśvaraṃ vaṭakalpavr̥kṣa-lāṃchita vijayadhvajaṃ caṃdra]guttakulakama
35. ḷa(la)mārttaṃḍaṃ । kadanapracaṃḍaṃ । haṃnirbaragaṃḍaṃ । śaraṇā-gatavajrapaṃ
36. jaraṃ vikramādityaputra vīra guttarasadēvaru śivadēvara kāru
37. ṃṇyamaṃ paḍedu ḷiṃgōtsavasamayadalli kaṃnādēviyaru
38. muktikṣēttradalli pratiṣṭheyaṃ māḍisida kallidēvarige sarvvaśrīkāryārtha-māgi śrīmanma
39. hāprabhu vūliyahaḷḷiya muddagauḍaniṃ śakha(ka)varuṣa 1184neya
40. duṃdubhi saṃvatsarada kārtika śu ॥ 15 sōmavāradaṃdu voḍeyara
41. pāda samakṣamadalli sarvvanamaśyamāgi vūlihaḷiya jōyigauḍana kēyaṃ gu
42. ttarasadēvaṃ dhārāpūrvakamāgi koṭṭa
43. gaṃgana mattaru 1 mane 1 tuḍike 1
44. sarvanamaśyamāgi koṭṭa yere baḍagaṇa (vo)lanalli gaṃgana mattaru 1 mane 1 tuḍike 1
45. gōpeyalliya baila mattaru 1 ... mattaru 1 yiṃtī dharmava si(śi)vadēvara gaṇaṃga
46. ḷu pālisuvaru.

Inscription No. VI

1. Oṃ nama[ḥ] śivāya । mudadi pā
2. lisugurvvīpadamaṃ caṃdrārkkatārakaṃ
3. bara[ṃ] girijāvadanāṃbujātamitraṃ tridaśēśvara mu
4. ktanātha dēvara dēvanu ॥ svasti śrīmatu yādava
5. rāya nārāyaṇaṃ prauḍhapratāpa cakravartti śrī
6. vīra mahādēvarāyana besadiṃ ॥ svasti śrīmanu (śrīman)
7. mahāpradhānaṃ sarvādhikāri toṟagaleya śrī dēvarsa
8. ru kaṭakadiṃ baṃdu ॥ svasti śrīmadārūḍha vīrabhra(bra)ti śiva
9. yōgasiddha śivadēvarige sāṣṭāṃgapraṇāmapūrvvakaṃ
10. biṃnapaṃgeyidaniṃteṃdaṃ ॥ voṃdu grāmava koḍu nīneṃdaṃ
11. yadukula nru(nṟ)pōttamaṃ mahadēvaṃ । yiṃdada patikarisalu
12. bēkeṃdoḍe śivayōgasiddha nagutiṃtendanu ॥ tribhuvanaveṃdu
13. du paḻliya prabhutvavēṃ ślāghyave yadalldu māṇeṃdabhayaka
14. ra siddhanenalā śubhalakṣaṇa dēvarāja maraḷiṃteṃdaṃ ॥ vr̥ ॥ dēvaru ko
15. ṭṭadolladiralappudu dēvaṇi māḍi siddhiyiṃ śrī vibhavagaḷiṃ manu
16. ja lōkadadhīśvararittoḍolladeṃdeviralappuduttama padārthacayaṃga
17. ḷanalladātmajarbhāvakarārttattaḍadanollevenippudu dharmmavappude eṃ
18. damr̥tōdara prabhava dēvanr̥paṃ nuḍidoṃdu vākyadoḻu baṃdakhiḷā-gamārtthaṃ
19. nelasiddudu śāstrada sarvvasaṃpadaṃ saṃdudu vaidikārtthavoḍanirddu dha
20. rmmada permavettudēnendapeneṃdu taṃnoḷanumānisutaṃ śivadēvarraṃ-(reṃ)
21. daparu ॥ ārādhisuvaṃ nīnolidārādhisikoṃbanīśvaranuvēnānumanārādhisu
22. kayikoṃbaṃ vīrēśvaranendu siddhanēmisalolaviṃ ॥ ā dēvarājaṃ ॥ uttara dakṣiṇa paścima
23 duttuṃgāsanada rāyarārādhise varavitta śivadēvaraṃ śrī guttānvaya rāja
24. guruvanārādhisidaṃ adeṃteṃdaḍe ॥ svasti śrīmanmahā maṃḍaḷēśvaraṃ
25. ujjayanipuravarādhīśvaraṃ caṃdraguptānvayaṃ guttakuḷakamaḷamārttaṃ-ḍa kadana
26. pracaṃḍa pannirbbaragaṇḍa maṃḍaḷikabhayiravaṃ śaraṇāgata vajrapañ-jaraṃ śrī sparśaliṃ
27. ga gaḷaganāthadēva śrī pādapadmārādhakarappa guttarsadēva । hiriyadēva । jōyi

28. dēvaṃgaḷa । avara tāyvarappa maiḷādēviyara kayyalu dhāreya koṇḍu gottoḷalnā
29. ḍaprabhu gāvuṃḍagaḷanoḍaṃbaḍisi śakavarṣa 1187 raktākṣi saṃvatsarada puṣya ba 15
30. ādivāra śravaṇa nakṣatra bya(vya)tīpātaṃgūḍidarddō(rdhō)daya puṃṇyatithiyalli dēvarsaru
31. māḍidārādhaneya kramaveṃta[ṃda]ḍe ॥ gottoḷala baḍagavoladalli yerega
32. ṃgana mattaru 1 hiriya keṟeya keḷage gadde gaṃgana kaṃba 10 mane 1 tu
33. ḍike 1 hoṃnavattiya mūḍavoladalli yere gaṃgana mattaru 1 । mane 1 ।
34. tuḍike 1 ॥ yālūra keṟeya baḍagalere gaṃgana mattaru 1 । mane 1 ।
35. tuḍike 1 । ulihaḷḷiyalli vūra mūḍa [de]seyalli kaṃba 50 teṃka[de]seyali kaṃba 50
36. aṃtalli yeregaṃgana mattaru 1 । mane 1। tuḍike 1 ॥ hāhanūra paḍuva vo
37. lanalli yeregaṃgana mattaru 1 । mane 1 । tuḍike 1 ॥ nageyūra vola
38. nalli yere gaṃgana mattaru 1 mane 1 tuḍike 1 ॥ vōlaguttūra mūḍala vola
39. nalli yere gaṃgana mattaru 1 mane 1 tuḍike 1 ॥ kaṃnavaḷḷiya baḍagavolanalli ye
40. re gaṃgana mattaru 1 mane 1 tuḍike 1 ॥ agaḍiya baḍaga holadalli yare(yere) gaṃgana
41. mattaru 1 tuḍike 1 mane 1 ॥ hādaragēriya volanalli yere gaṃgana
42. mattaru 1 mane 1 tuḍike 1॥ imtī hattu grāmaṃgaḷalli dēvarsaru śrī śi
43. vadēvarige samārādhaneyaṃ māḍida dharmavu ācaṃdrārkkaparyaṃtaṃ
44. sarvvanamasyavāgi gottoḷalnāḍa prabhugāvuṃḍagaḷu salisuvaru ॥

Inscription No. VII

1. svasti śrī sa(śa)kavatsara 1210neya sarvvadhāri saṃvatsarada srā(śrā)vaṇa su(śu)ddha 5
2. sōmavāradaṃdu svasti śrī rāmapratijñā paraśurāma yā
3. davakuḷ(ka)akamaḷa(la) kaḷikāvikāsabhāskara dvārāvatīpuravarādhīśvara viṣṇu vaṃ
4. sō(śō)dbhava māḷaviya mallāhitarāyamadaṃ gurjjararāyavāraṇāṃkusa(śa) te
5. luṃgarāyasirakamaḷapūṟṇasaṃdōhamardana ... bhōjabhūpāḷa vyā
6. ḷavidrāvaṇa lakhumidēvakaṃsa ... ityādi samasta rājāvaḷī s
7. virājamāna śrīmatu yādavanārāyaṇa bhujabaḷa praviḍapratāpacakra
8. vartti śrī rāmacaṃdradēvarāya rājyavijayōdayada mahāpradhāna[masināstiha ?]

9. ...śrīmaṃnā ... na kāḷē pravarttamānēkaṃnnāḍadēsē guttoḷaladēsē
10. taṃ madhyē gōpanāmagrāmē tuṃgabhadrāyāṃ taṭamadhyē muktikṣētr śrī siddhasi(śi)va
11. dēvanāmnī muktēśvaradēvasaṃnnidhau śrīmaṃmahāmaṃḍalēśvara arirā
12. ya vibhāḍa kadana[pracaṃḍa] ... sthāpanācariya ... hōsaṇarāyadisāpaṭṭaṇa ... ni rāyarakṣāpāḷaka
13. sakaḷasainyādhipati rāṇaka śrī saḷiva ākhyō dēvaṇnayya prapautrāya siṃhadēvasai
14. nyādhipati pautrāya ballāḷadēvasaiṃnyādhipatiputrāya śrī sāḷive siṃmdēvasai
15. nyādhipati [nāma] ... sāḷiveyākhya kīrtstaṃbha pratiṣṭādharmō yāvatu
16. caṃdrārkkamēdinau tāvatu stirōbhūt maṃgaḷa śrī śrī
17. nūra ... yasyōdda ... nēna mahā ... sitadaṃ ... kēṇa । nāḷāyi
18. ... sarōruha ... prabhāṃ ... kaḷāpa ... kāṃ ...
19. ... tika kāṃti ... haṃsa ... kāḷa ... gaḷita ....
20. ... matā । avyādavyāhatajapaṃ ... ārati bhāsayaṃ
21. ... bhukaṃ khaṭvāṃga hasta sara ... kṛttisuḷavāḷaṃ khaḍugahastaṃ ...
22. ... gataṃ । vāmahastaṃ dinakara caṃdrākṛtumāḷādi āvṛtaṃ siraṃ sarpayajñōpa
23. vītaṃ । kaḷākōvidakāraṃ mahādēvaṃ namōstute ॥ 3 ॥ kṛdhā
24. dapiṃ mēsti ghanamēdinīmahimāliṅgamahatā mahēṃdramērau maṃdarādrau maḷyāy
25. magiḷa ... sōmavakṣyā pa । ratvaṃ ... dapakṣapadatvaṃ ...
26. ... mahā kaṃtuvāhana ... jyāyāprērita bhṝ ... kṣārahaṃ ॥ 4 ॥
27. tatvādi ... sphurati vasūdēvamaṃ ... prāṇipraṇitasarasīkṛtapadaṃ
28. maṃ nyasta ... vaiva ... nimityāṃ vikṛtacakṣukhyātavallabhaḥ kāminau
29. ...statē samalatu sīmāya vidhānyā ... hāyāvattā ...
30. bhūdhārabhayabhavaḥ cāmaratōmaraṃ । yāvadgrāma karāmarana
31.rāṃ । rā ... yaṇaṃ.samudrabhōgabhuvana ... rāya nityana ...
32. brahaṃ । kṛtabṛōtama ... caṃdramasta ... samudra
33. hara ... mana ... tṛgaṃ ... kṣētraturvimala ... munayō ... vyōmarasvinaḥ।
34. ... vasuṃ sivāya ... kṣama bhagavān pārvatīsvarapate ... ॥7॥

Inscription No. VIII

1. śrī ōṃ namaḥ । si(śi)vāya । srī(śrī si(śi)vadēvaprabhu
2. vē sa(śa)raṇu । svasti śrīmatu yādavarāya
3. nārāyaṇaṃ bhujabaḷapravuḍhapratāpa

4. cakravartti śrī vīra rāmacaṃdradēva vijayarā
5. jyōdayada 24neya kharasaṃvatsarada pu
6. sya(ṣya) bahuḷa amava(vā)se ādiva(vā)ra ya(a)rddhōda
7. ya sūryagrahaṇadalli svasti śrīmatu rā
8. yarājaguru mahāvīrabrati nūṟeṃṭu
9. navabratanisṭaraha gō(go)peya si(śi)ddha si(śi)vadēvara prāṇa
10. liṅga muktēsva(śva)radēvara tuṃgabhadre paścimavā
11. hini dakṣiṇa vāraṇāsiya gō(go)peya
12. nūṟippattiṃbara ṣa(sa)ṃnnidhiyalli yi muktanā
13. thadēvarige । svasti śrīmanu mahāpradhānaṃ sa
14. rvvādhikāri parasu(śu)rāmadēvara nirūpadiṃ sa
15. rbbādhikāri habbarsadēvarsaru suṃkada
16. sitāḷahegaḍe ā muktanāthadēvara purada
17. staḷasuṃka kāruka telligaruṃ magga teṟe aṃgaḍi
18. mukhyavāgi aṣṭabhōgatējasāṃmya 25. e
19. ttina suṃka mayideṟe mūlesuṃkavanu
20. sarbba(rvva)mānyavanu ācaṃdrārkkavāgi sī
21. meyaṃ mudresahita dhārāpū
22. rvvakavāgi koṭṭanu ॥ maṃgaḷa mahā śrī ।
23. svadattam(ttāṃ) paradattaṃ(ttāṃ) vā yō harē
24. ti(ta) vasuṃdharā(ṃ) ॥ ṣaṣṭirvarṣasahaśrā(srā)
25. ṇāṃ(ṇi) viṣṭāyāṃ jāyatē kri
26. miḥ ॥ maṃgaḷa mahā śrī śrī śrī
27. śrī muktanātha sa(śa)raṇu ॥

BIBLIOGRAPHY

Architecture in Dharwar and Mysore, photographed by the Late Dr. Pigou, Bombay Medical Service, A. C. B. Neill Esq. and Colonel Biggs Late of the Royal Artillery, with an historical and descriptive memoir by Colonel Meadows Taylor and Architectural notes by James Fergusson, published for the Committee of Architectural Antiquities of Western India under the patronage of Premchund Raichund, London, John Murray, 1866.

Ajitāgama, ed. N. R. Bhatt, Publications de l'Institut français d'Indologie No. 24, 1-3, Pondicherry, 3 vol. 1964, 1967, 1991.

Kriyāsāra of Nīlakaṇṭha Śivācārya, ed. vol. I by R. Ramasastri and N. S. Venkatanathacharya, vol. II & III by S. Narayanaswamy Sastry, Oriental Research Institute Series—95, 99, 100, Oriental Research Institute, Mysore, 1964, 1957, 1958.

Mayamata, Traité sanskrit d'architecture, text and French translation by B. Dagens, 2 vol., Publications de l'Institut français d'Indologie No. 40, Pondicherry, 1970, 1976.

Nandimath S. C., "A Broken Stone Inscription from Chaudadanapura" in*Prof. P. B. Desai Felicitation Volume, Studies in indian History and Culture,* Karnatak University, Dharwar, 1971, pp. 76-84.

Rauravāgama, ed. N. R. Bhatt, Publications de l'Institut français d'Indologie No. 18, 1-3, Pondicherry, 3 vol. 1961, 1972, 1988.

Sadashiva Wodeyar, "Two Ancient Towns of Karnataka", in *Prof. P. B. Desai Felicitation Volume, Studies in indian History and Culture,* Karnatak University, Dharwar, 1971, pp. 258-61.

Śivadēvavijaya by Śarīf Kavi, edited by M. G. Namjumdaradhya, Prabodha Pustakamale, Cikkapete, Bangalore, 1949.

Śaivaratnākara of Jyotirnātha, ed. by H. P. Malledevaru, Oriental Research Institute Series—180, Oriental Research Institute, Mysore, 1992.

Vātulaśuddhāgama (with Kannaḍa Translation), ed. by H. P. Malledevaru, Oriental Research Institute Series—155, Oriental Research Institute, Mysore, 1988.

Vīramāheśvarasaṅgrahaḥ of Nīlakaṇṭhanāgānāthācārya with the commentary Karnāṭakabhāṣābhūṣaṇa of Śrīdharāṅka, ed. by M. S. Basavarajaiah, Oriental Research Institute Series—176, Oriental Research Institute, Mysore, 1991.

Virāgamottaram, ed. by H. P. Malledevaru, Oriental Research Institute Series—168, Oriental Research Institute, Mysore, 1988.

GENEALOGY

I. Gutta Chieftains of Guttavaḷal

- Māgutta
  - Gutta I
    - Mallidēva (Mallugi, Mallabhūpa)
      - Vikramāditya I = Siriyadēvi (1162-63)
        - Jōyi II (1177-82)
        - Gutta II = Padmaladēvi
          - Vikramāditya II = Paṭṭamahādēvi & Sōvaladēvi (1182-1233)
            - Tuḷuvaladēvi
            - Gutta III
            - Jōyi III (1238-41)
            - Vikramāditya III = Maiḷaladēvi (1248)
              - Vikramāditya IV
              - Gutta IV (1259-65)
              - Hiriyadēva
              - Joyidēva IV
                - Vikramāditya V (1283)
          - Vijayamahādēvi = Siṅgidēva
    - Jomma I (Jōyi I) (1124)

II. Jaṭā Cōḷa's family

- Jaṭā Cōḷa
  - Jomma
    - Dāsa = Candabbarasi
      - Attirāja (Mallidēva is his māva, father-in-law or maternal uncle)
      - Caṇḍarasa
        - Mācale (d.) = Māra Nāyaka
          - Kāmeya Nāyaka

INDEX OF INSCRIPTIONS

(References to inscriptions and their lines)

GENERAL INDEX

(References to pages)

LIST OF PLATES

A. Drawings.

B. Photographs.

Plate III.

1. Temple of Muktēśvara, south façade, central niche.
2. Temple of Muktēśvara, north façade, north-east angle of the vimāna; image of Vīrabhadra.
3. Temple of Muktēśvara, north façade, north-west angle of the raṅgamaṇḍapa.
4. Modern wooden processional car in the Maṭha of Cauḍadānapura; the photograph shows the extremities of the beams, with a connecting band, which support the entire superstructure.

Plate IV.

1. Temple of Muktēśvara, north façade, *pañjara.*
2. Temple of Muktēśvara, north façade, reduced replica of a temple in an angle of the *vimāna.*
3. Temple of Muktēśvara, north façade, motif of lion head and arch over a pañjara.
4. Temple of Muktēśvara, north façade, upapīṭha, first and second plinths.
5. Temple of Muktēśvara, north façade, *upapīṭha* (*kumuda* and *kapota*), *adhiṣṭhāna.*

Plate V.

1. Temple of Muktēśvara, north wall.
2. Temple of Muktēśvara, north wall of *raṅgamaṇḍapa*, north-west angle.
3. Temple of Muktēśvara, ibidem, detail : Mahēśvara.
4. Temple of Muktēśvara, south wall of *raṅgamaṇḍapa*; the inner representations of rafter ends in the eave (east side) are seen; on the back wall under the lion head on the left is seen the image of a Vīraśaiva worshipping his Liṅga held in his left hand, presumably Śivadēva.

Plate VI.

1. Temple of Muktēśvara, east porch, door lintel, east façade.
2. Temple of Muktēśvara, east porch, right doorjamb, east façade, inferior part.
3. Temple of Muktēśvara, east porch, right doorjamb, east façade, superior part.
4. Temple of Muktēśvara, vimāna, 1st and 2nd levels of the tower, south façade.

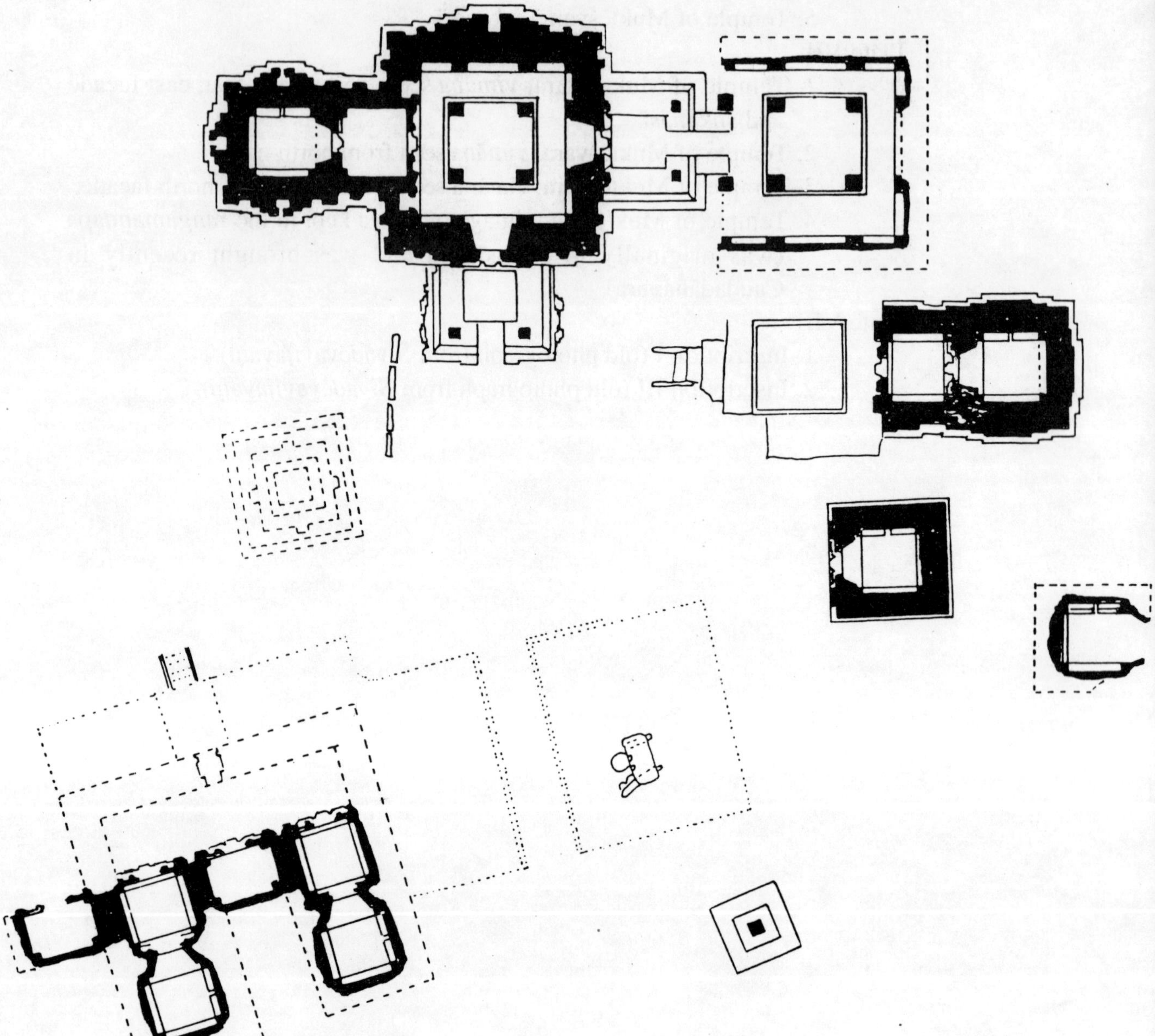

Plate 1. Cauḍadānapura. Temple of Muktēśvara, site plan c. 1925 (from Cousens's plan), approximate scale: 1/200.

ಮಹಾದೇವಭೂವಲ್ಲಭರಿಂ ಜನಿಸಂ। ತಿಕ್ಕಿನದೇಗಾಂಸುಮದುಳಿಪ್ಪ। ಲಾಂಛನಯುಕ್ತ
ಳದೇವತೆಲಕತಿರ್ಗಾಳೋಳ್॥ ಅಂತಿರಲು ತತ್ರ ಮದರ್॥ ಪದರಿದರ್ ವಭೂತಯಸಂ। ಪರ
ಮಂಶಲ್ಲರನನರನಿಕಂನ್ನದೇವಿಗೆ। ಮದದಿಂ ದರತ್ರ ಬೆಲ್ಲ। ಳದೇವಂ ಜಂಗಮಸುಮ್ರ
ಕಸುಗಾಸದ್ಭಾವಂ॥ ಅಂಸತಿ ಕಂನ್ನದೇವಿಯ್ಯು॥ ಶ್ರೀ ಸುಖನಂ ಪದರಿಳಾನವಿಭೂಷಾದಿಗಳ್॥
ಬಾನಗಾಂನಿನವಗಾಂಗಳ। ಗೊನರಿನದಿಮಾ ದಿಶಾದಿ ಸುಖಸುತ್ರಿಪ್ರೆಳ್ಗಳವಗಳವದನತ್ರ
ರವುಗಳ ಶಮಾರ್ಗರಯುದಿನಿಜಪತಿ। ಧರ್ಮದ್ಭಜದೇವಲಾಕ। ವನಿತಾನೆಯುದಲ್। ಧರ್ಮಗ
ದೇವಿಕಂಸ್ಥಳಿ। ಕಮಗರಿಯುಂ ಪಾಯುಬಜ್ಜ್ಯಗಂಗೆಯು ವನ್ನಂ॥ ಪರಮಗುರುಕಬ್ರಾಳ್
ಗ। ಬರಿರಿರಿಯನಿಗಾನಗಾಕ್ಲೆಯುಂ ಬನಸದನ। ಭೃತಿಯುಮನಿಯುಪ್ಪಮು ಕ್ಕಿ। ಳ್ಳ
ರಂಗ ದೊಳ್ಳಲ್ಲಿತುಂಗಭದ್ರೆಯತಡಿಯಪ್ಪೊಳ್ಗಳ ಯುಂತ್ರನೆ॥ ಅಂ ನೆನನೆನದೇವಿಸದ್ಗುಣ।
ತಾನೇನಂತೆಮಾರಿದವಿ। ಚಿತ್ರವಸುಸುತ್ತಂ। ಮಾನಿನಿ ಕಂನ್ನದೇವಿಯು। ರಾನಂದದಿ ಬಂದು ಮ
ತ್ರ ಸಾಧನಕಂಡರ್॥ ಅಂತಾ ಮುಕ್ತಿಹೇತ್ರದಲ್ಲದರ್ ಪ್ಪಿಂಗದಿಲಂಗ ಜಂಗಮಾರ್ಚನೆ
ತ್ಪರೆಯಾಗಿರ್ಪ॥ ಶ್ರೀ ವಯಿಷ್ಣವಿ ।

। ಶ್ರೀ ಪರಶಕಾನ್ನದೇವಿ। ಭುವನಂವರಿಯಲ್ ತ್ರಿಕಲಿದೆವರಸ್ವಾಮಿನಿದಳ್। ಸ್ವಸ್ತಿಶ್ರೀ ಮ
ತುಯಾದವನಾರಾಯಣ ಪ್ರೌಢಪ್ರತಾಪ ಚಕ್ರವರ್ತಿ ಮಹಾದೇವರಾಯರಾಜ್ಯ
ಪ್ರವರ್ಧಮಾನ । ಮಹಾಮಂಡಲೇಶ್ವರಂ ಪೃಜ್ವಿಯನಿಪುರ
ವರಾಧೀಶ್ವರಂ। ಸತ್ರಕುಲಕಮಲಮಾರ್ತಾಂಡಂ। ಕದನಪ್ರಚಂ
ಡಂ। ಹಾಂನಿಬರ್ರಿಗಂಡಂ ಶರಣಾಗತವಜ್ರಪಂಜರಂ ವಿಕ್ರಮಾದಿತ್ಯಪುತ್ರ
೨೮ ಪುಂಣ್ಯಮಂ ಪಡೆದು ಅಂ ಗೊಸ್ವವನಮುಯುದಲ್ಲಿ

ಮುಕ್ತಿಹೇತ್ರದಲ್ಲಿ ಪ್ರತಿಷ್ಠೆಯಂ ಮಾಡಿದಕಲ್ಲದೇವರಿಗೆನವರ ಶ್ರೀಕಾರ್ಯಧರ್ಮ
ಮಾಗಿ ಶ್ರೀಮನ್ಮಹಾಪ್ರಭು ಪೂಲಿಹಳ್ಳಿಯ ಮುದ್ದಗಾದನಿ ಶಖವರುಷಗಳ
ನೇಯ ದುಂದುಭಿ ಸಂವತ್ಸರದ ಕಾರ್ತಿಕ ಶು ೧೫ ಸೋಮವಾರ ಚಂದ್ರಗ್ರಹಣದೆಯ
ರಪಾದನ ಮುಷ್ಟಮದಲ್ಲ ಸರ್ವನಮಸ್ಯವಾಗಿ ಪೂಲಿಹಳ್ಳಿಯ ಚೋಯ ಗಾದನ
ಕೆಯಂ ಸುತ್ತರನದೇವ ದಾರಾಪೂರ್ವಕವಾಗಿ ಕೊಟ್ಟ
ಗಂಗನ ಮತ್ತರುಗ ಮನೆಗ ತುದಿಕೆಗನ ಸರ್ವನಮಸ್ಯವಾಗಿ ಕೊಟ್ಟಯ ಕಬದಗಾಪ್ರೊ

Folio 239 verso

Plate 6. Inscription No. II, copy preserved in Walter Elliot's Collection, (with the courtesy of The Royal Asiatic Society, London).

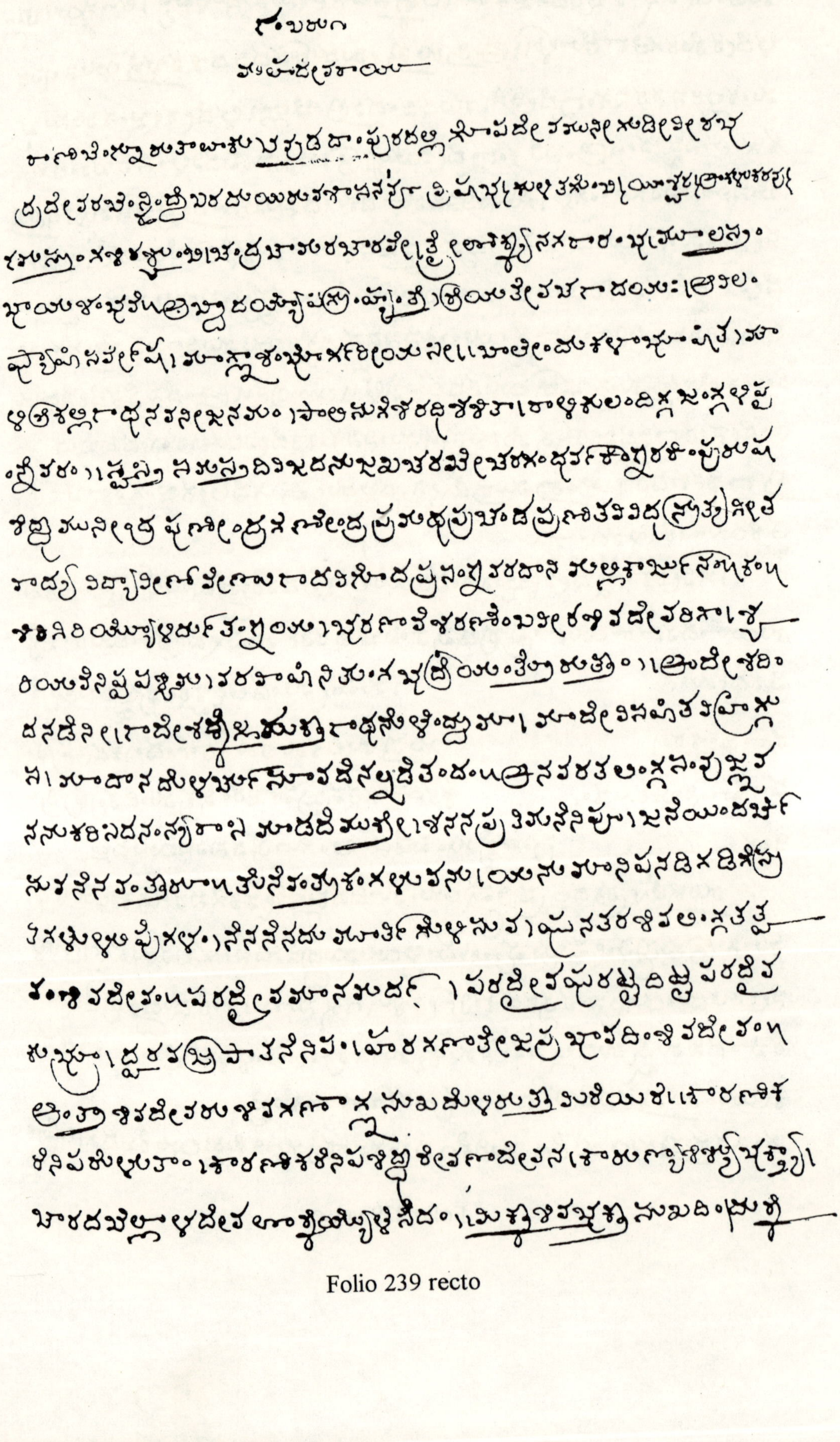

Folio 239 recto

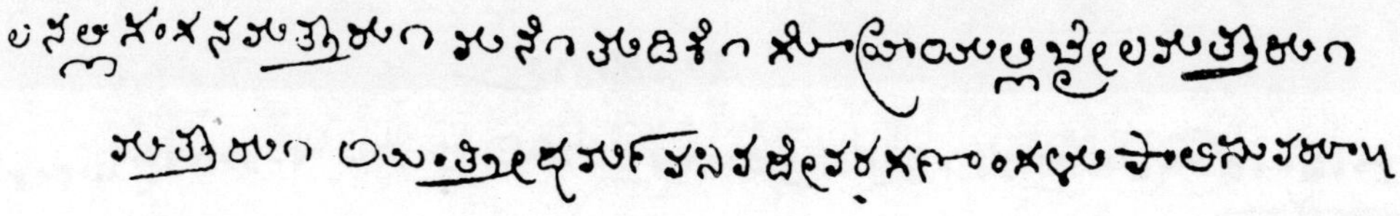

Folio 240 recto

Plate 7. Inscription No. V, copy preserved in Walter Elliot's Collection (with the courtesy of The Royal Asiatic Society, London).

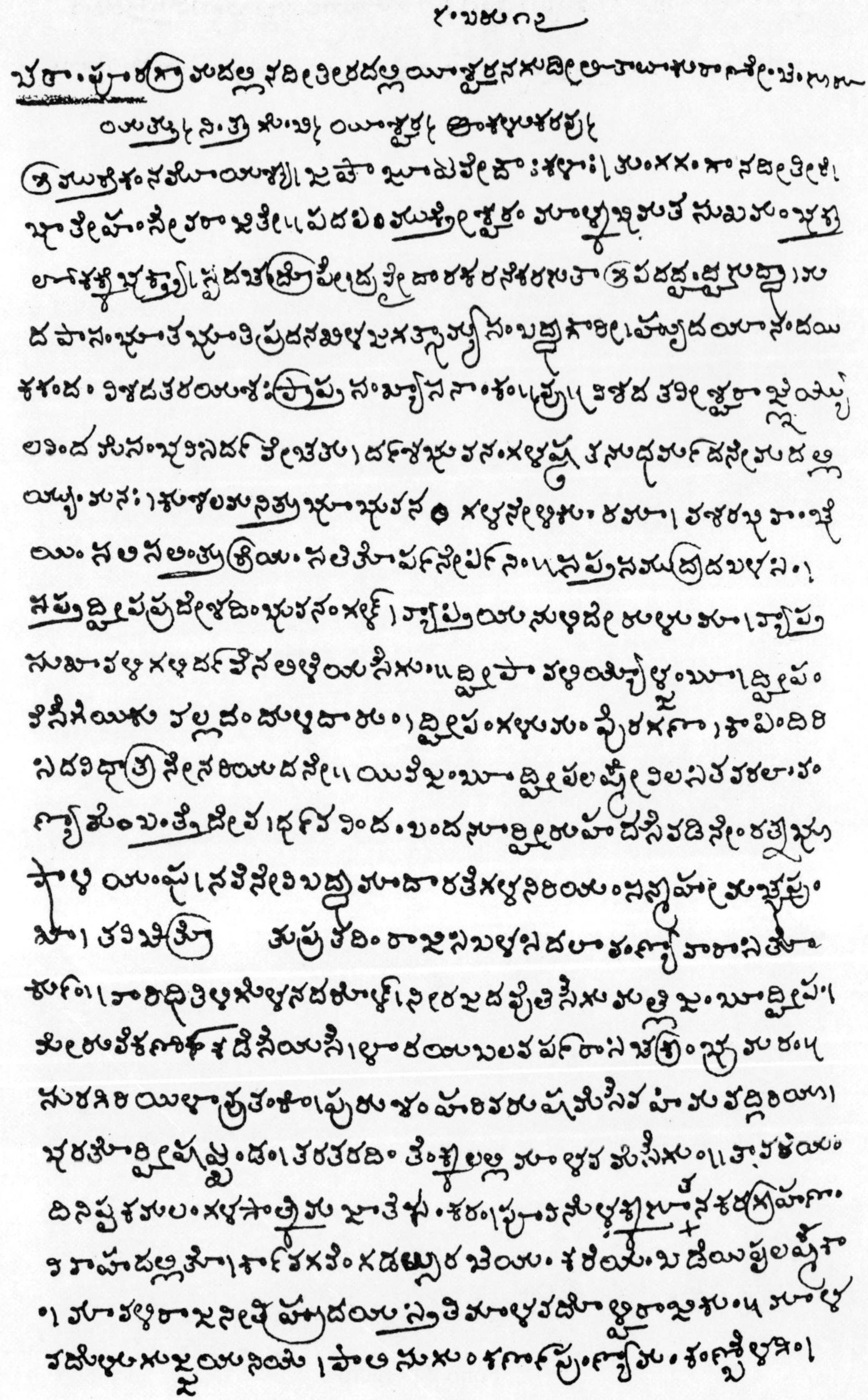

Folio 345 verso

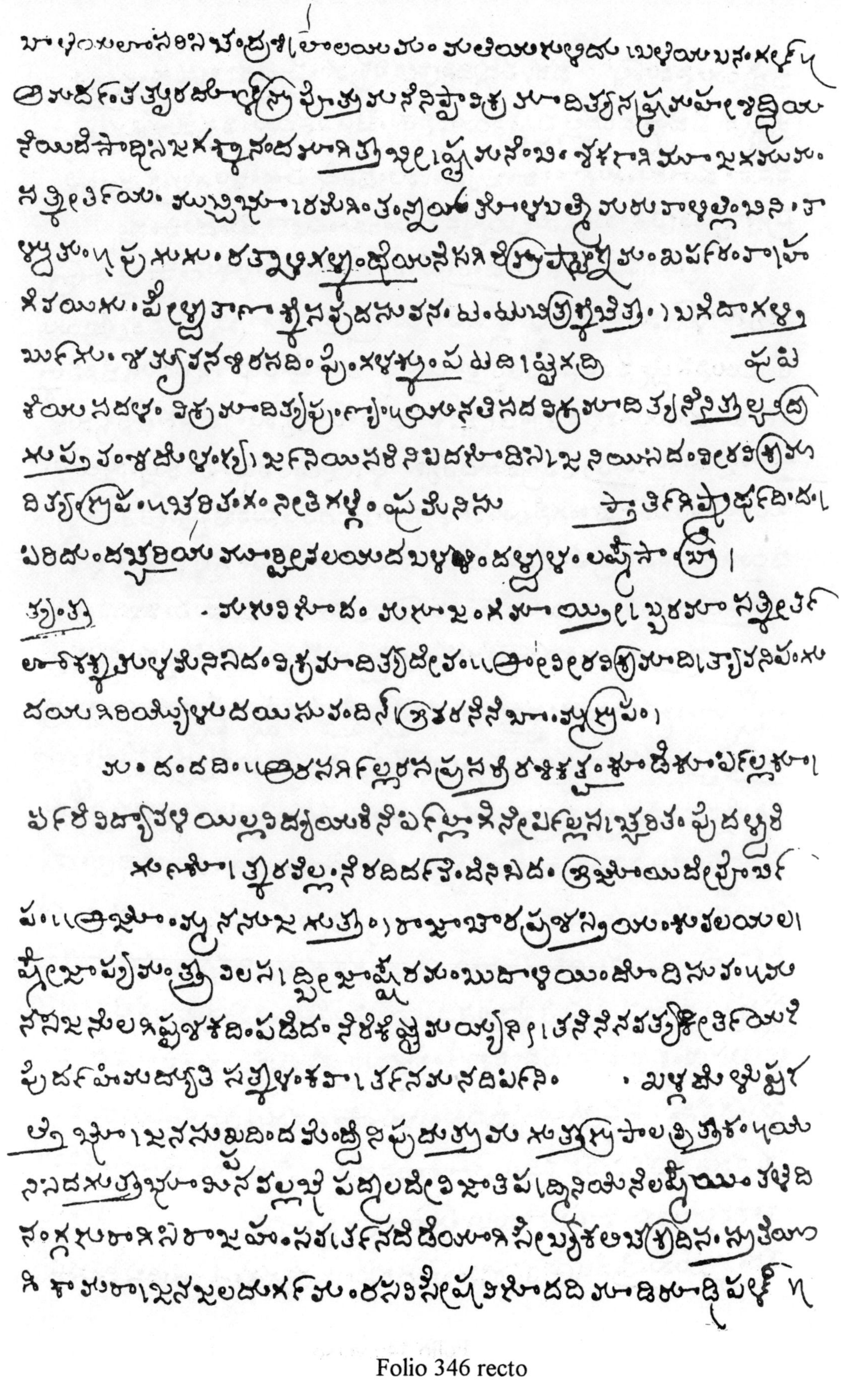

Folio 346 recto

పద్మేంయునివర్గళ్ల   దశ। పద్మాదినీశిలశిక్రుపం॰ పృష్ఠదగా। పద్మశ్రపసంత్రి
శ్రేష్ఠన। పదేన్న దరదల్ల పృష్ఠనయువినితు॰ షే॥ వినయం విశ్రపుశ్రత్రపుణ్యా
పనిషా పయుంరు॰ గున్నాం రాజ్యపుం। పుండనదేవపూంశుగళ్ళుంత్రె నల్లరికి
పుణ్యాం చేతనం బల్లపేని। య్యునయుం భూంష్ణా పుందుపాస్త్ర

ధర్మప్రవర్తనపుం॰ దింత్రహావీరవిశ్రుపుగెల్లళుగ్ంప్రాజ్ఞసామ్రా
జ్యగోళ్॥ పొయునెయోళ్ల ళ్గ నహాయుత్రిత్రితనగాత్రిం॰ దం॰ నరేంద్రాయు
తే। యునిసత్నీనపునం సతత్త పుయుధా ఋపంతధావిలపుం। దినినిల్లా
పనుళుం॰ పుయూవిళనితాం తేజః పుంజనం రాజ్యపేం। దెనిసల్ విశ్రపుళ
శ్రీరాజ్యనుగువింత్రే విశ్రపూదిత్యగోళ్॥ జయపధుపం ప్యూ॰ స్మయ్యూ॰
బంయునుతిపర్ధపాంగనెయుర్గళాం నదిం। బంయునుపచల్లనీతితతిగల్ల
డెయుల్ నుపదత్రపంచపుం। బయునుపపూగనాతిగళవేష్ణగళం
బయుత్రిపర్గతి। ప్రియువెనిపాపరాజ్యనువినిం మినుపం॰ విభువీరవి
క్రాపం॥ స్పైస్త్ర నపుధినతపంచపుహాశబ్ద పుహాపుండలేశ్వరం। పపుగల్ల
త్రిష్టేలాం॰ చితవిజయుధ్వజం॰ భువనష్ణోశ్రదష్టదష్ణాం భుజచాంద్రి
గుప్తాం॰ న్నయునుధాం॰ న్నయు పూర్ణచంద్రం॰। విభవా పుశేంద్రం॰। హారచరణా
నఖికిరణాసాంద్రచంద్రికాచకోరం॰ గురుపదయుగ్మాదరధ్యాగంది తపు
యుగ్మేర॰ పూనినిపూనన సర్వస్వపుం॰ నూరికారం। రణాంగోళ్ ధీరం॰ । వ
యుశపుండళశభయురవం। శ్రీనందితయుగ్మవతీనయునశయురవం। పంనిర్గర
గణాస   రం॰। శ్రీమహాదిత్యం విశ్రకిక్రుపూదిత్య॰ బనపసేగారం
దుష్టనిగ్రహశిష్టప్రతిపాలనదిం పాలిసుత్తం సుత్తవెళలనెలివీదిగో
ళలునుఖసంగ్రధాకిగో దదిం రాజ్యంగెయ్యుత్తమిరె॥ భూపాలపదాబ్జ
భృంగనెనిపం॰ సద్గుశ్రయ్యుక్తయుం। భూపాలనపుంత్రయుక్తనెనిపం
తంనపుదతప్పవీరపత్తదిం। భూపాలనదష్టదష్టణాం భుజాంధ్ర॰ దనిజం
తాకిగల్లా। భూపాలగాయుశ్రీగణాజగద్విఖ్యాత   ॥౫౪
తదం॰ న్నయుపుం॰ త్రెనె॥ ఆతప్పరాజనంబం దరనం। నతప్పదకణాకి యునినిమినుప

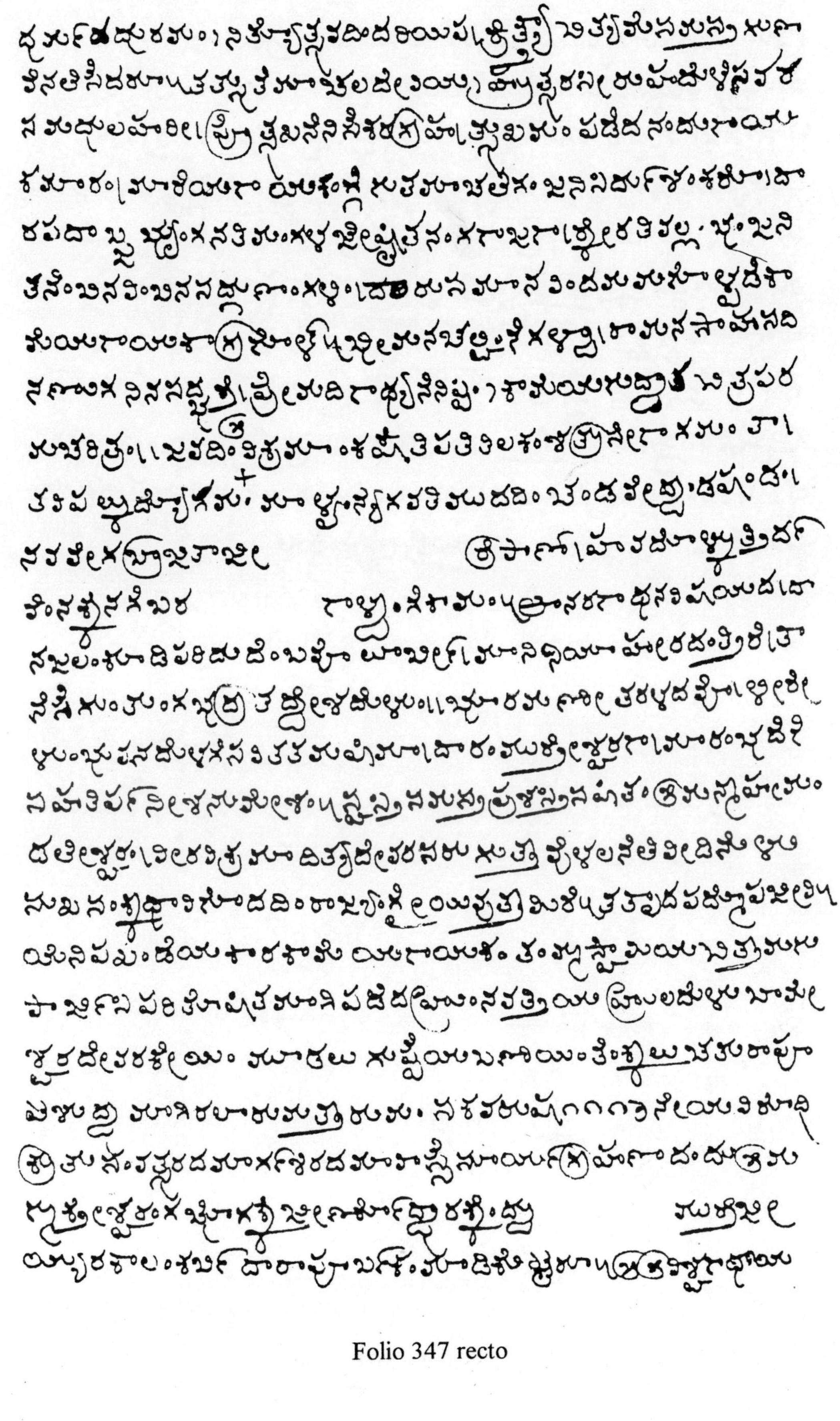

Folio 347 recto

ಕಲು ॥ ಯಿಂತೀ ಧರ್ಮವಂ ಪ್ರತಿಪಾಲಿಸಿದವರು ಪ್ರಯಾಗೆ ವಾರಣಾಸಿ
ಯು ಪುಷ್ಕರ ತೀರ್ಥಂಗಳಲು ಸಾವಿರ ಕವಿಲೆಯ ಕೋಡುಗಳಿಗೆ ಹೊನ್ನ ಕಟ್ಟಿ
ಸಿ ಸಾಸಿರ ವೇದಪಾರಗರಿಗೆ ಕೊಟ್ಟ ಫಲವನೆಯ್ದುವರು ಸ್ವದತ್ತಾಂ ಪರದತ್ತಾಂ ವಾ ।
ಯೋ ಹರೇತಿ ವಸುಂಧರಾಂ । ಷಷ್ಟಿರ್ವರುಷ ಸಹಸ್ರಾಣಿ । ವಿಷ್ಠಾಯಾಂ ಜಾ
ಯತೇ ಕ್ರಿಮಿಃ ॥ ವಿರೋಧಿಕೃತು ಸಂವತ್ಸರದ ಪುಷ್ಯದ ಬಹು ಪಾಸ್ಸೆ ಸಂಕ್ರ
ಮಣಾಂ ಕೂಡಿದಲ್ಲಿ ಶ್ರೀ ಮುಕ್ತೇಶ್ವರದೇವರ ತ್ರಿಕಾಲ ದಾಹಾರಕ್ಕೆ ... ಸಂಗ
ಹಾಸಂಡ ತೀರ್ಥಕ್ಕೆ ವಿರಪೇ ಮಾಡಿ ದೇವರ ಸಮುಖ ಹಾಜನ ಗಳಸ
ನಿಧಾನದಲ್ಲಿ ಕೊಟ್ಟ ಗದ್ದೆ ... ಹಾರಂ ... ಪತ್ರಿಯ ಹಾಳ
ಕಲ್ಲದೇವರ ಗದ್ದೆ ಯಿಂತೀ ಸ್ಥಳಂ ಮೂರ ಣಾಂ ಬಿಟ್ಟ ಗದ್ದೆ ಕಂಬ ಯಿಂತೀ
ಧರ್ಮವಂ ತಪ್ಪದೆ ಪ್ರತಿಪಾಲಿಸುವರು ಕುಲಹಾಂ ದರಾದಿಯಾಗಿ ಮಾಡಿದರು
ಸಹಿತ ಮುಕ್ತೇಶ್ವರಾಯ

Pl. II 1. Temple of Muktēśvara seen from west (behind the south porch are seen the dome of Kallidēva shrine and the shrine No. 3).

Pl. II 2. Temple of Muktēśvara seen from south (the river is seen behind the temple, on the left and through the eastern porch).

Pl. II 3. View of the site from the south-east angle; from left to right: shrine No. 4, a corner of shrine No. 3, Kallidēva shrine No. 2; in the background the dome of Muktēśvara temple and its southern porch.

Pl. II 4. View of the site from the north: *kīrtistambha* and shrines No. 6-9.

Pl. III 1. Temple of Muktēśvara, south façade, central niche.

Pl. III 2. Temple of Muktēśvara, north façade, north-east angle of the vimāna; image of Vīrabhadra.

Pl. III 3. Temple of Muktēśvara, north façade, north-west angle of the raṅgamaṇḍapa.

Pl. III 4. Modern wooden processional car in the Maṭha of Cauḍadānapura; the photograph shows the extremities of the beams, with a connecting band, which support the entire superstructure.

Pl. V 1. Temple of Muktēśvara, north wall.

Pl. V 2. Temple of Muktēśvara, north wall of *raṅgamaṇḍapa*, north-west angle.

Pl. V 3. Temple of Muktēśvara, ibidem, detail: Mahēśvara.

Pl. V 4. Temple of Muktēśvara, south wall of *raṅgamaṇḍapa;* the inner representations of rafter ends in the eave (east side) are seen; on the back wall under the lion head on the left is seen the image of a Vīraśaiva worshipping his Liṅga held in his left hand, presumably Śivadēva

Pl. VII 1. Temple of Muktēśvara, *vimāna* seen from south-east, east façade and *śukanāsi*.

Pl. VII 2. Temple of Muktēśvara, *vimāna* seen from north-east.

Pl. VII 3. Temple of Muktēśvara, *vimāna* seen from north-east, north façade.

Pl. VII 4. Temple of Muktēśvara, image of Sūrya kept in the *raṅgamaṇḍapa* (was originally in Narasipura and was brought recently in Caudadānapura).

Pl. I 1. Temple of Muktēśvara seen from south-west angle. Photograph of Pigou and Dixon, 1866 (Courtesy of The Royal Asiatic Society, London).

Pl. I 2. Temple of Muktēśvara seen from south-east angle. Old photograph published in *Śivadēvavijayam*.

Pl. IV 1. Temple of Muktēśvara, north façade, *pañjara*.

Pl. IV 2. Temple of Muktēśvara, north façade, reduced replica of a temple in an angle of the *vimāna*.

Pl. IV 3. Temple of Muktēśvara, north façade, motif of lion head and arch over a *pañjara*.

Pl. IV 5. Temple of Muktēśvara, north façade, *upapīṭha* (*kumuda* and *kapota*), *adhiṣṭhāna*.

Pl. IV 4. Temple of Muktēśvara, north façade, *upapīṭha,* first and second plinths.

Pl. VI 1. Temple of Muktēśvara, 'east porch, door lintel, east façade.

Pl. VI 2. Temple of Muktēśvara, east porch, right doorjamb, east façade, inferior part.

Pl. VI 3. Temple of Muktēśvara, east porch, right doorjamb, east façade, superior part.

Pl. VI 4. Temple of Muktēśvara, *vimāna,* 1st and 2nd levels of the tower, south façade.

Pl. VI 5. Temple of Muktēśvara, *śukanāsī.*

Pl. VIII 1. Inscription I (old photograph from *Śivadēvavijayaṃ*).

Pl. VIII 2. Inscription III (old photograph from *Śivadēvavijayaṃ*).